Globalization and Education

Globalization and Education

Integration and Contestation across Cultures

edited by
NELLY P. STROMQUIST
and
KAREN MONKMAN

ROWMAN & LITTLEFIELD PUBLISHERS, INC.
Lanham • Boulder • New York • Oxford

ROWMAN & LITTLEFIELD PUBLISHERS, INC.

Published in the United States of America
by Rowman & Littlefield Publishers, Inc.
4720 Boston Way, Lanham, Maryland 20706
http://www.rowmanlittlefield.com

12 Hid's Copse Road, Cumnor Hill, Oxford OX2 9JJ, England

British Library Cataloguing in Publication Information Available

Library of Congress Cataloging-in-Publication Data

Globalization and education : integration and contestation across cultures / edited by
Nelly P. Stromquist and Karen Monkman.
     p.   cm.
Includes bibliographical references and index.
ISBN 0-8476-9918-8 (cloth : alk. paper)—ISBN 0-8476-9919-6 (pbk. : alk. paper)
     1. Education—Economic aspects—Cross-cultural studies.   2. Education—Social
aspects—Cross-cultural studies.   3. Globalization—Cross-cultural studies.   I.
Stromquist, Nelly P.   II. Monkman, Karen.
LC65.G46   2000
306.43—dc21   00-027241

Printed in the United States of America

∞ ™ The paper used in this publication meets the minimum requirements of American
National Standard for Information Sciences—Permanence of Paper for Printed Library
Materials, ANSI/NISO Z39.48-1992.

Contents

Preface   vii

Abbreviations and Acronyms   xv

Part 1   Conceptual Issues

1   Defining Globalization and Assessing Its Implications on
    Knowledge and Education   3
    Nelly P. Stromquist and Karen Monkman

2   Globalization and Internationalism: Democratic Prospects for
    World Education   27
    Phillip W. Jones

3   Globalization and Educational Reform   43
    Martin Carnoy

4   Educational Reform: Who Are the Radicals?   63
    Val D. Rust

5   Globalization and Curriculum Inquiry: Locating, Representing,
    and Performing a Transnational Imaginary   77
    Noel Gough

6   Globalization and the Social Construction of Reality: Affirming or
    Unmasking the "Inevitable"?   99
    Catherine A. Odora Hoppers

Part 2   Globalization Impacts in Various Educational Sectors

7   Alternative Responses to Globalization from European and South
    African Universities   123
    Jan Currie and George Subotzky

8 Globalization of the Community College Model: Paradox of the
Local and the Global 149
Rosalind Latiner Raby

9 Local/Global Labor Markets and the Restructuring of Gender,
Schooling, and Work 173
Jane Kenway and Peter Kelly

10 Globalization, Adult Education, and Development 197
Shirley Walters

Part 3 National Case Studies of Globalization Impacts

11 Globalization and Universities in the Commonwealth Caribbean 219
Anne Hickling-Hudson

12 Internationalization in Japanese Education: Current Issues and
Future Prospects 237
Lynne Parmenter

13 Globalization and Decentralization in Sub-Saharan Africa: Focus
Lesotho 255
William M. Rideout, Jr.

14 Globalization and Educational Policies in Mexico, 1988–1994: A
Meeting of the Universal and the Particular 275
Rosa Nidia Buenfil

15 South African Higher Education in Transition: Global Discourses
and National Priorities 299
Crain Soudien and Carol Corneilse

16 The Impacts of Globalization on Education in Malaysia 315
Molly N. N. Lee

17 "Hanging onto the Edge": An Australian Case Study of Women,
Universities, and Globalization 333
Jill Blackmore

Index 353

About the Editors and Contributors 359

Preface

The origins of this publication can be traced to 1997 when its two editors selected "globalization" as the theme for the western regional conference of the Comparative and International Education Society (CIES). We felt that although the concept had attracted considerable interest in the academy and throughout most of the world, it had been examined primarily as an economic and technological phenomenon, not from an educational or cultural perspective. Besides, empirical evidence was scarce.

During the years since, globalization has attracted the attention of educators in the industrialized countries, which are now examining the effects of new technologies on knowledge and the role of the university in creating new technologies. The expanding interest in the intersection of education and globalization has brought up several new topics: training, higher education, culture, the environment, industrialization strategies, information management, migration, labor, multinational affairs, and rural and agricultural development.

While education is gaining widespread attention, it must acquire more support if it is to assess the impact of globalization on Third World countries and on the interplay that is occurring between central and less-developed countries on such modalities as adult education, vocational education, and higher education. Innovations affecting the community college, decentralization, restructured curricula, and the role of the university in the economy are emerging as powerful new agendas closely linked to globalization initiatives.

From the western regional CIES conference, we selected the paper by Martin Carnoy—who presented the keynote speech of the conference—and the contributions by Val D. Rust, Phillip W. Jones, Rosalind Latiner Raby, Lynne Parmenter, and William M. Rideout, Jr. We solicited other papers through contacts we made at subsequent CIES and American Educational Research Association (AERA) conferences in San Diego and Montreal and through knowledge of colleagues engaged in this topic. Our thinking has benefited from colleagues working in diverse parts of the world and focusing on diverse areas of interest in education. We have benefited also from the expanding literature on globalization and knowledge, which bears clear implications for educational systems of the future.

In fundamental ways, the forces of globalization challenge the previous approaches and theories of national development. In the minds of some observers, globalization is an exaggerated form of global capitalism; in the view of others, it is a wake-up call to look for alternative forms to the new social and cultural arrangements that are being spontaneously generated by globalization.

This book is organized in three parts. The first addresses conceptual and theoretical issues underlying such notions as globalization, internationalization, and multilateralism. The second presents empirical data from various countries and provides examples of shifts and transformations within a specific level or modality of the educational system. The third looks at the totality of educational changes, taking the nation as the unit of analysis. These country-level case studies bring together in concrete and detailed ways the impacts of globalization at the multiple levels of the modalities of the education system.

We remind the reader that we are not considering the media in this book even though it is a very important aspect of globalization. The absence of media chapters is not due to our lack of recognition of their importance but rather to the scope of the book, namely, concentrating on education, albeit defined in broad terms.

In the first part of this book—on conceptual and theoretical issues—we begin with an essay defining globalization and assessing its implications for all levels of education. We find that two actors are imposing themselves on educational policy agendas: the market and the transnational corporation. The changes they are encouraging affect not only the formal educational system but also the construction and restructuring of local cultures. Amid substantial transformation in the economy and culture, however, it can be said that exploitive ideologies and policies regulating the relations between women and men are finding new uses in the globalized economy and demonstrating a resistance to significant alteration. Globalization is promoting increased knowledge, a byproduct of the constant and rapid exchange of information made possible by computer-mediated technologies. This new type of knowledge, following the observations made by Castells, is likely to generate winners and losers at individual and national levels—even though the current discourse of globalization glosses over this possibility, preferring to talk instead of opportunities for persons and countries to develop their "comparative advantage."

Martin Carnoy explores the question of how globalization and its "ideological package" affect the overall delivery of education. He looks beyond what occurs in the classroom in relation to global economic phenomena and considers the "ideological package," which globalization carries with it, and a broader notion of schooling. He sees three effects of globalization: (1) the pressure to reduce the growth of public spending on education and find other sources of funding; (2) the rate of return to higher levels of education increases pressure to produce more secondary graduates qualified for tertiary education; and (3) international comparisons of educational systems (e.g., TIMSS), encouraging a focus on quality. When this is the focus of reform, the ways education is delivered are thereby changed. While Carnoy sees that national educational policies are informed by financially driven reforms, which redistribute schooling, accentuating a more unequal distribution of income and highly valued knowledge, he also argues that nations can condition the ways that globalization is brought into education. "There is much more political space to develop alternatives than the ideologies of globalization allow."

As Jones notes in his chapter, globalization has not engendered a camaraderie, so it is not about internationalism. He explores the tension between globalization—a focus on global economic integration through processes related to the free market—and internationalism—promotion of global peace through intergovernmental relations—and how these tensions emerge in the educational policies of the United Nations Childrens Fund; the United Nations Educational, Scientific, and Cultural Organization; and the World Bank. Sources of funding condition educational policies, both of which reflect to a greater or lesser degree the logic of globalization or internationalism. The World Bank, for example, which raises capital commercially and therefore operates as a free agent, promotes particular preconditions for educational policy and practice that mirrors its globalization agenda. Democratic ideals inherent in public schooling become diminished in favor of economic viability, including shifting responsibility to parents for support of schooling. In addition to examining intergovernmental organizations, Jones invites readers to analyze the globalization–internationalism tensions in the work of international nongovernmental organizations (NGOs).

Val D. Rust's chapter raises the issue of what it means to be politically radical. In analyzing the orientations of conservatives and liberals in the former Soviet Union and the European welfare states, Rust suggests that the conservatives are promoting radical change while the liberals want to maintain the status quo, thus reversing the traditional notions of who is radical and who is conservative. He then proceeds to examine two educational issues—the public vs. private school debate and the comprehensive school movement—in light of his assertions. He finds that the efforts to maintain and support viable public systems of education are coming from voices on the Left; they seek to maintain the status quo. It is the Right that promotes the use of vouchers and privatization in schools. Similarly, the Left is now defending the welfare state and its related public systems of education, which try not to favor the elite at the expense of others. The Right questions the viability of the comprehensive school due to the perceived breakdown in educational standards and discipline; its members seek change. The "radicals of the past are now attempting to defend their past achievements, while the radicals of the present" want to see a breakdown "of the welfare state and many of the traditions that characterize modern states" including comprehensive education and public schooling.

Noel Gough looks at globalization from a cultural perspective. He asks not what globalization is, but how it works and what it does. He examines meanings that curriculum workers exchange under the sign of globalization, particularly in relation to the increasing *awareness* people have of the growing reality of transnational processes and communications (but not necessarily linked to the realities themselves). While he sees little overt influence of globalization on curriculum theory—on concepts and methods of academic curriculum inquiry—he does recognize a multifaceted phenomena in which "the transnational imaginary of cultural globalization is *simultaneously* represented in curriculum policies and school programs, expressed by teachers and students, circulated in popular media, and deployed in the construction of school knowledge." How these various discourses relating to curriculum will interact and influence school curricula is yet to be seen.

Completing the first part of the book, Catherine A. Odora Hoppers offers a provocative reflection on how globalization is muffling previous debates over unfair and unequal relations between poor and rich nations. She points out that while education as a key institution in the provision of skills and human capital formation is being preserved, globalization is erasing two other important functions of education: the transmission of the normative heritage of particular societies and the development of critical thought. Odora Hoppers finds that through the influence of international development agencies, there is a tendency toward a "geopolitics of sameness," characterized by a uniformity of assumptions, diagnoses, and prescriptions. Accordingly, Sub-Saharan African countries are construed as being in permanent "crisis" and therefore urged, and even forced, to follow external advice, often conveyed by technocrats sensitive to financial institutions from abroad but much less aware of the values of African solidarity and self-determination.

The second part of the book, which focuses on higher education, vocational education, community colleges, and adult education, begins with a chapter by Jan Currie and George Subotzky. The authors zero in on universities in selected countries. They find that the introduction of managerial practices in the university is creating a negative impact on both internal decision making and on the university's external mission of serving the common good. They argue that in the three national contexts they have studied (France, Norway, and South Africa) political, economic, and cultural conditions are conducive to trying alternatives to the increasingly dominant Anglo-American neoliberal tradition of limiting university knowledge to the economic production. The authors propose several democratic decision making practices and community partnership service as alternatives to the entrepreneurial model and as essential spaces to preserve a critical stance toward the unfolding developments in society.

Rosalind Latiner Raby considers the North American community college model of postsecondary education and its diffusion in many countries. She discusses why this model is of interest outside the United States and how it is implicated in international development education. She discusses also the nature of the symbiotic relationships between donor and recipient colleges and how both institutions are influenced by these relationships.

Jane Kenway and Peter Kelly's chapter examines the tripartite relationship of gender, schooling, and work, offering what they call "an eagle's and a worm's view" of vocational education and training (VET). Relying particularly on Giddens's framework for analyzing the "altered context of political life," they detect four restructuring processes affecting gender and work, the child/adult transition, the school/work linkage, and the redefinition of the local community. With the assistance of macro and micro data, Kenway and Kelly show that these restructuring processes intersect in important ways with traditional notions of gender and social class. Young people face new situations for which VET is not preparing them or for which VET may introduce problems of its own. The authors challenge VET educators and policymakers to be sensitive to individual students' biographic projects and to macrosocial and economic conditions by which gender ideologies and practices are simultaneously being eroded and magnified.

Shirley Walters looks at how adult education is being shaped by globalization processes and how adult education practitioners are responding to new and often contradictory pressures, using the South African situation as a case in point to ground the discussion. Historical trends in adult education and terminology (adult education, training, lifelong learning, adult learning) are outlined and the interrelationships between development and adult education are discussed. She introduces the concepts of competitive and cooperative globalization, linking each to alternative adult education paradigms. Competitive globalization relates to economic development and requires adult education and training to serve these purposes. In contrast, cooperative globalization is concerned with human values and full participatory democracy. Adult education institutions, as other social institutions, are involved in the transformation of society, in the creation of the new South African citizen, and in determining how the local and the global will coexist. Walters argues that "the potential of adult learning will only be fully realized through collective struggles across national and regional boundaries, where some of the benefits of globalization, like the new communications technologies, can be used to forge new visions of a world which are both utopic and viable."

Part three of this book presents seven case studies of particular countries or regions—Mexico, South Africa, Lesotho, Malaysia, Japan, Australia, and the English-speaking Caribbean.

Anne Hickling-Hudson covers ongoing developments affecting universities in the English-speaking Caribbean. A notable feature concerns the expansion of access to higher education, primarily through the creation of private universities; the establishment of much more market-oriented degrees, often in non-university institutions; and the acceptance of partnership programs with foreign universities, often using new communication technologies. The universities in the Caribbean are found to be rapidly moving into standardization of their programs to be ready for a more mobile professional labor force. Hickling-Hudson welcomes the growing democratization of universities and other forms of postsecondary education in the region, but suggests ways by which Caribbean institutions may be able to combine traditional as well as modern, and Western as well as non-Western, contributions. In her view, universities and colleges in developing countries "must work even harder than their counterparts in the wealthy world to reinvent themselves on their own terms."

Lynne Parmenter looks at 1998 educational reforms that pertain to international goals in Japanese elementary and junior high schools. Educational discourse in Japan—one of the strongest beneficiaries of globalization—uses the terms _globalization_ and _internationalization_ interchangeably and ambiguously. Parmenter's review of the current reform documents, however, shows us that the thrust of these reforms is to develop "Japanese people who can live in international society." The current reforms move from the notion of "us and them" to a concept of "living with" people of different cultures. However, national identity remains a primary concern. Hope comes in (1) the form of "integrated study time," where subject boundaries can be transcended and teachers are able to shape the curriculum, including the incorporation of international issues and experiences, and (2) the possibility for many of the more general moral values specified in the educational reforms to be extended to the international sphere to "provide a solid foundation for the construction of world citizenship."

William Rideout examines how the concept of decentralization, which he finds heavily endorsed and spread by the World Bank, has been played out in Sub-Saharan Africa. Focusing primarily on Lesotho, but also highlighting conditions in the Democratic Republic of Congo, Senegal, and Cameroon, he demonstrates that various forms of educational decentralization have preceded the current trend and that community and parental participation have often been used to provide resources unavailable from the central governments. In recent times, de jure decentralization has often not become a reality or has distorted and even destroyed previous forms of de facto decentralization. In Rideout's view, the positive aspects of decentralization reside in its potential to promote bottom-up options. This implies that although globalization seems to call for a uniform type of educational decentralization, local realities must be allowed to prevail.

Displaying strong familiarity with postmodernist thought and analysis, Rosa Nidia Buenfil deconstructs educational policies in Mexico in the last decade. Her chapter focuses on reforms to modernize the educational system through concepts such as quality, equity, and productivity. The new Mexican policies are found to reiterate many of the global recommendations by the World Bank, such as decentralization, curricular reform along worker productivity lines, and the revalorization of the teachers' role. Buenfil's key finding is that at the local level different sets of actors in the educational system (e.g., the ministry of education, the teachers' unions, and the classroom teachers) produce a different reading of the modernization policy, a process Buenfil terms "resignification." Importantly, global meanings and discourses are being reshaped by local realities because these new interpretations create spaces for "ethical and political intervention."

Crain Soudien and Carol Corneilse's chapter also focuses on higher education. Taking South Africa as the key referent, the authors examine recent developments in the University of Cape Town. In the process of restructuring, due in part to declining government subsidies, faculties and departments were asked to redesign their offerings. While the criteria for the new programs included "excellence," "equity," and the "need for transcending the legacy of apartheid," in actual outcomes, academic programs that emerged are those approved on the basis of their ability to respond to market needs. This became evident when a "Foundation Semester" in the humanities with an African Studies emphasis became hotly debated and university administrators found its content not supporting or congruent with the globalization process South Africa is undergoing. The intervention by administrators on curriculum matters is unprecedented and signals new configurations of power in the academic world.

Centering on Malaysia—recognized as one of the few successful industrializing countries, where "globalization of the economy" has been the basis for its growth—Molly N. N. Lee examines how globalization forces have affected the entire educational system of her country. Schooling has expanded preschool attention to accommodate the increasing number of working mothers, secondary schooling has seen the reintroduction of English (a move Lee interprets as the need to produce a "globally oriented workforce"), and higher education has expanded by permitting the establishment of previously prohibited private and foreign universities. Lee observes that other globalization forces are also operating simultaneously with measures to globalize the educational system following Western trends. In the case of Malaysia, they take the form of Islamic education, to preserve what is seen as part of the Malaysian and regional identity.

We close the book with a chapter on Australia by Jill Blackmore, who introduces the case of an industrialized country whose path may not be drastically different from less powerful countries in the developing world where structural and other policies associated with globalization affect both marginalized countries and individuals. In Australia these policies have transformed gender relations by changing the nature of the state and its relation to the individual, household, and community. The welfare state, which has been an important site for political action for women, used to discipline the market; now the market disciplines the state. At the same time, universities take on a more corporatist model, limiting the ways that research, teaching, collegiality, and participatory governance can occur. Attention to equity within educational institutions becomes obscured. Globalization has threatened feminism's mode of engagement with the welfare state—an important site for political activism—and its public agencies such as universities—a critical forum for the production of multiple, including hegemonic, knowledges.

With this book, we seek to raise the discussion on globalization both to a more theoretical level and to a greater level of concreteness by referring to specific instances of the globalization forces and the responses to them in selected countries. The emerging terrains of convergence, dissonance, and conflict should help us visualize with greater clarity the implications of globalization for education and knowledge in the twenty-first century.

Abbreviations and Acronyms

AACC	American Association of Community Colleges
ABET	Adult Basic Education and Training
ACIIE/Stanley	American Council on International/Intercultural Education/Stanley Foundation
ACTI	Association of Caribbean Tertiary Level Institutions
AD	Associate Degree (AD)
ANC	African National Congress
APE	*Association des Parents d'Eleves* (Association of Parents of Students)
APF	Academic Planning Framework
ASC	Advisory School Committee
ASEAN	Association of Southeast Asian Nations
CBO	Community-Based Organization
CCID	Community Colleges for International Development
CEPAL	Economic Commission for Latin America and Caribbean
CNTE	Coordinadora Nacional de Trabajadores de la Educación
CONFINTEA V	Fifth International Conference on Adult Education
Congo/K	Democratic Republic of Congo
CSL	Community Service Learning
DAWN	Development Alternatives with Women for a New Era
DEETYA	Department of Employment, Education, Training and Youth Affairs [Australia]
DSE	Deutsche Stiftung fur internationale Entwicklung
EEP	Equal Employment Policies
EPRC	Education Policy Review Commission
EU	European Union
FDI	Foreign Direct Investment
FTZ	Free Trade Zone
GEAR	Growth, Employment and Redistribution Strategy [South Africa]
GLOSAS	Global Systems Analysis and Simulation Project
GOL	Government of Lesotho

GU	Global University
HDI	Human Development Index
HECS	Higher Education Contribution Scheme
HICOM	Heavy Industries Corporation of Malaysia
HSC	High School Certificate [Australia]
IBP	International Best Practice
ICC	Intercultural Communicative Competence
ICEED	International Consortium for Economic and Educational Development
IDRC	International Development Research Centre
ILRIG	International Labour Research and Information Group
IMF	International Monetary Fund
ISA	International Sociological Association
IT	Information Technology
MC	Management Committee [Lesotho]
MOE	Ministry of Education [Lesotho]
MSC	Multimedia Super Corridor [Malaysia]
NAFTA	North American Free Trade Agreement
NATO	North Atlantic Treaty Organization
NCHE	National Commission on Higher Education [South Africa]
NGO	Nongovernmental Organization
NQF	National Qualifications Framework [South Africa]
OCDE	Organización de Cooperación y Desarrollo Económico
ODHEC	Organization for the Development of Higher Education in the Caribbean
OECD	Organization for Economic Cooperation and Development
OUS	Office of University Services, University of the West Indies
PAN	Accion Nacional Party [Mexico]
PAS	Parti Islam Se-Malaysia
PMR	Penilaian Menengah Rendah [examination]
PP	Private Providers
PPEALC	Principal Education Project for Latin America
RDP	Reconstruction and Development Program [South Africa]
SAP	Structural Adjustment Program
SCC	Sinclair Community College [Ohio]
SEP	Secretaría de Educación Pública
SNTE	Sindicato Nacional de Trabajadores de la Educación
SOSE	Studies of Society and Environment
SPM	Sijil Pelajaran Malaysia [examination]
TAFE	Technical and Further Education [college]
TIMSS	Third International Math and Science Study
TNC	Transnational Corporation
UCCA	Universities and University Colleges Act 1971 [Malaysia]

UCT	University of Cape Town
UG	University of Guyana
UMNO	United Malays National Organisation
UN	United Nations
UNAM	Universidad Nacional Autónoma de México
UNCTAD	United States Commission on Trade and Development
UNDP	United Nations Development Program
UNEP	United Nations Environment Program
UNESCO	United Nations Educational, Scientific, and Cultural Organization
UNICEF	United Nations Childrens Fund
Utech	University of Technology
UWI	University of the West Indies
VET	Vocational Education and Training
WREDO	Western Region Economic Development Organization [Australia]

Part 1

Conceptual Issues

1

Defining Globalization and Assessing Its Implications on Knowledge and Education

Nelly P. Stromquist and Karen Monkman

GLOBALIZATION DEFINED

Globalization, a contemporary term that has entered the consciousness of most people by now, is a phenomenon that comprises multiple and drastic changes in all areas of social life, particularly economics and culture. Not surprisingly, its meaning varies depending on the angle that is emphasized when defining it. Globalization can be discussed in economic, political, and cultural terms. It can be expressed in neoliberal economic perspectives, critical theory, and postmodernity. It has been applied to cover debates centering on convergence/divergence, homogenization/heterogenization, and local/global issues. Despite its ability to capture in its unfolding changes the involvement of the entire world in one way or another, globalization remains an inexact term for the strong, and perhaps irreversible, changes in the economy, labor force, technologies, communication, cultural patterns, and political alliances that it is imposing on every nation.

While some observers are quick to point out that external influences have always impacted the world's nations, most people recognize that the degree of interconnectivity and speed brought about by current technologies, economic actors, and economic production vastly surpasses such previous exchanges on Planet Earth. Not only are speed and consumption needs greater than ever, but new actors have emerged and their actions heavily impact on others. As Harvey has nicely encapsulated, under contemporary capitalism we have a "time-space compression" (cited in Castells, 1997, p. 434). English is emerging as the global language, and social/economic transactions are being formulated within what Castells calls the "network society," a rise in horizontal connections among re-

3

lated institutions in diverse localities and dependent on computer-mediated technologies.

A useful definition of globalization is that offered by Gibson-Graham (1996, p. 121): "a set of processes by which the world is rapidly being integrated into one economic space via increased international trade, the internationalization of production and financial markets, the internationalization of a commodity culture promoted by an increasingly networked global telecommunications system." This economic space is increasingly connected to cultural influences and to political relations that are also global in nature.

The economic features of globalization involve an export orientation to production, the ample use of subcontracting, and the (usually unintended) growth of the informal sector. Its political features include the emergence of a minimalist state with mediating rather than intervening roles and a trend toward privatization of industrial production and services; some would claim that globalization has also brought the dissemination of democratic norms and pluralistic parties for nation-states. A global culture is thus emerging, characterized by high respect for industry and technology and the exercise of a new social and technical division of labor. As Castells clarifies, the economy is becoming global, not in the sense that similar events are occurring in different countries but in the sense that there has developed "an economy with the capacity to work as a unit in real time on a planetary scale" (1996, p. 92).

Globalization has many faces. In the area of economics, practices favoring free trade, private enterprise, foreign investment, and liberalized trade prevail. In the social area, new consumption patterns and lifestyles with consequences for migration, family relations, and social organization have arisen. At cultural levels, the flows of people, goods, information, and images reflect the influence of communication processes (Featherstone, 1990), and new identities and imaginaries are taking shape. At the political level, there is increased acceptance of pluralistic systems, multiparty democracy, free elections, independent judiciaries, and the call for human rights (Ghai, 1987). Some observers are skeptical that these practices and norms will alter the real economic order. González Casanova (1996) sees the term *globalization* as a rhetoric device for the reconversion of dependency, as it hides the effects of economic policies that are creating major social problems in many developing countries. As Amin (1996) notes, globalization affects not only trade but also the productive system, technology, financial markets, and many other aspects of social life. So far, because there are still people outside the modern economy, globalization has not affected the lives of every person in every country, but increasingly, it appears that ultimately all groups will be brought into conformity with the structure and goods of globalized society.

NEW ACTORS IN THE GLOBAL ECONOMY

The unfolding dynamics of globalization have brought several major players into the economic and political decision making process. The first of these is unquestionably the market; the others, the more tangible ones, are the transnational corporations (TNCs) with indisputable roles in the market and politics.

The Market

Today, with the demise of the centrally planned, socialist economies, great promise and reliance are placed on the role of the market to release creative energies and minimize inefficiencies. Through competition of firms, the market is expected to enable production to reach its highest volume and quality. Competitiveness, then, is a major principle in the globalized market.

Castells (1996) identifies sources of competitiveness in the global economy. They operate through four distinct processes: (1) the technological capacity of a country or the articulation of science, technology, management, and production; (2) access to large, integrated, affluent markets such as the European Union, North American Free Trade Agreement, or Japan; (3) a profitable differential between production costs at the production site and prices at the market of destination (including not just labor costs but land costs, taxes, and environmental regulations); and (4) the political capacity of national and supranational institutions to guide the growth strategy of those countries or areas under their jurisdiction (pp. 103–5). What this list shows clearly is that knowledge is one component in the attainment of competitiveness; as we will see later, it might not always be accessible.

Having observed the workings of the market, Gibson-Graham (1996, p. 144) concludes that "it is not all or only capitalist," and that "commodities are not all or only products of capitalism." This position is accepted by several others. For instance, Castells (1996) asserts that global markets are not truly global except for a small but growing segment of professionals and scientists. But he goes on to affirm that "labor is a global resource in at least three ways: firms relocate to find the labor supply they need, be it in terms of skills, costs, or social control; firms everywhere may require highly skilled labor from everywhere; and labor will enter any market at its own initiative, coming from anywhere" (p. 93).

The power exercised by markets may not benefit all. And this is the problematic situation, as no market self-regulatory apparatus exists. Financial markets behave in extremely speculative ways; not only do they not engage in productive investments, but they have triggered currency devaluation of entire countries (e.g., Brazil, Mexico, Thailand, and Russia), with corresponding consequences in reduced national wealth, thus leading to limited public policies. One million children in Asia were unable to return to school after the market crisis precipitated there in the late 1990s.

A feature of contemporary markets is their clustering in regional blocs to attain benefits of scale, coordinate production, and target specific populations. Three such blocs have emerged (Europe, North America, and East Asia) and they are preparing themselves for increasing competition.[1] Together with the global market, we are seeing the creation of macroinstitutions to facilitate economic and political exchanges. Examples are the growing influence of the International Monetary Fund (IMF) and World Bank in numerous countries (McGuire and Campos, 1997), the recent creation of the World Trade Organization (WTO), and the redefinition of NATO to address sociopolitical problems within European countries. On the other hand, world institutions such as that needed for the creation of a new international economic order are now being fostered. Through structural adjustment programs coordinated by the World Bank and the IMF, the process of capital accumulation continues while impacting negatively on the process of distribution and reallocation of the social product (Oomen, 1997).

Transnational Corporations

Some forty thousand large firms qualify today as transnational corporations (Moghadam, 1999). TNCs are both the primary agents and major beneficiaries of globalization (Ghai, 1987; Gibson-Graham, 1996). It is estimated that four hundred TNCs own two-thirds of the planet's fixed assets and control 70 percent of world trade (Robinson, quoted in McLaren, 1999, p. 17). Through access to highly mobile capital, TNCs have created global factories, relying on the cheapest combination of labor and skills for selected tasks. TNCs thus have generated increasingly integrated and interdependent systems of capital–labor flows across regions and between states. With the support of international financial institutions, TNCs can engage in substantial and speedy capital investment, technology transfer, financial exchanges, and increased trade (Moghadam, 1999).

The emergence of institutions that are less publicly accountable, such as multinational corporations, banks, and media conglomerates, has produced a society in transition with new philosophies about government (Independent Commission, 1996, p. 257). Blackmore (in this volume) warns that, "Whereas the welfare state previously disciplined the market within its national boundaries, in a globalized context, the state is now disciplined by international markets."

The emergence of TNCs as major players has implications for education. With business and profitability as the main referent, "social and public service interests are devalued" and "appropriate knowledge becomes increasingly narrowly defined" (Kempner, 1998, p. 455). At local levels, there is an increased presence of business in cooperation with the schools, determining what constitutes quality and what is needed.

CULTURE

The impact of globalization on culture is universally felt. However, there are opposing viewpoints about current developments. Most observers see a tendency toward homogeneity of values and norms; others see an opportunity to rescue local identities.

Through the mass media (TV, film, radio, video), not only is English becoming the global language, but there has developed a tendency, particularly among elites and middle classes all over the world, to adopt what might be termed an "American way of life." Among French intellectuals the opinion prevails that globalization is leading to superficialization and uniformization, impelled by the anglophone world. Such is the view of literary critic and writer Alex Maugey (cited in Namer, 1999). Through the mass media, the computer, and the role of research in industrialized countries, the English language is becoming dominant. What impact will this have on local cultures?

For Cvetkovich and Kellner (1997), the cultural forces reflected in the global media influence roles, identities, and experiences. In their view, old identities and traditional ways of seeing and being in the world have been challenged, and new forms are being constructed out of the "multifarious and sometimes conflicting configurations of traditional, local, national, and now global forces of the present time" (p. 10). They argue that "although global forces can be oppressive and erode cultural traditions and identities they can also provide new material to re-work one's identity and can empower people to revolt against traditional forms and styles to create new, more emancipatory ones" (p. 10). Among those who see less possibility for homogenization are Wilson and Dissanayake (1996, p. 6, from Gough, herein), who describe a "transnational imaginary" as

the *as-yet-unfigured* horizon of contemporary cultural production by which national spaces/identities of political allegiance and economic regulation are being undone and imagined communities of modernity are being reshaped at the macropolitical (global) and micropolitical (cultural) levels of everyday existence (emphasis in original).

Nonetheless, globalization fosters a greater synchronization of demands as well as a greater similarity in taste and preference within the national markets. In a way, this homogeneity is necessary to ensure a more standardized, and thus easier to produce, supply of products and services such as leisure and foreign travel.

It is likely that globalization is creating forces that will divide people economically, but it might also generate forces with the potential to offer new bases for solidarity (Kenway, 1997). While the world is becoming smaller and more homogeneous at some levels, in a variety of ways local cultures are making efforts to retain their identity and, in some cases, even to rediscover it. One such example concerns recent developments in Latin America. While for many years there raged a debate as to whether the indigenous question should be about social class or ethnicity, indigenous organizations have opted for the second position, which does not deny or ignore the exploitation Indians face but prefers to act by affirming their ethnic identity (Stavenhagen, 1997). Some scholars argue that the renaissance of the local might be emerging as a defense against the impossibility of joining the global on favorable terms. In any case, efforts to recapture traditional identities and values come as unintended effects of globalization.

The prevailing values that are emerging bring a twist to traditional definitions. "Flexibility" for instance, means less the ability to accept cultural differences than the ability to adjust economically and adapt innovations in the production of goods and services. While there have been significant changes in production processes, which have now moved into "post-Fordist" forms, current labor practices and work organization continue to have a hierarchical network structure. Moreover, large companies in central countries offer their workers reward systems based on seniority and cooperation with firm-based unions; but firms in developing countries, which Castells terms those "in the periphery of the network," treat labor as expendable and exchangeable, relying on temporary workers and part-time employees, among whom women and poorly educated youth are the majority. In Japan, for instance, networked business groups lead both to flexible cooperation and to highly segmented labor markets that induce a dual social structure, organized mainly along gender lines (Castells, 1996, p. 175). In other words, production forms seem to have changed more than the values and norms attached to the way production is organized.

Culture and Gender

An important dimension of culture regards the formation of masculinity and femininity. Institutions such as armies, bureaucracies, and even the stock market have served to export norms of violence, aggressiveness, and domination that established masculinity as the dominant norm (Connell, 1998). These forms of masculinity have not disappeared but are assuming what seems at first sight "gender-neutral" (though not gender-equalizing) forms under representations of "markets," "individuals," and "choice." But, as Connell reminds us, the emerging global mass media, especially the electronic media, is a major venue for the globalization of gender imbalances. Through popular entertainment, stereotyped gender images as well as prevailing modes of Western masculinity and criminality circulate in large volume (Connell, 1998). On the other hand, through the widespread diffusion of communication technologies, ideas about gender equality and equity have circulated very fast. The "personal is political" is a universally accepted tenet among many women; this principle "politicized masses of women never before active and enabled many who were already active to develop more independent and self-defined relationships to politics" (Miles, 1996, p. 3). Globalization, therefore, has introduced contradictory ideas in the reproduction of gender ideologies and practices in society: it has provided the space for critique and alternative social visions and at the same time transfers representations of women and men that are not only highly genderized but also solidify very traditional views of these two sets of social actors.

Applying the gender construct to the production arena, several observers assert that globalization is creating two distinct economies: a masculinized world of high technology and finances that involves production that serves the public sphere and a mostly feminized economy consisting of sexualized and racialized services in the private sphere. Given its structure and functioning, the latter expression of globalization does not distinguish between the private and public spheres of the women workers and thus institutionalizes abuse and exploitation and sustains the highly technical form of production, which relies on cheap work. For example, most migrant workers in domestic service receive lower salaries than their nonimmigrant counterparts, but in both cases, women fill these jobs.

The most positive feature of globalization for women has been their incorporation into the labor market. According to Organization for Economic Cooperation and Development (OECD) data, this incorporation in the seven major national economies grew about 30 percent from 1970 to 1990, a growth that Castells calls a "massive incorporation of women in paid work" throughout the world (1996, p 253). Yet, this incorporation has taken forms that have not been particularly advantageous to women. In Japan, the second major industrial power in the world, women massively enter the labor force in their early twenties, stop working after marriage to raise their children, and return later to the labor force as part-timers. This structure of the occupational lifecycle is reinforced by the Japanese tax codes, which make it more advantageous for women to contribute in a relatively small proportion to the family income than to add a second salary. While the strict labor participation pattern of Japan is not found to the same extent in the United States, the U.S. tax code also penalizes two-income families (read, wives with large salaries).

Castells (1997) finds that in several countries women are often being promoted to multiskilled jobs that require initiative and education. He believes that since new technologies demand an autonomous labor force able to adapt and reprogram its own tasks, women with the pertinent skills will benefit in the new informational economy. This possibility certainly is there. Yet, women comprise the majority of part-time and temporary employment in OECD countries, and longitudinal data reveal that women are increasing their share of this type of participation. Part-time jobs represent about one-fifth of the jobs in OECD economies; under globalization, these jobs also have a tendency to increase. Flexible time and part-time work favor women because they accommodate women's needs to combine their child rearing tasks and their working lives. It should be obvious, however, that this "accommodation" tends to reproduce highly gendered social relations.

Displaying powerful insight, Connell (1998, p. 15) remarks that the "individual" of neoliberal theory has in general the attributes and interests of a male entrepreneur, while the increasing and unregulated power of transnational corporations places strategic power in the hands of particular groups of men.[2] He considers it not surprising that the "installation of capitalism in Eastern Europe and the former Soviet Union has been accompanied by a reassertion of dominating masculinities and, in some situations, a sharp worsening of the social position of women."[3] Supporting this observation, Craske (1998) maintains that the neoliberal project that accompanies current globalization processes depends on women retaining their "traditional" family-oriented identities without undermining their availability for the labor market to provide low-wage competition.

Patriarchal structures are not changing very much. Even though there is talk of the "new man" [sic] in industrialized societies, a study conducted of the division of labor within families in Western Germany found that though the patriarchal structures are modernizing in the sense that women are encouraged to enter the labor force and the public arena, reproductive (i.e., domestic and menial) work is being redistributed between different groups of women. In the German context, young, better qualified, and wealthier German women and men are increasingly likely to delegate reproductive work to other less qualified, socially disadvantaged, and/or foreign women (Rerrich, 1996). Feminist thinker Eisenstein states:

> Global capital sends Avon to brazil [author states country names in small letters to highlight the decreased importance of the nation-state], fancy lingerie to argentina, prostitution and porn to eastern europe. There is little new here, but there are now new ways of doing it. Transnational corporations defy economic borders while utilizing and adapting old formations and constructions of race and gender. The question is whether capital itself will erode the racialized/gendered borders that it depends on (1997, p. 144).

Today women predominate in labor-intensive and low-wage textile and garment industries, as well as electronics assembly and pharmaceutical production (Moghadam, 1999). Further, as production increasingly requires more sophisticated technology, women workers tend to be replaced by men or are recruited at a slower pace, as evidence from Mexico, Spain, and Italy shows (Moghadam, 1999). Women entering the informational field are finding greater possibilities in such areas as software and system design, information searching, and service provision, but they still represent a minority compared to men. All over the world, home-based work (carried out by women) is an important source of employment. In seven African countries, 55 to 77 percent of enterprises are home-based, a fact not captured by official statistics (Chen, 1998). Because of these negative, or at best modest, trends for women in the current globalized economy, Chen advocates that "feminists scholars of all kinds and economists should unpack markets" (p. 30). Given the type of access and location of women in the globalized labor market, it seems that women will need to have comparatively higher levels of education to compete with men for the better jobs, as parity in primary and secondary education is not sufficient under conditions of social discrimination. Aided by such recognition, women are the social actors most strongly promoting broader projects of social justice. Moghadam (1999) finds that the massive entry of women into the labor force has been accompanied by the expansion of women's organizations of all types: union, grassroots, feminist, women-led nongovernmental organizations (NGOs), and networks working on women and the global economy. Other observers argue that with pressures for survival, women are making fewer demands for social justice, an example of this being the limited pressure on schools to promote gender sensitivity.

For many women who face survival problems or deteriorating economic conditions under globalization forces, migration has arisen as a strategy to increase their income. A case in point is the growing migration among women from Latin America to Holland, Spain, and Germany, as domestic workers and prostitutes, and to Germany, England, and Switzerland, as janitors.[4]

KNOWLEDGE UNDER GLOBALIZATION

It is obvious that a rapid and sustained shift is occurring in the ways we learn and do things. Boundaries in time and space are being crossed with great ease; people know of events much quicker than ever before, and they can be in distant places with great ease. A positive expectation about the new speed of information and human diffusion is that the invisible hand of the market now also moves faster and with greater efficiency, which will both increase the satisfaction and welfare of consumers and exercise pressures for greater efficiency among firms that wish to remain in the market.

Globalization increases interaction, and this creates opportunities for new learning—but also for old learning. Among the new learning, we have now what is called the "cult of technology" and conversely the diminution of respect for spiritual and cultural values (Maugey, cited in Namer, 1999). While some ideas indeed are being exchanged freely, it is a struggle to offer and disseminate ideas with weak connection to the market.

According to Giddens (1994), with the rise of multiple technologies and globalization dynamics, there are no permanent structures of knowledge or meaning today. The process of translation and adaptation calls for many changes, and this in turn produces changes in intended as well as unintended ways. Giddens predicts the arrival of an era of reflexivity, caused by the growing proportion of people who are knowledge seekers. Since knowledge will be increasingly subject to revision, we might find "doubt" to be a feature of globalization (cited in Kenway, 1997). Giddens is perhaps only partly correct. Science and technology are fields that today receive much respect. But they are also fields whose "knowledge" is predicated on positivistic science with claims of certainty and precision. Such tendencies would generate an impetus for knowledge as certainty. In the social sciences, in fact, we are seeing a tendency toward the understanding of knowledge as precise, decontextualized, and thus fragmented. Such a trend is evident in the current attempts by agencies such as the World Bank to create "knowledge management systems" whose fundamental premise seems to be that knowledge can be reduced to a minimal and yet valid expression.

In a globalized world, as technology becomes its main motor, knowledge assumes a powerful role in production, making its possession essential for nations if they are successfully to pursue economic growth and competitiveness. This search for technological knowledge makes sense at one level, but at another perhaps sets countries on an impossible path. Often, one hears the assertion that workers can be transformed into owners of capital as knowledge can be put into their heads (Curry, 1997), an assertion predicated on the assumption that knowledge is more accessible than the other factors of production: land and capital. But what this argument ignores is the great chasm that poverty creates between the poor and the international circuits of production, distribution, and access to knowledge.

In addition to the increased speed of circulation of knowledge there has been growth in the quantity, quality, and density of knowledge embodied in the design, production, and marketing of even ordinary products (Curry, 1997). Consequently, knowledge will be increasingly embedded in technical capital. Countries that depend on natural resources extraction will build only minimal technical capital (Curry, 1997). Extrapolating from this trend, it follows that the knowledge composition of capital will be differentially distributed. If so, the fundamental relation between labor and capital may remain the same as before, even though the knowledge component of capital may be today far more sophisticated than in the past.

GLOBALIZATION AND FORMAL SCHOOLING

The principle of competitiveness has brought about much more salience to education than in previous decades since education is intimately linked to the development of technological capability. Rhoades and Slaughter (1991) note that educational reform in the United States is being argued in terms of "preparing better students for the workplace," which will render the curriculum an additional form of contemporary cultural production through which the concept of the transnational is expressed.

The increasing importance of the global market has had several repercussions on formal schooling. First, criteria employed in firms for efficiency and productivity are being extended to schooling, sometimes in an inappropriate fashion. Second, focus has shifted from child-centered curriculum to economy-centered vocational training. This trend is evident in leading nations such as Japan, the United States, the United Kingdom, Germany, and Scandinavian countries and in important new players such as China and Russia (Walters, 1998). Third, education is losing ground as a public good to become rather another marketable commodity. The state has become limited in its responsibility to schooling, often guaranteeing basic education but extracting in turn user fees from higher levels of public education, as any other service in the market. Fourth, teachers' autonomy, independence, and control over their work is being reduced while workplace knowledge and control find their way increasingly in hands of administrators. McLaren (1998) asserts that this situation is clearly affecting U.S. teachers.

In primary and secondary education today we see an almost unstoppable trend toward privatization and decentralization, both of which decrease the collective concern and bring heterogeneity of purpose and publics as unquestioned values. To serve the technological needs of the market better, new forms of flexible training in vocational and technical education are emerging through private offerings. Among the unintended consequences of these dynamics are (1) fields less connected to the market losing importance, e.g., history vis-à-vis math and science; (2) pedagogies less linked to the market losing importance, e.g., classroom discussions based on critical theory as opposed to problem-solving tasks; and (3) on a broader scale, issues of equality and equity concerning women and ethnic minorities losing ground to the consideration of such issues as efficiency (often reduced to performance in math and reading tests).

Much is being made of the need for individuals to have knowledge, and particularly technological knowledge, to move their countries into higher levels of economic competitiveness. But what is not taken into account in this argument are the contradictory demands that a technological society might make on its internal labor force. Individuals who will benefit from the new reality by virtue of their mastery of technological knowledge will likely transfer menial forms of service to others. Activities such as housecleaning, laundry, food preparation, and gardening will not only increasingly have to be conducted by these "others" but will possibly be subject to demands for higher quality. In other words, a "knowledge society" must count on a cadre of individuals whose knowledge is low enough to accept menial tasks or whose social conditions are such that they cannot claim the more dignified, higher-paying tasks for themselves. Extrapolating these dynamics into the future, it might be said that schooling will be used to differentiate students in early phases and that, if this does not create a sufficient pool of local workers, migration will supply the missing labor. There is already evidence of migration of trained people from poor economies to wealthier countries, such as Peruvians with college degrees working in Chile as nannies, high-school graduates from Paraguay working in menial jobs in Argentina, women from various Caribbean and Latin American countries serving as maids in Europe and the United States, and Filipino women with college degrees working as maids in Kuwait. The "brain-drain" phenomenon occurs because the educated are the ones who will have the most facility in obtaining information and conducting the paperwork needed for migration. But globalization welcomes them less for their higher levels of education than for their willingness to take on the low-skill jobs.

Higher Education

Globalization and its sophisticated use of technology implies a salient role for postsecondary education. TNCs have been making broad demands on universities for engagement in research and development, but it must be remembered that some of these companies are moving into their own direct involvement in R&D, portending a consequent reduction of the role of universities in technological development. In the field of microelectronics, the most definite globalization industry, this is certainly the case.

In a situation where universities will be linked more to the market and less to the pursuit of truth, it is likely that the definition and establishment of quality will become the prerogative of managerial rather than academic enterprise (Cowen, 1996). It is also likely that universities will become more "client" or "customer" focused. This orientation is not necessarily bad because responsiveness to adult needs has always been a good principle; but under globalization it is likely that the "client" will increasingly be powerful donors or contractual industrial clients and students from upper- and middle-class families, who might move the university toward reproducing distinctions of class or reducing its areas of knowledge to those research topics of interest to clients and donors (Simpson, 1998). The requirement to produce "consumer satisfaction" will place further emphasis on market-oriented effectiveness (Chaffee, 1998). Guided by a climate of knowledge as production, the university may become hostile or indifferent to subjects dealing with ethics, social justice, critical studies, and gender studies.

Life in the university will likely change under globalization. Intellectuals (read college professors) will become less the guardians of the search for truth, and administrators will assume a dominant role. In this regard, norms that have traditionally been part of university life may come under questioning. One such norm is tenure. In recent years several doubts have been raised about its "effectiveness." One example is reflected in the statement by Keith (1998, p. 165), who asserts that "The tenure system can be seen as an obstacle to change since it protects faculty who may be doing a good job but not the job that most needs to be done."

Entrepreneurial cultures now permeate university life in the prevailing "surveillance/appraisal" practices in British higher education and, in an emergent fashion, in the United States. In the United Kingdom there is now a Research Assessment Exercise and a Teaching Quality Assessment program that not only conduct frequent appraisal of faculty performance but also reduce such performance to a few indicators (McNeil, 1999). As universities compete with each other, and intramural rivalries grow between schools or departments within these universities, this norm of competing individualism will gradually limit attention to other areas of academic life that are not income-producing. Evaluations have an important role to play in universities, but if conceived in terms of marketability they can lead to distorted forms of academic performance.

Since the main beneficiaries of globalization are the TNCs, as well as individuals with professional, technical, and managerial skills (Ghai, 1987), the university is becoming a highly contested terrain. One new form of contestation might be preemptive, via the creation of a highly differentiated postsecondary system, characterized by a small number of elite universities with highly competitive admissions on one side, compensated by an expanding range of other, more accessible, types of postsecondary education.

This trend of affairs is now quite visible in Latin America, where universities are losing their monopoly over higher education. Many new institutions are emerging, usually simple in character and with no commitment to research. In Latin America today 85 percent of higher education institutions are not universities but a mixed bag of institutions and academies; at present 60 percent of the enrollment is still in universities, but this is likely to decline over time. Students are also moving into private universities, many of which offer relaxed entrance requirements. In Colombia, Brazil, Chile, El Salvador, and the Dominican Republic between 50 and 65 percent of the enrollment involves private institutions (Yarzabal, 1998, p. 304). The privatization of higher education offers several advantages to the proponents of a more competitive national economy. It reduces the financial burden of the government; satisfies aspirations for higher education of a large number of students (even though the prestige of their university may be much lower than that of the established universities); ensures that fields of study that are directly market-related will be offered in those institutions; and last, but of critical importance, contributes to the depoliticization of the university since students in private universities are readily inculcated by "careerist" as opposed to "critical" norms. In Latin America, the number of students in graduate programs (particularly Ph.D.) is expanding. Countries such as Mexico and Brazil have at least fifty thousand master's and doctoral students. This development is limited to universities with high prestige; new private universities are moving toward concentration on undergraduate and technical education. For those more concerned with the role of the higher education in defining societal goals, the privatization of higher education puts it squarely in the productive sphere and weakens the principle of education as a public good, for its future marked class distinction will not permit all graduates to gather knowledge of similar type and quality or to reap similar rewards from postsecondary education.

Gender Studies

Gender or women's studies in universities tend to be small programs serving a reduced number of students, but they are also crucial places in the production and transmission of critical knowledge. In the area of gender studies globalization is also producing contradictory effects. With the greater circulation of information, some values, such as human rights, including the rights of women, are becoming increasingly accepted as topics to be examined within the academy. There is also a greater diffusion of gender studies in universities and much more contact among women-led NGOs with each other and with academics in their national societies. Yet, as Blackmore (this volume) argues, globalization has affected the ties between feminists and the welfare state and has weakened feminist work within the university. She notes that

> Discourses of globalization have been used to justify reshaping the nature of universities, which had been strategic sites for feminist political activism. The welfare state, while still patriarchal, had provided some advantages for women, and universities, while still highly conservative, provided an intellectual counterpoint to the wider women's movement.

Adult Education

The education of poor adults who never went to school or who did not learn sufficiently when they did has suffered from chronic neglect by governments. There is ample consensus that adult education has existed without policy support, with little funding, and seldom more than a handful of projects dedicated to capacity building.

Efforts to serve marginalized and poor adults have long resulted more from grassroots support than governmental assistance. Bhola challenges adult educators to re-invent globalization by infusing it with a new ideology and disabusing it of the idea of profit above people. If the educators are successful, globalization could create a valuable space to build human solidarity and share responsibility for the future of the human race (Bhola, 1998). This challenge is in fact being taken seriously. The International Conference on Population and Development (in Cairo, 1994) called for a massive program of adult education, particularly addressed to women. The Social Summit in Copenhagen (1995) sought a new social contract at the global level to "fight poverty, to create productive jobs, and to strengthen the social fabric." This contract certainly would have implications on the education and training of adults. The Fifth International Conference on Adult Education (in Hamburg, 1997) was the first to combine representatives of government and civil society. Its agenda, not surprising, included an expanded set of issues—human rights, democracy, indigenous people, female empowerment—though no financial commitments by either governments or donor agencies (Bhola, 1998). UNESCO has very limited funds to engage in effective mobilization in favor of adult education. But the fact is that today—for various reasons, some of them related to changing global conditions—adult education has greater nongovernmental advocates than ever before.

THE STATE AND PUBLIC POLICY

Most discussions of the state under globalization highlight the relationship between the state and the market and are typified by very divergent views. Neoliberalism offers a negative view of the state in developing countries, characterizing it as corrupt, self-interested, and incompetent (Mosley et al., 1991). Measures of privatization, deregulation, decentralization, and integration into the global economy have, not surprisingly, coincided with a decrease in public expenditures (González Casanova, 1996). This decrease is in part fueled by ideology; in part it is caused by the new economic dynamics. With international pressure mounting for the free exchange of products, ultimately there will be no taxes on imports and thus less revenue for the state. The challenge for many governments today is how to modify the tax structure to gain greater contributions from domestic sources.

Though reduced revenues and rising costs appear likely to leave national governments with less wealth than in the past, assumptions about the diminishing role of the state do not automatically follow. Some perceive the state as rendered powerless and obsolete by globalization while the market economy progressively fulfills the state's functions. The creation of regional blocs and the roles states play in them are taken as further indications of the diminished role of states. But a larger number of observers consider that though globalization is bringing a change in the role of the state, it will remain an important actor (Featherstone, 1990; Kofman and Youngs, 1996; Hirst and Thompson, 1996). The new state will be less concerned with the welfare of its citizens than the creation of legal norms that enable the protection and coherence of the market.

Some indeed argue that the state creation is not to be seen as an impediment to globalization, but instead as an integral part of its emergence. For instance, the development of national systems of education have been intimately connected to globalization processes. National systems of education share many characteristics that reflect globalizing processes of convergence:

> almost universally, children are expected to attend school for more or less uniform periods of time, schools are age-graded and divided into primary and secondary levels, teacher training is increasingly at a post-secondary level, and the same basic curriculum is found across regions (Rust, this volume).

With the end of the Cold War, globalization, and structural adjustment programs in many countries, there has been a considerable expansion of private direct and portfolio investment from North to South and a simultaneous reduction in public-sector foreign aid programs (McGuire and Campos, 1997). State development policies have changed in nature and today seek to accumulate information for production and constrain dissent, while giving less time to modify or even consider structures of power and social inequalities. The new outlook has made social policy secondary to the market and has "atomized the social," centering on the interests of the individual as consumer rather than as citizen (Bustelo and Minujin, 1998).

Castells (1996) makes a contribution to the debate on the state by clarifying that "firms are motivated not by productivity but for profitability. Political insti-tutions, in contrast, are oriented, in the economic realm, toward maximizing competitiveness" (p. 81). If "competitiveness is an attribute of collectives, such as countries and regions, rather than firms," as Castells asserts (p. 86), then the state will continue to have a crucial function in economic life. The growing interde-pendence of economies (especially capital markets and currencies) limits the pos-sibilities of exclusively national economic policies. However, in many instances rapid technological change relies on both entrepreneurial innovation and deliber-ate government strategies to target technologies with potential to provide a coun-try a comparative advantage and to support related research. Summarizing this effectively, Castells forecasts that, "The new economy based on socioeconomic restructuring and technological revolution will be shaped according to political processes played out in and by the state (Castells, 1996, p. 90).

Also considering the future trajectory of the state, Lechner (1997) argues that it will continue to exercise three key coordinating functions: (1) its regulatory function, by legally ordering relations between different processes and actors (particularly crucial under a globalized economy that needs protection of private property and enforcement of contracts); (2) its function of representation, which involves reflecting the prevailing social order and offering symbolic images of units of society; and (3) its function of leadership, by channeling societal differ-ences into a shared view of the future.

Significant trends in educational policy are evident. First, the state is altering the educational labor market in terms of supply by fostering private schools, en-abling parental "choice" through voucher mechanisms, and demanding competi-tive performance of schools and in terms of demand by redefining education as a commodity or a private rather than social good (Blackmore, 1997).

Second, social expectations regarding educational policies have been trans-formed. Education used to be the state's greatest manifestation of social policy. An inspiring article by Weiler (1981) noted that the state uses education as a compensatory instrument of political legitimization, for in so doing it gains the good will of citizens without major changes in the economic and social structure. Today, such a strategy is no longer seen as relevant or crucial to state survival.

Reversing the question, it can be asked, What can education do for the state under globalization? Education is being set up as a critical element in economic well-being and competitiveness, yet—as in the past—it continues to be one factor among several. With the globalization of labor, TNCs follow the cheapest bidder internationally; while the skills of the labor force are important, usually lower levels of schooling are sufficient. For those countries able to generate high techni-cal knowledge among their university graduates, retention of talent at the highest levels is seen as one of the main challenges of globalization for Third World countries. Two factors operate against retention: one is the imitation factor that leads a Third World professional to compare himself/herself to others in the in-dustrialized countries. For example, a Mexican CEO complains that he earns "merely" $450,000, while his counterpart in the United States earns one million dollars per year. The other is the industrialized countries' ability to attract foreign knowledge on instant demand, as is seen in the current influx of microelectronics engineers.[5]

Green (1997) reviews various arguments about whether globalization processes will serve to effectively end national education systems or act as a force to widen curriculum and education policy. Like those who do not see the state disappearing under globalization, Green also does not anticipate the disappearance of national systems of education. Instead he sees national interests active in influencing the internationalization process in education (i.e., making it more sensitive to the needs and visions of other societies), in the marketing of education across national borders, and in citizen formation through schooling. He does forecast an increasing convergence in curriculum among European nations and an active exchange of faculty and students across national boundaries. Even the marketing of education, Green argues—a dynamic associated with globalization process—is done mostly within national contexts.

Third, it appears that the time and space for educational policies (and other types of policy) have been drastically altered. Those involved in policy making observe that globalization is shortening times and budget cycles; thus, there has been an acceleration in the design of such policies, with little time to reflect because responses are needed with greater urgency. While in the past the "horizon" of social policy was four to five years, today many programs arise and die in a twelve-month period; these programs also command fewer resources than in the past. Policy has moved from "strategic planning" to "continued responsiveness" in order to provide more market sensitivity. Policy formation in an increasing number of countries is accompanied by "ministerialization" (minister and advisers) rather than by bureaucrats (i.e., regular and stable government officials).

The influence of business and its accompanying values and norms are spreading throughout the world. What consequences will this ultimately have for education? Will teaching concentrate on transmitting knowledge about production, profit, and self-gratifying consumption? What is the possibility of introducing alternative forms of knowledge?

WINNERS AND LOSERS?

The prevailing discourse on globalization is rather optimistic. By and large, most people see advantages to the new open, highly connected, competitive, far-reaching process of economic and cultural exchanges. On a closer look, the tidal wave of globalization has impacted the lives of citizens of all countries with different degrees and a mix of positive and negative directions.

Castells (1996) acknowledges that the global economy is deeply asymmetric. He clarifies that this asymmetry is not in the form of a single center with semiperipheric and peripheric countries or the simplistic opposition of North and South, but rather more variegated and elusive. Nevertheless, a group of countries that corresponds approximately to membership in the OECD accounts for an overwhelming proportion of the world's technological capacity, capital, markets, and industrial production.[6] Continuing his insightful analysis, Castells holds that the structure of the new global economy is "characterized by the combination of an enduring architecture and a variable geometry" (p. 145). The "architecture" to which he refers are the three major economic blocs (the European Union, NAFTA, and the Asian Pacific) with the "variable geometry" ranging, with increasing polarization, from the productive, information-rich, affluent areas to the impoverished areas producing raw materials and engaging in easily supplantable labor procedures.

At one level, the terrain under globalization is "a space of flows, an electronic space, a decentered space, a space in which frontiers and boundaries have become permeable" (Robinson, cited in McLaren, 1999, p. 11). But at another level, this space seems highly fixed. Amin contends that the center (i.e., the most powerful industrial nations) holds five monopolies: technology, worldwide financial markets, global natural resources (in terms of access), media and communications, and weapons of mass destruction (Amin, 1996). A crucial question is, Can we change the nature of these monopolies? A more specific question for us, as educators, is, Can education help break or at least weaken these monopolies?

Analyses of the distribution of wealth in countries conclude that globalization has not increased wages except in the United States. Wealth has grown tremendously, and its allocation has been highly clustered. Within industrialized countries, "the new and wealthy class is the technological aristocracy and a cadre of business executives who work in the interests of corporate share price" (McLaren 1998, p. 434). Economic growth no longer guarantees poverty alleviation or employment generation, and both developed and developing regions must face high unemployment and a difficult job market, particularly among the youth (Development Alternatives with Women for a New Era, DAWN, 1995).

Economic changes have altered the relations between human beings and the nature of their lives. Guided by this awareness, DAWN, one of the largest women-led nongovernmental organizations, maintains that

> Indices of social development cannot be reduced to literacy, education, health or expenditures on social services. It must include the prevalence of violence, its promotion in the media, gross inequalities in consumption, dislocation of children from their homes, the unrepresentative character of the institutions associated with political and economic management (1995, p. 2002).

COUNTEREFFORTS TO GLOBALIZATION

At present, capitalism is seen as the only economic reality. Further, as Gibson-Graham (1996) underscores, the discourse on globalization presents capitalism as an incombatible force. These authors encourage us to deny the inevitability and reality of the power of TNCs over workers and communities and to explore ways in which we can render these TNCs vulnerable.

The challenge to seek different development paths and economic identities calls for the strengthening of the state. About 85 percent of total North–South private capital flows to only twelve developing countries. Clearly, the state (read nationwide and coordinated strategies) is needed to move some developing countries to better economic positions.

The alternatives being proposed are few and need greater development. A United Nations Development Program Independent Commission argues that a new social contract is needed and that it must go beyond security, justice, and well-being to include an expanded citizenship with a sense of belonging, meaningful participation, and a stronger civil society. Amin, a well-known development scholar, calls for an "Alternative Humanist Project of Globalization," attentive to "disarmament; equitable access to the planet's resources; open, flexible economic relationships between the world's major regions; [and] correct management of global/national dialectics in the areas of communication, culture, and political policy" (1996, p. 6). Cardoso (1996), the current president of Brazil and a former student of development processes, calls for an ethic of solidarity by the governments to create new associational forms between society and the state, which he sees as the best way to reduce the marginalization of the poor.

CONCLUSION

Though still not a precise concept, what we understand as "globalization" is bringing forth numerous and profound changes in the economic, cultural, and political life of nations. These changes will deeply affect how education is defined, whom it serves, and how it is assessed.

Globalization forces seem to be introducing a mix of homogenizing tendencies, but they are also opening space for new identities and contestation of established values and norms, many detrimental to the achievement of true social justice. A dichotomous perspective of the effects of globalization, looking only at the extremes of the globalized and nonglobalized economies, might miss the important dynamics that occur in both global and local dimensions and the interaction between the two levels. Local groups often reshape their local identities when they meet challenges related to globalization processes, but they do not abandon these identities to become entirely globally oriented. What was "local" becomes redefined as a modified form of "local" that can work in conjunction with the supralocal forces. It is in the way these forces mesh that hope for a positive transformation lies.

Today more than ever, there is a need to ask, Education for what will prevail in the globalization age? Will it be only to make us more productive and increase our ability to produce and consume, or will it be able to instill in all of us a democratic spirit with values of solidarity? This solidarity will have to recognize the different interests among men and women and among the dominant groups and disadvantaged groups.

NOTES

1. Countries such as Mexico under NAFTA have increased their production of goods enormously (even though it reflects other firms posing as Mexican). Exports increased from $82 billion in 1993 to $160 billion in 1998, yet poverty and maldistribution are also increasing. Some say the pie is getting bigger, but this is difficult to accept given the constant growth of the informal sector and illegal immigration to the United States.

2. Developing countries are fighting for integration in the global economy and trying to serve as sites for relocation of production.

3. Connell (1998) reminds us that the study of the growing masculinization of the economy will need not only life-history and ethnographic methods that have so far been so central to the study of masculinities but also the use of teams to investigate institutions, markets, and mass communications, as issues of scale and complexity are involved.

4. According to the European Commission, the sexual traffic in Europe involves between two hundred thousand and five hundred thousand women from Latin America, Africa, Asia, and Eastern Europe. Calculations based on International Labor Organization data for four countries (Indonesia, Malaysia, Thailand, and the Philippines) indicates that prostitution accounts for between 2 and 14 percent of their GNP (Lim, 1997).

5. The United States has almost doubled its visas for high-technology foreign workers in a period of six years, going from 60,000 in 1993 to 115,000 in 1999. The two largest groups of such workers come from India (46 percent) and China (10 percent).

6. OECD plus the four newly industrialized countries of Asia represent about 73 percent of the world's manufacturing production. In 1990 the G-7 countries accounted for 90.5 percent of high-technology manufacturing and 80.4 percent of global computing power (U.S. National Science Board, 1991, cited in Castells, 1996, p. 108).

REFERENCES

Amin, Samir. 1996. The Future of Globalization. *Social Justice*, vol. 23, nos. 1–2, pp. 5–13.

Bhola, H. S. 1998. World Trends and Issues in Adult Education on the Eve of the Twenty-first Century. *International Review of Education*, vol. 44, nos. 5–6, pp. 485–506.

Blackmore, Jill. 1997. Level Playing Field? Feminist Observations on Global/Local Articulations of the Re-gendering and Restructuring of Educational Work. *International Review of Education*, vol. 43, nos. 5–6, pp. 439–61.

Bustelo, Eduardo, and Alberto Minujin. 1998. Política Social e Igualdad. In Eduardo Bustelo and Alberto Minujin (eds.), *Todos Entran: Propuesta para Sociedades Incluyentes*. Bogota: United Nations Childrens Fund and Santillana, pp. 67–117.

Cardoso, Fernando Henrique. 1996. Consecuencias Sociales de la Globalización. *Política* (Univ. of Chile), vol. 34, pp. 5–17.

Castells, Manuel. 1996. *The Information Age: Economy, Society, and Culture. Vol. I: The Rise of the Network Society.* Malden, MA: Blackwell.

———. 1997. *The Information Age: Economy, Society, and Culture. Vol. II: The Power of Identity.* Malden, MA: Blackwell.

Chaffee, Ellen. 1998. Listening to the People We Serve. In William Tierney (ed.), *The Responsive University: Restructuring for High Performance.* Baltimore: Johns Hopkins University Press, pp. 5–31.

Chen, Marty. 1998 (April 2). Gender and the Economy. Proceedings of a Workshop on Gender and Development. Washington, D.C.: The World Bank, mimeo, pp. 30–31.

Connell, Robert. 1998. Masculinities and Globalization. *Men and Masculinities*, vol. 1, no. 1, pp. 3–23.

Cowen, Robert. 1996. Performativity, Post-Modernity and the University. *Comparative Education*, vol. 32, no. 2, pp. 245–58.

Craske, Nikki. 1998. Remasculinization and the Neoliberal State in Latin America. In Vicky Randall and Georgina Waylen (eds.), *Gender, Politics, and the State.* London: Routledge, pp. 100–20.

Curry, James. 1997. The Dialectic of Knowledge-in-Production: Value Creation in Late Capitalism and the Rise of Knowledge-Centered Production. *Electronic Journal of Sociology*, vol. 002–003. <http://www.sociology.org/content/vol002.003./curry.html>.

Cvetkovich, Ann, and Douglas Kellner. 1997. *Articulating the Global and the Local: Globalization and Cultural Studies.* Boulder, CO: Westview.

DAWN. 1995. Rethinking Social Development: DAWN's Vision. *World Development*, vol. 23, no. 11, pp. 2001–4.

Eisenstein, Zillah. 1997. Women's Publics and the Search for New Democracies. *Feminist Review*, no. 57, pp. 140–67.

Featherstone, Mike. 1990. Global Culture(s): An Introduction. In Mike Featherstone (ed.), *Global Culture: Nationalism, Globalization and Modernity.* London: Sage, pp. 1–13.

Ghai, Dharam. 1987. Economic Globalization, Institutional Change, and Human Security. In Staffan Lindberg and Arni Sverrisson (eds.), *Social Movements in Development: The Challenge of Globalization and Democratization.* Houndmills, UK: Macmillan Press, pp. 25–45.

Gibson-Graham, J. K. 1996. *The End of Capitalism (As We Knew It): A Feminist Critique of Political Economy.* Cambridge, MA: Blackwell.

Giddens, Anthony. 1994. *Beyond Left and Right: The Future of Radical Politics.* Stanford, CA: Stanford University Press.

González Casanova, Pablo. 1996. Globalism, Neoliberalism, and Democracy. *Social Justice*, vol. 23, nos. 1–2, pp. 39–48.

Green, Andy. 1997. *Education, Globalization and the Nation State.* New York: St. Martin's and Basingstone, UK: Macmillan.

Hirst, Paul, and Grahame Thompson. 1996. *Globalization in Question.* Cambridge: Polity Press.

Independent Commission on Population and Quality of Life. 1996. *Caring for the Future: Making the Next Decades Provide a Life Worth Living.* Oxford: Oxford University Press.

Keith, Kent. 1998. The Responsive University in the Twenty-first Century. In William Tierney (ed.), *The Responsive University: Restructuring for High Performance*. Baltimore: Johns Hopkins University Press, pp. 162–72.

Kempner, Ken. 1998. Post-Modernizing Education on the Periphery and in the Core. *International Review of Education*, vol. 44, nos. 5–6, pp. 441–60.

Kenway, Jane. 1997. Education in the Age of Uncertainty: An Eagle's Eye-View. Paper commissioned by the Equity Section, Curriculum Division, Department for Education and Children's Services, South Australia, mimeo.

Kofman, Eleonore, and Gillian Youngs (eds.). 1996. *Globalization Theory and Practice*. New York: Pinter.

Lechner, Norberto. 1997. The Forms of Social Coordination. *CEPAL Review*, no. 61, pp. 7–17.

Lim, Lin. 1997. *The Sex Sector: The Economic and Social Bases of Prostitution in Southeast Asia*. Geneva: International Labor Office.

McGuire, James, and Mauro Campos. 1997 (June 3). Rethinking Development: Concept, Policies, and Contexts. Workshop Proceedings. Los Angeles: University of Southern California.

McLaren, Peter. 1998. Revolutionary Pedagogy in Post-Revolutionary Times: Rethinking the Political Economy of Critical Education. *Educational Theory*, vol. 48, no. 4, pp. 431–62.

———. 1999. Traumatizing Capital: Oppositional Pedagogies in the Age of Consent. In Manuel Castells, Ramon Flecha, Paulo Freire, Henry Giroux, Donaldo Macedo, and Paul Willis (eds.), *Critical Education in the New Information Age*. Lanham, MD: Rowman & Littlefield, pp. 1–36.

McNeil, Maureen. 1999 (May 13–15). The Challenges of a "New Equity Context" for British Education Approaching the Millennium. Paper presented at the international conference on Gender Equity Education organized by the Women's Research Program, Population Studies Center, National Taiwan University, Taipei.

Miles, Angela. 1996. *Integrative Feminisms: Building Global Visions 1960s–1990s*. New York: Routledge.

Moghadam, Valentine. 1999. Gender and the Global Economy. In Myra Ferree, Judith Lorber, and Beth Hess (eds.), *Revisioning Gender*. Thousand Oaks, CA: Sage, pp. 128–60.

Mosley, Paul, Jane Harrigan, and John Toye. 1991. *Aid and Power: The World Bank and Policy-Based Lending. Vol. I: Analysis and Policy Proposals*. London: Routledge.

Namer, Claude. 1999 (August 10). Estamos en vías de una mundialización salvaje. *El Comercio*, p. C3.

Oomen, T. K. 1997. Social Movements in the Third World. In Staffan Lindberg and Arni Sverrisson (eds.), *Social Movements in Development: The Challenge of Globalization and Democratization*. Basingstoke, UK: Macmillan pp. 46–66.

Rerrich, Maria. 1996. Modernizing the Patriarchal Family in West Germany. *The European Journal of Women's Studies*, vol. 3, no. 1, pp. 27–37.

Rhoades, Gary, and Sheila Slaughter. 1991. The Public Interest and Professional Labor: Research Universities. In William Tierney (ed.), *Culture and Ideology in Higher Education: Advancing a Critical Agenda*. New York: Praeger, pp. 187–211.

Simpson, Christopher (ed.). 1998. *Universities and Empire: Money and Politics in the Social Sciences during the Cold War*. New York: The New Press.

Stavenhagen, Rodolfo. 1997. Indigenous Organizations: Missing Rising Actors in Latin America. *CEPAL Review*, no. 62, pp. 63–75.

Walters, Shirley. 1998. *Globalization, Adult Education, and Training*. London: Zed Books.

Watson, Keith. 1998. Memories, Models and Mapping: The Impact of Geopolitical Changes in Comparative Studies in Education. *Compare*, vol. 23, no. 1, pp. 5–31.

Weiler, Hans. 1981. *Compensatory Legitimation in Educational Policy: Legalization, Expertise, and Participation in Comparative Perspective*. Stanford, CA: Institute for Research on Educational Finance and Governance, School of Education, Stanford University.

Wilson, Rob, and Wimal Dissanayake (eds.). 1996. *Global/Local: Cultural Production and the Transnational Imaginary*. Durham, NC: Duke University Press.

Yarzabal, Luis. 1998. La Educación Superior en América Latina. *Memoria: I Congreso Internacional de Educación*. Guanajuato: Gobierno del Estado.

2

Globalization and Internationalism: Democratic Prospects for World Education

Phillip W. Jones

THE CONCEPT OF GLOBALIZATION

My model of globalization starts with its most obvious and fundamental feature—the organization and integration of economic activity at levels that transcend national borders and jurisdictions. I use the word *jurisdictions* advisedly, given the sheer force of much of the globalization process as it transcends the taxation and regulatory discipline conventionally the concern and responsibility of national governments. This is the sense considered by such analysts as Hirst and Thompson (1996, p. 176), who explore globalization in terms of the attainment of century-old ideals of the free-trade liberals, who looked to "a demilitarized world in which business activity is primary and political power has no other tasks than the protection of the world free trading system." In highlighting the essentially ungovernable quality of any emerging globalized economy, I do not join those who see in globalization the collapse of the state or the erosion of governmental participation in economic life. On the contrary, the logic of globalization implies the active involvement of state mechanisms in order to ensure the unfettered operation of markets, both capital and labor. Reconstituted states, in fact, begin to behave like economic entrepreneurs in a free market. One of the ironies of globalization is its reliance on the state to make possible the free operation of markets implying, as Hirst and Thompson (1996, p. 3) put it, that global markets are "by no means beyond regulation and control."

Use of the term *globalization* in this focused sense began, of course, within the business world itself and referred to globalization as a means of conducting business more efficiently, profitably, and discreetly. It will cause no surprise to claim

27

that an integral part of this aim was the intention to open up the world's markets and minimize the supervisory role of public authorities within them. Much of the globalization process came to be dependent on the adoption of reduced roles for government, not only as regulator but also as provider of public services funded in large measure through taxation. With many nations revealing interesting differences in how economic rationalist agenda were promoted and applied within them, at a global level the promotion of a "New World Order" has taken on a distinct form and character of its own. While arguments might rightly persist about the current and likely extent or intensity of globalization, clarity is needed when considering the logic of globalization and any claims made about its effects. A new division of labor among nations is only one aspect of this, whereby the economic outlook for various groups of nations varies enormously.

At its heart, the story of globalization is as much the story of changes within individual nations as changes in economic relations between and among them. This is an emphasis taken up by many commentators who, like Robertson, see a tying up of the universal and the particular as part of a "globewide cultural nexus . . . [bound up by a] universality of experience" (Robertson, 1991, p. 76). Here we see how necessary it becomes to move beyond a straightforward reductionist view of economic integration in any analysis of globalization. Hall, for example, insists upon an emphasis on how the global articulates with the local and upon a view of globalization that recognizes the inevitability of persistent multiplicity and diversity among cultures rather than the inevitability of bland homogenization (Hall, 1991a and 1991b). Adopting a bottom-up view of globalization is necessary, claims Hall, if we are to avoid the simplicity of a reductionist view of globalization as "monolithic, non-contradictory, uncontested" (Hall, 1991a, p. 32). At the same time, Hall and I seem aligned on how the global affects the local: "I think of the global as something having more to do with the hegemonic sweep at which a certain configuration of local particularities try to dominate the whole scene, to mobilize the technology and to incorporate, in subaltern positions, a variety of more localized identities to construct the next historical project" (Hall, 1991b, p. 67).

What made globalization agenda feasible were, of course, the communications and information revolutions, combined with increased mobility of persons, services, and goods. They can usefully be seen as the tools of economic integration, as prominent means whereby the creation of a new world economic order is facilitated. Discussion of globalization and its effects cannot get far without reference to them, and it becomes problematic if we insist too much that they be recognized as conceptually distinct from globalization itself. Their own logic does not imply globalization, yet globalization as we are experiencing it would not be possible without them. Such issues come to the heart of the ultimate incompatibility of world systems understandings of globalization as championed by Wallerstein and his followers with what Robertson claims to be "more wide-ranging, open and fluid" (1992, p. 15) concepts of global unification, demanding not an economic focus but a "cultural focus":

> We have come increasingly to recognize that while economic matters are of tremendous importance in relations between societies and in various forms of transnational relations, those matters are increasingly subject to cultural contingencies and cultural coding. Even more relevant in the present context, it is becoming more and more apparent that no matter how much the issue of "naked" national self-interest may enter into the interactions of nations there are still crucial issues of a basically cultural nature which structure and shape most relations, from the hostile to the friendly, between nationally organized societies (Robertson, 1992, p. 4).

If classical Marxism has inspired those who, like Wallerstein, insist on the primacy of the economic as the determinant of the political and the cultural, the legacy of Parsons in the work of Robertson and others cannot be overlooked either, with its insistence on culture as the engine of the economic and the political. Waters (1995, p. 3) has perhaps made some progress: while he characterizes globalization as a weakening of the constraints of space and time on economic, political, and cultural arrangements, he suggests that the dominance of relationships between the three "systems" are themselves determined by space and time. Waters, like Hall, in looking to the transcending of national boundaries, accepts the likelihood of a single world society and culture, territoriality being an increasingly weak organizing principle. But at the same time, Waters insists on how "extremely abstract" this universality is likely to be, being erected on a fundamental "tolerance for diversity and individual choice." He sees a globalized world as unlikely to be "harmoniously integrated although it might conceivably be. Rather it will probably tend towards high levels of differentiation, multicentricity and chaos" (Waters, 1995, p. 3). Little (1996, p. 428) has succinctly organized various aspects of Waters' ideal-typical patterns of globalization (Waters, 1995, pp. 94, 123, 157) along the following lines.

Economic globalization
- freedom of exchange between localities with indeterminate flows of services and symbolic commodities
- the balance of production activity in a locality determined by its physical and geographical advantages
- minimal foreign direct investment
- flexible responsiveness of organizations to global markets
- decentralized, instantaneous, and "stateless" financial markets
- free movement of labor

Political globalization
- an absence of state sovereignty, and multiple centers of power at global, local, and intermediate levels

- local issues discussed and situated in relation to a global community
- powerful international organizations predominant over national organizations
- fluid and multicentric international relations
- a weakening of value attached to the nation-state and a strengthening of common and global political values

Cultural globalization
- deterritorialized religious mosaic
- a deterritorialized cosmopolitanism and diversity
- widespread consumption of simulations and representations
- global distribution of images and information
- universal tourism and the "end of tourism"

Although it is easy to overstate the speed and intensity of economic globalization, it is important to appreciate its impact to date. The various agenda of globalization by nature are mutually reinforcing and increasingly leave participants who refuse to "play ball" isolated and, yes, at a comparative disadvantage. Second, and in the same way, can be seen the multiplier effect of globalization on the processes that promote it—communications, information technologies, and mobility. Each intensifies as it is called into play, and each becomes a more dominant aspect of our lives and of the world scene. The enormous implications for culture have, rightly, been the object of much consideration (if somewhat restricted in Waters's typology just considered).

The political character and consequences of globalization are also the object of a great deal of discussion. Conventions of the nation-state, governance, accountability, and the public versus private domain become unsettled. Governments are called upon to, and indeed do, revise their role and reduce the scope of their work. Notions of the public good shift in order to accommodate reduced expectations about accountability, regulation, and taxation, which in turn lead to not only reduced but transformed expectations about what public services and infrastructure consist of. Social relations are scrambled, frequently in ways that promote reckless individualism. Identity, diversity, responsibility, accountability—each fails to escape the impact of fundamental assaults on democratic institutions, and on the careful balances of self-determination at individual, communal, and national levels (a useful discussion is Strange, 1997).

What I especially wish to take up here are the effects of globalization on international order. I have already referred to the establishment and reinforcement of divisions of labor that impose structural divisions between winners, losers, and those somewhere in between, contrary to the "win-win" rhetoric so prevalent in globalization discourse (for an extended analysis see Burbach, Nunez Soto, and Kagarlitsky, 1996). Such structural inequalities can only have profound implications for the world's prospects for peace, the acceptance of human rights, environmental integrity, and the self-determination of peoples. The yawning chasm between individualistic capitalism and democracy gives rise to concern about the application of democratic principles and practices at the international level as well as the local. Further, there need to be considered the effects of globalization upon those fragile commitments to international peace and well-being effected through international organization, the promotion of international standards and norms, and the promotion of international law (for an overview see Cox, 1994 and 1997). Globalization has collided with them head on, and it is a far from trivial matter to gauge the damage done to the world's prospects.

INTERNATIONALISM AND GLOBAL ORDER

The vast literature on internationalism is bound together by its focus on international order, with its traditions revealing varying degrees of both idealism and practicability. Hedley Bull's famous characterization of international order cannot be ignored—as activity (and commitment to activity) designed to promote specified goals of the "society of states," goals that he ranked in descending order of priority: first, preserving commitment to the society of states itself; second, preserving the sovereignty and independence of individual states; and, third, promoting peace (Bull, 1977, pp. 3–22; see also Goldmann, 1994, p. 210). Permeating this focus on international order are what might be called commonsense notions of international community, international cooperation, international community of interests, and international dimensions of the common good, of the kind that frequently find their way into dictionary definitions of internationalism.

Given the idealism surrounding much of the internationalist stance, it is important to appreciate the degree to which its focus on order enables consideration of means as well as ends. Whether emphasis is placed on the creation and application of international law, communications and exchanges at the international level, or the conduct of business through international organizational frameworks, internationalism looks to ordered, structural means of giving practical expression to outward-looking, universalist stances. They stand in stark contrast to both vague utopianism and inward-looking isolationism.

If deterrence lies at the heart of conventional interpretations of the internationalist ideal and their applications in international order, the problem of the causes of war remains as a separate and crucial issue. If the early advocates of international organization promoted agenda based on disincentives to embark on war, they overlooked much of the classical liberal explanation of war and its causes that was developing at the same time. The promotion of peace by the promotion of free trade comes to the heart of matters when the tensions between globalization and internationalism are considered. Goldmann (1994, p. 10) sums it up well, drawing on the work of Silberner (1946, pp. 280–83):

The key to the classical liberal analysis of war was the conviction that war was due to a false conception of the national interest. Free trade was immensely preferable to war, it was argued, contributing not only to the material prosperity of nations but also to the intellectual and moral progress of mankind [sic]. It would strengthen the peaceful ties that unite nations and the pacific spirit among men [sic]. Freedom of commerce would thus substantially reduce the risk of war or even eliminate it altogether.

Goldmann goes on to sum up some key ideas in classical liberal-economic pacifism (1994, p. 12). "Uninhibited international commerce, to the minds of many liberals," was associated with

1. the growing realization that, in each nation, free trade was to the advantage of everybody but a small minority;
2. the growing realization that nations had a common interest in peaceful relations with one another and in each other's welfare; and
3. the growth of those forces or classes in society with especial interest in peaceful international discourse and the decline of elements less interested in the maintenance of peace (the state apparatus, particularly the military).

Over a century later, such a summary seems fresh and relevant to current debates. At the heart of such thinking was the severing of the link between economic development and military opportunism. Balances of power, at the end of the day, would shift in favor of those with vested interests in peace. I have argued elsewhere how such expressions came to be interpreted in light of the League of Nations experience, the breakdown of economic order associated with the depression of the late 1920s and 1930s, and World War II itself (Jones, 1993). The major conceptual development, in terms of the midcentury ordering of the international world, was the emphasis placed on functionalism, seen profoundly in the design of the United Nations system. Not only did functionalism provide the emerging system with a practical emphasis, it also bedded down the principle of the transfer (or, at the very least, the replication) of state functions to international organizations, in the name of the great quantity of business that governments needed to transact among themselves at more than the bilateral level. The great pillars of peace, progress, and human rights emerged as the cornerstones of what international organization was there to promote, and despite disappointments about degrees of success, it is fair to say that such impulses remain at the heart of popular folklore about the purposes and functions of the international system.

DEMOCRACY, ORDER, AND PROSPECTS FOR PEACE AND WELL-BEING

An essential element in much thinking on the logic of internationalism is its affinity with democracy, to the extent that internationalism is, for many, best understood as a product of democratic institutions at work. As soon as internationalism finds expression in ordered, structural ways, the democratic requirement is readily accommodated, it being evident that just as domestic political institutions might be shaped along democratic lines, so too can those that make and give effect to decisions at the international level. Goldmann (1994, p. 53) takes up the point:

> Just as opinions are freely formed and expressed within democracies, and just as democratic leaders are expected to be influenced by them, opinions can be formed at the international level and ought to influence international politics—an assumption to this effect is implicit in internationalist reasoning. . . . And just as democracy presumes pluralistic diversity within a consensual framework, cooperative links ought to multiply across national borders so as to promote both transnational diversity and consensus on fundamentals.

This stance leaves considerable room for internationalists to disclaim any interest in establishing a world state, democratic or otherwise. It is a peaceful and cooperative interstate system that defines international order, despite the inevitable tensions between respecting sovereign independence while applying democratic principles at the international level (Goldmann, 1994, p. 54). Invoking both Immanuel Kant and Woodrow Wilson, Goldmann acknowledges the ways in which internationalist agenda go hand in hand with democratic change at the domestic level: "It accords with the tradition of internationalist thinking to consider law, organization, exchange, and communication to be more likely to lead to peace and security if states are democratic than if they are authoritarian" (1994, p. 54).

This comes to the heart of the matter if the negative impact of globalization on domestic democratic institutions is extended to the international arena. It is of fundamental interest to consider the extent to which international peace, security, and well-being depend upon the maintenance of democratic institutions and practices at the domestic level. The question also brings us to consider the possibility and extent to which the international framework as currently and recently effected (since 1945) is an expression of hegemony exercised on behalf of Western capitalism. If so, it is also worth considering whether globalization, by weakening international frameworks, is in fact pushing them into less powerful and thereby less hegemonic positions. The posthegemonic character of emerging international frameworks becomes a key element in any consideration. The way forward may well be to consider which elements of present-day international structures are best seen as aligned with the democratic impulses of the internationalist ideal and which others can only be seen as the vanguards of globalization. The likelihood is strong that a highly differentiated system of intergovernmental structures is emerging, some elements lying beyond the accountability demanded by the logic of internationalism.

My concern with the preservation of democracy brings me back to the interplay between the global and the local. My starting point here is to dissuade any reader of the notion that the international economic interdependence deriving from globalization has anything to do with the logic of internationalism, that is, the free association of sovereign states. On the contrary, globalization brings with it an economic dynamic that is associated with a profound shift in how we regard sovereignty and the very idea of statehood. They are eroding, and quickly. It is an extremely complex moment in history, to see the erosion of national economies, of national identities and cultures, and of nationhood. Hall (1991a) thoughtfully invites us to compare the rise of nationhood, with its aggressive and frequently racist stances, with responses to its decline, which indeed might be similarly aggressive and xenophobic:

> One of the things which happens when the nation-state begins to weaken, becoming less convincing and less powerful, is that the response seems to go in two ways simultaneously. It goes above the nation-state and it goes below it. It goes global and local in the same moment (Hall, 1991a, pp. 26–27).

Going global implies, perforce, the emergence of new patterns of economic organization—new structures, new systems, new modalities. The primary criterion that seems to be applied to them is that of freedom from state supervision and regulation, both domestically through (national) governments and internationally through intergovernmental mechanisms. But such patterns produce— require?—their own forms of cultural expression. We see emerging a global culture, which, as a form of mass culture, is intimately bound up with the economics and politics of globalization. To call it a homogenized culture, however, may be grossly misleading. While such populist writers in organization "theory" as Schwartz propel us into coming to terms with the mass culture of the "new global teenager" (Schwartz, 1996, pp. 118–34) we might be better advised to ponder the tolerance of cultural globalization for diversity. That is to say, while capital and power remain uncompromisingly centered, that concentration requires no mandatory expression in narrow cultural terms. Hall also takes up the point:

> It does not attempt to obliterate. . . . It has to hold the whole framework of globalization in place and simultaneously police that system: it stage-manages independence within it, so to speak. You have to think about the relationship between the United States and Latin America to discover what I am talking about, how those forms which are different, which have their own specificity, can nevertheless be repenetrated, absorbed, reshaped, negotiated, without absolutely destroying what is specific and particular to them (Hall, 1991a, pp. 28–29).

The logic of globalization tolerates, indeed requires, the promotion of cultural (and possibly political) difference and diversity. Globalization will build on diversity and needs to work through patterns that seem paradoxical—both global and decentered—forms of social organization that convey powerful symbolic images of choice, freedom, diversity. Globalization might build a unitary world, but one that celebrates difference while at the same time neutralizing it—reducing difference and diversity ultimately to matters of lifestyle, consumption, seeking pleasure, rather than the essential requirements of democracy. Will globalization's embracing of difference and diversity foster a cruel misunderstanding of freedom?

At this point I wish to return to the question of war and take up once again the question of which patterns of world order might be more likely to prevent outbreaks of war. In fact, I would prefer to push the matter more vigorously and ask more positively about the world's prospects for peace, attracted as I am to that notion of peace as "human rights in action." The classical liberal agenda for peace, to make the point again, looks to economic incentives, whereby a free, global marketplace makes warfare superfluous. It is here that a fascinating juxtaposition can be contemplated between globalization and internationalism. Let me use Goldmann (1994, p. 158) to set the scene:

> The fact that democratic states do not fight each other has been characterized as "one of the strongest nontrivial or nontautological generalizations that can be made about international relations" [Russett, 1990, p. 123]. The absence of war between democratic states, in the words of another scholar, "comes as close to anything we have to an empirical law in international relations" [Levy, 1989, p. 270]. . . . The association between democracy and absence of war cannot be accounted for in terms of other variables like wealth, economic growth, and common alliances . . . insofar as can be ascertained, the absence of war between democracies is in fact related to the democratic form of government.

A range of explanations is evident, naturally enough, it being remembered that the point being made is that democracies appear unlikely to wage war upon each other (we need little reminding of their capacity to embark on hostilities with others). Nineteenth-century pacifism emphasized the popular will, the disinclination of citizens to agree that war was in their interest, whereas more contemporary explanations might look more to institutional checks and balances in democratic states, that division of powers that includes the need for public debate, making it "difficult for democratic leaders to move their countries into war" (Ember, Ember, and Russett, 1992, p. 576). The democratic impulse, it can be assumed, revolves around norms of tolerance and mutual respect. Democratic institutions, at the same time, can be relied upon to be more cautious, or at least to be less inclined to impulsive or hasty actions. If such are "rules of thumb" within democratic societies, can such norms be expected to prevail between democratic peoples?

Such reasoning, when pushed, can take us into very dangerous territory, with its implied dismissal of international peace-building in favor of appeals to democracy pure and simple, that is, that international peace is a matter of domestic politics after all. Where the argument is misleading, in my view, is that it fails to distinguish precisely enough between the operation of democratic principles at the international level and the openness of international relationships. Openness (of markets, communications, etc.) is not to be understood as democracy, and the blurring of the two has led directly to a recycling of the neoliberal evocation of the operation of untrammeled free markets as the world's best hope for peace and security.

Goldmann's reminder that "it is not necessary that all or even most states [be] democratic in order for internationalism to work" (1994, p. 160) is useful in this context. Yet it is a giant leap to proceed from the premise that universal democracy is not a necessary precondition for internationalism to work to any claim that widespread economic integration might suffice. Rightly, Goldmann calls for further research on how domestic and international relations interact in order to produce certain policy outcomes:

> The old issue of cooperation and war is linked to one that is more up-to-date: the internationalization of domestic politics and the domestic-politicization of international politics. The more politics become what Putnam calls a two-level game [Putnam, 1988], and the more intertwined international and domestic politics become in other ways, the greater the likelihood that peace and security will be affected by international cooperation. By the same token, the more we learn about the links between politics at the international and national levels in different types of political systems, the greater our ability to specify the conditions under which cooperation will play a part in inhibiting war (Goldmann, 1994, p. 161).

MULTILATERAL AGENDA IN EDUCATION

Education has not remained innocent of the differentiation now so evident within the present-day multilateral system. I have outlined elsewhere the essence of the multilateral argument as it affects education, as well as outlining the prominent organizational arrangements (Jones, 1993). Part of the picture is the stark contrast between the declared educational policies of several agencies, whose differences stem not so much from their constitutional mandates as their funding bases. In fact, a compelling case can be made that agency policy is a direct product of how its funds are secured, an understanding of which can also provide insight into an agency's stance in relation to the globalization/internationalism divide.

The United Nations Children's Fund (UNICEF), for example, relies massively upon voluntary contributions (whether from governments, nongovernment organizations, or private bodies and individuals). Accordingly, its analyses of need tend to be dramatic, its projections tend to be alarmist, and its solutions tend to be populist. Its annual survey "The State of the World's Children" can be relied upon to provide a strong example (for example UNICEF, 1997). Importantly, UNICEF rhetoric about prospects for the well-being of children and their careers is notable for the way in which the agency's sources of funds mirrors the agency's view about the provision of social services.

The United Nations Educational, Scientific and Cultural Organization (UNESCO), by contrast, relies on compulsory levies imposed by formula upon governments, the wealthiest of which invariably combine to render UNESCO as low-cost an organization as possible. Accordingly, the cash-strapped UNESCO can afford expansive rhetoric it need not match with funded operations. Further, UNESCO's insistence that its policies and programs be constructed on the basis of universality and consensus renders inevitable the much-vaunted generality of UNESCO stances. A good example is the report on education for the twenty-first century prepared by Jacques Delors and the commission he chaired, a report that projected a concern for democracy, social inclusion, and human-centered development in a way which reflects UNESCO's "niche" in the international system (UNESCO, 1996).

By contrast again, the World Bank, which raises its loanable capital commercially and administers itself through its trading profits, can remain aloof from the need to ask any government, nongovernmental organization (NGO), or private entity for funds (although its soft credit arm—the International Development Association, IDA—is so dependent). The World Bank is a free agent as far as intergovernmental structures are concerned, its obligations resting with the international markets that provide its loanable capital.

The matter today might well involve the extent to which this or that agency is better seen as an expression of conventional internationalism or has shifted ground in terms of its place in a globalized world. To risk bluntness, the World Bank provides a clear-cut example of how the logic of internationalism can be disposed of in favor of the logic of globalization. Not that this has recently occurred, the essentially banking nature of the World Bank determining its fundamental character at its conception at Bretton Woods.

Despite the often neglected fact that it is both an intergovernmental organization and a specialized agency of the United Nations, the World Bank functions with a stark degree of independence. At the same time, it provides a fascinating window onto the world of international finance, a world that lacks a storefront but nevertheless operates in terms of ideology with strong social content. I have argued at length, in fact, that we cannot understand World Bank education policy independently of its position as bank (Jones, 1992). What has recently emerged, however, is a willingness to bring its ideology of globalization to center stage in its statements of education policy. This stands in stark contrast to the three earlier decades of educational involvement, when Bank rhetoric about its education portfolio failed to acknowledge its fundamental debt to its economic and fiscal basis (see also Jones, 1997).

This basis establishes, in the view of the Bank, a set of preconditions for successful educational policy and practice, which override any views about educational processes the Bank might wish to promote. These preconditions, of course, are precisely the agenda of globalization, championed by a bank that seeks to consolidate its own role at the heart of an integrated world economy. Its chance came in large measure with the end of the Cold War, at which time the Bank rapidly switched to the "transition economies" of Eastern Europe as its priority region, displacing Sub-Saharan Africa with its chronic debt and persistently negative growth rates (although its enthusiasm for "structural adjustment" along the logical lines of globalization was universally applied to its member countries from the early 1980s). Yet it was only in 1995 that Bank education policy as officially codified embraced the globalization agenda in its *Policies and Strategies for Education: A World Bank Review,* the first formal statement of Bank education policy since 1980 (World Bank, 1995; for extended commentary see Jones, 1997; Burnett, 1996; Lauglo, 1996; Bennell, 1996; Samoff, 1996; Burnett and Patrinos, 1996).

The Bank's preconditions for education can only be understood as an ideological stance, promoting an integrated world economic system along market lines. It attempts to find intellectual grounding in human capital theory, an attempt I have discussed earlier (Jones, 1992, pp. 233–38), and champions public austerity and a reduced role for government in the provision of education. In painting a picture of the preconditions for successful educational development, the Bank is in effect depicting its view of the ideal economy.

It is an economy that at best can only tolerate public education. The role of government is that of protector of the poor and the disadvantaged, provider of market information about educational provision, "compensator" for market failures in education, and setter and monitor of standards in education. It is an economy in which the management of education "by central or state governments . . . allows little room for the flexibility that leads to effective learning" (World Bank, 1995, pp. 3–6). It is an economy in which "educational priorities should be set with reference to outcomes, using economic analysis, standard setting, and measurement of achievement through learning assessments" (World Bank, 1995, p. 8). What is euphemistically termed "household involvement" in education, understood in terms of maximizing household choice in education, is placed at a premium in such an economy. The "risks" involved are easily identified, and it is, accordingly, an economy in which fundamental difficulties and obstacles to equity can be easily managed. It is an economy that can afford to pass to communities and households some of the costs of education. "Even very poor communities are often willing to contribute toward the cost of education, especially at the primary level" (World Bank, 1995, p. 105). It is an economy that has shed the disagreeable effects of centralized control over education. Centralized control only fosters centralized teachers' unions, for example, which "can disrupt education and sometimes lead to political paralysis" (World Bank, 1995, p. 137). It is an economy in which decentralization fosters reform, in which parental and community control, "when accompanied by measures to ensure equity in the provision of resources, can offset much of the power of vested interests, such as teachers' unions and the elite." At least in urban areas, decentralization "can be enhanced by the use of market mechanisms that increase accountability and choice."

For the first time there is unambiguous consonance between the Bank's economic, political, and ideological goals and those of its education sector. Explicitly, the market is looked to for provision of accountability. Choice transcends democracy. Freedom is trivialized.

What I have not attempted here is a comprehensive survey of multilateral frameworks in order to assess the differential alignments within them in terms of the globalization–internationalism divide. However, it is no trivial matter to ponder their democratic bases and to consider which elements might or might not contribute to a posthegemonic future. Also remaining for consideration is the emergence of a large array of international nongovernmental organizations (INGOs) many of which, although by definition outside formal intergovernmental structures, nevertheless are beginning to exercise considerable economic, political, and cultural influence. With rapidly shifting balances of power, important issues arise about the world's prospects for peace, security, and well-being. Should the domestic operation of the marketplace be deemed a threat to the application of democratic principles to the decisions that concern people and the lives they lead, then the global marketplace should come under the same scrutiny insofar as the people of the world look to some form of international order to enhance the prospects for putting human rights into action.

Those interested in promoting or studying education in international perspective will find a more complex world order than ever before, with the logic of internationalism under threat from an increasingly differentiated and anarchic framework for the conduct of international relations. Of particular importance is the need to think afresh about the nature and importance of democracy, democratic institutions, and accountability as a basis for democracy. Should our past reliance—at the international level—have been placed in intergovernmental structures and mechanisms in order to safeguard and promote democracy, it will be important to assess the democratic prospects of a globalizing world and to think afresh about education and its interactions with nationalism, statism, governmentalism, and internationalism.

NOTES

This chapter first appeared in *Comparative Education*, vol. 34, no. 2, 1998, pp. 143–55.

REFERENCES

Albrow, Martin, and Elizabeth King (eds.). 1990. *Globalization, Knowledge and Society*. London: Sage.

Bennell, Paul. 1996. Using and Abusing Rates of Return: A Critique of the World Bank's Education Sector Review. *International Journal of Educational Development*, vol. 16, no. 2, pp. 235–48.

Brown, Phillip, and Hugh Lauder. 1996. Education, Globalization and Economic Development. *Journal of Education Policy*, vol. 11, no. 1, pp. 1–26.

Buell, Frederick. 1994. *National Culture and the New Global System*. Baltimore: Johns Hopkins University Press.

Bull, Hedley. 1977. *The Anarchical Society: A Study of Order in World Politics*. London: Macmillan.

Burbach, Roger, Orlando Nunez Soto, and Boris Kagarlitsky. 1996. *Globalization and Its Discontents: The Rise of Postmodern Socialism*. London: Pluto Press.

Burnett, Nicholas. 1996. Priorities and Strategies for Education—A World Bank Review: The Process and the Key Messages. *International Journal of Educational Development*, vol. 16, no. 2, pp. 215–20.

———, and Harry A. Patrinos. 1996. Response to Critiques of Priorities and Strategies for Education: A World Bank Review. *International Journal of Educational Development*, vol. 16, no. 2, pp. 273–76.

Cox, Ronald W. 1994. The Crisis in World Order and the Challenge to International Organization. *Cooperation and Conflict*, vol. 29, no. 2, pp. 99–113.

——— (ed.). 1997. *The New Realism: Perspectives on Multilateralism and World Order*. London: Macmillan for the United Nations University Press.

Ember, Carol R., Melvin Ember, and Bruce M. Russett. 1992. Peace between Participatory Polities: A Cross-cultural Test of the "Democracies Rarely Fight Each Other" Hypothesis. *World Politics*, vol. 44, no. 4, pp. 573–99.

Goldmann, Kjell. 1994. *The Logic of Internationalism: Coercion and Accommodation*. London: Routledge.

Haggard, Stephan. 1995. *Developing Nations and the Politics of Global Integration*. Washington, D.C.: Brookings.

Hall, Stuart. 1991a. The Local and the Global: Globalization and Ethnicity. In Anthony D. King (ed.), *Culture, Globalization and the World System: Contemporary Conditions for the Representation of Identity*. Binghamton: Department of Art and Art History, State University of New York, pp. 19–39. [Also London: Macmillan; and Minneapolis: University of Minnesota Press.]

———. 1991b. Old and New Identities, Old and New Ethnicities. In Anthony D. King (ed.), *Culture, Globalization and the World System: Contemporary Conditions for the Representation of Identity*. Binghamton: Department of Art and Art History, State University of New York, pp. 41–68. [Also London: Macmillan; and Minneapolis: University of Minnesota Press.]

Hirst, Paul, and Grahame Thompson. 1996. *Globalization in Question*. Cambridge: Polity Press.

Hutchinson, John. 1994. *Modern Nationalism*. London: Fontana.

Jones, Phillip W. 1992. *World Bank Financing of Education: Lending, Learning and Development*. London: Routledge.

———. 1993. United Nations Agencies. *Encyclopedia of Educational Research*, sixth edition. New York: Macmillan, pp. 1450–59.

———. 1997. On World Bank Education Financing. *Comparative Education*, vol. 33, no. 1, pp. 117–29.

King, Anthony D. (ed.). 1991. *Culture, Globalization and the World System: Contemporary Conditions for the Representation of Identity.* Binghamton: Department of Art and Art History, State University of New York. [Also London: Macmillan; and Minneapolis: University of Minnesota Press.]

Lauglo, Jon. 1996. Banking on Education and the Uses of Research: A Critique of World Bank Priorities and Strategies for Education. *International Journal of Educational Development,* vol. 16, 2, pp. 221–33.

Levy, James S. 1989. The Causes of War: A Review of Theories and Evidence. In Philip E. Tetlock (ed.), *Behavior, Society, and Nuclear War,* vol. 1. New York: Oxford University Press, pp. 250–80.

Little, Angela W. 1996. Globalization and Educational Research: Whose Context Counts? *International Journal of Educational Development,* vol. 16, no. 4, pp. 427–38.

Pannu, R. S. 1996. Neoliberal Project of Globalization: Prospects for Democratization of Education. *The Alberta Journal of Educational Research,* vol. 42, no. 2, pp. 87–101.

Prendergast, Renee, and Frances Stewart (eds.). 1993. *Market Forces and World Development.* London: Macmillan.

Putnam, Robert D. 1988. Diplomacy and Domestic Politics: The Logic of Two-Level Games. *International Organization,* vol. 42, pp. 427–60.

Robertson, Roland. 1990. Mapping the Global Condition: Globalization as the Central Concept. *Theory, Culture and Society,* vol. 7, nos. 2–3, pp.15–30.

———. 1991. Social Theory, Cultural Relativity and the Problem of Globality. In Anthony D. King (ed.), *Culture, Globalization and the World System: Contemporary Conditions for the Representation of Identity.* Binghamton: Department of Art and Art History, State University of New York, pp. 69–90. [Also London: Macmillan; and Minneapolis: University of Minnesota Press.]

———. 1992. *Globalization: Social Theory and Global Culture.* London: Sage.

Russett, Bruce M. 1990. *Controlling the Sword: The Democratic Governance of National Security.* Cambridge, MA: Harvard University Press.

Sachs, Jeffrey D., and Andrew M. Warner. 1995. Economic Reform and the Process of Global Integration. *Brookings Papers on Economic Activity,* vol. 1, pp. 1–118.

Samoff, Joel. 1996. Which Priorities and Strategies for Education? *International Journal of Educational Development,* vol. 16, no. 2, pp. 249–71.

Schwartz, Peter. 1996. *The Art of the Long View: Planning for the Future in an Uncertain World.* New York: Doubleday.

Silberner, Edmond. 1946. The Problem of War in Nineteenth-Century Economic Thought. Princeton, NJ: Princeton University Press.

Stewart, Frances. 1996. Globalization and Education. *International Journal of Educational Development,* vol. 16, no. 4, pp. 327–33.

Strange, Susan. 1997. Territory, State, Authority and Economy: A New Realist Ontology of Global Political Economy. In Robert W. Cox (ed.), *The New Realism: Perspectives on Multilateralism and World Order.* London: Macmillan for the United Nations University Press, pp. 3–19.

UNICEF. 1997. The State of the World's Children. New York: UNICEF.

UNESCO. 1996. Learning: The Treasure Within. Report of the International Commission on Education for the Twenty-first Century chaired by Jacques Delors. Paris: UNESCO.

Wallerstein, Immanuel. 1990. Culture as the Ideological Battleground of the Modern World System. *Theory, Culture, and Society*, vol. 7, pp. 31–55.

———. 1991. The National and the Universal: Can There Be Such a Thing as World Culture? In Anthony D. King (ed.), *Culture, Globalization and the World System: Contemporary Conditions for the Representation of Identity*. Binghamton: Department of Art and Art History, State University of New York, pp. 91–105 [Also London: Macmillan; and Minneapolis: University of Minnesota Press.]

Waters, Malcolm. 1995. *Globalization*. London and New York: Routledge.

World Bank. 1995. *Policies and Strategies for Education: A World Bank Review*. Washington, D.C.: World Bank.

Worsley, Peter. 1990. Models of the Modern World System. *Theory, Culture and Society*, vol. 7, nos. 2–3, pp. 83–96.

3

Globalization and Educational Reform

Martin Carnoy

The rapid development of industrializing economies in Asia and new information technologies have contributed to the emergence of a truly global economy in the last ten years. A global economy is not a world economy. That has existed since at least the sixteenth century (Braudel, 1979). Neither is it an economy where trade, investment, and resource exploitation take place worldwide. It is not even an economy where the external sector is dominant. For example, neither the United States nor the bloc of western European countries (taken as a whole unit) show foreign trade as a major part of their economic activity. A global economy is one whose strategic, core activities, including innovation, finance, and corporate management, function on a planetary scale on real time (Carnoy et al., 1993; Castells, 1997).[1] And this globality became possible only recently because of the technological infrastructure provided by telecommunications, information systems, microelectronics machinery, and computer-based transportation. Today, as distinct from even a generation ago, capital, technology, management, information, and core markets are globalized.

Two of the main bases of globalization are information and innovation, and they, in turn, are highly knowledge intensive. Internationalized and fast-growing information industries produce knowledge goods and services. Today's massive movements of capital depend on information, communication, and *knowledge* in global markets. And because knowledge is highly portable, it lends itself easily to globalization.

If knowledge is fundamental to globalization, globalization should also have a profound impact on the transmission of knowledge. According to Harvard educator Noel McGinn, this has generally not been the case (McGinn, 1997). Education, he argues, appears to have changed little in most countries at the classroom level—even in those most involved in the global economy and the information age. Beyond occasionally used computers in classrooms, teaching methods and national curricula remain largely intact. McGinn explains this phe-

43

nomenon by focusing on one of the most important educational reforms associated with globalization, the decentralization of educational administration and finance. He shows how that reform, for various reasons, seems to have little or no effect on educational delivery in classrooms.

Insightful as it is, McGinn's analysis misses the mark. I agree that educational decentralization is a major manifestation, if not of globalization itself, certainly of an ideology closely identified with and pushing the development of the global economy in a particular direction. So we need to ask how this larger ideological package, that includes but is not limited to decentralization, affects education. I also agree that the way knowledge is delivered in the classroom is an important aspect of knowledge production. But it is only one part of the knowledge production process. In assessing globalization's true relationship to educational change, we need to know how globalization and its ideological packaging affect the overall delivery of schooling.

Using this broader interpretation, globalization is having a major impact on education in three crucial ways:

- In financial terms, most governments are under pressure to reduce the growth of public spending on education and to find other sources of funding for the expected expansion of their educational systems.
- In labor market terms, the payoff to higher levels of education is rising worldwide as a result of the shifts of economic production to knowledge-intensive products and processes. Governments are also under increased pressure to attract foreign capital, and this means a ready supply of highly skilled labor. This, in turn, places increased pressure on governments to expand their higher education and, correspondingly, to increase the number of secondary school graduates ready to attend postsecondary institutions. In countries that were previously resistant to providing equal access to education for young women, the need for more highly educated low-cost labor tends to expand women's educational opportunities.
- In educational terms, the quality of national educational systems is increasingly being compared internationally. This has placed increased emphasis on math and science curricula, standards, testing, and on meeting standards by changing the way education is delivered.

WHITHER GLOBALIZATION?

Globalization is a hotly disputed concept. Most of the discussion focuses on whether transnational institutions have replaced national economies and national states as the locus of world development. The argument against the globalization thesis is based on two major assertions (Amin, 1998): the first is that "transnational" corporations are not transnational but "multinational" (Carnoy, 1993).[2]

Transnational means that they transcend any national space. *Multinational* means that they have offices in many different countries but retain a very high fraction of their assets in their home base economy. Multinationals therefore depend heavily on those nations' economic policies for their overall health. For example, the most transnational of major corporations, IBM, with a global innovation network and highly internationalized management, floundered badly when its core U.S. business suffered in the 1990–92 recession. Only a total restructuring at home helped IBM recover. Similarly, Japanese banks, also highly multinationalized and riding high globally in the 1980s, have fallen on hard times since the slowdown of the Japanese economy. This suggests that these global corporations are still situated nationally, since their core activities cannot transcend the economic health of their principal location.

The second argument against globalization is that national economic regulation is still the main form of public economic intervention and control. This is so because a high fraction of a nation's economic activities remain almost entirely domestic and distinctly unglobalized (health, construction, education, retail and wholesale, restaurant, bar, and many other services). If national states choose not to exercise their power to regulate and redistribute, it is because they are subjected to domestic pressures generally orchestrated by national capital, not by transnationals.

But these assertions, while valid critiques of those who would claim that national economies and national states are no longer important, miss the point. Besides the fact that multinationalization of firms has certainly increased—multinational firms now account for one-third of the world's economic output and two-thirds of world trade, with 32 percent of world trade composed of intra-firm trade, unreported in standard trade statistics (United States Commission on Trade and Development, UNCTAD, 1993)—the essence of globalization is not contained strictly in trade and investment figures nor in the percentage of a national economy that is national, but a new way of thinking about economic and social space and time. Firms, workers, students, and even children watching television or using the Internet at school are reconceptualizing their "world," whether that world is defined as a market, a location for production, a place to work, a source of information, a place to vacation, or a source of environmental problems. The reconceptualization of space and time into what Manuel Castells has called the "space of flows" (Castells, 1996) is partly the result of history (world wars that enlarged nations' geopolitical space, for example) and secular advances in "ordinary" technology, such as the speed of transportation. Yet, the reconceptualization is also profoundly affected by new information and communication technology that allows real time interchange of knowledge between the most distant points on our globe. Information networks are also increasingly individualized, and this too has a profound affect on the way knowledge and information are transmitted and interpreted, and the way social life is organized. An entrepreneur working at home can access masses of information about markets, products,

prices, and contacts with other producers worldwide without relying on interme-
diaries. Students in schools can interchange e-mail with students in a distant
country instantaneously, bringing them together in real time and space. Individual consumers or political organizers can reach out globally at extremely low (and
falling) cost to get or supply information pertinent to their activities. This both
creates enormous possibilities for global interaction and puts a growing premium
on the individual's ability to get and interpret information.

Is the power of the national state diminished by globalization? Yes and no. Yes,
because increasing global economic competition makes the national state focus
on economic policies that improve global competitiveness, at the expense of policies that stabilize the current configuration of the domestic economy or possibly
social cohesion (Castells, 1997). Yes, because the national state is compelled to
make the national economy attractive for the mass of capital that moves globally
in the "space of flows," and that may mean a reduction of public spending and
the introduction of monetary policy that favors financial interests rather than
workers and consumers (Castells, 1997).

But no, because ultimately national states still greatly influence the territorial
and temporal space in which most people acquire their capacity to operate globally and where capital has to invest. National states are largely responsible for
the political climate in which businesses conduct their activities and individuals
organize their social lives. Some analysts have called this underlying context for
social and economic interaction, "social capital" (Coleman, 1988). Others have
focused on "trust" (Fukuyama, 1995). National public policy has an enormous
influence on social capital and trust. Even the World Bank, supposedly a global
institution, has "rediscovered" the national state as crucial to national economic
and social development (World Bank, 1997). It makes a huge difference to a nation's economic possibilities when the national state is capable of formulating coherent economic and social policies and carrying them out. It makes a huge difference if the national state can reduce corruption and establish trust, and it is
difficult to imagine achieving greater social capital in most places without a well-
organized state.

FINANCING EDUCATION IN THE GLOBAL ECONOMY

Globalization means increased competition among nations in a more closely intertwined international economy, a competition that is continuously enhanced by
more rapid communication and computer technology and by a way of business
thinking that is increasingly global rather than regional or national. One of the
main products of such competition is to make national states increasingly aware
of their "business climate." The conditions of doing business in a country are
responsible for attracting foreign capital and for the ability of local businesses to
accumulate profit.

The International Monetary Fund (IMF) has played an important role in setting the conditions for national states to develop economically in this global context. A major part of the IMF package for countries preparing themselves for "sound" economic growth is to reduce the size of public deficits and shift national resources from government control to the private sector. This, in turn, means the reduction of public spending relative to the private sector. Since educational spending is such an important fraction of public sector spending in most countries (about 16 percent), reducing public spending inevitably means reducing the relative spending on education, at least for a number of years. The longer-term lending counterpart to the IMF, the World Bank, has provided a set of Structural Adjustment Loans (SALs) to help countries through this trying economic period and sector loans specifically aimed at cushioning the downturn in relative educational spending. But these loans are "conditioned" to making certain kinds of educational reforms.

Globalization has therefore had its most direct impact on education through what I have described elsewhere as "finance-driven" reforms, and the main vehicle for these reforms has been the World Bank, with major support from the finance ministries of national states. This should not be surprising. The Bank is a financial institution, concerned primarily with reducing the cost of public service delivery. For example, the latest World Bank Educational Sector Paper (1995), which traditionally summarizes the Bank's recommendations for educational strategies in donor countries, focuses attention on the need to expand education and increase its quality, but in the context of limited public resources for education. Among other strategies, the Bank paper recommends (1) the shift of public funding for education from higher to lower levels of education; (2) the expansion of secondary and higher education through increased privatization; (3) the reduction of public spending per pupil in countries with "high" teacher–pupil ratios in primary and secondary education (less than 1:40) through increasing class size; and (4) the increase of the quality of education through relatively costless "efficiency" reforms, such as decentralization.

Decentralization

It is in this context that we have to assess the impact of decentralization on education in countries going through "globalization reforms" (McGinn, 1997). The main argument for decentralization is that if municipalities and, in some places, schools, are given greater educational decision making autonomy, this will devolve local control over curriculum and teaching methods to local communities and the teachers and principals of the schools themselves. The assumption is that increased flexibility and control allows for a better fit between educational methods and the clientele served, as well as greater accountability for educational results. If the local educational authorities see themselves and are seen as responsible for educational delivery, reformers reason, educational quality will improve.

Decentralization is therefore cast as a reform that increases productivity in education and hence contributes significantly to improving the quality of a nation's human resources—largely through bringing educational decision making closer to parents' needs and giving local authorities greater educational decision making autonomy. Although decentralizing the management and financing of highly bureaucratic, centralized systems of education should lead to more innovative and efficient educational service delivery, with more accountability to parents, there is little evidence that educational quality improves as a result. For example, in the United States, where there has been a concerted push to move control of educational decisions down to individual schools, extensive evaluation shows that school autonomy itself has produced no significant student achievement gains (Malen et al., 1989; Hannaway and Carnoy, 1993).

Privatization

For many, an extension of such reforms is public school choice and the privatization of educational delivery (UNESCO, 1993). Although the reason why parents would want to have school choice is usually the composition of the local (urban) school student body and the resulting "undesirable" conditions in the school, choice proponents argue that the threat of parent exit would motivate teachers and principals to improve school quality. Similarly, a major argument for privatization is its positive effect on interschool competition and school accountability, hence school quality (West, 1997). Although World Bank analysts claim that private schools are much more cost-effective than public (Jimenez et al., 1988; Lockheed and Jimenez, 1996), the evidence supporting this claim is controversial. Recent research in Chile suggests that in a country where more than one-third of all primary school pupils attend voucher-subsidized private schools, public schools turn out to be, in the 1990s, more effective than subsidized private schools when the socioeconomic background of students attending schools is accounted for, and private school cost-effectiveness is only slightly higher (Carnoy and McEwan, 1997). Private schools that cater to students from less-educated families are least likely to do better than their public school counterparts. Further, in most countries, including Chile, private schools lower their costs, mainly by selecting out "higher cost" students and by "free-riding" on the system of public education; i.e., by hiring a higher proportion of part-time teachers (many who also work in public schools) than public schools. To estimate the "true" cost-effectiveness of private education, we would need to cost out private educational delivery under conditions of totally private management of the educational system.

Finally, the Chilean data do not bear out the often mentioned claim that competition between private and public schools results in improved public school performance. Using panel analysis, we found that although competition per se may have had some positive effect on average public school performance, this was swamped by the opposite influence of "cream skimming," where private schools skim off the better-performing students from public schools (McEwan and Carnoy, 1998). To the contrary, the one significant positive effect on Chilean public school performance over time has been central Ministry intervention through providing new materials and teacher training to the lowest-performing schools (McEwan and Carnoy, 1998).

In turn, the principal argument for privatizing higher levels of education is that many countries simply will not be able to finance the expansion of secondary and higher education with public funds given future increases in demand. Thus, for education to expand at those levels, developing nations will have to rely on families to finance a high fraction of school costs privately. This can be done in two ways: (1) by allowing the creation of accredited private secondary schools and universities in much larger numbers and (2) by limiting the public assistance given to all schools, including public institutions, and requiring increased fees to cover the gap between the cost per student and public assistance per student. The Bank has also focused on increasing community contributions to schools, in both pecuniary and nonpecuniary forms. All of these reforms essentially push for increased financing of schooling through user fees, whether the users be the community or individuals. The more highly privatized a level of schooling, the greater the user fee component. The Bank has explicitly argued that for "efficiency" and "equity" reasons (see below), user fees should be a much greater proportion of total financing the higher the level of schooling.

Better Performance or Less Government Spending?

The decentralization reforms we observe as part of the globalization process are therefore couched in the rhetoric of increasing productivity by giving more control to local actors over educational decision making. But in truth the reforms are inexorably entwined with reducing the central government contribution to public education. This difference between rhetoric and reality is important. In narrow economic terms, globalization does produce greater efficiency, since it enables capital to seek out high returns and to employ productive forces and knowledge wherever they might exist. The decentralization rhetoric reflects that possibility for education. Decentralization can conceivably improve educational productivity. But in the present historical context, globalization is accompanied by an ideology that makes financial austerity a condition of economic progress. Free-market ideology also dominates the educational thinking of those spreading decentralization reforms, who, in turn, are largely representatives of financial institutions that are willing to put resources behind their beliefs. Free-market ideology is not just concerned with economic efficiency. It is inherently opposed to government activism, on the grounds that government bureaucracies are inescapably inefficient. Since decentralization reform is dominated by these ideological considerations, not the imperative of raising educational productivity, globalization shapes education in terms of goals that are at best tangential to achieving educational improvement and certainly outside the everyday world of educational practice. In a nutshell, globalization enters the education sector on an ideological horse, and its effects on education are largely a product of that financially driven, free-market ideology, not of a clear conception for improving education.

Brought in as a financial, free-market ideology, globalization does have major effects on education. In the 1980s, many Latin American and African countries, saddled with high-interest debt and forced to undergo major financial restructuring, accepted structural adjustment packages from the IMF and World Bank. These required the reduction of public spending, including spending on education (International Labour Office, 1996). Although data are scarce on the effect of structural adjustment policies (SAPs) on educational quality, one study suggests that in Costa Rica, SAPs in the 1980s lowered promotion rates in secondary school significantly, and this was related to lowering costs per pupil (Carnoy and Torres, 1994).

With financially driven decentralization, lower-income regions often end up having to lower the cost of schooling more and to put their already more at-risk school population in a worse situation than higher income regions. This is what appears to have happened in Chile in the 1980s after the 1981 voucher reform. But lower-income regions are not only faced by lower levels of physical resources that they can bring to bear on educational delivery. They also lack the human resources for managing educational systems. So in the name of the persuasive argument that bringing educational delivery closer to the clients makes education more relevant and responsive to local needs, financially driven decentralization reform is likely to reduce access and quality of education in those regions with the least resources.

Financially driven decentralization reform is also likely to put increased pressure on teacher salaries, especially in the lowest-income regions, hence to create resistance among the very educational actors needed to improve the quality of education. Especially because teachers continue to work largely unsupervised behind the closed doors of classrooms, focusing so heavily on top-down cost-saving deflects attention from a second fundamental reality: if nations hope to increase the cognitive skills of their young populations through schooling they will have to rely on autonomous, motivated, and skilled professional teachers. How these teachers regard themselves, how well they are prepared to do their job, and how committed they are made to feel to their pupils' academic success are keys to producing both basic and advanced learning in any society. This requires a heavy dose of public sector involvement, and not just at the basic education level. Teacher recruitment, education, and technical assistance through in-service training are almost universally public sector—financed and managed. If they are to be improved, it is the public sector that will be responsible.

Since globalization is articulated in the form of finance-driven decentralization reforms, its main effect on the educational systems of many developing countries is to increase inequality of access and quality. It also puts enormous pressure on regions and municipalities to go after teacher salaries in order to reduce costs, creating conflict with the very group needed to produce favorable educational change. Many of the reforms implicit in structural adjustment are actually needed, but their form of implementation results in a series of negative impacts that could be avoided by more coherent focus on school improvement rather than on simple financial objectives. This requires national state interpretations of how to improve educational process and practice within the context of globalization rather than on globalization's financial imperatives themselves.

LABOR AND GLOBALIZATION

Is labor also globalized? With the exception of the upper layers of professional labor, it does not seem to be. In 1993, despite global panic about "floods" of immigrants, only about 1.5 percent (eighty million workers) of the global labor force worked outside their country, and half of them—surprisingly—were concentrated in Sub-Saharan Africa and the Middle East (Campbell, 1994). Free movement of citizens in the European Union resulted in only 2 percent of its nationals working in another Union country in 1993. That proportion has been unchanged since the mid-1980s.[3] Notwithstanding the public perception in the United States and Europe concerning the invasion of cheap labor from the South and East, immigrants as a proportion of the total population only surpassed 5 percent in Germany (about 7 percent), and in France, the proportion was lower in 1992 than in 1986. In the United Kingdom, it was only slightly over the 1986 level (Carnoy and Castells, 1997, Appendix I). The United States was always an immigrant society, and current trends are consistent with an earlier period of open immigration (Portes and Rambaut, 1996). Yet, the main concern with immigration in the United States and Europe is less in the numbers than in the ethnic composition of immigrants. Immigrants today are less European, and the higher birth rate of non-European immigrant populations once they are in the host country makes societies increasingly multicultural and multiethnic.

Although the "coloring" of predominantly white societies does not necessarily imply a global labor market, increased multiculturalization of Eurocentric societies is one important manifestation of globalization. In the United States, for example, business is behind much of the political push for open immigration for both high- and low-skill workers. Not surprisingly, information technology companies are among the most active lobbyists for increased immigration. They see a large supply of highly skilled engineers and computer programmers in India, China, and Europe who can fill their needs at lower wages than those demanded by U.S. high-end workers. U.S. (and Japanese) universities also now depend heavily on foreign science and engineering graduate students to do research on government-funded projects (Carnoy, 1998). Foreign countries, too, have an interest in sending their students (and lower-skilled workers) to the United States, Europe, and Japan, so that they can learn and bring back the latest technological skills and earn higher wages and remit money back home.

And even if labor does not circulate globally to the same degree as do money and goods, the new dynamics of trade and investment, led by multinational corporations and transnational networks of firms, have increased the interdependence of labor markets (Bailey et al., 1993). Some economists claim that the impact of trade on employment and wages in the United States is very positive (Krugman and Lawrence, 1994),[4] but most believe that foreign trade has had a significant negative impact on the wages of less-educated workers (Bluestone, 1995). One estimate shows that between 1960 and 1990, skilled workers in the North benefited from the process of globalization, both in employment and wages, but unskilled workers lost out in the competition from developing countries. Demand for unskilled labor in the North fell by 20 percent, and wages declined (Wood, 1994). Others have shown that the potential of mobility for firms in the global economy provides management with extra bargaining power in obtaining concessions from the labor force in the North (Shaiken, 1993). Whereas indirect effects of globalization are not always visible, they do affect bargaining relations. They tend to reduce labor's share of economic surplus but simultaneously preserve jobs that cannot be easily exported, such as highly skilled jobs or those located in nontradable services.

So even without a unified global labor market or a global labor force, there is global labor interdependence in the new economy. Such interdependence is characterized by hierarchical segmentation of labor, not between countries but across borders. The new model of global production and management is tantamount to the simultaneous integration of work and disintegration of workers as a collective.

GLOBALIZED MARKETS AND THE GLOBALIZATION OF SKILLS

In practice, segmentation across borders means that globalized finance and investment create a worldwide demand for certain kinds of skills—namely language, mathematics reasoning, scientific logic, programming—associated with higher levels of education. Globalized science-based technology firms are increasingly using scientists and engineers trained at least partially in newly industrializing countries' (NICs) universities to staff their innovation activities both in the developed countries and in the NICs themselves. At the same time, national states, particularly in the NICs of Asia, are increasing their scientific and technological higher education rapidly in the hope of capturing innovation rents as innovation continues to globalize.

But the effect on global skill formation does not end there. Developed countries' universities' science-technology training and research, almost entirely under the aegis of national state-sponsored research and development programs, are becoming increasingly internationalized, drawing heavily on first degree programs for graduate students in the NICs (Carnoy, 1998). The highly skilled scientists and engineers coming out of these graduate programs are available for globalized innovation, including innovation in enterprises owned and managed by NIC entrepreneurs and states.

Globalized demand for certain types of higher-level skills puts upward pressure on the payoffs to the higher educated around the world, particularly in those economies more closely tied into the globalization process. In the past generation, most countries have undergone rapid expansion of their primary and secondary education systems. This is not universally true, but thanks to a generalized ideology that basic education should be available to children as a right, even financial constraints in many debt-ridden countries, such as those in Latin America, did not prevent them from increasing access to basic and even secondary education (Castro and Carnoy, 1997). University education has also expanded, but given the bias of global demand for the higher educated, the tendency is to push up rates of return to investment in higher education relative to the payoffs in investing in primary and secondary schooling. Estimated rates of return in countries such as Singapore, Malaysia, Hong Kong, the Republic of Korea, and Argentina, as well as in a number of the Organization for Economic Cooperation and Development (OECD) countries, show rates of return to university education as higher than to either secondary or primary.[5]

Higher rates of return to higher education mean that those who get that education are benefited relatively more for their investment in education than those who stop at lower levels of schooling. In most countries, those who get to higher levels of schooling are also those from higher social class background. In addition, with increased emphasis on decentralization and privatization, higher socioeconomic status (SES) students are those who get access to "better" schools, in regions that are more likely to spend more per pupil for education, particularly in those schools attended by higher SES pupils. Competition for such higher-payoff education also increases as the payoff to higher education increases, because the stakes get higher. Higher SES parents become increasingly conscious of where their children attend school, what those schools are like, and whether they provide access to higher levels of education. The total result is therefore that schooling becomes more stratified at lower levels rather than less stratified, especially under conditions of scarce public resources. National economic competition on a global scale gets translated into subnational competition in class access to educational resources.

In addition to raising the payoff to higher levels of education, globalization appears to have raised the rate of return for women's education. In many countries rates of return for education for women are higher than for men (Ryoo et al., 1993; Psacharopoulos, 1989). The reasons for the increased participation of women in labor markets are complex, but two main factors have been the spread of feminist ideas and values and the increased demand for low-cost semiskilled labor in developing countries' electronics manufacturing and other assembly industries. The worldwide movement for women's rights has had the effect of legitimizing equal education for women, women's control over their fertility rates, women's increased participation in wage labor markets, and women's right to vote (Castells, 1997; Ramirez et al., 1997). The increased demand for low-cost labor and greater sense by women that they have the same rights as men have brought enormous numbers of married women into the labor market worldwide. This, in turn has created increased demand for education by women at higher and higher education levels. So globalization is accentuating an already growing trend by women to obtain as much or more education than men.

This does not mean that women receive wages equal to men's. That is hardly the case. Nor does it mean that women are obtaining higher education in fields that are most lucrative, such as engineering, business, or computer science. That is also far from true. Women are still vastly underrepresented in the most lucrative professions even in the most "feminized" countries, such as Sweden or the United States. But globalization seems gradually to be changing that, for both positive and negative reasons. The positive reasons are that flexible organization in business enterprise requires flexible labor, and women are as or more flexible than men, and that information technology and telecommunications are spreading democratic ideas worldwide. The negative reason is that women are paid much less than men almost everywhere in the world, and it is profitable for firms to hire women and pay them lower wages. Yet, both sets of reasons gradually seem to be driving both the education and the price of women's labor up relative to men's. For example, the percentage of women in science and engineering university faculties is increasing worldwide. Although such increased "professionalization" of women may have costly effects on family life, it does serve to democratize societies and greatly raise the average level of schooling.

GLOBALIZATION AND WAGE INEQUALITY

Rising relative rates of return to higher education are not just the result of new technology and the increasing demand for higher-order skills. Because globalization is heavily influenced by the movement of financial assets, it is set in the context of a particular ideology of economic development, an ideology that puts financial considerations first. "Conservative" economic policies without the presence of strong institutional factors favoring labor–business cooperation, such as in Germany, Japan, Scandinavia, and Austria, tend to put the lower-educated at increased disadvantage as protections to labor are reduced and protectionist policies dismantled.

Globalization does not necessarily lead to increased wage inequality between the more and less educated. But the pressure on governments to put their economies' financial houses in order to compete in the global economy produces policies that tend to hurt the lower educated more than the higher educated. In the context of the ideological packaging surrounding globalization, this has produced a strong bias against raising wages, a strong bias against social wages, and a bias in favor of financial policies that keep unemployment higher than it otherwise might be.

As a result, governments that buy into the globalization package tend to

- Turn away from welfare state policies with their corporatist overtones and toward the private market. Part of this shift results from voters' perception of the declining power of the state to influence markets in an increasingly global economy (Castells, 1997). But part comes from a major effort by corporations to raise the share of private profits in gross national product (Bowles et al., 1983; Carnoy et al., 1983).
- Take strong anti-union policies, setting a tone for bargaining that put employers in the driver's seat.
- Lower minimum wages as part of policies to "increase employment," particularly of youth, even though there is considerable evidence that raising minimum wages has little effect on youth unemployment, at least in the United States (Card and Krueger, 1995). Combined with severe anti-inflation policies that produce high levels of unemployment, declining real minimum wages put increasing pressure on the pay of lower-skilled workers.

Thus, institutional settings and resulting government policies and firm behavior can affect not only income distribution, but also the wages of certain groups of workers. The institutional argument is supported by studies that show earnings inequality rising less than in the United States, for example, especially at the low end of the earnings distribution, than in countries such as Canada, France, and Germany. Workers in those countries were exposed to similar changes in the relative demand for low-skilled workers as in the United States but faced more amenable labor legislation and better employer–labor relations (Freeman and Needels, 1991; Freeman and Katz, 1995). These studies conclude that rising minimum wages and the maintenance of more balanced bargaining power between employers and labor were crucial in keeping low-skilled wages from falling significantly.[6]

Between the rising demand for higher skills resulting from technological change and the increasing income inequality resulting from government policies associated with anti-labor, pro-high private profits, globalization inexorably pushes up rates of return to higher education and increases the demand for schooling. The good side of this trend is that it accelerates the increase in nations' human capital and may increase labor productivity. The bad side is that when accompanied by greater inequality in access to high-quality education, children from lower-income families with less-educated parents are even less likely to get access to social mobility than in the past.

GLOBALIZATION, SCIENCE CULTURE, AND EDUCATIONAL MEASUREMENT

Globalization has also produced an increased emphasis on teaching science and mathematics and on educational measurement. The high value of information technology and other science-based industries has pushed countries to increase emphasis on science and mathematics education. This has been stimulated by the spread of a science and math culture (Schofer et al., 1997) and also the strong effort by many countries to attract foreign high-tech investment and build up domestic high-tech industries (Carnoy, 1998). How much real increase has taken place in science and math education is questionable, but the rhetoric surrounding the issue has increased greatly.

Furthermore, there is a much greater focus in many countries on comparing performance in these subjects with student performance in other countries. With increased economic competition and the increased availability of information technology, data takes on greater value and increased use. Performance in real time is enhanced as an outcome; quantitative measurement appears easier, and its results become increasingly the means of communication about performance. An important element of such performance is linked to "efficiency." The application of this thinking, part and parcel of globalized thinking, to education takes the form of tracking the quantity and quality of education through data collection. The most recent expression of this is collecting data on student performance as a measure of the quality of education, largely with the intention of using such results to improve educational efficiency.

The measurement of quality linked to improving educational efficiency cannot be separated from the financially driven reforms discussed above. Much of the discussion of student performance is in the context of educational spending and how to reduce it without impacting "quality." The implication is that public educational delivery is inefficient, and part of its inefficiency can be picked up by measuring student performance to make the "system" aware of how well or badly students are doing.

The new emphasis on measuring and comparing school outcomes across countries and within countries has not occurred spontaneously. Rather, it has been pushed by international organizations such as the International Association for Evaluation of Educational Achievement (IEA), the OECD, and the World Bank. All these organizations share a globalized view of education and efficiency, which includes a highly quantitative view of progress. They also share an explicit understanding that "better" education can be measured and that better education translates directly into higher economic and social productivity. With more intensive economic competition among nation-states, the urgency of improving productivity is translated by these organizations into spreading the acceptance of inter- and intranational comparisons on standardized tests of student knowledge.

Although only in its beginning stages, the use of national and international tests in a comparative way is already having observable policy effects. In the United States, for example, the Third International Math and Science Study (TIMSS) has accentuated a national discussion of mathematics curricula and put teeth behind many states' use of standards and accountability. A number of Latin American countries have also begun to test students and will participate in the next TIMSS. In Chile, national testing has gone on for at least fifteen years, but it is only in the past five years, with the new global emphasis on efficiency and measurement, that the testing has started to define the "meaning" of education and educational change, with schools consciously aware of their test results and organizing themselves around improving scores.

The use of student tests in the "global" conception of measurement and efficiency is, however, currently rather confused. This is due largely to the push by international organizations such as the World Bank and Inter-American Bank for comparative data to reform systems in keeping with system efficiency, mainly in financial terms. Although articulated in terms of making education more "efficient" or in terms of improving education, these ways of collecting and using the data are not necessarily consistent with improving schooling.

Another way of using testing is linked directly to school improvement, not for system reform or saving money. In the best of cases, school personnel participate in designing and applying the tests, and the tests are directly linked to knowledge transmission goals set either at the national or regional level. Important aspects of school efficiency can certainly be understood through such tests, but efficiency here is less concerned with resource allocation per se, as with process and use of resources. In Chile, for example, national testing of fourth and eighth grade students was originally, in the 1980s, used simply as a way to stimulate competition among private and public schools competing for students and the voucher funds attached to each student. Available evidence suggests that this use of tests had no positive effect on student achievement. However, in the 1990s, the use of national testing linked to central government school improvement programs did apparently increase test scores in lower-scoring schools catering to low-income students.

Global notions of efficiency and measurement can therefore have a positive effect on educational output. For this to happen, however, these notions must be passed through local filters and have as their specific purpose school improvement even if school improvement requires more resources, which is likely the case in most developing societies. The distinction between this type of application of measurement to raising efficiency and the use of testing to develop national policies for resource use with the intention of decreasing per student public resources available for education is subtle and is mainly rooted in how the state, rather than international organizations, interprets the role of measurement in conditioning educational change.

CONCLUSION

National education has been significantly affected by globalization even though we may not necessarily observe these effects (beyond a few computers in the schools) in most of the world's classrooms. The effects are expressed through changes in the payoffs to different levels of education and the implication that has for the value attached to different levels and kinds of knowledge in each society. They are also expressed through the educational policies implemented at the national level in the context of a globalized economy. The influence of financially driven reforms tends to redistribute access to schooling away from lower-income students, accentuating the more unequal distribution of income and more highly valued knowledge. Decentralization is a form of restructuring that *can* have positive effects on educational productivity. But in the context of attempts by anti-public spending ideology, decreases in public involvement in education couched as school decentralization are likely to have the opposite effect on quality. Finally, educational measurement as used by international organizations (and often adopted by national states) reinforces these trends by employing testing to justify finance-driven reforms rather than school improvement.

All of these effects of globalization on education are passed through the policy structures of national states, so it is these states that ultimately decide how globalization affects national education. I would argue that there is much more political and even financial space for the national state to condition the way globalization is brought into education than is usually admitted. Testing and standards are a good example of this space, and decentralization and school autonomy are others. States can provide schooling access more equally, improve the quality of education for the poor, and produce knowledge more effectively and more equally for all within a globalized economy. That they generally choose not to do so is at least partly the result of ideological preference rather than helplessness in the face of new competitive pressures and new, globalized thinking. Although it is difficult to counter strong, worldwide ideological trends and, indeed, the objective reality of financial globalization, my argument is simply that there is much more political space to develop alternatives than the ideologues of globalization allow.

NOTES

1. Real time is, in entertainment parlance, "live," meaning that information is exchanged or communicated as it is produced.
2. For an early definition of transnationals, see Barnet and Muller (1974).

3. *Newsweek,* special issue on "Jobs." June 4, 1993.
4. For a response, see Cohen, 1994.
5. For a list of studies that make these estimates, contact the author.
6. Other economists claim that "shadow" income inequality is much higher in France and Germany if unemployment rates are taken into account. In other words, the earnings of low-skilled workers would fall if those employed would "share" the existing set of jobs with the unemployed.

REFERENCES

Amin, Ash. 1998. Globalization and Regional Development: A Relational Perspective. *Competition and Change*, vol. 3, pp. 145–65.

Bailey, Paul, Aurelio Parisotto, and Geoffrey Renshaw (eds.). 1993. *Multinationals and Employment*. Geneva: International Labour Office.

Barnet, Richard, and Ronald Muller. 1974. *Global Reach*. New York: Simon and Schuster.

Bluestone, Barry. 1995 (Winter). The Inequality Express. *The American Prospect*, no. 24, pp. 81–95.

Bowles, Samuel, David Gordon, and Thomas Weiskopf. 1983. *Beyond the Wasteland*. New York: Doubleday.

Braudel, Fernand. 1979. *The Wheels of Commerce*. Volume II of *Civilization and Capitalism*. New York: Harper and Row.

Campbell, Duncan. 1994. Foreign Investment, Labor Immobility and the Quality of Employment. *International Labour Review*, vol. 2, pp. 185–203.

Card, David, and Alan Krueger. 1995. *Myth and Measurement*. Princeton, NJ: Princeton University Press.

Carnoy, Martin. 1993. Multinationals in a Changing World Economy. In Martin Carnoy et al., *The New Global Economy in the Information Age*. University Park: Pennsylvania State University Press, pp. 45–96.

———. 1998. The Globalization of Innovation, Nationalist Competition, and the Internationalization of Scientific Training. *Competition and Change*, vol. 3, pp. 237–62.

Carnoy, Martin, and Manuel Castells. 1997. *Sustainable Flexibility*. Paris: OECD.

Carnoy, Martin, Stephen Cohen, and Fernando H. Cardoso. 1993. *The New Global Economy in the Information Age*. University Park: Pennsylvania State University Press.

Carnoy, Martin, and Patrick McEwan. 1997. Public Investments or Private Schools? A Reconstruction of Educational Improvements in Chile. Stanford University School of Education (mimeo).

Carnoy, Martin, Derek Shearer, and Russell Rumberger. 1983. *The New Social Contract*. New York: Harper and Row.

Carnoy, Martin, and Carlos A. Torres. 1994. Educational Change and Structural Adjustment: A Case Study of Costa Rica. In Joel Samoff (ed.), *Coping with Crisis*. London: Cassell with UNESCO, pp. 64–99.

Castells, Manuel. 1996. *The Rise of the Network Society*. London: Blackwell.

———. 1997. *The Power of Identity*. London: Blackwell.

Castro, Claudio de Moura, and Martin Carnoy. 1997. *La Reforma Educativa en America*

Latina. Washington, D.C.: Inter-American Development Bank, Department of Social Programs and Sustainable Development.

Cohen, Stephen S. 1994 (July–August). Reply to Krugman. *Foreign Affairs*, vol. 73, no. 4, pp. 194–97.

Coleman, James. 1988. Social Capital in the Creation of Human Capital. *American Journal of Sociology*, vol. 94, supplement, pp. S95–S120.

Freeman, Richard, and Lawrence Katz. 1995. *Differences and Changes in Wage Structures*. Chicago: University of Chicago Press and NBER.

Freeman, Richard, and Karen Needels. 1991 (September). Skill Differentials in Canada in an Era of Rising Labor Market Inequality. Cambridge, MA: National Bureau of Economic Research, Working Paper 3827.

Fukuyama, Francis. 1995. *Trust*. New York: Free Press.

Hannaway, Jane, and Martin Carnoy. 1993. *Decentralization and School Improvement*. San Francisco: Jossey-Bass.

International Labour Office. 1996. *The Impact of Structural Adjustment on the Employment and Training of Teachers*. Geneva: International Labour Office (JMEP/1996/II).

Jimenez, Emmanuel, Marlaine Lockheed, and Nongnuch Wattanawaha. 1988. The Relative Efficiency of Public and Private Schools: The Case of Thailand. *World Bank Economic Review*, vol. 2, no. 2, pp. 139–64.

Krugman, Paul, and Robert Z. Lawrence. 1994 (April). Trade, Jobs, and Wages. *Scientific American*, pp. 44–49.

Lockheed, Marlaine, and Emmanuel Jimenez. 1996. Public and Private Schools Overseas: Contrasts in Organization and Effectiveness. In Bruce Fuller and Richard Elmore (eds.), *Who Chooses? Who Loses?* New York: Teachers College Press, pp. 138–53.

McEwan, Patrick, and Martin Carnoy. 1998. Competition and Sorting in Chile's Voucher System. Stanford University, School of Education (mimeo).

McGinn, Noel. 1997 (March). The Impact of Globalization on National Education Systems. *Prospects*, vol. 28, no. 1, pp. 41–54.

Malen, Betty, Rodney T. Ogawa, and Jennifer Krantz. 1989 (May). What Do We Know about School-Based Management. School of Education, University of Utah (mimeo).

Portes, Alejandro, and Ruben G. Rumbaut. 1996. *Immigrant America: A Portrait*. Berkeley: University of California Press.

Psacharopoulos, George. 1989. Time Trends of the Returns to Education: Cross-National Evidence. *Economics of Education Review*, vol. 8, no. 3, pp. 225–39.

Ramirez, Francisco, Yasemin Saysal, and Susan Shanahan. 1997 (October). The Changing Logic of Political Citizenship: Cross National Acquisition of Women's Suffrage Rights, 1890 to 1990. *American Sociological Review*, vol. 62, pp. 735–45.

Ryoo, Jai-Kyung, Martin Carnoy, and Young Sook Nam. 1993 (March). Rates of Return to Education in Korea. *Economics of Education Review*, pp. 71–80.

Schofer, Evan, Francisco Ramirez, John Meyer. 1997. Effects of Science on Economic Development. Paper presented at the annual meetings of the American Sociological Association, Toronto.

Shaiken, Harley. 1993 (Fall). Beyond Lean Production. *Stanford Law & Policy Review*, vol. 5, no. 1, pp. 41–52.

UNCTAD. 1993. *World Investment Report 1993: Transnational Corporations and Integrated International Production*. New York: United Nations.

UNESCO. 1993. *World Education Report, 1993*. Paris: UNESCO.

West, Edwin G. 1997 (March). Education Vouchers in Principle and Practice: A Survey. *World Bank Research Review*, vol. 2, no. 2, pp. 83–103.

Wood, Adrian. 1994. *North–South Trade, Employment and Inequality*. Oxford: Clarendon.

World Bank. 1995. *Priorities and Strategies for Education: A World Bank Sector Review*. Washington, D.C.: World Bank.

———. 1997. *World Development Report: The State in a Changing World*. New York: Oxford University Press.

4

Educational Reform:
Who Are the Radicals?

Val D. Rust

POLITICAL GLOBALIZATION

Global relations imply that economic, political, and cultural activities have disengaged themselves from territorial authority and jurisdictions and have begun to transcend the nation-state and function according to their own imperatives and interests (Hobsbawm, 1994; Giddens, 1994). Interpreters of globalization have shown the greatest interest toward economic developments, but globalization goes far beyond economic processes and includes political and cultural processes. The focus of this essay shall be on some globalizing developments within the political sphere. Interpreters of political globalization typically focus on the surrender of sovereignty on the part of nation-states and the emergence of larger political units (European Union), multilateral treaties (North American Free Trade Agreement), and international organizations (United Nations, International Monetary Fund) (Waters, 1995, p. 97). They find the rational consequence of these trends to be a system of global governance with the decline of state powers and authority (Held, 1991, pp. 207–9). Such a scenario seems reasonable, but actual political developments are not so clear. While state autonomy is apparently in decline, as yet no global political unit is in place that regulates and coordinates cultural and economic globalism. However, a more subtle kind of political globalization is taking place. Certain interpreters claim that an incipient common, global political culture has emerged; this political culture takes different forms, depending on the orientation of the interpreter. For example, Francis Fukayama (1992) claims that the collapse of the former Soviet Union signals the triumph of global political liberalism. His view is reinforced by certain educational specialists, who find strong evidence that education policy and norms are becoming globally more and more uniform. The goal of every country is to have all children

63

attend school for a certain period of time. The structural ideal of schools is to be vertically age-graded and divided into primary, lower secondary, and upper secondary levels. Instructors increasingly possess postsecondary teaching credentials. Essentially the same curriculum is taught in every environment. Children are trained to contribute to the global economy (see, for example, Meyer and Hannan, 1979).

In this paper I would like to raise the question of what it means today to be politically radical with regard to educational change. Anthony Giddens (1994, p. 1) reminds us that the idea of political radicalism has long been bound up primarily with socialist thought. And to be radical has usually been associated with a view that history promises innovative possibilities, that humankind can and will break away from its constraining past. Of course, some radicals have been revolutionaries who have believed that only through revolution could a necessary sharp separation from the past be realized. Yet Giddens claims, and I concur, that the notion of revolution has never been the defining feature of political radicalism; rather, it has consisted mainly of the idea of progress. History is there to be seized, to be molded, to be developed and organized in such a way that the human condition is made better.

Because I specialize in the European sphere, much of my frame of reference must be seen from that vantage point, though some of my references will pertain to the United States and other parts of the world that have been engaged in recent educational reform activities. However, since Louis Hartz (1955) it has been difficult to think of the United States as anything other than having a "liberal" tradition, though recent advocates of the so-called "silent majority" and the "new right" have successfully challenged such a label.

It is useful to begin by reminding ourselves of the many political "isms" that are a part of our discourse. They might easily be compressed to five, three, or even two categories, particularly the Left and Right. And they might just as easily be expanded into a dozen categories. Clinton Rossiter (1982) has made a distinct contribution to an understanding of the implied continuum, whatever its number of categories, in that he does not see the political spectrum proceeding along a straight line (right to left) but around the rim of a circle, so that the first and last categories are closest of neighbors.

The conventional view of the political Left and Right is shown in figure 4.1.

Rossiter's view is of a circle, and the line of division between any two of the categories is in fact no line at all but an imperceptible gradation; within each category there are any number of possible minor deviations. Graphically, it might be shown as in figure 4.2.

Of course, one finds revolutionary radicalism and revolutionary reactionism at

Left ⟵⟶ **Right**

Figure 4.1

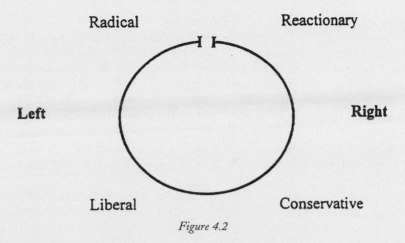

Figure 4.2

the extremes of the continuum, but the Western tradition has not experienced those political extremes as much as the more tempered radicalism and reactionism. Even those representing these more tempered versions are so dissatisfied with the existing order that they are committed to thoroughgoing change, and thus they are willing to initiate deep-cutting reforms. The main difference in the two is that radicalism looks toward new historical designs, while the reactionaries maintain a certain reverie for the past. They believe those in the past were somehow better off than we are at present and if we continue into the future as we have been going our condition will only get worse. The solution for the reactionary is to roll back the social process, to restore certain virtues that defined society and mankind. It ought to be clear from the above scheme that liberals and conservatives are closer neighbors with each other than they are with the so-called extreme Left and Right.

Some fascinating and even surprising global developments have occurred in recent years, calling for elaboration. Conservatism, or at least the new Right, in many of its influential guises in Europe, and to some extent elsewhere in the world, has come to embrace what it has traditionally repudiated. Although it may sound like a contradiction of terms, many conservatives are now active radicals with respect to tradition. Conservatism has become radical, and it has forced socialism to become conservative.

THE FORMER SOVIET UNION

The Soviet Union long claimed that it epitomized revolutionary radicalism. Its leaders proclaimed that they had broken from the tradition of social-class relations and were moving toward a state of equality, community, peace, and brotherly love. The revolutionary process systematically attempted to destroy most conventional institutions and historical traditions and reconstructed all aspects of life (Sinyavsky, 1990). Comparative education provides a good example of the extent to which the Soviets and their satellites claimed they had broken with the past. A major debate ran in the 1950s and 60s regarding the role of comparative education. Many socialists said the only legitimate use of comparative education was within the socialist sphere, because the capitalist countries were at a different (lower) level of social development. Their capitalist educational systems were incommensurable with the socialist systems, and, therefore, comparison was inappropriate and useless. Indeed, they believed the Soviet Union had achieved a radical break with the traditional, Western economic, political, and intellectual model.

By the late 1920s the Soviet Union was able to expand its industrial and manufacturing base, and shortly after World War II it could claim to have the second largest economy in the world. And the economy continued to grow until the end of the 1950s. At that time the world's manufacturing system began to shift away from heavy industry toward high-value-added, knowledge-intensive, and consumer-driven industries (Kennedy 1993, pp. 232–33). The state planners of the Soviet Union were unable to adjust to the new demands, and the Soviet economy began to stagnate; by the early 1980s it had reached a crisis point. Even though attempts were made to maintain the status quo, throughout the region under the control of the Soviet Union, some changes did occur. Even before Mikhail Gorbachev gained the international spotlight, certain central and eastern European countries had already begun charting a course that veered from the Soviet model. Such divergence became gradually public. In contrast to the Soviet Union, there was a limited private sector in the economies of Hungary and Poland, as well as the GDR, at least in the craft and service sectors. Also, cultural life never reflected a total *Sovietization*. National and regional consciousness were always realities, and the everyday life of people in many respects remained consistent with their traditions. These activities took place, however, with a keen awareness that the Soviet Union remained the dominant regional power, and it was possible that the Soviet Union would assert itself at any time, so these reforms were always tempered by the *realpolitik* that pervaded central and eastern Europe. It is for this reason that Gorbachev's policies of *glasnost* and *perestroika* are now seen to have been so significant in terms of the events of the past decade. During the early period of *glasnost* and *perestroika*, the Soviet Union chose to retain its commitment to the ideology it had supported for the past seventy years, and its leaders spoke of a renewed socialism, rather than of a fundamental shift in orientation. As the movement for reform gained momentum, the political leaders of socialism and communism found themselves to be on the defensive, and as the region marched toward its ultimate collapse, the leaders became symbols of conservatism. They were increasingly seen as defenders of a form of authoritarian dogmatism, deriving from a revolution betrayed, and when the collapse began, these conservative forces were swept away in quick and rapid succession. Since that time, those associated with leadership in the former Soviet Union continue to symbolize the conservative forces on the political spectrum. They are known by the pejorative label "Conservatives."

THE WELFARE STATE

We understand the welfare state to connote a government that plays a key role in the protection and promotion of the economic and social well-being of its citizens. In the European context, the welfare state traces its roots back to the nineteenth century and the rise of labor movements in the various national settings. In Germany, for example, Otto von Bismarck inaugurated the world's first general pension, health, and disability insurance systems in the 1880s, as a means of accommodation, while trying to contain the movement for social welfare by banning the Social Democratic Party. Thus, as early as the 1880s, the Germans made reference to the state in connection with welfare measures. The Scandinavian countries probably have the best-developed welfare states, and it is no accident that these countries also have a history of the strongest labor movements in Europe. The term *welfare state* (in English) was first used during World War II, but many English had long been attempting to engage the government in activities conducive to the welfare of the people, including the English Poor Law of 1834 (Einhorn and Logue, 1989; Wilensky, 1976).

It was only after World War II that the notion of the welfare state came into common usage, and by 1960 it had reached its peak currency. Almost all economically "advanced countries" became committed to some form of public responsibility for the well-being of the people through welfare legislation. Even when labor governments were voted out of office, the new regimes made no attempt to dismantle existing provisions, and the welfare state became linked to the idea of ever-increasing prosperity.

In the late 1960s certain basic notions of the welfare state began to be called into question. In Scandinavia, for example, conservatives claimed welfare measures undermined social morality and limited individual freedoms. In Great Britain, conservatives added to this list the claim that it undercut efficiency and productivity in the free-market system (Einhorn and Logue, 1989, p. 265). In the United States, conservatives claimed government programs such as the "war on poverty" contradicted institutions considered to be central to any healthy society, including the family, the church, and the workplace (Trattner, 1984). While most of these criticisms came from the Right, the Left also began to call certain facets of the welfare state into question, particularly the notion that welfare programs treated symptoms and not causes (Einhorn and Logue 1989, pp. 172–76).

By the end of the 1970s, attacks against the basic assumptions of the welfare state had been so successful that the concept fell into disrepute, and in the past twenty years the notion that the government plays the role of patriarch in the national family has been largely discredited. According to Giddens (1994), the welfare state project has foundered in part because it came to embody the failed aspirations of socialism. For example, one of the basic premises of socialism has been that the national wealth and resources would be more equitably distributed (Marshall, 1965). This never happened, and in fact, the middle class and even the upper classes have been the beneficiaries of welfare as much as and in many cases even more than the poorer classes, because "the welfare state actually became in some part a vehicle helping to promote the interests of an expanding middle class" (Giddens, 1994, p. 149).

But the important issue in our discussion is that advocates of the welfare state have become the political conservatives. Socialists are now the defenders of the status quo; they have lost their role as creators of a new history, of being progressive, of molding and organizing the world in such a way that the human condition is thereby improved. Their lot has been reduced to the modest task of preserving the accomplishments of the welfare state. Of course, this is a noble and important task, but the socialists are no longer the radicals of society, but the conservatives, attempting to preserve the significant and valuable achievements of the welfare state.

PUBLIC VS. PRIVATE EDUCATION

We recall that prior to the modern age in Europe, education was mainly an institution of the church. It was only with the rise of the modern nation-state that education came under government control. Without exception, nation-states turned to formal schools in order to achieve their purposes. Schools intended to produce leaders, and clerics have existed almost from the beginning of recorded history in the West. Other institutions that provided some limited cultural or professional training have also existed from time to time, but institutions whose sole mission was systematically to mold the lives of all the young of a culture are recent indeed. On the one hand, the nation-state took on many educational tasks that other institutions in traditional societies had carried. Wilhelm Flitner, for example, identifies four main historical roots in the German Volksschule. They are: (1) basic skills in reading, writing, and computation; (2) catechetical instruction, or religious and moral indoctrination; (3) enlightened learning in the vernacular; and (4) a patriotic and loyal identity with the Volk or nation-state (Flitner, 1941). The primary schools in other Western lands reflect a similar heritage. On the other hand, the nation-state turned to the elite secondary schools, such as the Great Public School of Great Britain, the Lycée of France, and the Gymnasium of the German states, to prepare the future leaders for higher education studies and statesmanship. And the state would play a substantial role in this educational process. This was considered to be a radical move at the time, and those defending tradition fought against such an activist role on the part of the state.

In Germany, Johann Friedrich Herbart (Rust, 1977), for example, opposed the adoption of state schools. He maintained that mass schooling could not impart genuine education, which could only be realized within the setting of the family and household. He maintained that schooling was little more than a second-class substitute for genuine education and cannot be an all-encompassing educational institution, especially for individuals. Whereas true education concentrates on the unique personality, the establishment of moral development, and inner freedom, the school would cripple the individual. Schooling "cannot be produced like goods in a factory" (p. 146). His model was taken from the so-called Hauslehrer (home teacher) tradition in Germany and consisted of individual tutoring.

Of course, private schooling was also schooling. Today a good deal of variation has come to exist in terms of the number of young people engaged in schooling in the private sector. In the Netherlands almost 71 percent of young people attend schools sponsored by nongovernment groups, but the norm is less than 20 percent.[1] From the time of the reformation through the early stages of the modern era, the church controlled education, and a significant element of every country's educational history is the story of the struggle of the political leaders to overcome that church monopoly by instituting either a public monopoly or some form of public regulation of all schooling.

Eastern Europe was the most extreme in its attempts to break down private interests in education. In fact, the only countries in Europe that eliminated all private schooling were in eastern Europe. All communist countries followed the lead of the Soviet Union, where one of the first decrees after the revolution was to remove the schools from the control of the church and place them under the control of regional and local councils (Soviets) (Bereday et al., 1960, p. 51). In East Germany, for example, in the first school law to be issued during the Soviet occupation period, private schools were abolished. The communist forces held that private schools were seedbeds of privilege and represented a denial of democratic principles (Hearnden, 1974, p. 59). Not only were the churches eliminated from the schooling picture, but radical leaders of socialism claimed all private initiative in schooling was a vestige of capitalistic free enterprise, which must be prohibited in favor of a single, unified, state-run system of schooling.

No western European country has eliminated private schools, although Norway and Sweden might be described as having thoroughgoing public school monopolies, because all private schools are tightly controlled by the state and only a very small percentage (1–2 percent) of the population attends schools under private sponsorship. These countries have allowed private schools to exist, but only if they have the same general purposes as public schools and actually help the public sector to satisfy its aims. In this respect, private schools have not been considered to be genuine alternatives, even though they are supported in large measure by the state, because they actually provide some stimulus to the public sector in terms of reform endeavors. Until recently, private schools have been bound to follow school law as vigorously as the public schools, and in Norway, secondary schools have only been allowed to exist as a part of general county school plans.

That is now rapidly changing. In the former Soviet Union and in central Europe one of the main reform agendas has been to allow private institutions to come into being. Privatization has become attractive in all of central Europe and in the former Soviet Union. Throughout Europe, the major thrust of schooling has been to provide greater parental choice, and the most radical orientation has been to create certain variations of voucher systems, which allow parents, at public expense, to choose whatever school they wish. The most popular alternatives are those that stem from the so-called progressive education era, including the Montessori schools, Freinet schools, Waldorf schools, Dalton-Plan schools, etc., which have a decided orientation toward humanistic education. However, other alternatives are on the horizon, including traditionally conservative institutions such as Islamic-oriented religious schools, national-oriented schools, and community schools. One of the dominant themes of institutions, particularly in higher education, are those that promise to prepare young people to deal successfully with the West and free enterprise. I have been working for many years with Khazar University, in Baku, Azerbaijan, which has attempted to align itself with American higher education. The language of instruction at Khazar University is English, and the most popular subjects are business, English, and management.

The contemporary reform movement has clear new Right roots and is economically driven. Its leaders have little interest in social welfare issues such as social-class or racial integration. They wish to create schools that prepare youth for a free-market economy. Significantly, they have also adopted a free-market model for schools, claiming that schools themselves must be subjected to a competitive format. This competitive format allows parents to make choices about where they may send their children to be schooled. The assumption behind this notion is that competition will strengthen the quality of schools, that when a school possesses a monopoly it experiences no competition and has no incentive to improve itself or make itself more attractive to the students. If schools are in competition with each other, goes the argument, then the good schools will attract pupils and the poor schools will decline and eventually die.

This notion means, however, that the leaders of the movement today must destroy certain norms that are central to the conservative tradition. In Europe, for example, the private school tradition emphasized a humanistic, even classical, tradition and refused to cater to the industrial imperatives of modern society (Rust, 1991). Now the mission of the school is becoming free market–driven and aligning itself with economic imperatives in ways that were previously unacceptable to the old conservative class. The opposition to the new movement includes the teachers unions, the liberal and labor parties, and other groups that have until recently been identified for their sympathies with the Left. They are now the conservatives in school reform as they attempt to curb the efforts of the radical Right.

In the United States, the cherished idea of the neighborhood school is now giving way to the opportunity to choose between schools. The new radicals, including not only the Christian Coalition and Catholic bishops, but the Republican Party National Committee, claim that parents are the best judges about which schools serve the needs of their children, parents know what is necessary for their children to receive the best education, and the neighborhood school is about to die. There are three levels of activity regarding parental choice. At the first level, parents are given the opportunity to decide which school within a school district their children will attend. For example, I live in a school district that has eighteen primary schools, each of which is quite distinct. Two are very traditional schools that stress the basics; two are year-round schools; some might be defined as high-tech schools, with cable television, extensive computer use, etc.; and some stress the arts. The parents in my district are allowed to determine which their children will attend. At the second level of activity, parents may actually place their child in a school outside the school district boundary, if they can demonstrate that a particular school is important for the child's talents and interests. At the third level of activity, parents are working to obtain the right to enroll their children in private schools using public funds to pay most of the tuition costs. This is a radical departure from our historical background. Even in America, which has a strong tradition of separation of church and state, because almost all of our private schools are religiously sponsored, they have never been allowed to use public funds. However, recent studies have demonstrated that children who attend private schools usually perform better than those who attend public schools, so leaders of the present movement wish to make private school available without great cost to parents. Such a movement, supported by the new Right, has never been a part of the schooling tradition of America, and it signals a radical departure from American tradition.

Of course, the most extreme course of action parents are choosing is home schooling. This has not caught on in Europe, but it is gaining great attention in the United States. We now have professors of home schooling in certain universities and departments of education of America, and it does not look like the trend will diminish in the near future.

The opposition to these radical proposals in America includes both the American Federation of Teachers (AFT) and the National Education Association (NEA). Sandra Feldman, president of the AFT, in reference to vouchers, explains, "Vouchers do not mean reform no matter what name you give them. What they do mean is a radical abandonment of the public schools and public education" (in Suarez, 1998). President Bill Clinton agrees that any endeavor to diminish the importance of public education must be stopped. His secretary of education, Richard W. Riley, states, "Vouchers are a pessimist's response to the problems facing some of our public schools." He feels the way to overcome these problems is to promote parental involvement in the public schools and their class-rooms rather than abandoning them for the private sector (Policy News, 1997). It is clear that the unions and Democrats are the current conservatives in American school reform, attempting to maintain the current trajectories.

COMPREHENSIVE SCHOOLING

From the beginning of state-supported schooling in Europe, schools were intended to address the needs and interests of a special social class. At the most basic level, schooling was divided along a dualistic frame, where the elites attended one type of school and the masses attended another. This social-class consciousness was heavily loaded with modern industrial imperatives. Even the traditional lower-class schools of premodern Europe were not as consciously social-class oriented as the schools of modernity. Aries (1962, p. 306) has demonstrated that even the French "charity schools did not give rise to education reserved for the lower classes." Rather, from their earliest origins, "they attracted a well-to-do clientele of craftsmen, merchants, and burgesses, and were often competitive with the grammar schools in their ability to attract pupils." It would also be inappropriate to connect the small circulating schools of rural Europe with lower-class schooling. The hosts of these schools were always the holders of large farming estates who sent their children, together with the children of tenant farmers, to learn to read and become somewhat civilized.

And so we must connect the segmented school system of early modernity with an intentional social-class bias. With the rise of the labor movement, the major cultural symbol of educational reform in western Europe has inevitably been some form of comprehensive school structure that would provide a common schooling experience. Following the Russian revolution and the beginnings of the Soviet regime, a single comprehensive school became a political priority, which served as the model for all of central and eastern Europe. In East Germany, for example, the ten-year polytechnical school became the centerpiece of the entire educational system. It advocated, to the extent possible, grouping pupils together from all social and economic levels and providing them with a general polytechnical education. That is, its intent was to prepare young people to work productively in the socialist state and to tie theoretical and academic schooling together with practical and vocational schooling.

The process of educational reform in western Europe was much more difficult to achieve; however, Norway and Sweden adopted a common primary school even prior to the turn of the last century. France made such a decision in the 1930s, and just prior to the end of World War II Great Britain joined most western European countries by adopting a policy of common primary schooling.

After World War II the focus of liberal reform in Western Europe shifted to the secondary level, and reform also became tightly linked to research. That is, educational research was put into the service of reform. Sweden led the way when it adopted a plan for a universal, basic, common nine-year school as early as 1949 (Boucher, 1982), and the research community worked to develop an appropriate institutional structure. Sweden was followed by other countries such as Italy, Norway, and France, and other western European countries have engaged in comprehensive school reforms with varying degrees of success, although the German-speaking countries remained very reluctant to move away from the dualistic tradition.

In some countries the liberal reform agenda continues to take priority, but the growing reform agenda deviates radically from the trends of the past century and a half. The principles of the current educational reforms are differentiation and pluralism. This is nowhere more evident than in central Europe, where the trend is to make unity and equity the exception and multiplicity the dominating theme of reform (Panov, 1994). On the basis of new and modified educational laws it is clear that commitments are toward an extension and diversification of secondary schooling, as well as a stronger inner differentiation of specific educational institutions. In addition, individualized instruction claims a stronger place in schooling programs (Schirokova, 1992). In Russia, for example, after 1992 a multiplicity of state school types began to emerge. Many are private and take a variety of forms. At the secondary level one finds *gymnasien* (grades 5–11/12), *lycéen* (grades 8–11/12), experimental schools focusing on modified instructional approaches, free-time programs, and social and psychological services, as well as many special schools focusing on specific fields of study. Although these institutions suggest a borrowing from western Europe mentality, a good deal of discussion is found in the pedagogical literature concerning the strong Russian tradition of the *gymnasium*; attempts are made to identify this type of schooling with the general cultural and national heritage of the Russian people (Kondratjeva, 1994, p. 80).

Dramatic structural change is also occurring in western Europe. Led by the model of the new states of the Federal Republic of Germany, the Germans have begun to reject the three-pronged (academic, technical, and general) school structure in favor of a dual structure. Because the Hauptschule is becoming a dumping ground for children in the West it is seen to have little viability. In fact, in 1996 the old German state of Saarland had taken steps to abolish the Hauptschule altogether.

Recent developments have thrown the old socialists into the role of conservative. For example, with the fall of the Soviet Union, many socialists have come to concentrate their energies on protecting the welfare state in the face of the strains to which it has become subject. Some socialists, it is true, continue to say that authentic socialism has never been tried, arguing that the disappearance of communism is a windfall rather than a disaster. However, this thesis is threadbare, and although the educational adjustments taking place throughout the region are significant, there is a striking uniformity of educational changes taking place, all related in one way or another to a rejection of the communist ideology that has dominated education for the past four decades. In addition, there is a uniformity even in the language of reform. It is clear that a good deal of sharing has occurred in the various countries of the former Soviet bloc, as they have attempted to work out their individual education reform agendas. The major obstacles to these endeavors come from those who continue to defend the old Soviet principles, although even they are giving up the rhetoric of communism in favor of a more tempered socialism.

Throughout Europe, the major victim in this political shift has been the comprehensive school, which has come to symbolize the ills of contemporary schooling, including the perceived decline in educational standards, the breakdown of discipline among youth, and the subversive ideologies that reformers claim have crept into the schools. In fact, scholars such as Achim Leschinsky and Karl Ulrich Mayer (1990) contend that the comprehensive school has not contributed to greater social equality in countries such as France, Great Britain, and Sweden. To this point, no clear alternative to the comprehensive school has been crafted, but the reform thrust of this past century is clearly being called into question, and the radicals of the past education reforms have been put on the defensive as the new radicals forge their own agenda. While the old radicals of the Left are cast in a defensive and conservative role regarding comprehensive schooling, it is crucial to point out that they do have outlets toward which they turn their energies in a positive way: to the new social movements, such as those concerned with feminism, ecology, peace, or human rights. But even Anthony Giddens (1994) recognizes that the new social movements cannot readily be claimed for socialism. Of course, some movements stand close to socialist ideals, but they do not constitute a united front, and in fact their objectives often oppose one another. They usually reflect narrow, focused interests, and their leaders rarely are able to work with leaders of other narrow, focused interests. Even feminists are not able to organize themselves into a united front, because they tend to represent radical, liberal, socialist, and other orientations (Stromquist, 1990). The "radical" groups on the Left are radical in ways quite different from socialists of the more general variety.

CONCLUSION

The global relations of the world of the late twentieth century, one must conclude, have turned themselves upside down. The radicals of the past are now attempting to defend their former achievements, while the radicals of the present promise to give a new and different kind of direction to history by getting rid of the welfare state and many of the traditions that characterize modern states. They are the ones who think they can take control of their won destiny and the destiny of the world. I am not convinced their mission will be successful. I certainly doubt if it ought to succeed, but I recognize the energy behind their endeavors and the curious mix of old and new in what they are attempting to achieve.

NOTES

1. Some difficulty comes with using the term *private* as a label for nongovernment schools. To the Danes, *private* implies profit, and only nonprofit bodies are now allowed to establish nongovernment schools. Belgians use the term *free school* to designate institutions that provide a religiously based educational program. It is also important to keep in mind that *public school*, as Americans use the term, is inappropriate in many contexts. In Great Britain, a public school is actually an independent school that holds a special status in society. The terms *public* and *private* in this chapter shall be used to refer to institutions that are sponsored by government and nongovernment bodies respectively.

REFERENCES

Aries, Phillip. 1962. *Centuries of Childhood*. New York: Vintage.

Bereday, G. Z. F., W. W. Brickman, and G. H. Read. 1960. *The Changing Soviet School*. Boston: Houghton Mifflin.

Boucher, Leon. 1982. *Tradition and Change in Swedish Education*. Oxford: Pergamon.

Einhorn, Eric S., and John Logue. 1989. *Modern Welfare States: Politics and Policies in Social Democratic Scandinavia*. New York: Praeger.

Flitner, Wilhelm. 1941. *Die vier Quellen des Volksschulegedankens*. Stuttgart: Ernst Klett Verlag.

Fukuyama, Francis. 1992. *The End of History and the Last Man*. New York: Free Press.

Giddens, Anthony. 1994. *Beyond Left and Right: The Future of Radical Politics*. Stanford, CA: Stanford University Press; and London: Polity Press.

Hartz, Louis. 1955. *The Liberal Tradition in America*. New York: Harcourt Brace.

Hearnden, A. 1974. *Education in the Two Germanys*. Oxford: Blackwell.

Held, David (ed.). 1991. *Political Theory Today*. Stanford, CA: Stanford University Press.

Herbart, Johann Friedrich. 1818. Über Erziehung unter öffentlicher Mitwirkung. *Pädagogische Schriften*, edited by W. Asmus. Düsseldorf: Helmut Küppers, Vol 1.

Hobsbawm, Eric. 1994. *The Age of Extremes: A History of the World, 1914–1991*. New York: Pantheon.

Kennedy, Paul. 1993. *Preparing for the Twenty-first Century*. New York: Vintage.

Kondratjeva, M. A. 1994. The Gymnasium of the Fatherland: Historical Experiences and Contemporary Problems [Russian]. *Pedagogika*, vol. 57, no.1, pp. 75–80.

Leschinsky, Achim, and Karl Ulrich Mayer (eds.). 1990. *The Comprehensive Experiment Revisited: Evidence from Western Europe*. Frankfurt a/M.: Peter Lang.

Marshall, T. H. 1965. *Class, Citizenship, and Social Development*. New York: Anchor.

Meyer, John, and Michael T. Hannan. 1979. *National Development and the World System*. Chicago: University of Chicago.

Panov, V. 1994. From Pluralism to Unity [Russian]. *Narodnoie Obrasovanije*, vol. 76, no. 6, pp. 19–23.

Policy News and Information Service. 1997. School Vouchers. October 13 on the Internet, <http://www.policy.com>.

Robertson, Roland. 1992. *Globalization: Social Theory and Global Culture*. London: Sage.

Rossiter, Clinton. 1982. *Conservatism in America*. Cambridge, MA: Harvard University Press.

Rust, Val D. 1977. Personalized Teacher Education: The Example of Herbart. *Educational Studies*, vol. 8, pp. 221–29.

————. 1991. Educational Reform in International Perspective. *New Education*, vol. 13, no. 1, pp. 27–35.

————, Peter Knost, and Jürgen Wichmann (eds.). 1995. *Education and the Values Crisis in Central and Eastern Europe*. Frankfurt a/M: Peter Lang.

Schirokova, G. 1992. A Multifunctioning System of Preschool Education [Russian]. *Doshkol'noie Vospitanije*, vol. 67, no. 2, pp. 25–30.

Sinyavsky, Andrei. 1990. *Soviet Civilization: A Cultural History*. Boston: Little, Brown.

Stromquist, Nelly P. 1990. Gender Inequality in Education: Accounting for Women's Subordination. *British Journal of Sociology of Education*, vol. 11, pp. 137–54.

Suarez, John M. 1998. *School Vouchers—Yesterday, Today and Forever*. Secular Humanist Bulletin, vol. 14, no. 2.

Trattner, Walter I. 1984. *From Poor Law to Welfare State*. New York: Free Press.

Waters, Malcolm. 1995. *Globalization*. London: Routledge.

Wilensky, Harold. 1976. *The New Corporatism, Centralization, and the Welfare State*. London: Sage.

5

Globalization and Curriculum Inquiry: Locating, Representing, and Performing a Transnational Imaginary

Noel Gough

GLOBALIZATION AND CURRICULUM INQUIRY

The act of curriculum inquiry, for me, usually begins from a position informed by narrative theory and poststructuralism, one corollary of which is that I rarely feel any obligation to start an essay by providing stipulative definitions. In this essay, globalization is not a subject and/or object to be constrained by definition, but a focus for speculation—for generating meanings. To paraphrase Clermont Gauthier's (1992, p. 185) orientation to his critique of action research, I want to know how globalization works, and what it does, but not what it is. I am interested in what curriculum workers (teachers, administrators, academics, researchers) *do,* and do *not* do, with the meanings that we exchange under the sign of globalization, and in working toward a defensible position on the meanings we should attempt to select, generate, and reproduce through our curriculum practices.

Miriam Henry and Sandra Taylor (1997, p. 47) identify two aspects of globalization—"the facts concerning transnational processes and communication" and "an increasing awareness of this reality"—and I will focus here on the second. There is, of course, no unitary "reality" of globalization, and I suggest that whatever "awareness" may be "increasing" is a somewhat inchoate apprehension of complex, multiple, proliferating, and immanent realities, overlaid (and further complicated) by our own reflexive "awareness" of the need to be—and to be *seen* to be—aware that globalization is, indeed, worthy of our attention. My own attention is drawn to those traces of globalization that Rob Wilson and Wimal

Dissanayake (1996, p. 6) describe as a "transnational imaginary," namely, "the *as-yet-unfigured* horizon of contemporary cultural production by which national spaces/identities of political allegiance and economic regulation are being undone and imagined communities of modernity are being reshaped at the macropolitical (global) and micropolitical (cultural) levels of everyday existence" [emphasis in original].

Like Madeleine Grumet (1981, p. 115), I take curriculum to be "the collective story we tell our children about our past, our present, and our future" and there- fore see curriculum work as one form of "contemporary cultural production" through which this transnational imaginary may be expressed. As it coheres around the concept of *globalization*, the appearance of this transnational imagi- nary in the Australian literature of educational inquiry has, for the most part, been restricted to discussions and debates about the economic management, mar- keting, and organization of education and training (see, for example, Kenway, Bigum, and Fitzclarence, 1993; Kenway et al., 1994; Lingard, Knight, and Por- ter, 1993) and broad questions of national schooling policy (see, for example, Henry and Taylor, 1997). For these scholars, economic restructuring—driven by the need for Australia to respond to international economic and technological trends—appears to be the master discourse informing policy decisions at all levels of education. While I do not dispute their judgments, we should not necessarily assume that the institutional force of globalization within particular national and state policy discourses carries similar weight in other discursive communities. Transnational economic exchanges predate the spread of global capital, and imagining that they now constitute some kind of irresistible force transforming all aspects of late twentieth-century life may exaggerate the reach and extent of global economic integration. For example, Richard Barnet and John Cavanagh (1994, p. 383) estimate that about 80 percent of the world's population lives out- side global consumer networks. More importantly, specific local expressions of globalization,[1] such as the inclusion of schooling in Australia's federal (Labor) government's microeconomic reform agenda during the late 1980s, should not necessarily be taken as inevitable consequences of global economic processes that will routinely be found in other local discourses.

Furthermore, local expressions of the transnational imaginary of globalization are not restricted to the economic arenas of social life, such as those concerned with the production, exchange, and consumption of goods and services, and re- lated issues of industry and employment. Global relations are also expressed in and through mass media and converging information technologies and the social institutions and movements through which we monitor and regulate our concerns about many quality of life issues including health (such as the global traffic in drugs and disease) and environmental issues (for example, global climate change). Globalization is expressed in our apprehension of new and increasingly complex patterns of interconnectedness—cultural processes that destabilize relationships between social organization and the spaces and places in which technologies, materials, media, and meanings are produced, exchanged, and consumed.

Economic globalization clearly has consequences for both national and local curriculum policies, but evidence of the ways in which it may be informing and (dis)organizing curriculum practices at the school level is chiefly anecdotal. For example, Henry and Taylor (1997, p. 56) observe that the pressures of microeconomic reform have already encouraged education systems and some schools "to wheel and deal where they can in the attempt to become more competitive and cost-effective":

> Schools buy in pre-packaged American software, and there are increasing pressures for schools to seek corporate sponsorship for all manner of things—from school bands through to computer laboratories. Increasing numbers of schools ply the Asian market for fee paying students. This commercial logic is essentially anarchic, with unpredictable effects on curriculum and schooling practices.

Despite these uncertainties, globalization has so far had very little overt influence on curriculum theory—on the concepts and methods of academic curriculum inquiry. For example, there is no mention of globalization in either of the two major synoptic texts published in the curriculum field during recent years (namely, Jackson, 1992; Pinar et al., 1995). This relative silence in the literature of curriculum theorizing is evident even in works that are explicitly postmodernist in their approach. Thus, for example, despite passing references to the work of Fredric Jameson (1991), neither William Doll's (1993) *A Post-Modern Perspective on Curriculum* nor Patrick Slattery's (1995) *Curriculum Development in the Postmodern Era* acknowledges the global market forces of "late capitalism" as a possible influence on curriculum theory and practice.

Precisely how school curricula will change in response to the new restructuring agendas driven by economic globalization remains a very open question, especially as these are combined with, and complicated by, the increasing (and interconnected) effects of global media culture on what young people learn (in and out of schools). While it is possible to make some informed guesses about how globalization will manifest itself in changing school curricula (and in whose interests), there are many gaps in our current knowledge of the dynamics of a transnational imaginary in curriculum work and in the theoretical resources that may assist us in identifying problems and opportunities as they emerge. In beginning to map these gaps, my methodological (dis)position is to understand curriculum as a deconstructed (or deconstructing) text (see Gough, 1994a), an orientation to inquiry succinctly characterized by the literary critic Barbara Johnson's response (as quoted by Imré Salusinsky, 1987, p. 81) to an invitation to define deconstruction:

> One thing I could say is that the training most people get from the beginning, in school and through all the cultural pressures on us, is to answer the question:

"What's the bottom line?" What deconstruction does is to teach you to ask: "What does the construction of the bottom line leave out? What does it repress? What does it disregard? What does it consider unimportant? What does it put in the margins?" So that it's a double process. You have to have some sense of what someone's conception of what the bottom line would be, is, in order to organize the "noise" that is being disregarded.

Thus, for Johnson, deconstruction is less an academic argument about signs and meanings than a vocabulary and a set of practices oriented toward uncovering what she calls "noise"—that which is disregarded or marginalized by our dominant cultural myths and narratives. I will examine three sources of "noise" that might complicate any attempts to locate the transnational imaginary of globalization in the microdynamics of curriculum work, namely, (i) the sedimented history of global perspectives in school curricula, (ii) popular expectations that globalizing technologies such as the Internet will transform schools and their curricula, and (iii) the "internationalization" of the field of curriculum studies itself. I have chosen these three facets of globalization in curriculum discourse precisely because they are so different. While new global media networks (re)present themselves to us as leading edges of contemporary cultural transformations (see N. Gough, 1996; and Gough, 1997), existing global perspectives in school curricula occupy the "trailing edges" of these changes; the internationalization of curriculum studies makes us aware that what counts as a "leading" or "trailing" edge of cultural change may vary substantially between different local knowledge traditions.

BEFORE GLOBALIZATION: GLOBAL PERSPECTIVES IN THE CURRICULUM

Global issues and concerns have long functioned as topics or themes in specific learning areas such as history and geography, and efforts to give more emphasis to global perspectives in school curricula are well documented. For example, during the latter years of the 1980s, global themes became an explicit focus of a number of curriculum development initiatives in such relatively new curriculum areas as development education (*Living in a Global Environment*, Fien, 1989), peace studies (*Educating for Global Responsibility*, Reardon, 1988), world studies (*Global Teacher, Global Learner*, Pike and Selby, 1987; *Making Global Connections*, Hicks and Steiner, 1989; and the World Wide Fund for Nature's *Global Environmental Education Programme*, Huckle, 1988).[2] Recognition of the global dimensions and significance of issues such as peace, environment, and industrialization in developing nations also led some international organizations (such as the United Nations and its various satellites and subsidiaries, including the United Nations Educational, Scientific, and Cultural Organization (UNESCO), to attempt to influence school curricula through a variety of transnational curriculum development and/or teacher professional development projects. For example, the UNESCO-United Nations Environment Program (UNEP) International Environmental Education Program, which commenced in 1974 and is still active, has sponsored many projects that have sought to promote educational action in response to concerns about the quality of the global environment (however, this program has also been criticized for perpetuating a neocolonialist discourse in environmental education rather than promoting genuine international collaboration and cooperation; see Greenall Gough, 1993).

Many of these curriculum development initiatives valorized variations on a familiar slogan—"Think global. Act local"—though none, to my knowledge, recognized the irony of recycling a phrase that seems to owe much of its popularity to Theodore Levitt (1983, p. 92), who used it to encapsulate his advice that "the globalization of markets is at hand" in an article for the *Harvard Business Review*.[3] But while global themes in the curriculum are undoubtedly one consequence of the success of transnational social movements, there is very little evidence that they express a transnational imaginary that has contributed to any significant changes in the key meanings that are mobilized in school-based curriculum deliberations and debates. (See, for example, A. Gough, 1997; and N. Gough, 1994b.) For example, it is obvious that environmental education has been understood in schools as an incremental addition or alternative to conventional curriculum content, but there is little or no evidence of it challenging the "container" metaphor of curriculum. Yet this is precisely what might be expected if "think global" had become a powerful imperative in thinking about school curriculum change, since it can be argued that all notions of "containment" are destabilized and subverted by recognizing the complexity and multiplicity of the global environment's interconnections (thus, for example, we can no longer simply "throw garbage away," because in global environmental terms there is no "away").

However, the point I wish to develop here is concerned with the ways in which global perspectives in national and state curriculum specifications function as a kind of "noise" in any transformations of school curricula that might (or should) be taking place in response to economic globalization and to broader cultural expressions of a transnational imaginary. For example, in 1995 the Australian state of Victoria's Board of Studies published its *Curriculum and Standards Framework* (CSF) as a basis for curriculum planning in years P–10 and for reporting on student achievement. The eight-volume CSF (its contents are organized into the eight key learning areas "agreed to nationally" by the former Australian Education Council) includes in its outcome statements references to many of the same global issues and concerns that have previously functioned as topics or themes in subjects such as history and geography. Moreover, the CSF can itself be understood as a product of a centralizing tendency in educational restructuring that has been animated by economic globalization.[4] However, while the CSF is undoubtedly influencing the rhetoric of school curriculum policies and priorities, any references to globalization that are expressed in (or implied by) its outcome statements comprise only a relatively small sample of the possible meanings that actually circulate among teachers and students in schools.

For example, we have little knowledge of how teachers in the Studies of Society and Environment (SOSE) key learning area (KLA) deploy concepts of globalization or other expressions of a transnational imaginary to "explain economic decisions made by governments,"[5] although a content analysis of syllabus documents and textbooks would undoubtedly provide us with some clues as to which explanations they are likely to privilege. John Fien and Jane Williamson-Fien (1996, p. 125) provide a recent overview of "best practice" in teaching global perspectives in SOSE in which they assert that "few Australian syllabuses provide students with [a] comprehensive view of the world as an interconnected and interdependent system." However, a consideration of what these authors omit from their discussion and recommendations sheds useful light on the new complexities that globalization introduces to the SOSE curriculum. Fien and Williamson-Fien (1996, p. 129) argue that "the role of global education in a country such as Australia is to create public awareness and understanding of the nexus between development and lifestyle issues, and to promote values and lifestyle choices consistent with the core principles of life in a democracy." These authors unabashedly write from a socially critical standpoint on the role of the industrial development paradigm in building nation-states, but they do not seem to recognize that the terms of the political debates in which they engage are rapidly changing. One set of such changes is usefully summarized by Philip McMichael's (1996, p. 26) list of five premises underlying his argument that globalization has displaced the institutional and ideological relations constructed by the development project.

> First, development is perhaps the "master" concept of the social sciences, and has been understood as an evolutionary movement bringing rising standards of living—a logical outcome of human rationality as revealed in the European experience; second, the development project was a political strategy to institute nationally managed economic growth as a replicable pattern across the expanding system of states in the post–World War II world order; third, the paradigm of developmentalism offered a broadly acceptable interpretation of how to organize states and international institutions around the goal of maximizing national welfare via technological advances in industry and agriculture; fourth, this paradigm has collapsed with the puncturing of the illusion of development in the 1980s debt crisis, the management of which dismantled development institutions; and fifth, debt management instituted a new organizing principle of "globalization" as an alternative institutional framework, with the underlying message that nation-states no longer "develop;" rather, they position themselves in the global economy.

Fien and Williamson-Fien (1996, p. 129) argue that "global education is based upon the assumption that the social and structural changes needed to make this a more peaceful, just and ecologically sustainable world" will not occur without "a fundamental re-education of the Western public." But, as McMichael's analysis suggests, the "social and structural changes" that might constitute socially just and ecologically sustainable responses to *post*-developmentalist capitalism are not necessarily those that have been seen to be desirable in forms of global education that take a socially critical position on development. This is not to say that a socially critical stance toward industrial development is obsolete but, rather, that it may not be sufficient. McMichael may be overstating the extent to which globalization has ideologically displaced development, and in some nation-states it might even be argued that the development project has been intensified by global trends toward economic integration. My point is simply that globalization has added a new layer of complexity to, and may even have changed the character of, the educational problems and issues that "global education," as Fien and Williamson-Fien portray it, seeks to address. Fien and Williamson-Fien's (1996, p. 129) elaboration of their position also raises questions about the susceptibility of the language of opposition to the development paradigm to appropriation by the new rhetoric of globalization; they write: "if it is true that the rich must live more simply so that the poor may simply live then, in the words of Trainer" (1988, as cited in Fien and Williamson-Fien, 1996): "the key . . . must be the education of publics in overdeveloped countries regarding these critical themes, so that eventually they will support the necessary restructuring of the global economy and the economies of their own countries."

I suspect that many readers of Trainer's words could easily accommodate them to the dominant discourses of economic "restructuring" with which Australia and many other Organization for Economic Cooperation and Development (OECD) countries have been preoccupied since the mid-1980s; some will undoubtedly recognize that Trainer is likely to be anticipating a very different type of "restructuring" from that which might be indicated by the OECD's economic agenda. My concern here is that the extant (or remnant) language of "global education," as promulgated by even its most critical practitioners, may be a little too hospitable to the new imperialism of economic globalization.

GLOBALIZING MEDIA TECHNOLOGIES:
AN AIRPORT FICTION

Popular understandings of globalization are replete with apparent contradictions, including a curious tolerance of—or indifference to—extravagant claims about its significance and consequences in various arenas of social life. On the one hand, as Henry and Taylor (1997, p. 46) observe, "there is a good deal of hype around the notion of globalization," while on the other hand, as Malcolm Waters (1995, p. 1) notes, " 'globalization' is far less controversial than 'postmodernism.' " I want now to examine a specific form of transnational imaginary that is routinely expressed in expectations about the transformative effects of globalizing technologies on schools and their curricula. The critique of expectations requires a different methodology from the critique of historical legacies. As I argue elsewhere (Gough, 1998), our purposes in educational inquiry are sometimes better served by (re)presenting the texts we produce as deliberate fictions rather than as "factual" narratives that "reflect" educational phenomena and experiences. Following Donna Haraway (1994), I also argue that some modes of fiction can help us to produce texts that diffract the storylines of educational inquiry and thus move research efforts beyond reflection and reflexivity: "Diffraction is an optical metaphor for the effort to make a difference in the world" (Haraway, 1997, p. 16).

I will begin by juxtaposing two stories referring to new information technologies that were carried on the front page of *The Age*, Wednesday 27 November 1996. One of these stories, appropriately located on the far right (of the page), reported suggestions by Victoria's minister for education, Phil Gude, for a novel approach to streamlining the delivery of government schooling.

SCHOOL HOURS MAY BE CUT
    The State Government has begun a review of school education policy that could lead to children spending fewer hours in class and more time learning from home.
    The Education Minister, Mr. Phil Gude, yesterday flagged the new policy—tentatively called Schools of the Third Millennium—which will build on the Government's contentious Schools of the Future program. . . .
    Mr. Gude said the Government had begun examining what the next generation of schools required.
    He singled out the impact of new technology which, he said, raised the question of whether children should spend as much time at school as they do now.
    "When you get the interlinking capabilities between the home and the workplace—called the school—could there be more work done in a domestic arrangement?" he asked. "What impact will that have on the structures and the natures of the physical building of the school?"
    As part of the work on the new policy, Mr. Gude will call a meeting of architects and builders within the next few months to review the design of schools.

The item goes on to report that the minister will travel to the United States early next year, "where he hopes to pick up ideas for the new policy" and, further, that the Education Department is looking at British examples of secondary schools that "have a strong technology and business focus and have corporate sponsors." In this item, which conjures up images of children wired to the World Wide Web through their home computers while the minister shops for (duty free?) educational policies in the global marketplace, a transnational imaginary is clearly at work.[6]

I can only admire the minister's bravery (gall?) in announcing a school education policy that invites comparison with Colleen McCullough's (1985) novel *A Creed for the Third Millennium*—for this is educational policy as airport fiction, cheerfully flaunting its cliché-ridden commercialism and superficiality, with formulaic phrases like "new technology" and "corporate sponsorship" pushing enough buttons to entertain (but not to tax, in any sense) the business-class passengers who are the real constituency of Victoria's present government. No doubt the minister's plan to call a meeting of architects and builders to review the design of schools will keep some of his customers satisfied, but can you imagine the response of architects and builders if the minister for planning and development announced that he would kick-start a review of major infrastructure projects by calling a meeting of school teachers and other educators? Like the "Schools of the Future" program that preceded it, we can expect a "Schools of the Third Millennium" policy to use deceptively forward-looking language to dress up the present Victorian government's preferred approach to managing public schooling. "Schools of the Future" are nothing more than self-managing schools—an attempt to recreate in the government system the kind of competitive corporatism that has long been the norm for private schools. In other words, "Schools of the Future" reflect the past practices of private education and the economic ideology of the present government. The phrase "Schools of the Future" is a purely token gesture, using language that appears to herald a new and bold vision of education to disguise what is at heart a deeply conservative approach to public schooling. "Schools of the Third Millennium" heralds a similarly retrogressive vision, with "the impact of new technology" being used as yet another excuse to reduce the costs of public education. A deeply conservative approach to social policy also underlies any serious consideration of reducing the length of the school day. Who will supervise the work that the minister expects to be done "in a domestic arrangement?" Cutting school hours would seriously disrupt many families' domestic and income-producing activities—with the exception, of course, of another (local) imaginary: the virtually extinct traditional nuclear family in which one parent (usually male) "works" and the other parent (usually female) undertakes "home duties," which will henceforth include increased responsibility for children's compulsory schooling.

As I contemplated the minister's vision of homes of the future, and of what might actually be achieved by students using "the interlinking capabilities" provided by the new information technologies "in a domestic arrangement," my attention was drawn to another item on the same page.

WOMAN WANTS TO DOWNLOAD BABY
Sandy Indlekofer-O'Sullivan wants to have a baby through the Net.
While sex with the prospective father is fine, romance is not, the Wollongong businesswoman declares on her Internet babies page appealing for a cyberspace father.
"I am simply wanting to have a child without being married," she says.
Yesterday she said she had received about 100 insemination offers from as far apart as Sydney and the Netherlands.
She wants to meet the men first, but if all goes to plan the baby [will] arrive by late 1998.

Ms. Indlekofer-O'Sullivan, who also makes a living setting up websites, said the Internet with its 120 million users seemed like a normal way to go about what she freely admits is not a normal process.

I am sure Phil Gude would have applauded Ms. Indlekofer-O'Sullivan's marketing skills in placing a double-column block advertisement for her website construction service on the front page of *The Age* at absolutely no cost to herself—another win for small business and free enterprise—and, as the minister's own pronouncements demonstrate, you don't have to make sense to make news. These items have two things in common. First, both items point toward the changes that the new information technologies are making to what we now think of as "natural" or "normal." (There is a particularly interesting reversal of current expectations in Ms. Indlekofer-O'Sullivan's characterization of her public appeal to 120 million Internet users to satisfy her maternal yearnings as "a normal way to go about what she freely admits is not a normal process." I would have thought that using the Internet as a global do-it-yourself introduction agency was not yet a "normal" way to go about the entirely normal/natural process of finding a sexual partner for procreational—or, for that matter, recreational—purposes, which, advances in teledildonics notwithstanding, still require partners to be in the same locality. I very much doubt that these are the kinds of "interlinking capabilities" that Phil Gude had in mind.) Secondly, both items perpetuate stereotypical expectations about what might actually be achieved by the convergence and proliferation of new information technologies. But whereas downloading a baby is an absurd exaggeration of what can be accomplished by information technology (Internet delivery hardware does not, and will not for the foreseeable future, have sufficient bandwidth to download even a virtual reality game, let alone a baby, and in any case it is not exactly what Ms. Indlekofer-O'Sullivan has in mind), cutting school hours has just enough plausibility to be taken seriously, despite the simplistic reasoning that connects new information technologies with a reduction in school hours. This is not to say that the minister's suggestion is in itself "nonsense" (as the leader of the opposition, John Brumby, is reported to have said in a follow-up news item on page 2 of *The Age*, Thursday 27 November 1996). I have no quarrel with Phil Gude raising questions about the impact of changing media technologies on "the structures and the natures" of school buildings—the difficulty I have is with (i) his premature foreclosure on the purposes and functions of schooling as a social institution by treating it as just another "workplace" and (ii) his attempt to short circuit the types of social, cultural, and educational inquiries that these questions warrant by first seeking responses from architects and builders.

One question we must ask is, Why should this particular "revolution" in media technologies be expected to transform schooling when previous communications revolutions have not? The modern school is, both culturally and materially, an enduring monument to a print-dominated culture. But while the domination of print has been eroded by a succession of electrical and electronic media technologies that have resulted in massive social and cultural change, these have resulted in only superficial modifications to the ways schools are built, organized, and operated. Our social relations and cultural values have been irreversibly transformed by the telegraph, the telephone, broadcast radio, the cinema, and especially by television. None of these, not even television, has changed the institutions of schooling to anything like the extent that each has changed society at large. In 1960 Marshall McLuhan wrote a short essay titled "Classroom without Walls," which described succinctly and persuasively why and how teaching and learning in schools should change in relation to the pervasive effects of mass televisual media. McLuhan's (1960) critique of print-dominated schooling has gained considerably in its forcefulness during the past four decades, not only because the effects he described have intensified and accelerated, but also because they have been extended and diversified by the convergence of broadcasting, computing, and telecommunications.[7]

We are no longer a print-dominated culture and have not been for many years. We have been a television-dominated culture for more than a generation, but when politicians bemoan the alleged decline in literacy standards, it is still only print literacy they are talking about, rather than the dispositions and skills needed for effective participation in the electronic culture of McLuhan's global village, in which "entire societies inter-communicate by a sort of 'macroscopic gesticulation'" (McLuhan and Fiore 1967, p. 17). Nevertheless, McKenzie Wark (1994, p. 47) provides a plausible reason for anticipating that computers might transform schooling in ways that television has not:

> We like to think we are a print dominated culture because there is a class issue attached to these two media. Watching too much TV equals "you're gonna screw your life up kid," equals "you're not gonna make it into the middle class," equals "you're a loser!" Learning to read and write equals "you're going to make it into the middle class" equals "you might get a job as opposed to you will" equals "that's good, that's fine, that's okay." So television is bad, video in the schools is bad. However there's a real kink in the way this is happening which occurs in the way people think about computers. Computers occupy that space that writing used to occupy in the fear and anxiety about the middleclassness of our kids. Computers equals work equals middle class skills equals good equals "let's get them into the schools right now!" We never even got the last generation of media technology properly into the schools, we are not educating anyone really on how we use our time, but we're going to get this new technology in there because you can attach the idea of the computer to the idea of work, to middle class values.

But in Victoria we now have the Phil Gude maneuver, which goes something like this: yes, computers equals work equals middle class skills equals good equals "let's get them into schools," *but* that's going to be way too expensive, so let's get computers into homes rather than schools—at parents' expense, of course—and, so long as they are "interlinked" with what's left of the schools, we can call what kids do at home "school work" (and, if only we really could download babies from the Internet, we could close a few more hospitals too).

GLOBALIZING LOCAL KNOWLEDGE TRADITIONS: THE "INTERNATIONALIZATION" OF CURRICULUM STUDIES

Curriculum studies is itself a form of contemporary cultural production through which the transnational imaginary of globalization may be expressed and negotiated, although it is more common for curriculum scholars to speak of the "internationalization" of the field. For example, the current guide for authors intending to submit manuscripts to the *Journal of Curriculum Studies* (JCS) includes the following advice:

> All authors are asked to take account of the diverse audience of *Journal of Curriculum Studies*. Clearly explain or avoid the use of terms that might be meaningful only to a local or national audience. However, note also that *Journal of Curriculum Studies* does not aspire to be international in the ways that McDonald's restaurants or Hilton Hotels are "international;" we much prefer papers that, where appropriate, reflect the particularities of each higher education system.

This advice[8] expresses a view of global/local relations that seems to resist "globalization"—understood as economic integration achieved through "free trade" in a deregulated global marketplace—while affirming "internationalism" (in the sense of promoting global peace, social justice, and well-being through intergovernmental cooperation and transnational social movements, agencies, and communities—such as the international community of curriculum scholars that produces and reads JCS).[9] I want to refine and amplify some of the tacit assumptions underlying this advice to authors, by considering ways in which diverse local knowledge traditions—as may still be represented in at least some local and national curriculum policies and syllabuses, as well as in some "indigenous" approaches to curriculum studies per se—can be sustained and amplified transnationally while resisting the forms of cultural homogenization for which McDonald's and Hilton Hotels are emblematic.

A literature that I have found useful in thinking about globalization and internationalization in relation to local knowledge production is, broadly speaking, that which Sandra Harding (1998b) calls post-Kuhnian and postcolonial science and technology studies (see also Harding, 1993, 1994, 1997, 1998a), and more particularly the work of David Turnbull (1993 and 1997; see also Watson-Verran and Turnbull, 1995). Turnbull argues that all knowledge traditions are spatial in that they link people, sites, and skills. His approach is thus to recognize knowledge systems (including Western science) as sets of local practices so that it be-

comes possible to "decenter" them and develop a framework within which different knowledge traditions can be equitably compared rather than absorbed into an
imperialist archive.

While both Harding and Turnbull share postcolonialist and anti-imperialist
positions, and assert that all knowledges are always situated and constituted initially within specific sets of local conditions and cultural values, their interests are
subtly different in ways that I find thought-provoking. Put crudely, Harding
seems more interested in the universalizing tendencies that accompany the
"travel" of knowledges beyond the localities in which they were initially produced, whereas Turnbull is more concerned with how trust is established between
heterogeneous knowledges that "arrive" (or are produced) in the same space. For
example, after reviewing the various implications of postcolonialist and feminist
science and technology studies for research epistemologies and methodologies,
Harding (1998b, p. 46) writes:

> the distinction between universally valid knowledge and merely local opinion—
> superstitions, folk knowledge, or indigenous knowledge systems—is much less useful
> than the older epistemologies supposed. If, as the post-Kuhnian, postcolonial and
> feminist accounts argue, all knowledge systems have integrity with the cultures that
> produce them and continue to find them useful, then nothing in principle is possible
> but local opinion—though some local opinions (e.g., the laws of gravity) definitely
> travel farther and retain usefulness longer than do others. . . . More productive is the
> project of seeking to understand the devices through which originally local knowl-
> edges (as all are) get to circulate and travel far from their origin, and how the most
> effective balances between these universalizing tendencies and the necessary localiz-
> ing tendencies have been and can be nourished and maintained.

Elsewhere, Harding (1998a, p. 182) again uses travel metaphors to capture her
sense of the ways in which "different modern scientific projects have maintained
valuable tensions between the local and the global":

> the most widely successful [knowledge systems], such as many parts of modern sci-
> ences, manage to travel effectively to become useful in other sets of local condi-
> tions—parts of nature, interests, discursive resources, ways of organizing the produc-
> tion of knowledge—that are different in significant respects from those that
> originally produced them. Without claiming a universality for them that we can now
> see is historically and conceptually misleading, how could we usefully think about
> valuable tensions between the local and this movability, or ability to travel, that has
> characterized parts of modern sciences in particular, but also parts of other knowl-
> edge systems (e.g., the concept zero and acupuncture)?

Turnbull detaches a knowledge tradition's "ability to travel" from any assumptions about its supposed "universalizing tendencies," preferring instead to find
ways in which different knowledge systems can coexist. An important aspect of
Turnbull's strategy is to abandon an "overly representational view of knowledge"

in favor of recognizing that all knowledge is "both performative and representational" (1997, p. 553). In other words, Turnbull is less interested in characterizing science's "ability to travel" by reference to the movement of its representations and abstractions (such as "the laws of gravity" or "the concept zero" to which Harding refers) and more concerned with the *activity* of knowledge production in particular social spaces:

> we can reconceive the social history of knowledge in a variety of intersecting and overlapping ways which move beyond simple contextualization. Science may be seen as a history of visualization or as a history of measurement and rational calculation. However, I would like to argue that a particularly perspicuous cross-cultural history of knowledge production is as a social history of space. That is as a history of the contingent processes of making assemblages and linkages, of creating spaces in which knowledge is possible (Turnbull 1997, p. 553).

Using such diverse examples as the building of gothic cathedrals in medieval Europe, the Polynesian colonization of the Pacific islands, the establishment of modern cartography, and rice farming in Indonesia, Turnbull shows how particular knowledge spaces can be constructed from differing social, moral, and technical components in a variety of cultural and historical contexts—or, following Gilles Deleuze and Felix Guattari (1987, p. 90), an "assemblage" of people, skills, local knowledge, and equipment linked by various social strategies and technical devices.

> From this spatialised perspective, universality, objectivity, rationality, efficacy and accumulation cease to be unique and special characteristics of technoscientific knowledge; rather these traits are effects of collective work of the knowledge producers in a given knowledge space. To move knowledge from the local site and moment of its production and application to other places and times, knowledge producers deploy a variety of social strategies and technical devices for creating the equivalences and connections between otherwise heterogeneous and isolated knowledges. The standardisation and homogenisation required for knowledge to be accumulated and rendered truthlike is achieved through social methods of organising the production, transmission and utilisation of knowledge. An essential component is the social organisation of trust (Turnbull, 1997, p. 553).

Turnbull here echoes Steven Shapin (1994, p. 36), who argues in his social history of science in seventeenth-century England that the basis of knowledge is not empirical verification (as the orthodox view of "scientific method" would have it) but trust: "Mundane reason is the space across which trust plays. It provides a set of presuppositions about self, others, and the world which embed trust and which permit both consensus and civil dissensus to occur." In a gesture toward Bruno Latour's (1987, 1993) "actor network theory," Turnbull (1997, p. 553) also suggests that the linking of heterogeneous components of a knowledge system is achieved by both social strategies and "technical devices which may include maps, templates, diagrams and drawings, but are typically techniques of spatial visualization."

Turnbull (1997, p. 553) argues that a major analytic advantage of this spatialized perspective is that, because all knowledge systems have localness in common, many of the small but significant differences between them can be explained in terms of the different kinds of work—of *performance*—that are involved in constructing "assemblages" from the people, practices, theories, and instruments in a given space:

> Some [knowledge] traditions move it and assemble it through art, ceremony and ritual; science does it through forming disciplinary societies, building instruments, standardising techniques and writing articles. In both cases it is a process of knowledge assembly through making connections and negotiating equivalences between the heterogeneous components while simultaneously establishing a social order of trust and authority resulting in a knowledge space. It is on this basis that it is possible to compare and frame knowledge traditions.

This is not the place to explore Turnbull's specific examples in detail, but his analysis demonstrates that the achievements of gothic cathedral building, Polynesian navigation, modern cartography, Indonesian rice farming, *and* modern (Western) science are, in each case, better understood performatively—as diverse combinations of social and technical practices—than as results of any internal epistemological features to which "universal" validity can be ascribed.

As already noted, the purpose of Turnbull's emphasis on analyzing knowledge systems comparatively in terms of spatiality and performance is to find ways in which diverse knowledge traditions can coexist rather than one displacing others. He argues that nourishing such diversity is dependent on the creation of "a third space, an interstitial space" in which local knowledge traditions can be "reframed, decentred and the social organisation of trust can be negotiated." The production of such a space is "crucially dependent" on "the reinclusion of the performative side of knowledge":

> Knowledge, in so far as it is portrayed as essentially a form of representation, will tend towards universal homogenous information at the expense of local knowledge traditions. If knowledge is recognised as both representational and performative it will be possible to create a space in which knowledge traditions can be performed together (Turnbull, 1997, pp. 560–61).

Turnbull's analysis suggests to me that resistance to the homogenizing effects of globalization and internationalization in the field of curriculum studies might be facilitated by emphasizing the performative rather than the representational aspects of curriculum inquiry. The "internationalization" of curriculum studies might then be understood not so much in terms of translating local representations of curriculum into a universalized discourse but, rather, as a process of creating transnational "spaces" in which local knowledge traditions in curriculum inquiry can be performed together.

It can be argued that international journals, through their social and technical protocols, traditions, and conventions, should more deliberately and reflexively aspire to be transnational performative spaces of this kind. In my role as an editor, I certainly want to examine carefully the extent to which the *Journal of Curriculum Studies* may already have succeeded in this respect, as well as determining or refining some of the textual strategies (for both authors and editors) that might advance the performative aspects of curriculum inquiry in such transnational spaces as *JCS*.

However, the implications of emphasizing spatiality and performance in curriculum inquiry extend well beyond the practices of writing for and editing scholarly journals. Indeed, the need for vigorously and rigorously recuperating local knowledge systems, in both their performative and representational idioms, has been amplified for me by some recent experiences of doing curriculum work in southern Africa, where many local knowledge traditions have been rendered invisible by the effects of universalizing imperialist discourses and practices. For example, in countries such as Zimbabwe and Malawi, the concept of a "good education" for the vast majority of African students, most of whom live in rural subsistence settlements, is equated with failing Cambridge University O-level examinations in English. The absurdity of this situation to Western eyes is captured by Doris Lessing's (1992, pp. 200–201) recollections of visiting a rural school in Zimbabwe in 1988, during which one member of her party lamented the country's unserviceable infrastructure and the lack of people skilled in—or being trained to be skilled in—mending broken valves, faucets, or pipes:

> The trouble is that all these poor bloody kids, in all the schools of Zimbabwe, have decided that only a literary education is worth having. Where do you find the ultimate bastion of respect for the Humanities? Not in Thatcher's Britain! No, in the bush, where generations of black kids have decided they are too good to be engineers and electricians, and are taking O-levels in English which they mostly fail. . . .[10]
>
> I was in an office in Harare. An American Aid worker was arguing that the education being given to the children was inappropriate, what was the point of teaching them the British syllabus, with books suitable for Europe? What was needed was a good basic technical education. A black woman who was waiting her turn turned furiously on her. She said, "I see you whites are still just the same. You don't want our children to have a real education. Oh no, that's for your children. We want a good education for our children, just the same as yours."

Thinking about this incident in terms of represented and performed curriculum is illuminating. The apparent point of disagreement between the Aid worker and the black woman is that the curriculum in question, "the British syllabus, with books suitable for Europe," represents "a real education . . . a good education" in Western and Zimbabwean contexts for the black woman but in only one context (Western) for the Aid worker (we could also say that the black woman imagines "a good education" transnationally whereas the Aid worker is imagining it locally). Many of us might want to argue that the represented curriculum is as "inappropriate" in Thatcher's Britain as in Mugabe's Zimbabwe. But both women might be able to agree that this British syllabus produces, in Turnbull's terms, a performative "equivalence," especially if it can be shown that (say) exhibiting perfect recall of the key events and protagonists in the English Reformation is a necessary condition for winning the class struggle in postcolonial Zimbabwe. As Lessing (1992, p. 212) writes, "In Zimbabwe today [1988] you need five [O-level] passes to get a job. With three you can train to be a nurse." A key curriculum problem here is the instrumental role of a curriculum in effecting social stratification—a problem that may be obscured by focusing on issues of superficial "appropriateness" or "relevance"—and if the performative function of the curriculum is, in effect, to make both black kids and white kids jump through white hoops, merely painting one set of hoops black does not resolve the problem.

One of the questions raised by Lessing's vignette is, Who is deploying a transnational imaginary here? Stereotypically we might expect the American Aid worker to have a more "global" or "international" perspective, but it is the black woman who seems to be assuming (or desiring) English O-levels to be part of the global economy of "a good education" and the Aid worker who wants to privilege (or "protect" in economic terms) local knowledge. The difficulty I perceive for the field of curriculum inquiry is that I suspect that our intellectual resources are presently geared toward defending the Aid worker's position rather than responding constructively and, in a literal sense, hopefully to the black woman.

TO BE CONTINUED

I have suggested that the history of global perspectives in curriculum, the anticipated impacts of new information technologies, and efforts to internationalize the field of curriculum studies can be understood as forms of "noise" disrupting and complicating attempts to locate a transnational imaginary in curriculum work, but in identifying them as such I am not suggesting that they should be "controlled" or suppressed. These "noises" are just as much an expression of a transnational imaginary as are the national curriculum policy instruments that are intended to better position Australian (or Zimbabwean) education in the global marketplace. But we need to know more about how these complicating discourses—whether they be history or hype—interact, shape one another, and shape school curricula.

In drawing toward some sort of closure to this chapter, it may suffice to say that curriculum inquiry advances by perturbations—by being challenged to respond to new problems and research questions. I have focused here on an emergent phenomenon—the ways in which the transnational imaginary of cultural globalization is simultaneously represented in curriculum policies and school programs, expressed by teachers and students, circulated in popular media, and deployed in the construction of school knowledge—and I suspect that the concepts and methods that will be most generative in advancing inquiries around this imaginary are more likely to emerge from a state of disequilibrium rather than stability. This essay is, I hope, a small contribution to sustaining instability in the conceptual and methodological landscape of curriculum inquiry.

NOTES

This chapter is an expansion of a paper published in the *Journal of Education Policy* (Gough, 1999), and I hereby acknowledge the prior publication of substantial portions of this chapter by Taylor & Francis Ltd. The research from which this chapter arises was supported, in its initial phases, by a seeding grant from the Faculty of Education, Deakin University, and is being conducted in collaboration with Annette Gough. Conversations with Jane Kenway and other members of the Deakin Centre for Education and Change have also advanced this inquiry, but I stress that the idiosyncratic positions taken here are my responsibility and are not necessarily shared by my colleagues.

1. I follow Philip McMichael (1996, p. 27) in using the term *local expressions* as shorthand for "the process by which local communities negotiate their social contexts, which includes global relations as embedded in institutions that condition local communities."

2. It is difficult to cite just one source for this multivolume program. Huckle's (1988) book is the teachers' guide to ten book-length units that make up one of four curriculum modules in the program.

3. Greig, Pike, and Selby (1987, p. 20) are typical of the authors of environmental education texts who render this slogan as "think globally, act locally" without citing or otherwise acknowledging any source. Of course, the imperative to think globally has a longer history. For example, in 1967 Marshall McLuhan noted that with the advent of an electronic information environment, "all the territorial aims and objectives of business and politics [tend] to become illusory" (McLuhan and Fiore 1967, p. 5).

4. According to Kenway et al. (1994, p. 318), two dominant restructuring tendencies have emerged in Australian educational systems' responses to economic globalization: a centralizing tendency concerned with curriculum and professional development, enabled by corporate federalism and the new nationalism, and guided by the principles of vocationalism and scientific rationality and a decentralizing tendency concerned with money, management, and industrial relations and guided by principles of deregulation, devolution, privatization, commercialization, and commodification.

5. This is a Level 5 learning outcome in the "Natural and social systems" strand of the SOSE KLA; see Victoria (1995, p. 18).

6. Six months later, another front-page item in *The Age* (3 June 1997, p. 1) indicated that the minister had also shopped for educational policies in New Zealand, Singapore, and Japan.

7. Steve Shaviro (1997, p. vii) is, I believe, entirely justified in asserting that Marshall

McLuhan and Andy Warhol are "the most significant North American theorists of postmodernism, even if neither of them used the term."

8. I was, in fact, responsible for this particular form of words, first incorporating them into the supplementary notes I prepared for authors in Australia and New Zealand shortly after I assumed the Australian editorship of JCS in 1986; however, I acknowledge that this characterization of the journal's "internationalism" paraphrases advice provided in a personal communication to me from the then general editor, William Reid.

9. For a discussion of the distinctions that may be made between globalization and internationalism see Phillip Jones's chapter in this volume.

10. Some of the reasons for their failure are not difficult to discern. As one of Lessing's (1992, p. 205) informants, a young teacher from England, recalls, "for instance, there was an exam paper set in Britain, one of the questions had the word 'shutter.' These people don't have shutters. One of the meanings of the word was a camera shutter. Most of them have never seen a camera, let alone used one."

REFERENCES

Barnet, Richard J., and John Cavanagh. 1994. *Global Dreams: Imperial Corporations and the New World Order*. New York: Touchstone.

Deleuze, Gilles, and Félix Guattari. 1987. *A Thousand Plateaus: Capitalism and Schizophrenia*. Translated by Brian Massumi. Minneapolis: University of Minnesota Press.

Doll, William E. 1993. *A Post-Modern Perspective on Curriculum*. New York: Teachers College Press.

Fien, John (ed.). 1989. *Living in a Global Environment: Classroom Activities in Development Education*. Brisbane: Australian Geography Teachers Association.

———, and Jane Williamson-Fien. 1996. Global Perspectives in Studies of Society and Environment. In R. Gilbert (ed.), *Studying Society and Environment: A Handbook for Teachers*. South Melbourne: Macmillan, pp. 125–40.

Gauthier, Clermont. 1992. Between Crystal and Smoke: Or, How to Miss the Point in the Debate about Action Research. In William F. Pinar and William M. Reynolds (eds.), *Understanding Curriculum as Phenomenological and Deconstructed Text*. New York: Teachers College Press, pp. 184–94.

Gough, Annette. 1997. *Education and the Environment: Policy, Trends and the Problems of Marginalisation, Australian Education Review No. 39*. Melbourne: Australian Council for Educational Research.

Gough, Noel. 1994a. Imagining an Erroneous Order: Understanding Curriculum as Phenomenological and Deconstructed Text. *Journal of Curriculum Studies*, vol. 26, no. 5, pp. 553–68.

———. 1994b. Playing at Catastrophe: Ecopolitical Education after Poststructuralism. *Educational Theory*, vol. 44, no. 2, pp. 189–210.

———. 1996. Virtual Geography, Video Art and the Global Environment: Postmodernist Possibilities for Environmental Education Research. *Environmental Education Research*, vol. 2, no. 3, pp. 379–89.

———. 1997. Weather™ Incorporated: Environmental Education, Postmodern Identities, and Technocultural Constructions of Nature. *Canadian Journal of Environmental Education*, vol. 2, pp. 145–62.

————. 1998. Reflections and Diffractions: Functions of Fiction in Curriculum Inquiry. In William F. Pinar (ed.), *Curriculum: Toward New Identities*. New York: Garland, pp. 94–127.

————. 1999. Globalisation and School Curriculum Change: Locating a Transnational Imaginary. *Journal of Education Policy*, vol. 14, no. 1, pp. 73–84.

Greenall Gough, Annette. 1993. Globalizing Environmental Education: What's Language Got to Do with It? *Journal of Experiential Education*, vol. 16, no. 3, pp. 32–39.

Greig, Sue, Graham Pike, and David Selby. 1987. *Earthrights: Education as if the Planet Really Mattered*. London: World Wildlife Fund and Kogan Page.

Grumet, Madeleine R. 1981. Restitution and Reconstruction of Educational Experience: an Autobiographical Method for Curriculum Theory. In Martin Lawn and Len Barton (eds.), *Rethinking Curriculum Studies: A Radical Approach*. London: Croom Helm, pp. 115–30.

Haraway, Donna J. 1994. A Game of Cat's Cradle: Science Studies, Feminist Theory, Cultural Studies. *Configurations: A Journal of Literature, Science, and Technology*, vol. 2, no. 1, pp. 59–71.

————. 1997. *ModestWitness@SecondMillennium.FemaleMan©MeetsOncoMouse™: Feminism and Technoscience*. With paintings by Lynn M. Randolph. New York and London: Routledge.

Harding, Sandra. 1994. Is Science Multicultural? Challenges, Resources, Opportunities, Uncertainties. *Configurations: A Journal of Literature, Science, and Technology*, vol. 2, no. 2, pp. 301–30.

————. 1997. Is Modern Science an Ethno-Science? Rethinking Epistemological Assumptions. In Terry Shinn, Jack Spaapen and Venni Krishna (eds.), *Science and Technology in a Developing World*. Dordrecht: Kluwer, pp. 37–64.

————. 1998a. *Is Science Multicultural? Postcolonialisms, Feminisms, and Epistemologies*. Bloomington: Indiana University Press.

————. 1998b. Multiculturalism, Postcolonialism, Feminism: Do They Require New Research Epistemologies? *Australian Educational Researcher*, vol. 25, no. 1, pp. 37–51.

———— (ed.). 1993. *The "Racial" Economy of Science: Toward a Democratic Future*. Bloomington: Indiana University Press.

Henry, Miriam, and Sandra Taylor. 1997. Globalisation and National Schooling Policy in Australia. In Bob Lingard and Paige Porter (eds.), *A National Approach to Schooling in Australia? Essays on the Development of National Policies in Schools Education*. Canberra: Australian College of Education, pp. 45–59.

Hicks, David, and Miriam Steiner (eds.). 1989. *Making Global Connections: A World Studies Workbook*. Edinburgh: Oliver and Boyd.

Huckle, John. 1988. *What We Consume: The Teachers' Handbook, Global Environmental Education Programme*. Richmond, Surrey: Richmond Publishing Company.

Jackson, Philip W. (ed.). 1992. *Handbook of Research on Curriculum*. New York: Macmillan.

Jameson, Fredric. 1991. *Postmodernism, or, The Cultural Logic of Late Capitalism*. London: Verso.

Kenway, Jane, Chris Bigum, and Lindsay Fitzclarence. 1993. Marketing Education in the Post-Modern Age. *Journal of Education Policy*, vol. 8, no. 2, pp. 105–23.

———, Janine Collier, and Karen Tregenza. 1994. New Education in New Times. *Journal of Education Policy*, vol. 9, no. 4, pp. 317–33.

Latour, Bruno. 1987. *Science in Action: How to Follow Scientists and Engineers through Society*. Translated by Catherine Porter. Milton Keynes, UK: Open University Press.

———. 1993. *We Have Never Been Modern*. Translated by Catherine Porter. Cambridge, MA: Harvard University Press.

Lessing, Doris. 1992. *African Laughter: Four Visits to Zimbabwe*. London: HarperCollins.

Levitt, Theodore. 1983. The Globalization of Markets. *Harvard Business Review*, vol. 83, no. 3, pp. 92–102.

Lingard, Bob, John Knight, and Paige Porter (eds.). 1993. *Schooling Reform in Hard Times*. London: Falmer Press.

McCullough, Colleen. 1985. *A Creed for the Third Millennium*. New York: Harper & Row.

McLuhan, Marshall. 1960. Classroom without Walls. In Edmond Snow Carpenter and Marshall McLuhan (eds.), *Explorations in Communication*. Boston: Beacon, pp. 1–3.

———, and Quentin Fiore. 1967. *War and Peace in the Global Village*. New York: Bantam.

McMichael, Philip. 1996. Globalization: Myths and Realities. *Rural Sociology*, vol. 61, no. 1, pp. 25–55.

Pike, Graham, and David Selby. 1987. *Global Teacher, Global Learner*. London: Hodder and Stoughton.

Pinar, William F., William M. Reynolds, Patrick Slattery, and Peter Taubman. 1995. *Understanding Curriculum: An Introduction to the Study of Historical and Contemporary Curriculum Discourses*. New York: Peter Lang.

Reardon, Betty A. (ed.). 1988. *Educating for Global Responsibility: Teacher-Designed Curricula for Peace Education, K–12*. New York: Teachers College Press.

Salusinsky, Imré. 1987. *Criticism in Society*. New York: Methuen.

Shapin, Steven. 1994. *A Social History of Truth: Civility and Science in Seventeenth-Century England*. Chicago: University of Chicago Press.

Shaviro, Steven. 1997. *Doom Patrols: A Theoretical Fiction about Postmodernism*. New York: Serpent's Tail.

Slattery, Patrick. 1995. *Curriculum Development in the Postmodern Era*. New York: Garland.

Trainer, F. E. [Ted]. 1988. Development Re-think. School of Education, University of New South Wales, Sydney, mimeo.

Turnbull, David. 1993. Local Knowledge and Comparative Scientific Traditions. *Knowledge and Policy*, vol. 6, nos. 3/4, pp. 29–54.

———. 1997. Reframing Science and Other Local Knowledge Traditions. *Futures*, vol. 29, no. 6, pp. 551–62.

Victoria, Board of Studies. 1995. *Curriculum and Standards Framework*. 8 vols. Carlton, Victoria: Board of Studies.

Wark, McKenzie. 1994. Understanding Media Culture, Student Identities and Learning. In Jane Kenway and Janine Collier (eds.), *Schooling What Future? Balancing the Education Agenda*. Geelong, Victoria: Deakin Centre for Education and Change, pp. 45–56.

Waters, Malcolm. 1995. *Globalization*. London: Routledge.

Watson-Verran, Helen, and David Turnbull. 1995. Science and Other Indigenous Knowledge Systems. In Sheila Jasanoff, Gerald E. Markle, James C. Petersen and Trevor Pinch (eds.), *Handbook of Science and Technology Studies*. Thousand Oaks, CA: Sage, pp. 115–39.

Wilson, Rob, and Wimal Dissanayake (eds.). 1996. *Global/Local: Cultural Production and the Transnational Imaginary*. Durham, NC: Duke University Press.

6

Globalization and the Social Construction of Reality: Affirming or Unmasking the "Inevitable"?

Catherine A. Odora Hoppers

It is possible today to think of globalization in terms of intensifying information and technology networks, corporate mergers, transnational capital, and a proliferation of group-level interactions that range from intense professional networks using the net and web, to chat groups and pornographic pedagogy, trade, and exchange. To some, this technology-driven superhighway system represents the ultimate level of human communication. Where human contact has failed, apparently the web will do. Where national state systems have failed to bring peace, maybe transnational capital and globalization will. Ostensibly, the temptation is to extend the optimism to issues that have so easily fallen within the cracks of capitalist forms of organization: gender and indigenous perspectives.

If globalization denotes something extensive, comprehensive, inclusive, universal, and "indiscriminate," then indeed we should all be beside ourselves with joy and bliss at its heralding, for, at last, our journey in search of justice, peace, human rights, equity, and equality should surely be at its end. Memory, hard and usually quite painful, however, warns us to meet globalization processes, at best, halfway, at worst, to use extreme caution and beware the nature of the beast.

For educationalists especially, positive, or potentially positive, aspects of globalization are quickly complicated by the role of education in what Berger and Luckman articulate as the "maintenance of the symbolic universe" (Berger and Luckman, 1967, p. 124), particularly in a context in which diversity and the right to "be" are rhetorically being affirmed but are continually under threat from the unresolved issues of Western hegemony. It is maintained that globalization is part of a subtle, calculated technology of subjection (Giddens, 1995) that consolidates and cements the gains of historical direct violence of colonial conquest, the structural violence of global economic relations, and the cultural or epistemic violence of discourses of concealment (Galtung, 1996; Odora Hoppers, 1998b).

THE PROBLEM: THE WEST AND THE "OTHER"

As globalization penetrates the big and small spaces of human life with a vengeance, and amnesia sets in undisturbed, reminders of the tenets undergirding the relations in this "global family" get harder to subject to rigorous scrutiny. On the other hand, it gets harder to simply wish away. Parallel to current talk of the information superhighway, global competitiveness, and untrammeled penetration of the structural adjustment programs in the poor countries, the social contract on a global scale continues to be defined in terms of "regime formation," "treaties," and "international coalition formation" (Bergesen, 1994). Education is still spoken as national development but not linked to new zones of intellectual struggle. Everywhere in "structurally adjusting" Africa, there is talk of reforming education—a reform talk that is a euphemism for tailoring education policy to fit with the requirements of neoliberalism.

In attempting to unmask these discourses, practices, and assumptions for whatever they are worth, it needs to be stated that for the vast majority of the countries as they exist today, the international system continues to reaffirm and reproduce the inequities that are so necessary for that limited, and provincial, version of progress and understanding of development not only to be writ larger, but to be thoroughly assimilated and routinized on a world scale. In most discourses surrounding global development, there is a total obfuscation of the fundamental elements of force and power and especially of the political and economic dominance of the European core (read Western powers) over the rest of the world (Bergesen, 1994).

The core struggle as captured, interestingly enough, in Huntington's thesis is that at the end of the twentieth century, the concept of universal civilization helps justify Western cultural dominance over other societies and the need for those societies to ape Western practices and institutions. Universalism, he states, is the "ideology of the West in confrontation with non-Western cultures" (Huntington, 1996, p. 66).

> The West is attempting, and will continue to attempt to sustain its pre-eminent position and defend its interests by defining those interests as the interests of the "world community." That phrase has become the euphemistic collective noun replacing the "Free World" to give global legitimacy to actions reflecting the interests of the United States and the other Western powers. The West is, for instance attempting to integrate the economies of non-Western societies into a global economic system which it dominates. Through the IMF and other international economic institutions, the West promotes its economic interests and imposes on other nations the economic policies it thinks appropriate (Huntington, 1996, p. 184).

The imposition is also accompanied by a near schizophrenic urge to monitor and keep the barbarians in check. In a recent article in *Le Monde Diplomatique*, Phillippe Riviere (1999) reviews the immense US$26.7 billion annual intelligence budget the United States alone maintains, which, in conjunction with the global technology and other Western powers, enables the United States to tap into, scrutinize, sort, select, and analyze hundreds of thousands of the world's telephones, faxes, and electronic mail messages as a matter of routine. This definitely has more to do with surveillance than with protecting individual liberties. Put in another way, it can be argued that what lingers on is apparently patriarchy's problem with alien men, the "Other" of which Miller (1991) has written. Knowing well that conquest and violence have characterized the history of the relationship between the West and other parts of the Third World, one is forced to reflect on the tension—both latent and overt—on the part of the conqueror, as to what exactly to do with the conquered.

> From its inception, patriarchy had a fundamental problem: how to deal with men not covered by the bonds of filial relationship. Patriarchy had defined humanity in terms of genealogical descent, and society in terms of relationships between the descendants of common ancestors. Persons with the same genealogical heritage were protected by a set of reciprocal rights, obligations and duties, constituting a covenant of kinship. Conversely, in patriarchal terms, non-kins were non-persons. They lacked genealogical pedigree and protection. They were aliens from rival lineages. They were outside the covenant of kinship (Miller, 1991, p. 121).

The problem for patriarchy then was, what to do with the conquered lineage?

The first practice that developed was for the triumphant lineage to kill all the members of the defeated lineage: men, women, and children. This was to ensure double death, death of the individual members and death of the lineage itself, with their descent line permanently cut. The dead lineage had a history but no future. For while the conquered men's potential to contribute to the wealth of the lineage could not be overlooked, their potential for disrupting the structure of power was real. The second practice in the ancient world was to make eunuchs of male captives. The original eunuch was a captive whose death sentence had been commuted. The male captive's life could be spared if his manhood was disposed of. Castration of all the vanquished males would achieve the same outcome as killing all the captives, or at least the men, in that it achieved the genealogical death of the defeated lineage while allowing the vanquished men to live. The third method was slavery. Patterson (cited in Miller, 1991, p. 127) defines slavery as the permanent, violent domination of natally alienated and (and thus) dishonored persons. The permanent loss of connection with one's lineage dishonored the individuals so affected and made them powerless and defenseless in lineage society. They were socially dead. The institution of slavery itself was based on two principles: marginality and integration. Slavery was institutionalized marginality, and, at the same time, slavery was institutionalized reintegration of natally alienated persons into the lineage system (Miller, 1991, pp. 130–34). Miller's analysis is valuable for the insights it provides in understanding the annihilation strategies used in the period following the colonial conquest of Africa, in modernization and globalization strategies.

REIFICATION OF DEVELOPMENT MODELS OF OLD

Globalization silences the debates over development models and over the notion of the Third World by routinizing Western hegemony and dressing it up as a new ubiquitous force in global development. The tolerated conception of development is the one in which non-Western societies are carefully theoretically incorporated into the linear progress developmental paradigm. Essentially a discourse of power and subjugation, it is constituted in a context of present global relations as a recipe for social change, stating as matter of fact, what was once, a matter of debate.

> The central thesis of developmentalism is that social change occurs according to a pre-established pattern, the logic and direction of which are known. Privileged knowledge of the direction of change is claimed by those who declare themselves furthest advanced along its course. Developmentalism is the truth from the point of view of the center of power; it is the theorization (or rather ideologization) of its own path of development, and the comparative method elaborates this perspective (Pieterse, 1991, p. 2).

Global space is transformed into a time sequence, with Europeans as the only contemporaries, the sole inhabitants of modernity: a perspective that served very successfully as a manual for imperial management of societies "at different evolutionary stages." Europe (now read the "West" or the "North") defines the world and gives names to phenomena in the genesis of the new world society brought forth in the wake of European expansion and conquest; industrial revolution; and, now, the advance of the world market. The naming process itself was an extension of the process of conquest making becoming "modern" mean becoming Western. The convergence between development methods, modernization, and the tenets of this democracy lies in the fact that social engineering from above ensures the political containment of the dispossessed.

The rule of market forces now in force further heightens the false understanding that the principal social objectives of all countries are consumption and accumulation, twin objectives to be enforced through the two complementary strategies of the carrot of consumerism through which a system of total demand is created and the competitive stick of enforced economic participation. In this second strategy, the resources and social structures that give independence or relief from the market are ruthlessly assaulted or sequestered, families and communities are ruptured, water and biomass expropriated in the name of economic progress and efficiency. "In a bizarre and profoundly irrational piece of sophistry, it is often claimed that those who are impoverished and immiserized by the forces of 'development' are actually (or will imminently be) its beneficiaries through some 'trickle down' process whereby some portion of the resources taken from them will be returned in more modern form" (Ekins, 1992, p. 205).

THE REAL THREAT TO DEMOCRACY IS THE CODIFIED INTERNATIONAL PIRACY

Behind the imperative of globalization stands the military, technological, and economic power of the West. These powers have rights without qualifications, including

- the right to *prop dictatorships* and undermine popular democracy if those democracies are not in step with the wishes of the Western powers;
- the right to *create a strong transnational state* that dictates economic policy including manufacturing, media and communications, and institutions in which a participant takes place in a fairly rigid hierarchy of domination, implementing orders from above, transmitting them downwards;
- the right to *construct the parameters of meaning*; and
- the right to *intellectual property*—the misnomer for the rising tide of doctrines designed to ensure that the U.S.-based corporations control the technology of the future, including biotechnology, which in turn will allow those state-subsidized private enterprises of the West to control health and agriculture as well as the means to life of all humanity (Chomsky, 1994).

Initially outlined by Winston Churchill, the earlier version of a "New World Order" talked of "satisfied nations" (read: genocidal nations) to be entrusted with the powers to govern the world:

The government of the world must be entrusted to satisfied nations, who wished nothing more for themselves than what they had. If the world government were in the hands of hungry nations, there would always be danger. . . . Our power placed us above the rest. We are like rich men dwelling at peace within their habitations (Churchill, 1951, p, 351).

Chomsky draws attention to vital Smithsonian footnotes. Over two hundred years ago, Adam Smith already stated that the rich follow the vile maxim of the masters of mankind. In Smith's day, he states, merchants and manufacturers were the principal architects of policy, which they designed to assure that their interests would be most peculiarly attended to, however grievous the impact on others, including the general population of their own societies (Chomsky, 1994). One can only guess what the world would have been like had the earlier Smith publication *Theory of Moral Sentiments*, which came out seventeen years before the now infamous *Wealth of Nations*, also received attention. In that book, Smith had developed a theory of human behavior and an implicit model of society based on the exercise of sympathy (i.e., our ability to imagine ourselves in "their" place). This vein of thought could have led to a very different application of economic analysis. The one book sank into obscurity, and the other became the free-market bible (Boulding, in Henderson, 1996).

The implications of the Smithsonian footnotes to which Chomsky refers have been noted by authoritative voices in the Third World. The South Commission for instance, observes that the core industrial powers have frequently resorted to a new form of colonialism, monopolizing control over the world economy; undermining the more democratic elements of the United Nations; and, in general, proceeding to institutionalize the South's second class status (The South Commission, 1990). Rather than strengthening the weaker countries, the industrialized countries (the North) used the plight of those developing countries to strengthen their dominance and influence over the development paths of the South, forcing the weak to reshape their economic policies to make them compatible with the North's design. The most powerful countries in the North have become de facto board of management for the world economy, protecting their interests and imposing their will in the South, where governments are then left to face the wrath, even the violence, of their own people, whose standards of living are being depressed for the sake of preserving the present patterns of operation of the world economy—that is, the present structure of wealth and power (The South Commission, 1990).

Chomsky reminds us that a particularly valuable feature of the rising de facto governing institutions is their immunity from popular influence, even awareness. They operate in secret, creating a world subordinated to the needs of investors, with the public "put in its place," and the threat of true democracy reduced. This reversal of the expansion of democracy over the past centuries is a matter of no slight significance as the former chairman of the Group of 77, Luis Fernando Jaramillo pointed out in his last address to that group:

> The strategy of the rich . . . is clearly directed at strengthening more and more the economic institutions and agencies that operate outside the UN system [which, with all its flaws remains] the only multilateral mechanism in which the developing countries can have some say. . . . [In contrast, the Bretton Woods Institutions that are being made] the center of gravity for principal economic decisions that affect the developing countries are marked by their undemocratic character, their lack of transparency, their dogmatic principles, their lack of pluralism in the debate of ideas, and their impotence to influence the policies of the industrialized countries whose dominant sectors they serve in reality. It is this "New Institutional Trinity" which would

have as its specific function . . . to control and dominate the economic relations that commit the developing world . . . while the industrialized countries will make their own deals outside normal channels . . . in G-7 meetings and elsewhere (in Chomsky, 1994, p. 179).

EDUCATION AND THE DIFFUSION OF CULTURAL ORIENTATIONS IN AFRICA[1]

Globalization is given further legitimacy through prescriptive action by groups or bodies operating at the international level. On the subject of prescriptive action, McNeely (1995) has argued that international organizations facilitate the process of diffusing cultural themes developed primarily in the West and apply pressure for these to be adopted worldwide as "universal" values. Development and education experts, McNeely argues, are part of an epistemic community already thoroughly imbued with the substantive ideology of this universalism, and are generally the foot soldiers in facilitating the symbolic and actual establishment of the universalist claims throughout the world. They are also responsible for constructing the requisite policy domains under the pretense that they are "neutral," "skilled" persons.

At the level of objectives of education, the fundamentally unresolved problems with the nature and philosophical basis underpinning education in Africa, take on a different flavor once globalization becomes a norm. Fägerlind and Saha have stated that education plays key roles in the development of an individual and of society. In its skills and human capital formation role, education provides a learner with new skills and knowledge that should enable her/him to function in a modern society. In its liberation role, education has been conceived of as a tool for illuminating the structures of oppression and equipping the learners with the tools to alter those oppressive structures in society (Fägerlind and Saha, 1989). However, there is a third role of education, which is the transmission of the normative heritage of a people from one generation to the next. A people's culture, wa Thiongo wrote, is the carrier of values evolved by that community in the course of their economic and political life. The values they hold are the basis of their world outlook, their collective and individual image of self, their identity as a people who look at themselves and to their relationship to the universe in a certain way (wa Thiongo, 1981).

In the context of Africa, the last two roles of education, that of liberation and that of transmission of the normative heritage of a people, are not only being rendered irrelevant to their use but, more accurately, are being buried alive. It is quite evident that by transmitting judiciously the normative heritage of only one culture, the Western, and transposing it onto all other people, education, as presently constituted, becomes a key carrier of a most insidious cultural and epistemic violence. As people's thoughts and cognition are shaped to enhance maximal congruency with the values and practices of Western society, and as this process is routinized and made to appear quite normal, discourses are formed to legitimize this normalcy, and any attempt to create or contemplate another discourse is quickly rendered as an anomaly.

Reward motivates further compliance, and it is of no surprise at all that in a study by Lewin et al. (1982) examining twenty-nine national education plans for the twenty-year period from 1966 to 1985, all these plans were uniformly found to express the major role of education in development, and all of them emphasized the role of education in labor force development and nation-building—all of which are consistent with "world cultural values" represented by UNESCO and World Bank education policies. The two organizations have also been primal technical agencies that have "assisted" in the drafting those plans, emphasizing the dissemination and the modalities for disseminating "world accounts" (McNeely, 1995).

Ki-Zerbo (1996) provides a refreshing African rejoinder to this gleeful process by arguing that as a system within a system, among other systems, education is closely linked with the functioning of the other subsystems, and is, in fact, the strategic pillar to the success of the other systems. Education, he states, is key to the preservation of the status quo, and in a situation of structural violence, education policy and practice become the main egalitarian mask and smokescreen for the massive violence being carried out in the other systems. In Africa, as the education subsystem is exogenous, it is organic by implantation, which means that its life cycle is closely guarded by the implanter. This makes education carry a "double mask," one of its relationship and link with the other subsystems such as the economy and Western ideology with which it has a dialectical relationship of mutual influence, and the other the mask of the dominating power.

Education in the African context, states Ki-Zerbo, is not just for the production of the "new self" but also for the reproduction of the social, economic, political, cultural structures. The drama (comic and tragic) of reproduction in the African context, and one for which education earns itself the trophy of being the chief conduit of structural violence, is that the reproduction is not of its own society, but of "another" society. The structural violence of the educational policy at the systemic level is in reproducing not just the "other society," but also in reproducing the violences of the other's subsystems into the conquered societies via its monopoly of/and influence over the mind space of the young (and old) of the conquered societies (Odora Hoppers, 1998b).

For women in non-Western contexts for instance, the education system of the Western type carries the double violation in that such an education is not only reproducing "another society" in general, but also that where in most precolonial societies women had the sacred role as mediator between the transcendent and humankind, the new mode of social reproduction now ensures that the space for social and cultural reproduction from an endogenous point of view is abrogated and supplanted by something else (Odora, 1993). As school is at once the site for reproduction, formation, and deformation, control of the mind space of the young is the main battlefield, making education become the most critical subsystem and key to the sustenance of the structural violence, from the point of view of its being the privileged site for legitimizing alienation from "self," and bondage and drugged identity with the prescribed "other-ness" (Ki-Zerbo, 1996).

GEOPOLITICS AND THE DEMARCATION OF WHAT IS A "PROBLEM" IN EDUCATION IN AFRICA

Another area in which reality is steadily being obscured is in the agenda setting and the demarcation of what constitutes a "problem" in education in Africa. For Africa, the interventions through donor conditionalities that persisted since the 1980s have gone to such an extent that a new de facto dependency has been institutionalized as part of what Ninsin refers to as the "big game involving a new colonialism which finds its greatest advantages in the nominal independence of the countries of the continent" (Ninsin, cited in Mohan, 1994, p. 526). In the new geopolitical terrain in place over Africa, Mohan states, the control exerted over African states is achieved without direct imposition of political power as of old. The new form of coercion for achieving consensus amenable to Western control is executed by supranational political agents working at "arm's length," relying now on more subtle means centered upon the creation and dissemination of knowledge; that is to say, abstract knowledge is used explicitly to create consensus for more concrete policy intervention (Mohan, 1994).

The area of research that informs policy has especially been identified by scholars as one such site in which hegemonic thought, visions, and meaning are constructed and in which manufacture of consensus in present-day Africa most effectively occurs. With the World Bank strongly leading the crew in establishing consensus for its (and the West's) neoliberal agenda, Samoff's studies reveal a new game of mind and policy control and manipulation, in which wealthy lender agencies set the research agendas and then base their policy discourses on this self-funded and "objective" research (Samoff, 1992a). Loxley and Seddon (1994) add: "The Bank is undoubtedly selective, not only in the way in which it deploys its statistical evidence in support of its own analysis, but also in the choice of 'successes' and 'failures' as examples to support arguments about the effectiveness of structural adjustment programs" (p. 489).

According to Samoff, it is no longer a world in which policymakers rationally survey a wide range of literature before making policy decisions. Indeed, the convergence in the relationship between research, funding, and policy does not begin at the point of funding, but further upstream and deeper at the level of meta-theoretical assumptions (Samoff, 1992a). Beginning with a definition of what is deemed wrong with Africa, one set of such pervasive assumptions on governance is that African countries are somehow in such a disarray that the state cannot fulfill its developmental role, therefore the Western transnationals and technical expertise should of necessity be called upon to fill this void (Samoff, 1992a). A sweeping generalization of what is worst in Africa becomes a strategic indulgence, with a strong tendency to stress the "internal" problems and blame the victims of the crisis—all too often by resorting to sociocultural explanations that suggest an intrinsic incapacity (Loxley and Seddon, 1994).

Geopolitics of sameness in the context of educational development is revealed in the striking uniformity and commonality of assumptions, the type of diagnosis, the content of prescriptions, and directions in the recommendations for action that nearly all bilateral and multilateral donors make to all their recipient countries. As if propelled by some higher order, all of them push for cost effectiveness and efficient management, numerical enrollment and retention, information and management, and all of them say that there is a "lack of capacity" for policy implementation at all levels. It should be recalled that such has been the historic preoccupation of Western intervention in Africa since independence. Thus it is interesting indeed that even after massive investments in training have been made by the recipient countries (following the donors' advice), the diagnosis seems to remain like the stylus on a damaged vinyl record, constant: it is a perpetual problem of incapacity (see Samoff, 1992b).

African education systems are labeled as having "deteriorated" in recent years, and quality of education, not just quantity, is the matter at stake. Quality is then dwelt on without considering the cultural relativity of such a concept, and especially without humility as to the fact that international standards of educational quality are conditioned by international technological, economic, and political relationships that are defined by the cultures of the powerful nations. It ignores that the framework of technical rationality within which the mainstream research that informs such interventions is itself a product of Western culture (Takala, 1994). Thus it can be stated that geopolitical reasoning works by the active suppression of complex geographical reality of places in favor of controllable geographical abstractions. In this frame, "research has shown" that all Sub-Saharan African countries have similar characteristics. The Third World is then affirmed with paternalism as a bloodless universality without aspirations, without dreams, without visions, without competencies (Naipul, cited in Mohan, 1994, p. 525).

From this perspective of authority, various "cures" to the "common for all" ailments are prescribed en masse as has happened with the Structural Adjustment Programs (SAPs). In fact they are not only prescribed, but in no time at all they become disseminated as the official descriptors in the discourse of all bilateral donors, and thereafter as the legitimate basis for new conditionalities. At the level of governance, the universalizing of Western liberal democracy under the influential diatribe of "good governance" is quickly routinized, the hegemony of the market is endorsed and disseminated, and decentralization to the advantage of privatization is legitimized (Mohan, 1994).

The donor agencies say the recipient countries should "own" their agenda now, but almost all the donors along with their activities remain opaque and most inaccessible to scrutiny by national governments of recipient countries. They say "transparency" is the key to good governance, but continue to insulate themselves and the premise of their diagnosis from any review by experts within the countries they support. They all want less government, privatization, increased school fees, and even "community participation" (Samoff, 1992b), but with no discussion as to other forms of learning other than the Western one that are also worth investing in, and which are important to a growing child in Africa.

It can be stated therefore that in the main, unlike in the colonial period in which political power was imposed in the form of an imperial state, consensus for intervention is achieved today via active supranational political agents relying on more subtle means centered around the creation and dissemination of knowledge. It is the task of these seemingly neutral and innocently technical institutions and intellectuals of statecraft (Mohan, 1994) to produce, transmit, and especially stabilize various development "truths" and ensure that they are posited and partaken of as "universal." The locus of the creation of the rules by which spoken and written statements are made meaningful continues, as in the colonial era, to have a distinctly geographical nature and entails modes and techniques of suppression of complex social, cultural, and geographical realities whenever these attempt to emerge and a permanent stranglehold on those that are already in existence (Loxley and Seddon, 1994).

STRUCTURAL ADJUSTMENT PROGRAMS AND THE REDEFINITION OF POLITICS AND GOVERNANCE IN AFRICA

Globalization had a "John the Baptist" of its own: the SAPs. Many African countries have been implementing SAPs for more than a decade. The process has involved a shift in aid programs with accompanying macroeconomic conditionalities (Havnevik and van Arkadie, 1996). It is also no longer any secret that donors are steadily shifting their ground, pushing conditionality beyond the areas of narrowly defined economic policy into institutional arrangements, ownership, privatization, changes in public service delivery systems, and political practice. This latter especially brings into question the issue of the political sovereignty of African countries, "indirect rule" through aid, and a call for a second liberation in Africa (Havnevik and van Arkadie, 1996; Mkandawire, 1996; Olukoshi, 1996; Fundanga, 1996).

The ensuing culture of surface partnership and structural subservience implies that government officials are not only subservient to often paternalistic donor officials, but political leaders are held accountable for policies designed elsewhere. It is also clear that African countries in the 1990s have very little influence over their own development agenda. Within national systems, adjustment-oriented "reforms" are promoted by manipulation through establishing alliances with ministers of finance to "get it moving." In the meantime, power in the recipient bureaucracies have shifted to the technocrats, recruited by external donors and placed in small units within key ministries with the responsibility for the coordination and promotion of SAPs.

Alongside calls for more democracy and transparency, critical decisions have been appropriated in the confidential milieu of donor–recipient negotiations. In the meantime, both the projects of nation-building and democratization are threatened by SAPs by weakening the capacity of the state to respond in a political way to the many demands on it and by riding roughshod over public opinion. It is the "anti-popular" content and political form—the foreign imposition and nontransparency of policymaking institutions—that have provoked the most negative response. African scholars argue that it is not in SAPs, but in resistance to it that democratic forces have been bred (Mkandawire, 1996; Olukoshi, 1996; Fundanga, 1996). It is no surprise that the governments that the World Bank has peddled as strong adjusters—Ghana, Ibrahim Babangida's Nigeria, and Uganda are essentially military regimes (Mkandawire, 1996).

SAPs are not only about the liberalization of domestic markets, but also about submission to the logic of global markets. The effect of the exigencies of global financial liberalization has been to strengthen the structural predominance of the entrepreneurial class by making the threat of capital flight a sword of Damocles hanging over policymakers. In the process, "market" has become reified into a neutral, apolitical, and a-historical institution. (Chaudry, in Mkandawire, 1996, p. 36). It is fetishized so as to acquire such human attributes as "anger," "disappointment," "displeasure," or "nervousness." In this fetishization of social arrangements, it is the "market" that insists on the devolution of power to the central banks to allay the market's suspicion that the government may not be seriously committed to orthodox market policies (Mkandawire, 1996).

A dramatic de-professionalization of public administration is also taking place with the emergence of the technocratic elite aligned to the external constituencies. These insulated international technocracies, ensconced in key ministries, wield enormous power. This further aggravates the tension between the practice of generating this cadre and the pressure on governments to become more transparent. The professional arrogance of these elite is fanned further by the heaps of praise accorded to them as the national salvation, in sharp contrast to the denigration that the domestic politicians and interest groups suffer at the hands of international financial institutions. On the other hand, the technocrats narrow the choices of the politicians by either being part of a transnational technocratic alliance or by identifying themselves with particular international models of crisis management, such as orthodox SAPs.

Politics is reduced to serving this technocratically defined "welfare function" instead of the technocrats devising the instruments necessary to meet a democratically specified "social welfare program." Mkandawire (1996) argues that SAPs have introduced a truncated democracy whose area of competence is severely restricted. It is a choice-less democracy, on an inflexible take-it-or-leave-it basis in which the silent compulsions of market forces reign unchallenged by human will and collective action (Olukoshi, 1996).

Holders of African debt, organized into the Paris and London Clubs, Olukoshi states, are treated to the same take-it-or-leave-it principle. Buffeted from all sides by pressures requiring them to reach agreements with the World Bank and the International Monetary Fund (IMF), African governments cave in one by one. They feel that they have lost control over the key aspects of economic decision making. Not only that, African governments are required to submit themselves regularly to monitoring missions from Washington, D.C. The gradual erosion of national sovereignty has only deepened with the almost complete takeover of the policy terrain by multilateral donors, with state officials reduced to mere implementers of the preferences that emanate, one way or the other, from the Bretton Woods twins (i.e., the World Bank and the IMF).

At another level, the requirements for meeting the demands of donor conditionality increasingly mean that public officials account more to the World Bank and the IMF than to the people. Public officials moreover, spend disproportionate amounts of time preparing reports, one after another, for the Bank, the Fund, a host of bilateral donors, and the Paris and London Clubs. This is in addition to time spent with a variety of evaluation/monitoring missions and in undertaking missions to the Bretton Woods institutions, the Paris and London Clubs, and with other donors to negotiate/justify further financing. The sum total of all of this is that governmental effectiveness is severely impaired (Olukoshi, 1996).

THE STIGMATIZED STATE AND EDUCATION POLICY

Olukoshi (1996) argues that the collapse of the former Soviet bloc, it would appear, has coalesced into a neoliberal triumphantism to create the impression of an inexorable march by all humankind toward "free" market policies and ideas. State policies and agencies are treated as the primary obstacle to the economic development of the continent. The critique of the postcolonial state built into the structural adjustment model opposes the public to the private, the rural to the urban, the formal to the informal, agriculture to industry in a one-sided manner. This is further developed by a copious borrowing from American behavioral political science writing on Africa tailored to the objectives of neoliberalism in Africa. For its part, the World Bank and its allied political economists perfected a set of referents with regard to the state. Some of these include descriptors such as: prebendal, crony, neo-patrimonial, overextended, lame leviathan, kleptocratic, parasitical, predatory, weak, soft, and rentier. All of these are denigrating terms (Olukoshi, 1996).

In other words, from being the cornerstone of development in the pre-adjustment period, the state, which a priori is defined as deficient, is now seen as the millstone holding back a system of market-led development. Where the state is to be mercilessly retrenched and put in its rightful place, the market is to be unbound and allowed to flower unrestrained (Olukoshi, 1996). To reiterate, application of conditionality is the primary means by which the multilateral donors who designed the adjustment framework seek to ensure that African states adopt and implement their reform program. As African governments can only expect to receive donor funds and support if they agree to adopt and implement policy reforms prescribed by the Bretton Woods institutions the IMF and the World Bank are well positioned to compel adoption of their favored policy options. The effectiveness of the leverage exercised over African countries is further reinforced by a system of cross-conditionality whereby bilateral donors agree to do business with governments only when they (the African governments) have made their peace with the World Bank and can produce a clean bill of health from the IMF.

Policy formulation experiences in Africa confirm the extensive presence of external donor agencies in the formulation of the policy documents and that all the education reforms being undertaken are impelled by the structural adjustment process. Ghana is interesting in that policy formulation and reform in education took a glaring swing in 1983 when the military regime veered away from its policies of self-reliance and undertook extensive adjustment programs with the support from the IMF and the World Bank (Fobih et al., 1996). In Guinea, following the launching of the Structural Adjustment Program in 1986, the state was removed from the productive sectors of the economy. At the end of 1988, with the support of the World Bank and other donors, government began two projects: Education I and II. By the end of the second project in 1989, as preparations for the SAP in education were already underway, a reasoning had been consolidated in the context of these projects to the effect that "experience" in "other countries" had shown that a coherent policy framework linked to macro adjustment programs "can lead to changes in the education sector that have a profound effect on the nation's schooling." In the context of an adjustment package financed by several funding agencies (French Cooperation, United States Agency for International Development, IMF, World Bank, and others), a policy declaration in Guinea was approved in 1989 that provided the basis for a multi-agency–financed education sector adjustment program. When the policy document was ready, it had to be approved by donors; when the Sectoral Adjustment was all in place, the Guinean government, through the minister of finance, affirmed their acquisition of the necessary concepts as required by the agencies. The minister addressed a special letter to the president of the World Bank, presenting "the relationship between the macroeconomic reforms to the proposed reform of the education sector" (Kamano, 1996).

The story of Uganda's involvement with the IMF and the World Bank began in 1987 when the then one-year-old government decided to abandon its policy of self-reliance in favor of the market economy espoused by the Bretton Woods institutions. The SAP that followed came amidst protests from civil society as to the negative effects that such a program would have on education, health, water and sanitation, child welfare, and other protection programs (wa Irumba, 1996). In 1987, an Education Policy Review Commission (EPRC) supported by the World Bank was appointed and a secretariat was set up. In terms of consultations, it is evident that in spite of what has been dubbed the "most extensive consultations ever," the EPRC held consultations only in urban areas. Rural communities; marginalized urban communities; and security agencies like the police force, the army, and the prisons department were not asked their views. The impressive list of 496 memoranda and resource papers does not show any involvement of the marginalized groups, but rather that of an educated elite.

In Benin, it was well recognized that many problems in education are symptoms produced by complex combinations of factors and cannot be fixed with simple, single-factor solutions. For this, the legacy of colonialism was spelled out in detail in the country report. Academic institutions were identified as being bastions of colonial conservatism and an elitist policy, such as using academic exams as the basis of selection. The whole educational system was identified as being an alienating one (Debourou, 1996). But when agencies came around to effect an educational reform, only enrollment was picked upon as a problem, with issues restricted to internal efficiency of the education system itself, planning problems, teacher qualifications, and the issue of quality (however defined). In the UNDP/UNESCO Education Policy Analysis project managed by a Beninese—but with "qualified" external expert assistance—there is no reference to designing the kind of reform policies that would address the factors related to colonialism.

RECONSTRUCTING REALITY: RECOVERING THE BASIS OF HUMANITY

The twentieth century has drawn to a close, and we take stock and look to a new millennium with both expectation and uncertainty. We grope to find a new foundation upon which to recover our sense of humanness. We seek to discover and foster tools that shall enable us to mature and muster courage and faith enough to cultivate the capacity to love (Fromm, 1975). We seek new directions in dealing with diversity: from the view of diversity as a tool for containment to diversity as a basis for human relations of respect. We seek to build bridges and affirm the value of holism in thought and practice. We commit to a new understanding of human rights: the right to know, the right to do, the right to be and become, and the right to live together (Delors Report, cited in Odora Hoppers, 1998a).

We seek an education that can enable people to bring to the field rich collective experiences and abilities and can permit these to be given place and name in the scheme of things. It is an education that builds capacities and fosters resistance to old models and roles. It is an education that can permit each human being to participate in naming the world on terms that he or she can understand (Odora Hoppers, 1998a).

Embodied in the African philosophy of *ubuntu*, a new universalism, which seeks to affirm a concept of development in which fear is replaced by joy, insecurity by confidence and materialism by spiritual values, promises to emerge. *Ubuntu* is humaneness, care, understanding, and empathy. It is the ethic and interaction that occurs in the African extended family. The *ubuntu* concept is found in proverbs from many African societies and communities such as "the stomach of the traveler is small," "a home is a real one if people visit it" (Zulu), "a bird builds its nest with another bird's feathers," and "the hands wash each other" (Xhosa). All these proverbs demonstrate an innate encouragement that sharing is good and a person is only a person because of other people (Boon, 1996). It is this philosophy that differentiates African society fundamentally from European and Western societies, which seek competition even unto death, exploitation until decimation, and relationships with "others" through conquest.

As we take stock and move to recover our sense of humanness and basis for practice, as we muster that courage to love, the one moral and ethical summons before us is to work tirelessly to help restore humanity to others so systematically separated from their own selves. This task is about recognizing and confronting the forms of epistemic violence of global proportions that has had unprecedented success in not just cultivating a sense of alienness, but also in decapitating peoples from their capacity to use their human powers to the fullest. But at another level, the task is also about understanding the fact that epistemic violence is not only diffuse but also extremely productive.

TAKING CUES FROM POSTMODERNIST
AND FEMINIST CRITIQUES

Rust (1991) states that as a critical discourse, postmodernism underscores contingency of meaning and challenges the major tenets of modern scientific and rational knowledge. For its part, globalization compels us to revisit two aspects of the postmodernism discourse and debate that are extremely relevant for the setting of new foundations for educational thought in the twenty-first century. These are the critique on the totalitarian nature of metanarratives; and the problem of the "Other" (Rust, 1991). The issue of "othering" is in large part associated with the notion of a culture of inner and outer imperialism, an imperialism that, although taken very much for granted by devoted moderns, no longer goes unchallenged. While self-determination and numerous liberation movements have adequately challenged "outer imperialism" with a substantial degree of success, the entire terrain of "inner imperialism" has not been seriously confronted. Thus, the fact that the core industrialized powers now aim at the control of thought of all "Others," by locking the spaces of their cognitive thought in what Lyotard (in Rust,

1991, p. 615) called "totalitarian and logocentric systems of thought," should be posited as a big part of the problem.

It is also at this point that the feminist sciences provide crucial theoretical and conceptual devices. At the core of a feminist dialectic is a sociology of knowledge, a conception that the world is known from the varied vantage points of actors differently situated in the social structure. This view that knowledge is anchored in and patterned by the knower's structurally situated vantage point leads one to the position that knowledge is itself the key problematique. This is particularly because people's perceptions of social reality are always partial and interest-based. Feminist sociology therefore seeks to understand how people come to their views of social reality, how they justify those views in the face of seemingly contradictory opinions and evidence, how they act on those views, condone their own behavior, or reconcile themselves to their social situation according to those views (Lengerman and Niebrugge-Brantley, 1988). Because women's experiences and knowledge, like those of Africans, have been obscured in the male bias of Western academe, including development theory and practice, the task is not just to add women or African experiences into the known equation but to work with new epistemologies and methodologies. This implies an open challenge to current knowledge production, a challenge to displace the neutral male subject of Western science and dissolve the division between research and practice (Harcourt, 1994).

As Foucault has posited, there is a need to develop new perspectives on society, knowledge, discourse, and power, which can equip us with such tools of analysis that are capable of discerning that slippery interface between modern forms of power and knowledge and rationality and institutions that have served to create new forms of domination that Hegelian and Marxist philosophies have been unable to grasp, "recognizing that systematizing methods produce reductive social and historical analyses, and that knowledge is perspectival in nature, requiring multiple viewpoints to interpret a heterogeneous reality (cited in Best and Kellner, 1994, pp. 34–35).

We should begin to ask, How can we attain that much rhetoricized goal of attaining a plurality of history of diversity in histories and render these capable of contesting for space in the face of the totalizing metanarratives of Westernization, of modernization, and of industrialization with all that these narratives have entailed? How, indeed, are we going to foreground the material context of subject construction that undergirds the global practices and discourses today? In short, we need to critically revisit that process by which individuals and nationalities as "subjects," get "subjected" to someone else through control and dependence, tied to their own identity by a conscience or self-knowledge. The formation of ideology has to begin with the development of a true conscience, which, in the first place, is free from the dominating presence of institutions and structures and, second, is one which is capable of undertaking transformative goals even in the absence of some large-scale uprising or massive revolution.

If Foucault is right that power is irreducibly plural, that it thrives at the local and capillary levels of society and is only subsequently taken up by larger institutional structures, then it follows that a change only in the form of the state, modes of production or class composition of society fails to address autonomous trajectories of power. Thus the key to micrological strategies . . . is that since power is decentered and plural, and so in turn must be forms of political struggle. A Foucauldian postmodern politics, therefore, attempts to break with unifying and totalizing strategies, to cultivate multiple forms of resistance, to destroy the prisons of received identities and discourses of exclusion (Best and Kellner, 1994, pp. 56–57).

The political task of genealogy, therefore, is to recover the autonomous discourses, knowledges, and voices suppressed through totalizing narratives. As Best and Kellner also argue, the subjugated voices of history speak through hidden forms of domination, and to admit their speech is necessarily to revise one's conception of what and where power is. The task of genealogy then becomes that of problematizing the present and exposing the operations of power and domination, working behind the neutral or beneficent facades. Writes Foucault: "It seems to me that the real political task in a society such as ours is to criticize the working of institutions which appear to be both neutral and independent; to criticize them in such a manner that the political violence which has always exercised itself obscurely through them will be unmasked, so that we can fight them" (1994 [1974], p. 171).

If "truth" is best understood not as correspondence or correctness of assertion, but as the absence of concealment, then the task of the critical social cartographers is to focus attention to the small and previously hidden narratives and on making the invisible visible. It becomes our responsibility to track omissions and understand mechanisms of power tied to the deletion of certain practical and intellectual work (Paulston and Liebman, 1993). Engaging in remaking the maps would reveal both acknowledged and perceived social inclusions while leaving space for further inclusions of social groups and ideas. Meadows (1997, p. 94) reminds us that

> To be human is to be born into a world that pulls out and pushes back the potentials inside us. I push and pull back trying to find or shape part of the world that supports my inborn potential. Sometimes the world supports me, sometimes it crushes part of me. What kind of a dance can I do with a culture that loads me with sludge and does not recognize my inner shine? All I can think to do is to tune into whatever I know of the light and life of the universe without denying the existence of my own failures.

NOTES

1. This section and those that follow draw from Odora Hoppers, 1998b.

REFERENCES

Berger, Peter L., and Thomas Luckman. 1967. *The Social Construction of Reality: A Treatise in the Sociology of Knowledge.* London: Penguin.

Bergesen, Albert. 1994. Turning the World Systems Theory on Its Head. In Mike Featherstone (ed.), *Global Culture: Nationalism, Globalization and Modernity.* London: Sage, pp. 89–97.

Best, Steven, and Douglas Kellner. 1994. *Postmodern Theory: Critical Interrogations.* London: Macmillan (and 1991, New York: Guilford).

Boon, Mike. 1996. *The African Way: The Power of Interactive Leadership.* Johannesburg: Zebra Press.

Chomsky, Noam. 1994. *World Orders: Old and New.* London: Pluto Press.

Churchhill, Winston. 1951. *The Second World War.* Vol 5. Boston: Houghton Mifflin.

Debourou, Djibbril M. 1996. The Case of Benin. In Association for the Development of African Education (ed.), *Formulating Educational Policy: Lessons and Experiences from Sub-Saharan Africa.* Paris: International Institution of Educational Planning (IIEP), pp. 39–61.

Ekins, Paul. 1992. *A New World Order: Grassroots Movements for Global Change.* London: Routledge.

Fägerlind, Ingmar, and Lawrence J. Saha. 1989. *Education and National Development: A Comparative Perspective.* 2nd ed. Oxford: Pergamon.

Fobih, Dominic Lwaku, Albert K. Koomson, and Ebenezer F. Godwyll. 1996. The Case of Ghana. In Association for the Development of African Education (ed.), *Formulating Educational Policy: Lessons and Experiences from Sub-Saharan Africa.* Paris: IIEP, pp. 63–84.

Foucault, Michel. 1974. Human Nature: Justice Versus Power. In Fons Elders (ed.), *Reflexive Water: The Basic Concerns of Mankind.* London: Souvenir Press.

Fromm, Eric. 1975. *The Art of Loving.* London: Unwin Books.

Fundanga, Caleb M. 1996. Practical Effects of Economic and Political Conditionality in Recipient Administration. In Kjell J. Havnevik and Brian van Arkadie (eds.), *Domination or Dialogue? Experiences and Prospects for African Development Cooperation.* Uppsala: Nordiska Afrikainstitutet, pp. 89–97.

Galtung, Johan. 1996. *Peace by Peaceful Means: Peace, Conflict, Development and Civilization.* London: Sage.

Giddens, Anthony. 1995. *The Consequences of Modernity.* Cambridge: Polity Press.

Harcourt, Wendy. 1994. Introduction. In Wendy Harcourt (ed.), *Feminist Perspectives on Sustainable Human Development.* London: Zed Books, pp. 11–25.

Havnevik, Kjell J., and Brian van Arkadie. 1996. Introduction. In Kjell J. Havnevik and Brian van Arkadie. *Domination or Dialogue? Experiences and Prospects for African Development Cooperation.* Uppsala: Nordiska Afrikainstitutet, pp. 13–23.

Henderson, Hazel 1996. *Creating Alternative Futures: The End of Economics.* New York: Kumarian Press.

Huntington, Samuel P. 1996. *The Clash of Civilizations and the Remaking of World Order.* New York: Simon & Schuster.

Kamano, Joseph Pierre. 1996. The Case of Guinea. In Association for the Development of African Education (ed.), *Formulating Educational Policy: Lessons and Experiences from Sub-Saharan Africa.* Paris: IIEP, pp. 85–101.

Ki-Zerbo, Joseph. 1996. Notes from personal interview with Catherine A. Odora Hoppers, Amman, Jordan.

Lengerman, Patricia M., and Jill Niebrugge-Brantley. 1988. Contemporary Feminist Theory. In George Ritzer (ed.), *Sociological Theory*. New York: Knopf, pp. 430–43.

Lewin, K., A. Little, and Christopher Colclough. 1982. Adjusting to the 1980s: Taking Stock of Educational Expenditures. In *Financing of Educational Development*. Proceedings from an International seminar held in Mont Sainte Marie, Ottawa, Canada: International Development Research Centre.

Loxley, John, and David Seddon. 1994 (December). Stranglehold on Africa. *Review of African Political Economy*, vol. 21, no. 62, pp. 485–93.

McNeely, Connie L. 1995. *Constructing the Nation State: International Organizations and Prescriptive Action*. Westport, CT: Greenwood.

Meadows, Donella. 1997. Untitled. In Frederick Franck, Janis Roze, and Richard Connolly. 1997. *What Does It Mean to Be Human? A Reverence for Life*. New York: Circumstantial Publications, pp. 94–96.

Miller, Errol. 1991. *Men at Risk*. Kingston: Jamaica Publishing House.

Mkandawire, P. Thandika. 1996. Economic Policy-Making and the Consolidation of Democratic Institutions in Africa. In Kjell J. Havnevik and Brian van Arkadie (eds.), *Domination or Dialogue? Experiences and Prospects for African Development Cooperation*. Uppsala: Nordiska Afrikainstitutet, pp. 24–47.

Mohan, Giles. 1994 (December). Manufacturing Consensus: Geo-Political Knowledge and Policy Based Lending. *Review of African Political Economy*, vol. 21, no. 62, pp. 525–35.

Odora, Catherine A. 1993. Educating African Girls in a Context of Patriarchy and Transformation: A Theoretical and Conceptual Analysis. Stockholm University, Institute of International Education.

Odora Hoppers, Catherine A. 1998a. The NQF, Equity, Redress and Development: A Human Centered Perspective. Keynote address to the CEPD/University of Witwatersrand conference on Reconstruction, Development and the National Qualifications Framework. Johannesburg, Center for Education Policy Development.

———. 1998b. Structural Violence as a Constraint to African Policy Formulation in the 1990s: Repositioning Education in International Relations. Stockholm University, Institute of International Education.

Olukoshi, Adebayo O. 1996. The Impact of Recent Reform Efforts on the African State. In Kjell J. Havnevik and Brian van Arkadie, *Domination or Dialogue? Experiences and Prospects for African Development Cooperation*. Uppsala: Nordiska Afrikainstitutet, pp. 48–70.

Paulston, Roland. G., and Martin Liebman. 1993. Invitation to Post-Modern Reflection on Critical Social Cartography. Paper presented at the Comparative and International Education Society Annual Conference, Kingston, Jamaica.

Pieterse, Nederveen J. 1991. Dilemmas of Development Discourse: The Crisis of Developmentalism and the Comparative Method. *Development and Change*. London: Sage, vol. 22, pp. 5–29.

Riviere, Phillippe. 1999 (January). How the United States Spies on Us All. *Le Monde Diplomatique*, pp. 2–3.

Rust, Val. 1991. Post-Modernism and Its Comparative Education Implications. *Comparative Education Review*, vol. 35, no. 4, pp. 610–26.

Samoff, Joel. 1992a. The Intellectual/Financial Complex of Foreign Aid. *Review of African Political Economy*, no. 53, pp. 60–87.

————. 1992b. Defining What Is and What Is Not an Issue. An Analysis of Africa Assistance Agency Africa Education Sector Studies. Stockholm: Swedish International Development Agency.

The South Commission. 1990. *The Challenge to the South*. Report of the South Commission. New York: Oxford University Press.

Takala, Tuomas (ed.). 1994. *Quality of Education in the Context of Culture in Developing Countries*. Tampere, Finland: University of Tampere.

wa Irumba, Katebalirwe Amooti. 1996. The Case of Uganda. In Association for the Development of African Education (ed.), *Formulating Educational Policy: Lessons and Experiences from Sub-Saharan Africa*. Paris: IIEP, pp. 141–64.

wa Thiongo, Ngugi. 1981. *Education for a National Culture*. Harare: Zimbabwe Publishing House.

Part 2

Globalization Impacts in Various Educational Sectors

7

Alternative Responses to Globalization from European and South African Universities

Jan Currie and George Subotzky

Globalization practices, such as entrepreneurialism, managerialism, and privatization, are increasingly evident in higher education. They are profoundly affecting institutional life in most parts of the world. More and more, institutions are being run as business enterprises in a managerialist fashion and are being pressured to generate new forms of income. They are also being held increasingly accountable for their responsiveness to social and economic needs, especially regarding their contribution to regional and national competitiveness in the global economy.

Under these conditions, the entrepreneurial university—characterized by strong partnership links with hi-tech industry, corresponding new organizational forms of knowledge production, and a managerialist mode of governance—has become the dominant model of institutional innovation (Clark, 1998; Slaughter and Leslie, 1997). This competitive, market-oriented model and the globalization practices that underlie it are in direct tension with the collegial ethos and with democratic institutional governance and tend to marginalize higher education concerns about community development, equitable social renewal, and the public good.

How universities respond to these trends, however, depends upon a range of interrelated factors. Among these are the political economy of the particular country and its position in the global economy and, linked to this, the degree of its acceptance of neoliberal economic reforms. Other factors include national culture, the structural features of the particular higher education system, and individual institutional mission and function.[1]

Given these dominant tendencies and the impact of globalization on higher

123

education, key questions arise. How can the broader social purpose of higher education be maintained in the face of the increasing prevalence of globalization practices? What organizational arrangements, especially regarding internal governance and external responsiveness, will provide the basis for maintaining concerns for democracy, social justice, and community development? In the competitive market ethos associated with these practices, what role will be played by institutions that are not at the cutting edge of innovation?

These issues are addressed in this chapter by approaching the concept of globalization in both its ideological and material forms and analyzing its impact on universities. We explore two sets of practices that may provide alternative models for universities to counter the seemingly inevitable drift toward globalization practices. One set of alternative practices relates to the internal organization of universities, and the other to the external responsiveness of universities to community development service.

The alternatives to the managerial model focus both on democratic internal governance practices and on external community service. We see the coupling of these as significant, as similar values underlie both. Maintaining democratic traditions ensures more collegial and participatory practices within the university. Likewise, community-oriented service partnerships, driven by the goals of social equity, embody democratic values and concerns for the public good.[2] Our main claim is that, together, these internal and external practices constitute important alternatives to the ubiquitous drift toward the entrepreneurial university, managerialism, corporate interests, and the private good.

France, Norway, and South Africa, in disparate ways, provide national contexts conducive to developing alternatives to the neoliberal model of "best practice" that is sweeping the world. This model has its origin in Anglo-American countries and is infused through supranational organizations, such as the Organization for Economic Cooperation and Development (OECD) and the World Bank (Lingard and Rizvi, 1998). France, Norway, and South Africa, with different traditions from those of the United States and Great Britain, have adopted some neoliberal economic reforms but have resisted others.

For example, despite OECD urgings to jettison the election system in Norwegian universities and to apply more modern managerial systems, these institutions have preserved their collegial forms of governance and have an election process that generates interest and debate beyond the university community (OECD, 1997, 1998b). French universities have also maintained their democratic traditions and have not adopted Anglo-American managerial styles of governance. In both countries, interviews with academics attest to their tenacity to retain democratic models of governance. In South Africa, given the strong socialist character of its struggle against apartheid, the post-apartheid government has voluntarily adopted many neoliberal structural adjustments favored by transnationals, the World Bank, and the International Monetary Fund (IMF). However, in the context of the vast disparities generated by apartheid, the imperatives of equity have given rise to a highly progressive constitution and public policy framework. This provides the opportunity for the nation and its higher education institutions to balance concerns for the redress of social injustices with neoliberal economic reforms. Research has suggested that one important way of achieving this balance is through the higher education–community service partnership model (Subotzky, 1998a, 1998b). In addition, given the enormous inequalities between historically advantaged (white) institutions and historically disadvantaged (black) ones, the issue of how non-research universities can position themselves within the competitive entrepreneurial model is starkly posed by the South African case. Important lessons can be gained by observing how higher education institutions in each of these countries is challenged by the reality of global trends, and also how the political economic conditions in each case have created some space to set and maintain alternative responses to globalization.

THE CONCEPT OF GLOBALIZATION AND ITS IDEOLOGICAL UNDERPINNINGS[3]

It appears that Roland Robertson (1992) was the first sociologist to use the term *globalization* in the title of an article in 1985. The term was barely used before 1980 but has rapidly assumed currency. A recent search for titles using "globali" on the Internet revealed a dramatic rise in hits, from two in 1986 to 196 in 1997 and a total of 692 hits over that period.[4]

While some authors have argued that globalization is not a new phenomenon (Hirst and Thompson, 1996; Frank, 1998), others argue that despite this, the use of the term, its ideological underpinnings, and the heightened sense of compression of the world in terms of space and time are new phenomena (Heydebrand, 1997; Koc, 1993). Arrighi concludes that "careful advocates of the globalization thesis concur with critics in seeing present transformations as not novel except for their scale, scope and complexity" (1998, p. 61).

Globalization is manifest in distinct but related economic, cultural, discursive, symbolic, and ideological dimensions. Among the signifiers of the process are the growth in world financial markets in which the foreign exchange market in 1992 was "sixty times larger than world trade" (Sassen, as quoted by Arrighi, 1998, p. 40). Bentley identifies "the dawn of the 'electronic age' and 'information society' as a convenient marker for distinguishing contemporary globalization from all its earlier forms" (Bentley, as quoted by Riggs, 1998). Along with citing the extensive use of the Internet and all related information technologies as an important marker of globalization, another is the downfall of the Soviet empire, which is linked to the dominant neoliberal discourse surrounding globalization. Koc (1993) concludes that globalization is not new, but only intensified in recent decades, and is accompanied by certain discursive practices:

What is new about globalization is its entry into our daily language as an expression of "reality." In this sense, I argue that globalization is not only a process but also a discourse, defining, describing and analyzing that process. I point out the neo-conservative ideology as the most prevalent influence in this discursive debate (Koc as quoted by Riggs, 1998).

The end of the Cold War implied a distinct ideological victory for the liberal market economy as the dominant paradigm in contemporary times. In considering the impact of globalization on higher education, it is therefore essential to identify the ideological currents and growing internal contradictions that underlie it.

Globalization, in its ideological dimension, is widely seen to be the outcome of doctrines aimed at serving the hegemonic interests of world capitalism (Smyth, 1994; Chomsky, 1997; Kraak, 1997; Orr, 1997). Following the minimalist government prescriptions of the neoliberal consensus, nations are urged to adopt structural adjustments that create conditions conducive to unregulated trade, the free flow of capital, speculative short-term investments, the repatriation of profits, and unfettered access to new markets. These policies entail reducing state control of the economy, restraining state spending, and encouraging the pursuit of export-led policies. Failure to follow these injunctions purportedly leads to loss of competitiveness in the global market. According to the monetarist-inspired rhetoric of globalization, governments are inefficient and, consequently, the demise of the welfare state is justified.

Critical concern for the effects of globalization on equity, social and financial stability, and the environment are growing (Mander and Goldsmith, 1996; Martin and Schumann, 1997). Critics argue that, in favoring the minority rich, globalization has widened the wealth gap. Through the integration of consumer markets, the process of globalization has created new inequalities and threatens peripheral consumer interests and rights as well as environmental conditions, especially in developing countries.

Within the neoliberal framework of globalization, the increasing determination of national economic policy by transnational corporations (TNCs) has resulted in the decline of national sovereignty (Smyth, 1994). Related to this, structural adjustment programs, in creating conditions that maximize TNC profits and short-term investment returns, are in direct tension with policies aimed at the redistribution of wealth and opportunity and meeting basic domestic needs, especially in developing countries (Chomsky, 1997). Autonomous by their very nature, TNCs are accountable to no one but their own shareholders. The vast global capital flows that characterize current short-term speculative investment trends can severely damage national short- and long-term interests.[5]

The underlying notion of the free market is also seen as something of a myth (Chomsky, 1997; Marais, 1998). Rapid and prosperous economic development— for example, until recently in the East Asian emerging economies and, as is shown below, in Norway and France—occurred precisely where the orthodoxy of neoliberal market principles was subverted, where the state controlled capital flight and assured greater equity, and where protectionism was retained.

Significantly, in response to recent turmoil in world financial markets, mainstream neoliberal economists (Sachs, 1998; Fischer, 1998) have called for a fundamental review of the global financial system and proposed some form of regulation of the large capital flows that have been so detrimental to emerging economies. Implicit in this call are crucial shifts in attitudes among establishment figures, which would have been unthinkable two years ago: that a liberalized and deregulated world economic system does not spell unparalleled global prosperity (Marais, 1998); that this flawed "free" market mechanism favors the minority, rich short-term speculators in the north to the vast detriment of developing countries; and that the growing global interdependence that is the consequence of globalization renders everyone vulnerable to market fluctuations resulting from short-term speculation.

Similarly, the seemingly sacred orthodoxy of the World Bank has recently been questioned from within by its prominent chief economist, Joseph Stiglitz, who has called for an end to the "misguided" debt relief policies of the IMF and the World Bank. He argues that "policies which underlay the Washington Consensus are neither necessary nor sufficient, either for macro-stability or longer term development" (Stiglitz, as quoted in Hanlon, 1998). The goal, he states, is equitable development "which ensures that all groups in society enjoy the fruits of development, not just the few at the top. And we seek democratic development." Stiglitz contends that "markets are not automatically better" and that "the dogma of liberalism has become an end in itself and not a means to a better financial system" (Stiglitz, as quoted in Hanlon, 1998).

It is important to note that these global developments do not manifest uniformly in different contexts; they are mediated by local and national conditions (Wolpe, 1995). Henry et al. argue that "there is no essential determinacy to the ways in which globalization processes work, since for various globalization pressures there are also sites of resistance and counter movements" (1997, p. 68). Following this logic, any study of globalization and higher education must seek not only to identify commonalities in higher education policy directions across national boundaries, but also the ways in which particular local contexts mitigate against wholesale or simplistic adoption of macro trends that serve selective interests.

As is the case with global economic relations, a totally deregulated market in higher education may not be the panacea that free traders imagine (see OECD, 1998a, on the benefits of open markets). The long-term value of the uncritical introduction of market-oriented managerial practices into public universities should therefore be seriously questioned. Increased competition, privatization, and managerial practices aim at more efficient universities. Yet efficiency at all costs and unmitigated business practices are in direct tension with existing practices and with the social purpose of higher education through its contribution toward the public good, social renewal, and basic development. Despite strongly encouraging a number of what we have categorized as globalization practices for its member countries, the OECD (1998b) has indicated some hesitancy in unleashing market forces totally on universities. This is evident in the following statement: "However, maximizing profit is not the purpose in education and it is necessary to ask whether the adoption of practices from the business world is consistent with the multiple services expected of educational institutions" (OECD, 1998b, p. 77).

THE EMERGENCE OF THE ENTREPRENEURIAL UNIVERSITY

In both its ideological and material forms, globalization has profoundly impacted on higher education. Universities have been affected by monetarist fiscal constraint and the general distrust of public sector agencies. The state has reduced university budgets, urging institutions to restructure and become leaner and more responsive to social and economic needs, while simultaneously demanding expanded enrollments to reduce unemployment. Governments have strongly encouraged universities to generate income from patents and innovations and to foster closer partnerships with industries to apply knowledge in the development of new products and services within the rapidly changed information-led economy.

Global trends in higher education have given rise to the "entrepreneurial" or "market" university (Dill, 1997; Orr, 1997; Slaughter and Leslie, 1997; Tierney, 1997; Clark, 1998). The entrepreneurial university is characterized by closer university–business partnerships; greater faculty responsibility for accessing external sources of funding; and a managerialist ethos in institutional governance, leadership, and planning. It thus entails increasing market-like behavior by both management and faculty. Universities are clearly functioning increasingly as market-like organizations and are therefore engaging in "academic capitalism" (Slaughter and Leslie, 1997). Universities are appointing new kinds of "knowledge workers" or "entrepreneurial scientists." Faculty across the board are being urged to assume fundraising roles, develop skills in interdisciplinary and team project management, and deal with the media and an increasingly better-informed general public.

As a result of new organizational forms of partnerships between higher education and industry, new modes of applications-driven knowledge production, which are characteristically interdisciplinary and heterogeneous in nature, have emerged (Gibbons et al., 1994). Under these prevailing market conditions, knowledge is being reconceptualized so as to value entrepreneurial research, especially that on the leading edge of science and technology and innovation, more highly than nonmarketable knowledge (Slaughter and Leslie, 1997). Conventional norms of academic freedom, critical reflection, peer-review evaluation, rewards, and curiosity-driven research are therefore in tension with income-generating market-like activities. Merit and rewards are increasingly being interpreted in terms of entrepreneurial activities. The devolution of budget responsibility to operating unit level threatens the concept of the university as a community in which individuals are primarily oriented toward the greater good of the organization. Undergraduate education in public research universities has declined as a result of the reduction of block grants, which are being expended more in market-oriented activities. Consequently, teaching and research are fragmented (Clark, 1997).

Faculty and disciplines far from the market are marginalized, as are concerns for the public sphere. The professional autonomy of faculty is infringed, and intellectual property rights have been eroded and commodified (Polster and Newson, 1998). Research shows that as a result of managerialism academics feel excluded from decision making and perceive that the academic function of the university has been made secondary to managerial imperatives (Currie and Vidovich, 1998). Although many universities have complied with these globalization trends, others have subverted these policy directives.

THE POLITICAL ECONOMIES OF FRANCE AND NORWAY

In general, European countries have not moved as far to the "Right" in their economic policies as has the United States (Kim and Fording, 1998). However, variations among these countries will arise, depending upon their current economic situation and the political party in power.

The two European countries under consideration, namely France and Norway, are more socialist in their political orientation in 1999, and they have higher levels of public sector expenditure per gross domestic product than the United States. The French and Norwegian governments have maintained a commitment to the welfare state, although certain aspects of this have disappeared in these societies. They both are moving toward the "Third Way," which is between the dogmas of free-market capitalism and big-government regulation. French prime minister Lionel Jospin (a Social Democrat) has adopted a managerial socialist administration that retains the principle of strong state regulation. As Barry James writes, "While being prepared to accept some ideas from the right, such as the privatization of state industries, Mr. Jospin has derided capitalism as 'a force that moves, but which does not know where it is heading' " (James, 1998, p. 1). It is, he believes, "the state's role to supply the necessary direction and protect fundamental values of egalitarianism and justice" (1998, p. 1). Jospin is quoted as saying recently that without the guiding hand of the state, there would be "an explosion of inequality, the erosion of the social bond, the menacing of our environment, the enfeebling of our cultural wealth, the loss of long-term perspectives" (James, 1998, pp. 1 and 7). Further, the French have a strong antipathy toward the Americans and their attempts to impose their model on the world, as evident in the response by French president Jacques Chirac to United States president Bill Clinton's advice on following the "American Model": "Would France strive to be like America? No, of course not. Each country has its own model" (*Time*, 1997, p. 37).

Norway is one of the very few countries in the world where public revenues exceed public spending. It is one of the few countries in western Europe that has voted not to join the European Union (EU). While the "no" vote has increased in each referendum, more recent polls are, however, indicating a shift in this opinion. Tjeldvoll and Holtet (1998) suggest that this should not be seen as a wish to withdraw from Europe but more likely an indication of Norway's self-confidence and a wish to preserve its culture. As stated by Tjeldvoll, "Just before the year 2000 and under the strong influence of a globalized market economy ideology, Norway is still a distinct welfare state. Education for all from kindergarten to university is free of charge and tertiary education is open to all who quality" (1998, p. 1).

The Norwegian Labor Party (equivalent to Social Democrats) is leaning in the same direction as the social democratic governments of France, Great Britain, and Germany, which would in many ways be parallel to the "Third Way." In 1999 the Labor Party was in opposition in Norway, and the country was administered by a minority government of three center parties, which had to rely increasingly on support from the Conservative Party and the extreme right-wing Progressive Party. Although there was still a high level of political consensus about welfare state principles, the largely informal coalition of the Conservative, Progressive, and Labor Parties continuously pushed in the direction of neoliberal market reforms. Interestingly, they were all in favor of joining the EU, which signals a change in policy. A poll taken in December 1998 showed, for the first time, a clear majority of the population in favor of joining the EU. Another change has been indicated by the minister of education in the minority government, who has given public signals that he prefers the "American Model." This may lead to greater privatization of universities and greater competition among universities in which tenure is more difficult to obtain.

DEMOCRATIC TRADITIONS IN FRENCH AND NORWEGIAN UNIVERSITIES

France's change toward greater participation in university governance originated in the 1968 student revolt. The 1968 *Loi d'Orientation* (Loi Faure or Law Giving Guiding Principles for Higher Education) created a democratic system in which all levels of staff and students participate in representative councils, including some external representatives from the community. These representative councils sit as one body to choose the university president, who is elected for five years and cannot serve a subsequent term.

With the first left-wing coalition in the history of the Fifth Republic in 1981, France received a government committed to democratization and participation as well as to reforming higher education. The government wanted to extend the research base, open the university to its region, and strengthen links to industry. The 1984 *Loi sur l'enseignement supérieure* (Loi Savary or Higher Education Law) regulated the governance and management structure of universities and introduced the concept of contracts concerning educational activities, which institutions sign with government. The composition of councils and the democratic process are stipulated in this law. The 1984 Higher Education Law also gave autonomy to universities and independence regarding research activities to researchers. This legislative framework provides the foundation for strengthening the democratization of French higher education.

In Norway during the mid-1960s, the process leading toward a more democratic decision making system began at the University of Oslo. This occurred before the 1968–69 student revolts as a result of an ongoing process initiated some years before. An interesting aspect of this process of democratization was that it was initiated by professors, rather than by students or other groups traditionally excluded from decision making. In 1972, professorial autocracy was replaced by a governance structure based on elected boards.

Other universities adopted a similar system, and in 1990 a new law incorporated all four universities and six colleges. The OECD review team, which visited Norwegian universities in October 1995, concluded that they were moving in line with international trends. The reviewers noted that "The recent legislation has resulted in streamlined governance arrangements, greater external participation in smaller governing bodies and increased executive power (OECD, 1997, p. 10). Norway now has a structure that blends executive power with its democratic tradition.

Case Studies of Avignon and Oslo

This section reports on findings of a study investigating a range of globalization practices affecting universities. In September and October 1998, Jan Currie and Arild Tjeldvoll interviewed academics and administrators at the Universities of Avignon and Oslo.[6] We focus in this chapter on responses to one question: Would you like to keep the value of democratically electing the president/rector, deans, and heads of departments?

Norwegian respondents were overwhelmingly in favor of democratic elections (100 percent). No one said that they would prefer appointed positions. All the French, except one, wanted elections. The one exception was a younger academic who favored appointing the president and heads of departments but still wanted to elect deans. A few respondents in both countries were in favor of democratic elections but also supported some changes to the current system in the areas of term of office and voter composition. Some noted the need for more training for leaders and for more decision making power to be given to those elected. The reasons given for wanting elections were varied. The following responses from both Avignon and Oslo academics indicate some of the underlying values that can be maintained in a democratic tradition:

> The university has survived for centuries and one of its strengths is its democracy. It ensures that there is a rotation of leadership within the institution. (Oslo 828)

> We should be able to have our say in our choice of leaders. This is important, that we are able to choose—we don't want just anybody presiding over us. Obviously, people don't always agree, but it is important that everybody gets to participate. (Avignon 921)

> I want to elect my leader because I want to know what kind of solidarity that person has with me. I want to know what kind of values that person has. (Oslo 805)

> Absolutely, I believe that this is the best way of functioning for an establishment like the university. This way of thinking is part of our history in France, we have had a democratic society for the last two hundred years so this is really part and parcel of our mentality. Our culture has an absolute, deeply founded respect for the system of democratic elections. People don't like the idea of having their leaders designated for them, apart from in the private sector, where money intervenes on all levels. If somebody is elected by his or her peers, this generally inspires a climate of mutual trust and respect. This gives a guarantee of their qualities. (Avignon 930)

Other respondents who favored democratic elections remarked on the need to rotate leadership, maintain a sense of solidarity, and ensure that policy was debated in the university community. They felt it was important to have someone who was familiar with the institution and someone of their own choice. Those who were elected spoke of it as being a positive starting point because it was an indication that they were accepted and not imposed upon the faculty. These responses indicate that faculty in these two universities in France and Norway have resisted the global trend toward increased managerialism.

In weighing the benefits and disadvantages of managerialist versus democratic governance, we draw from interviews in these two universities and in an American and an Australian university, which summarize the differences between the two practices of appointed versus elected deans. Appointed deans within a managerialist approach allow a free market for talent based on meritocracy. It allows new ideas and new "blood" to enter the university. It entails choosing a charismatic, inspirational leader—someone who can take charge and make tough management decisions. It tends to reflect a top-down, hierarchical, managerial structure. Decision making is streamlined into the hands of an autocratic few and tends toward secretiveness. Staff are not as involved and often do not know the direction of the organization. They tend to become more cynically alienated from the organization.

By contrast, elected deans within a collegial/democratic approach are leaders who are first among equals and are known quantities. On the other hand, they may be too well known and can be manipulated by friends and can destroy enemies. The limited term of elected deans (usually five years in Europe) means they have to return to previous positions among peers. This curtails the practice of destroying one's enemies. It allows for a rotation of leadership and a change of policies. Collegial decision making puts control into the hands of colleagues, or at least allows for democratic representation. Information flows more quickly, and workers feel involved. A more collective/community feeling and a desire to work for the goals of the organization are developed.

In determining which type of governance system to develop, there have been some interesting studies that suggest that a mixture of managerialism and collegiality can serve universities best. For example, de Boer, Denters, and Goedegebuure (1998) describe the Dutch pre-1998 system as a mixed system of leadership that may bring the best results. Their analysis suggests that while academic democracy is not all virtuous, the loss of participatory decision making processes is equally unfortunate.

Clearly, the neoliberal agenda will persist in universities in the near future. In this climate, leaders need to balance traditional academic values with pragmatic management. University leaders may need to be more cautious in adopting the crudest forms of managerialism and entrepreneurial practices so that democratic participation remains strong and curiosity-driven research remains an integral part of universities along with applied and community action research. The main challenge, as Rice (1998) recently put it, is to develop a "bilingualism" between the contrasting managerial and collegiate cultures within institutions. This implies instituting efficient management and entrepreneurship without succumbing wholesale to managerialism and entrepreneurialism, in which market assumptions and values dominate.

THE POLITICAL ECONOMY OF SOUTH AFRICA

Given its particularly politicized history, South Africa represents a vivid case of the challenge faced by all countries to respond to global pressures and simultaneously achieve a more equitable distribution of wealth and opportunity. It thus provides an interesting comparative case in which to observe these political economic tensions as a backdrop to understanding their impact on higher education policy.

South Africa completed in 1999 the first five years of its post-apartheid history. Since the 1990 unbanning of political opponents to apartheid and the release of

Nelson Mandela and other political prisoners, and the first democratic election in 1994, a progressive constitution and public policy framework have emerged to redress the ravaging injustices of apartheid. Simultaneously, South Africa has gradually reinserted itself in the international context, grappling with the challenges of positioning itself competitively as an emerging economy in the rapidly changing global scenario.

Given its deeply divided social order, South Africa remains a dual but interdependent society shaped by apartheid and largely determined along racial lines. This dual social structure consists of a relatively advanced, globally interconnected political economy dominated by the mainly white rich minority, which is linked to a relatively underdeveloped stratum comprising the poor, mainly black, majority. The former has depended on the latter in many critical ways for its existence and reproduction (Wolpe, 1995). Characteristic of this dual society is the extreme disparity in advantage and power between the rich minority and the poor majority. The tension in South Africa's macroeconomic policy manifests in its two-fold development imperative of simultaneously achieving global competitiveness and addressing the basic needs of its impoverished majority through the redistribution of wealth and opportunity.

Given the pronounced socialist leaning of the ruling African National Congress (ANC) during the years of its anti-apartheid resistance, the unanticipated moderateness of its current macroeconomic policy may appear somewhat anomalous. This bears testimony to the persuasive power of the neoliberal global consensus. Following the reforms of the old regime during the late 1980s, the new government has initiated a voluntary structural adjustment program designed to create a conducive climate for foreign investment, win World Bank and IMF favor, and assuage the concerns of local business. It has therefore positioned itself squarely within the prevailing neoliberal paradigm of unfettered capital flows and monetarist fiscal restraint, while retaining a broad moral and political commitment to the redistribution of wealth and opportunity and reconstructive development.

This duality manifests in two strongly contested and contradictory policies. The first is the redistributive development path embodied in the government's 1994 Reconstruction and Development Program (RDP)—an integrated program aimed simultaneously at meeting the basic needs of the people, thereby kickstarting growth through redistribution and sustaining this growth through the export-led high-tech competitive engagement in the global. The second path prioritizes globally oriented development and is premised on structural adjustments and redistribution through growth. It is linked to the government's 1996 Growth, Employment and Redistribution (GEAR) strategy, which aims at job creation through a projected growth rate based on increasing foreign investment. It is consistent with World Bank macroeconomic principles of budget deficit reduction and restricted social spending. To date, GEAR targets have not been reached, apart from reduction of the budget deficit.

While there has been constant rhetorical commitment to the RDP goals of meeting basic needs, not only have there been severe delivery problems and organizational haphazardness in grounding the RDP, but deep contradictions have also emerged in the formulation and implementation of macroeconomic and fiscal policy measures. For example, while offering relief to the low-income groups, the proportional tax burden has increasingly shifted from companies to individuals in order to create conducive conditions for investment.

These developments represent significant ideological shifts in government policy from its previously more unconditional commitments to the redistribution of wealth and have severely strained its alliance with trade unions and the South African Communist Party. In particular, recent sustained opposition by its partners to the GEAR strategy has been premised on the argument that it fundamentally favors the global development path at the expense of RDP concerns and the interests of the poor. The GEAR policy has come under sustained pressure from its alliance partners and others. Even the Church has opposed GEAR on the grounds that it does little to assist the poor. The ANC has subsequently agreed to modify GEAR targets but remains committed to its framework.

Clearly, South Africa must follow a "Third Way" complementary development path that accommodates global and redistributive concerns. Achieving this implies demonstrating considerable political will in critically challenging the neoliberal orthodoxy and justifying a strong role for the state in regulating transnational capital flows and in fulfilling its redistributive agenda. The state must actively drive basic development to complement the private sector's role in driving growth.

Higher Education Policy in South Africa

These wider tensions are embedded in emerging higher education policy in South Africa, which has undergone a fundamental restructuring. The 1996 report of the National Commission on Higher Education (NCHE, 1996) provided the framework for the reconstruction of the system and laid the foundation for the 1997 White Paper on higher education and the subsequent Higher Education Act. This framework borrows heavily from international policies on financing, quality assurance, and national qualifications models, mainly from the United Kingdom, Australia, and New Zealand. The new policy framework establishes the foundation for a unified, equitable, well-planned, program-based system. It aims to overcome the prevailing mismatch between higher education output and the demands of economic and social development, to ensure quality; reduce wasteful duplication through planning; and redress the severe race, gender, geographic, and institutional inequalities that are the legacy of apartheid.

Tensions among higher education stakeholders were high during the formulation of the NCHE report and the subsequent Green, Draft, and Final White Papers on Higher Education Transformation (Subotzky, 1998a). Mirroring the broader macroeconomic tensions outlined above, the main contestations were around the emphasis on the role of higher education in contributing toward global competitiveness as opposed to serving the basic needs of the poor majority. Significantly, the final White Paper shows numerous references to and a balanced consideration of both global and redistributive development priorities. According to the White Paper, higher education must "contribute to and support the process of societal transformation outlined by the RDP, with its compelling vision of people-driven development leading to the building of a better quality of life for all" (Department of Education, 1997, p. 7). It must also "provide the labor market, in a knowledge-driven and knowledge dependent society, with the ever-changing high-level competencies and expertise necessary for the growth and prosperity of a modern economy" (Department of Education, 1997, p. 7).

However, without exploring the basis upon which reconstructive community development can be institutionally operationalized, these goals remain unresolved, contradictory challenges. While numerous accounts in the literature characterize the new organizational and epistemological features of the "market" university, policy debates are relatively silent on the corresponding features of the reconstructive development function of higher education. A recent review of trends in the literature on *Higher Education and the Public Good* (Educational Resource and Information Center, ERIC, 1996, p. 1) suggests that "economic development is most represented in the literature, with political and social development significantly less discussed." New ways, it is suggested, "for higher education to support these goals regionally or locally—for example, through service learning or action research—should be studied."

NEW CONCERNS ABOUT THE CONTRIBUTION OF HIGHER EDUCATION TO THE PUBLIC GOOD

Renewed interest in the contribution of higher education to the public good and community development is part of a growing worldwide concern for recapturing the broader social purpose of higher education in the light of globalization practices. In response to evidence of the widening disparity between conventional academic practices and societal needs, the role of universities in fostering the public good has come under rigorous scrutiny recently (Fairweather, 1996; Tierney, 1997). This concern has been accompanied by a new emphasis on the policy dimension of research, establishment of collaborative linkages with government and the private sector, and reappraisal of the service and outreach function of higher education (Terenzini, 1996; Keller, 1998).

In a similar vein, Braskamp and Wergin (1997, p. 62) argue that, given the degree of social fragmentation in the environment, "higher education today has an opportunity unique in its history to contribute to our society." Despite the numerous roles that higher education has played in the progress of society, in

Boyer's words, universities are "increasingly viewed as a place where students get credentialed and faculty get tenured, while the overall work of the academy does not seem particularly relevant to the nation's most pressing civic, social, economic and moral problems" (Boyer, as quoted in Braskamp and Wergin, 1997, p. 62). There is increasing pressure to bridge the gap between higher education and society and "to become active partners in addressing and solving our social ills and be more competitive internationally" (Boyer, 1996, as quoted in Braskamp and Wergin, 1997, p. 62). Higher education institutions now need to "reorient themselves as active partners with parents, teachers, principals, community advocates, business leaders, community agencies, and general citizenry" (1997, p. 64). Higher education, in the view of these authors, will enhance its usefulness to society by "becoming a forum for critical community dialogues, by advancing practice-based knowledge and policies as well as upholding the creation of theory-based knowledge, and by utilizing faculty expertise in new ways—in short, by forming new social relationships" (Braskamp and Wergin, 1997, p. 64).

COMMUNITY SERVICE PARTNERSHIPS AND COMMUNITY SERVICE LEARNING

As part of these contemporary concerns, the community service partnership model—and within this, community service learning—has emerged as an important means by which higher education institutions can directly serve social development. Like the process of globalization, the idea of service in higher education is not new. It is, however, receiving much more intense focus currently as a policy option. Most institutions' mission statements identify community service as part of the universally recognized tripartite function of the modern university, namely, teaching, research, and outreach. Nonetheless, only recently has the partnership model provided a systematic operational basis for pursuing this goal as an institutionwide initiative that combines community development and academic benefits.

Community service learning (CSL) has grown rapid recently, especially in the United States (Bringle and Hatcher, 1996; Ward and Wolf-Wendel, 1997). CSL is defined as "a form of experiential learning in which students engage in activities that address human and community needs together with structured opportunities intentionally designed to promote student learning and development" (Jacoby in Ward and Wolf-Wendel, 1997, p. 1). Its distinguishing feature is the systematic integration of community service into the formal curriculum. CSL is closely associated with problem-based learning, the hallmark of innovative teaching, especially in the Health Sciences.

Claimed positive outcomes for students include more effective learning, especially with regard to lifelong learning; the linking of theory and practice; enhanced career goals; improved civic responsibility; changed perspectives on social issues and appreciation of others' cultural and socioeconomic situations and personal efficacy; exposure to other cultures and race groups; and critical reflection upon own attitudes (Perold, 1998). While these benefits are of course intrinsically valuable, they should ideally be integrated into a social change and partnership model to contribute also toward community development and integrate research activities. Recently therefore, greater emphasis has been placed on the community partnership model, of which CSL comprises a key component. This model involves the academic institution, community structures, and service providers (public, private, nongovernmental organizations, and community-based organizations) in a three-way partnership. Ideally, the concern is not only with the effectiveness of student learning and research opportunities, but also for community development, academic staff research, and curriculum development. The notion of partnership is therefore central to achieving these goals. As in all social relations, partnerships are vulnerable to unequal power relations. Within these "politics of partnerships," the interests of one partner (especially the academy) easily dominates. The ideal is to recognize and mediate the partners' differences in identities, roles, capacities, and interests through relations of mutuality and reciprocity. This implies building capacity toward the joint ownership, design, control, and evaluation of community service programs so that the interests and needs of all three collaborating partners are addressed.

Where successful, a partnership grounded on mutual relations provides reciprocal benefits. In the model, integrated service, learning, and research activities occur at an academic/service site located in the community. Context-rich opportunities are provided at these sites for experiential learning and applications-driven research (for students and staff alike, the latter both in disciplinary fields and in experiential learning), curriculum development, and community development. Service is enhanced and enriched by cutting-edge research findings.

In practice, however, this is a highly illusive ideal. A recent discourse analysis of the current literature on CSL indicates an alarming preoccupation with student outcomes and institutional interests (Ward and Wolf-Wendel, 1997) at the expense of symmetry, reciprocity, and mutuality in partnerships. The value of CSL appears to be perceived predominantly as a vehicle for achieving academic aims and bolstering the interests and power base of the academy rather than for fulfilling the goal of changing the social order.

Implications for Higher Education Institutions

To achieve the partnership ideal, therefore, a fundamental shift is necessary for academics from seeing the role of the university as providing applied knowledge to help for the solution of problems, to one in which the university is jointly responsible for social change in partnership with relevant bodies in the community. Under this new social contract the institution becomes an advocate for social justice (Braskamp and Wergin, 1997).

Based on experience in education outreach projects at the University of Illinois at Chicago (UIC), Braskamp and Wergin highlight lessons for higher education institutions in engaging in collaborative work within community partnerships.

Collaborative work often creates a conflict of institutional cultures; that political and community groups want to use the prestige of the university to enhance their agenda; that faculty members often have less *experiential* knowledge of the problem context than do teachers and reformers but compensate by using their theoretical perspectives; that failed experiments outside the academy are more visible than a failed experiment in a laboratory; that compromise is essential; that new forms of communication are needed to reach different audiences; that partnerships can be intellectually exciting and challenging; that faculty scholarship is enhanced; and that continuous support is needed for long-term impact. (Braskamp and Wergin, 1997, pp. 77–78)

They argue that the success of such ventures depends on substantial reorientation of the mission and focus of higher education, particularly at research universities.

These changes must begin, they contend, with a new social contract between higher education and the greater community, of which there is already growing evidence. Renegotiating the social contract implies dispelling the public perception that academic freedom is a smokescreen for furthering the private benefit of the individual and institutional interests. The role of the modern university is to become more responsive to social problems and function as a forum for the expression and negotiation of social discourse. Both of these functions have clear implications for the nature of faculty work and the focus of academic leadership.

While there are greater demands to address social ills, the academy remains currently on the one hand increasingly preoccupied with the market ethos, and on the other still largely inwardly turned toward maximizing quantifiable and rewarding publications output, which is the currency of conventional academic practice. This separation of the academy from society "has been conscious, deliberate, and defining" (Braskamp and Wergin, 1997, p. 80). Without including communities in defining research goals and agendas, higher education institutions "will become victimized by their own myopia" (1997, p. 80) or, we may add, narrowly market-oriented.

Encouragingly, against the tendency toward the increasing commercialization and privatization of faculty work Braskamp and Wergin identify the emergence of "public intellectuals." These activist academics want to influence public policy, notably by publishing in nonacademic publications, and integrate societal concerns into their personal and professional lives by establishing the social utility of research and by emphasizing new particularist epistemologies by which truth should not be separated from personal experience. Thus, "to the extent that the emerging perspectives of scholarship are both more political and more relevant, they parallel, without necessarily paying homage to, social forces pushing for change" (Braskamp and Wergin, 1997, p. 83).

A key insight is that "through partnerships, the research and instructional agenda can be intricately connected to the communities outside the academy" (Braskamp and Wergin, 1997, p. 87). This provides the principal means of linking academic freedom with social accountability and responsibility, of escaping the insular sanctuary of the academy and addressing the clamoring demands made on it by its social partners. In this way, the function of the modern university will be met: to be a "very active partner in shaping its social relationship with society, being responsive while retaining its core purposes and standards" (1997, p. 89). Braskamp and Wergin's account thus corroborates the partnership model as an alternative to the marketization of higher education.

Adopting the partnership model has clear implications and benefits for higher education. Its success depends on substantial shifts not only at the mission level, but also in terms of epistemological attitudes and academic practices, particularly at research universities. These changes entail a new social contract between higher education and the greater community. They thus constitute a complementary alternative to entrepreneurialism.

DEVELOPMENTS IN COMMUNITY PARTNERSHIPS AND CSL IN SOUTH AFRICA

Given its political history, a strong community service ethos emerged in South Africa during the 1980s, as activist faculty attempted to link their academic pursuits to the anti-apartheid struggle and make their expertise accessible to civil society (Cooper, 1992). Given this activist tradition, the current challenge is to ensure that academic knowledge, including its local and indigenous forms, is produced and disseminated so that practice can be improved (Kraak and Watters, 1995). In this way, rigor and relevance can be linked. These, as Cooper (1992) argues, are not necessarily contradictory, as is often claimed by disciplinary purists.

Community service is currently receiving close attention, partly in response to the government's recent decision to implement community service for medical and legal graduates and partly as the consequence of the argument that "community service in higher education has the potential to contribute to the reconstruction and development goals of the new government" (Perold, 1998, p. 2).

A review of the literature as well as recent case studies (Perold and Omar, 1997; Subotzky, 1998 and 1998b) reveals an interesting array of community service programs and community service learning opportunities. These clearly are contributing toward social upliftment in diverse ways and, central to our argument throughout, constitute complementary alternatives to the entrepreneurial university. Predictably, the most developed of these programs are in the health and other professional fields, but many also involve inter- and transdisciplinary elements.

It is noteworthy that while South Africa's historically black universities are generally very poorly disposed toward functioning as entrepreneurial institutions as a direct consequence of the multiple effects of apartheid, there is evidence of excellent community-oriented programs that serve as models for community development partnerships (Subotzky, 1997 and 1998a). The missions of historically disadvantaged institutions have always been closer to community concerns, and they have had close links to the communities they serve. Academics in these institutions can potentially combine their tacit and explicit knowledge of these contexts and thus turn disadvantage into comparative advantage (Kraak, 1997; Subotzky, 1997). This is evident in an interviewee's comment in a major recent study of historically black universities (Education Policy Unit, EPU, 1997):

We try to use our disadvantages and change them into advantages . . . especially if you look at our institution in the context of the new dispensation, the RDP and so on. I think we have an ideal opportunity to use our rural environment to do relevant research. Obviously we cannot compete with [the historically white research universities of] Wits or Cape Town in nuclear physics, and I don't think we should (EPU, 1997, p. 429).

However, all institutions are strategically positioning themselves within the new and increasingly competitive higher education context. Historically white universities, and especially the Afrikaans-speaking ones (which were historically more supportive of apartheid and whose future in the new South Africa is now threatened), are developing innovative community-oriented initiatives (Subotzky, 1998b). To take one instance: the historically white Afrikaans Pretoria University has established a semirural satellite campus in 1993, about fifty kilometers north of the capital, Pretoria. Here the university applies community service learning to provide a comprehensive teaching approach in which theory and practical experience are merged. The aim is to produce graduates better equipped to meet labor market demands.

In South Africa currently, the Community–Higher Education–Service Partnerships initiative is piloting partnership projects at eight institutions with the aim of replicating the model more widely. A noteworthy aspect of this project is that it is accompanied by a leadership capacity-building program at the master's level, in which three participating partners from each sector are enrolled. The modules of the program and the assignments within them are designed not only to build the necessary capacity in the three participating organizations, but also to form part of an integrated and systematic planning framework for implementation of the pilot projects. One module involves comparative crossnational research in the form of site visits to U.S. universities where community partnerships have been well established as institutionwide initiatives.

In summary, we agree with Ward and Wolf-Wendel (1997) when they argue that the gap between "needy" communities and "knowing" campuses must be dissolved and the charitable model must be supplanted by the social change model. This model focuses on the processes of building relationships within stakeholder groups to address collaboratively root causes of complex problems.

CONCLUSION

Clearly, the pressures and challenges of globalization and their impact on higher education are here to stay. However, their effect is neither uniform nor inevitable, and, where conducive political economic and cultural conditions prevail, they can be mediated. To do this successfully, alternatives to the increasing currency of globalization practices must be identified and strengthened. In highlighting two sets of such practices, we have argued that the combination of alternatives to internal management practices and external service activities may provide institutions with viable options in this regard.

The case study findings from the two European universities show that the professoriate resists moves toward greater managerialism in the universities. There was overwhelming support for democratic decision making and a more collegial model of governance. Nevertheless, global forces are beginning to penetrate these universities in the guise of public sector reforms (quality assurance and evaluation programs). What will actually happen in France and Norway is a rather open question. Because of the strength of the democratic cultural traditions in the two countries, as well as the strong position of the university as a public institution, it may very well take considerable time to change the institutions in a managerial direction.

Developments in the community partnership model in South Africa and elsewhere corroborate our contention that this model represents a significant countertrend to the entrepreneurial university. The innovations identified in the case studies are directed toward the solution of complex development problems and clearly involve new forms of applications-driven, transdisciplinary knowledge production. In this way, they serve as important sites for actualizing the social purpose of higher education and of countering the negative impact of globalization on higher education.

Despite the emphasis placed in this chapter on the value of community partnerships as a complementary alternative to higher education–industry research partnerships, two other aspects of the function of higher education must not be neglected. These are curiosity-driven research, which needs to remain a high priority within universities, and the role of the university in providing an independent critical voice in society. Regarding the latter, the maintenance of state-funded, autonomous institutions is vital to ensure that higher education is not narrowly driven by the agendas of industry or the policy priorities of the state. These institutions have a timely and important role to play in consolidating and disseminating critical perspectives on the contradictions and uncertainties appearing in the global market paradigm. Higher education institutions need to be seen to be actively working toward a more equitable society by championing and grounding the values of democracy and social solidarity in both its internal and external practices.

NOTES

This chapter has benefited from funding from the Australian Research Council and draws on work done by Tove Kvill and Arild Tjeldvoll in Norway and Claude Lacotte in France.

1. The features of national higher education systems can only be fully explained by reference to surrounding political economic conditions (Tierney and Kempner, 1997). However, this relationship is complex and cannot be treated in any depth in the context of this chapter.

2. It is important to stress that the higher education–community partnership model is proposed as a *complementary* alternative, and not simply as a dichotomous opposite to serving market needs. Along with curiosity-driven research, meeting market needs is undeniably an important function of contemporary higher education. However, this overwhelmingly favors selective private sector interests, which are dominant under prevailing neoliberal conditions. There is therefore an unavoidable ideological tension between managerial market-oriented higher education practices and those which foster participatory governance and address community concerns. Furthermore, promoting the community partnership model does not imply crudely championing equity over efficiency. A distinction can therefore be drawn between "entrepreneurship" and "entrepreneurialism." The first refers to efficient and innovative financial management measures such as cost reduction and diversified sources of income including the marketing, where appropriate, of academic services. This is not necessarily in conflict with democratic practices. Indeed, good management is a prerequisite for achieving democratic goals. The second refers to the dominance of market interests and managerial practices that marginalize democratic values and related internal and external practices.

3. This discussion benefits from the extensive work of Fred W. Riggs in developing a Home Page on the Internet on the concept of globalization and its discussion at a roundtable at the International Sociological Association World Sociology Congress in Montreal in July 1998 <http://www2.hawaii.edu/~fredr/glotexts.htm>.

4. This was a search of titles using "global" in the Social Science Citation Index by Jim Quigley on behalf of Henry Teune, April 1998, <http://www2.hawaii.edu/~fredr/glotexts.htm>. This number of hits represents a relatively high number of journal articles using "global" as a key term over that period of time.

5. The recent turmoil in the global financial market, which had deleterious effects on emerging economies, including South Africa, bears testimony to the vulnerability of developing countries to the damaging effects of hostile and manipulative short-term currency speculation.

6. Jan Currie interviewed all the respondents at the University of Avignon and most at the University of Oslo, and Arild Tjeldvoll made contacts with respondents and did several of the interviews at the University of Oslo. Claude Lacotte arranged the interviews at University of Avignon and translated the documents as well as organized the transcription

of all the interviews from French into English. Four interviews at the University of Avignon were done in English and the rest in French; all the interviews at the University of Oslo were done in English.

The interviewees comprised ten academics from the natural and physical sciences; ten from the social sciences; and ten from professional areas such as education, applied languages, business, and law in each university. Some of these were in elected positions as deans, heads of departments, vice presidents/pro-rectors, and president. In addition, at the University of Avignon, a retired secretary-general and the current secretary-general were interviewed. Those interviewed ranged from professors to lecturers (or their equivalent ranks in each country) and were a mixture of men and women (almost an equal number of each at the University of Oslo and slightly more males than females at the University of Avignon).

REFERENCES

Arrighi, Giovanni. 1998 (March). Globalization and the Rise of East Asia: Lessons from the Past, Prospects for the Future. *International Sociology*, vol. 13, no. 1, pp. 59–77.

Braskamp, Larry, and Jon F. Wergin. 1997. Universities and the New Social Contract. In William G. Tierney (ed.), *The Responsive University: Restructuring for High Performance*. Baltimore: Johns Hopkins University Press, pp. 62–91.

Bringle, Robert G., and Julie A. Hatcher. 1996. Implementing Service Learning in Higher Education. *Journal of Higher Education*, vol. 67, no. 2, pp. 221–39.

Chomsky, Noam. 1997 (May 27). Neoliberalism and Global Order: Doctrine and Reality. Seminar paper presented at the Centre for African Studies, University of Cape Town.

Clark, Burton R. 1997. Common Problems and Adaptive Responses in the Universities of the World: Organizing for Change. *Higher Education Policy*, vol. 10, nos. 3/4, pp. 291–95.

———. 1998. *Creating Entrepreneurial Universities: Organizational Pathways of Transformation*. Oxford: Pergamon/Elsevier Science.

Cooper, David. 1992. Extension Service Work at University. *Transformation*, vol. 18, pp. 139–48.

Currie, Jan, and Leslie Vidovich. 1998 (July 12–17). Globalization and Australian Universities: Policies and Practices. Paper presented at the World Congress of Comparative Education Societies (WCCES), Cape Town.

De Boer, Harry, Bas Denters, and Leo Goedegebuure. 1998 (Winter). Dutch Disease or Dutch Model? An Evaluation of the Pre-1998 System of Democratic University Government in the Netherlands. *Policy Studies Review*, vol. 15, no. 4, pp. 37–50.

Department of Education. 1997 (August). *Education White Paper 3: A Program for the Transformation of Higher Education*. Pretoria: Government Gazette No. 18207.

Dill, David D. 1997. Markets and Higher Education: An Introduction. *Higher Education Policy*, vol. 10, nos. 3–4, pp. 167–85.

Education Policy Unit (EPU), University of the Western Cape. 1997. *The Enhancement of Graduate Programmes and Research Capacity at the Historically Black Universities* (Final Research Report). Bellville, South Africa.

Educational Resource and Information Center (ERIC). 1996. Higher Education and the

Public Good. *Trends: Higher Education and the Public Good.* <http://www.gwu.edu/~eriche/library/public/htm>.

Fairweather, James. 1996. *Faculty Work and Public Trust: Restoring the Value of Teaching and Public Service in American Academic Life.* Needham Heights, MA: Allyn and Bacon.

Fischer, Stanley. 1998. Lessons from a Crisis. *The Economist,* October. <http://www.economist.co.uk/editorial/freeforall/current/sf1142.htm>

Frank, Andre Gunther. 1998. *ReOrient: Global Economy in the Asian Age.* Los Angeles: University of California Press.

Gibbons, Michael, Camille Limoges, Helga Nowotny, Simon Schwartzman, Peter Scott, and Martin Trow. 1994. *The New Production of Knowledge.* London: Sage.

Hanlon, Joe. 1998 (June 23). The World Bank Speech That Knocked Down Every Pillar, *Electronic Mail and Guardian.* <http://www.mg.co.za/mg/news/98june2/23june-worldbank.htm>.

Henry, Miriam, Robert Lingard, Fazal Rizvi, and Sandra Taylor. 1997. Globalization, the State and Education Policy Making. In Sandra Taylor, Fazal Rizvi, Bob Lingard, and Miriam Henry (eds.), *Educational Policy and the Politics of Change.* London: Routledge, pp. 54–77.

Heydebrand, Wolf. 1997. Globalization and the Rule of Law at the End of the Twentieth Century. In *1997 European Yearbook of Sociology of Law.* Milan: Giuffre.

Hirst, Paul, and Grahame F. Thompson. 1996. *Globalization in Question: The International Economy and the Possibilities of Governance.* Cambridge: Polity Press.

James, Barry. 1998 (September 25). The Elusive "Third Way" Europe's Socialists Rarely Agree on Definition. *Herald International Tribune,* pp. 1 and 7.

Keller, George. 1998. Does Higher Education Research Need Revisions? *The Review of Higher Education,* vol. 21, no. 3, pp. 267–78.

Kim, HeeMim, and Richard C. Fording. 1998. Voter Ideology in Western Democracies, 1946–1989. *European Journal of Political Research,* vol. 33, pp. 73–97.

Koc, Marc. 1993. La Globalización como Discurso. *Cuadernos Agrarios,* no 7, pp. 9–22.

Kraak, Andre. 1997. Globalization, Changes in Knowledge Production, and the Transformation of Higher Education. In Nico Cloete, Johan Muller, Malegapuru W. Makgoba, and Donald Ekong (eds.), *Knowledge, Identity and Curriculum Transformation in Africa.* Cape Town: Maskew Miller Longman, pp. 51–76.

———, and Kathy Watters. 1995. Investigating New Knowledge Production: A Western Cape Higher Education Case Study. Paper commissioned by Taskgroup 2 of the National Commission on Higher Education of South Africa.

Lingard, Robert, and Fazal Rizvi. 1998. Globalization, the OECD, and Australian Higher Education. In Jan Currie and Janice Newson (eds.), *Universities and Globalization: Critical Perspectives.* Thousand Oaks, CA: Sage, pp. 257–73.

Mander, Jerry, and Edward Goldsmith (eds.). 1996. *The Case against the Global Economy.* San Francisco: Sierra Club Books.

Marais, Hein. 1998 (September 25). Challenging the Free Market Dogma. *Weekly Mail and Guardian.* <http://wn.apc.org/wmail/issues/980925/NEWS54.htm>.

Martin, Hans-Peter, and Harald Schumann. 1997. *The Global Trap: Globalization and the Assault on Democracy and Prosperity.* Pretoria: HSRC Publishers.

National Commission on Higher Education (NCHE). 1996. A Framework for Transformation. Report of the National Commission on Higher Education. Pretoria, South Africa. Organization for Economic Cooperation and Development (OECD). 1997 (April). *Thematic Review of the First Years of Tertiary Education. Country Note: Norway.* Paris: OECD.

———. 1998a. *Open Markets Matter: The Benefits of Trade and Investment Liberalization.* Paris: OECD.

———. 1998b. *Redefining Tertiary Education.* Paris: OECD.

Orr, Liesl. 1997. Globalisation and the Universities: Towards the "Market University"? *Social Dynamics,* vol. 23, no. 1, pp. 42–64.

Perold, Helene. 1998. Community Service in Higher Education: Final Report. Johannesburg: Joint Education Trust.

———, and Rachmat Omar. 1997. Community Service in Higher Education: A Concept Paper. Johannesburg: Joint Education Trust.

Polster, Claire, and Janice Newson. 1998 (July 12–17). Re-claiming our Centre: Towards a Robust Defense of Academic Autonomy. Paper presented at the World Congress of Comparative Education Societies (WCCES), Cape Town.

Rice, Eugene. 1998 (November 4–7). *Where Love and Need Are One: The Changing Character of Faculty Work.* Keynote address to the annual conference of the Association for the Study of Higher Education, Miami, Florida.

Riggs, Fred, and Teune, Henry. 1998. The Concept of Globalization. Internet, <http://www2.hawaii.edu/~fredr/glotexts.htm>.

Robertson, Roland. 1992. *Globalization: Social Theory and Global Culture.* London: Sage.

Sachs, Jeffrey. 1998 (September 12). Making it Work, *The Economist,* <http://www.economist.com/tfs/archive_tframeset.html>.

Slaughter, Sheila, and Larry L. Leslie. 1997. *Academic Capitalism: Politics, Policies and the Entrepreneurial University.* Baltimore: Johns Hopkins University Press.

Smyth, John. 1994. A Policy Analysis of Higher Education Reform in Australia in the Context of Globalization. *Melbourne Studies in Education,* vol. 35, pp. 39–72.

Subotzky, George. 1997. Meeting the Dual Demands of Global Competitiveness and Redistributive Development: Constraints and Opportunities for the Historically Black Universities. In Nelleke Bak (ed.), *Going for the Gap: Reconstituting the Educational Realm—Kenton 1997.* Cape Town: Juta, pp. 119–34.

———. 1998a (July 12). Beyond Globalisation and the Entrepreneurial University: The Potential Role of South Africa's Historically Disadvantaged Institutions in Meeting the Imperatives of Reconstruction and Development. Paper presented at the World Congress of Comparative Education Societies (WCCES), Cape Town. Forthcoming in *International Review of Education.*

———. 1998b (November 4–7). Alternatives to the Entrepreneurial University: New Modes of Knowledge Production in Community Service Programs. Paper presented at the Annual ASHE-International Conference, Miami, Florida. Forthcoming in *Higher Education.*

Terenzini, Patrick. 1996. Rediscovering Roots: Public Policy and Higher Education Research. *The Review of Higher Education,* vol. 20, no. 1, pp. 5–13.

Tierney, William G. (ed.) 1997. *The Responsive University: Restructuring for High Performance.* Baltimore: Johns Hopkins University Press.

Tierney, William G., and Ken Kempner (eds.). 1997. *The Social Role of Higher Education.* New York: Garland.

Time Magazine. 1997 (July 7). Special Report on Globalization, p. 37.

Tjeldvoll, Arild. 1998 (March 18–22). Towards a Theory of the Service University. Paper presented to the Comparative and International Education Society (CIES) Annual Conference, State University of New York, Buffalo.

———, and Kirsten Holtet. 1998. A Service University in a Service Society: The Oslo Case. *Higher Education*, vol. 35, pp. 27–48.

Ward, Kelly, and Lisa Wolf-Wendel. 1997 (November). A Discourse Analysis of Community-Based Learning: Moving from "I" to "We." Paper presented at the Annual Conference of the Association for the Study of Higher Education (ASHE), Albuquerque, New Mexico.

Wolpe, Harold. 1995. The Debate on University Transformation in South Africa: The Case of the Western Cape. *Comparative Education*, vol. 31, no. 2, pp. 275–92.

8

Globalization of the Community College Model: Paradox of the Local and the Global

Rosalind Latiner Raby

Traditional four-year universities are criticized as being unable to meet the needs of a changing world, for "universities and university-level specialized institutions alone [cannot] cope with either the needs of the economy or the social demand for higher education . . . [hence] the existence of a recognized alternative to traditional universities [is] indispensable" (Cerych, 1993, p. 5). The resulting void left by the "demanteling of the sacred trust of traditional universities" (Kintzer, 1993, p. 4) is being filled by an explosion of nontraditional higher education institutions that favor higher education for the masses. More than four thousand such institutions, found in 180 countries, exist in "an amorphous field" that Kintzer (1994) consolidates under the rubric *nonuniversities*.[1] Despite the variety, the U.S. community college model remains the most emulated worldwide.

The nineteenth-century community college model, German Volkhochschulen, inspired formalized postsecondary, pre-university institutions throughout Europe, Canada, and the United States. However, it was not until a state tripartite system was created by the 1960 California Master plan that a prototype, in which the community college became an integral part of postsecondary educational structures, emerged. As variations of this prototype multiplied, a need for a definition inspired a 1971 Organization for Economic Cooperation and Development (OECD) conference, which was attended by delegates from Great Britain, France, Norway, the United States, and Yugoslavia. The final description closely resembled the U.S. community college model (OECD, 1971). In the next two decades, numerous imitations of this definition were cultivated. Variations arose in the 1980s in Egypt, Indonesia, Malaysia, and Mexico, while 1990s examples evolved in Armenia, Colombia, Hungary, India, Israel, Kazakhstan, Russia, South Africa, Tatarstan, and Thailand.

Proliferation of community college models across time and space is directly linked to cultural, economic, and philosophical globalization processes. Globalization, in this chapter, creates a condition whereby community college models have permeated the world, but in doing so effects both universality of experience as well as localized applications. A growing global demand to confront socioeconomic issues of labor and technology training, accessibility for the mass populace, and the "intransigence of university-dominated systems" (Kintzer, 1998, p. 1) facilitated this process. It is alleged that such education ensures opportunities that lead to employment, economic development, and prosperity and can contribute toward improved social conditions (Strydom and Lategan, 1998; Kintzer, 1998, 1994, 1979; Koltai, 1993). While the value of such an education, perceived and real, is at the core of much debate, the impact of the community college model in world higher educational reform movements cannot be underestimated. This chapter explores the effects that globalization has on the growth of community college models worldwide, analyzes why it is the United States community college model that is most emulated, and explores ramifications caused by the local and global dialectic.

U.S. COMMUNITY COLLEGE MODEL CHARACTERISTICS

Emulation of U.S. community college traits has affected higher education worldwide. The U.S. model is a publicly supported two-year institution, accredited to grant short-cycle certificates, award an associate degree as the highest degree, and prepare noncertificated graduates for midlevel labor markets. Varied programs enable students to participate directly in the workforce or transfer to a university to complete a bachelor's degree. Programs include vocational, technical in-service/retraining, English/acculturation for recent immigrants, liberal arts and science academics, remedial education, and community services that directly benefit the local community. Kintzer's (1998) identified internal traits of streamlined governance; flexible requirements; output of educational opportunities; technical, vocational, and occupational short-cycle curricula; and community connections, are found, in variation, in all community college models.

All students are eligible to enroll at age seventeen, regardless of educational attainment or socioeconomic status. As such, the student population mirrors the multicultural and multiethnic mixture of the local community. In 1998, over six million students in credit courses and four million in noncredit, continuing education courses enrolled in 1,200 U.S. community colleges. This represents 45 percent of the country's higher education students and 52 percent of continuing education students. Of students attending four-year universities, 51 percent of domestic and 25 percent of international students transfer from community colleges (Raby, 1999). Although, these institutions provide a wider range of educational choices and serve a greater proportion of youth in the United States than in any other nation (Keer, 1996), it is most significant, that for the vast majority of students, community colleges are their sole venues for higher education.

GLOBALIZATION AND COMMUNITY COLLEGES

A case study of community college models underscores the effects of globalization on localized interpretations of similar policy and structural designs that counter the notion of higher education as an elitist venture intended for only the few. McLaren discerns the global and the local as "mutually constitutioned parts of contradictory social wholes" (McLaren, 1999, p. 10). As similar policies, ideals, programs, and structures transverse from country to country, community college models share common qualities. However, it is the localized application that endows the uniqueness of each model. Thus, like two sides of the same coin, reverberations from the impact of globalization are found in formation of the similar and accentuation of universality of experience derived from emergence of new systems, structures, and modalities that combine economic, political, and cultural characteristics. On the other side of the coin, globalization simultaneously heightens localized connections that accentuate singularity of experience. Both sides of the coin render positive results, as well as negative repercussions.

GLOBALIZATION TO PROMOTE A REALM OF SAMENESS: U.S. DISCOURSES

Globalization as promoting homogenization, affects two trajectories: one that embodies the U.S. model and the other, community college models abroad. Globalization, in this venue, emphasizes universal reference, the "compression of the world," (Robertson, 1992, p. 8), and increases perceptions of interconnections that support deepening economic linkages; massive population shifts; information flows; and compression of technology, capital, and popular culture. For U.S. community college models, globalization encouraged acknowledgment of Others, an essential component of the college that is reflected in global values and global educational programs (Kintzer, 1998; Raby, 1999).

Global Values

Global values affect change in content, methods, and social context of U.S. community colleges with an explicit aim to better prepare students for citizenship, that supports and is supported by a global culture. A global identity arises from knowledge and awareness that reinforces global values and which distances individuals from constraints of ethnicity/nationalism. The Stanley Foundation is influential in this area with a goal to "create a world in which shared commitment to a common good and a sense of community amidst diversity are the firm foundation for peace and security" (Gordon, 1999, p. 1). Nationwide, community colleges are encouraged to adopt the 1996 global values list, designed by the American Council on International/Intercultural Education/Stanley Foundation (ACIIE/Stanley, 1996). These values are linked to the premise that students cannot be critical thinkers without a global perspective.

Global Educational Programs

Several educational programs[2] operate within globalizing contexts with a manifest aim to reinforce homogenization. International Development/Distance Learning programs share specifics on a tangential aim of community colleges, to prepare laborers to supply a flexible global economic workforce to those abroad. Emphasis is on personal development of individuals, whose employment is increasingly affiliated with international corporations, agencies, and institutions, and who are becoming part of the new diaspora of transculturals/transnationals (Willis, Minoura, and Enloe, 1997). A covert aim is to embody a philosophical promotion of sameness, as colleges abroad are transformed to mirror U.S. models. The Community Colleges for International Development (CCID) consortium specifically enables U.S. and Canadian community colleges to share expenses, expertise, and collaboration on large-scale international projects.[3]

International development programs include bilateral agreements of various durations that consult or supply support services to international institutions to develop midlevel management, paraprofessional, occupational, vocational, technical, and English language programs. Information exchange occurs through first-hand contact via student, administrative/ faculty exchanges and apprenticeships and international distance endeavors. CCID/LITE utilizes the Internet to provide "linkages among communities of interest in interactive international education to foster and support articulation and program standards" (CCID, 1998, p. 5). A common thread among all programs is reinforcing sameness by bringing U.S. community college education to those around the world who "want to learn what we have to teach" (Eskow, 1999, p. 3).

International development programs are not imposed upon another country, but rather result from specific requests by local educators, ministry of education representatives, and local entrepreneurs. For many, the value of a U.S. community college education is a highly regarded commodity (Eskow, 1999; Kintzer, 1998; Humphrys and Koller, 1994; Cohen, 1995; King and Fersh, 1992). Six junior university colleges, based on the U.S. model, were built after a 1969 visit by Sri Lanka's minister of education. A 1980 invitation from Taiwan's Ministry of Education created linkages between Taiwanese and U.S. colleges. A 1982 Paramaribo conference, with twenty-five Suriname educators, six Caribbean ministers of education, and CCID members, resulted in sustained Caribbean transnational cooperative efforts. A visit by the president of Jilin Institute of Architecture and Civil Engineering in Changchun, China, to Humber College in Toronto linked Interior Design Programs to help students "improve their English skills and to learn western design techniques and software packages" (Larin, 1999, p. 7). Due to an immense interest to adopt the U.S. model, the American Association of Community Colleges (AACC) developed a promotion campaign for those wanting to implement the U.S. concept in their own countries. Finally, in 1998, over 1,770 educators from eighty eight countries visited CCID-member colleges to specifically learn about daily operations (CCID, 1998). No other model receives the same attention as the U.S. model; Eskow (1999, p. 1) describes this aspect of technical and academic globalization as a competition in which "the U.S. model is the only player."

A quintessential manifestation of globalization is the international contract program that utilizes defined instruction, course numbers, titles, and catalogue description of accredited U.S. courses to develop branch colleges abroad. American College in Singapore exemplifies a credit-bearing, branch campus. These ventures vary with business and societal need, yet due to overwhelming cultural, economic, and political adjustments, few sustained programs exist (Yamano and Hawkins, 1996; CCID, 1999a). Virtual branch campuses, such as the World Community College, currently provide new dimensions, with connections to the Internet that "enhance the education of local students and local businesses in the course of the new focus on globalizing the college" (Eskow, 1999, p. 3).

Two rationales explain why U.S. colleges engage in development programs that contribute toward globalization of community college models. The humanitarian rationale delineates a link between global inequalities and differential access to sociopolitical, economic, and ideological power that is complicated by variables such as class, gender, and ethnicity. Development targets distributive justice for the less privileged and often takes the form of empowerment, consciousness-raising literacy, and health and technological assistance services (Cook, 1996). Assistance becomes a means to "apply our ideals, our sense of decency and our humanitarian impulse to the repair of the world, [as] investment in development is indeed investment in prevention" (Koltai, 1993, p. 2). Examples include CCID programs at the Center for Vocational Education in Madras, the Guyana project, the Sustainable Systems Program in Romania, and the First Global Community College Nong Khai-Udon Thani in Thailand (CCID, 1999a).

The privatization rationale implies that in the venue of supply and demand, community college models export practical experience and faculty talents as a means for revenue earning. Marketing expertise thus becomes more important than humanitarian conditions that fueled the ideology (Eskow, 1999; Schugurensky and Higgins, 1996). Privatization is the driving force behind CCID Intensive English Practicum in China; Workforce Development Center in Tomsk, Russia; Sustainable Systems Program in Romania; and the Suriname Telecommunications Company venture "for the purpose of developing an educational program that is designed to benefit not only the company, but anyone in Suriname seeking educational opportunities" (CCID, 1999a). Despite evidence that many projects have not proven to be money-producing ventures as envisioned, the lure of the potential for revenue earning sustains this rationale as the means to support current projects in Eastern Europe, the Pacific Rim, and Russia.

GLOBALIZATION TO PROMOTE A REALM OF SAMENESS: WORLD DISCOURSES

Homogenizing influences of economic productivity and democratic initiatives have heightened interdependent interactions between societies, resulting in what Robertson (1992, p. 8) refers to as the "Global System of Societies." This system embodies economic, political, social, and philosophical linkages, such that no country, nor community college model, exists alone. Globalization has created a phenomenon in which community college models are continually influencing this system, as well as being influenced by it. Eskow (1989, p. 6) maintains, "the image of the 'open door college' is the self-image of the community college," one that is vulnerable to globalization proclivities because it is purposefully marketed abroad and self-generated by those abroad who view its precise traits as desirable and hence readily adaptable.

Economically, globalization links education to national productivity, although the type and structure of education vary with a country's economic growth. In many regions, there is insufficient money to support mass numbers of students to attend universities for this education, not enough programs at these universities to branch into new occupational and technological fields, few qualified secondary graduates to fill these positions, and conditions whereby many of the poor lack accesses to even secondary education. Community college models aim to fill this void by targeting nontraditional audiences for workforce preparation. Yugoslavian Vise Skoles and the St. Louis Community College, Missouri, agri-business programs and economics training programs in banking and business management at Tomsk Polytechnic Institute Workforce Development Center exemplify this process. Similarly, access to economic development inspired Hungarian educational leaders to utilize community college models to "provide improved access to low-cost, relevant, work-related training for large numbers of people" (CCID, 1999b, p. 1). Because many of these models have recently been erected, their impact has yet to be fully realized.

Philosophically, globalization imparts ideals of democratic possibilities and social reform, despite evidence that "the process of globalization is often accompanied by efforts at dedemocratization" (McLaren, 1999, p. 11). In an attempt to counter a reality of inequity, community college models promote open access and low tuition to assist students whose academic background is lacking, who cannot afford university tuition, who are denied access due to minority status, and who do not fit a traditional profile. Access in this context is not a direct link to a university, but rather toward literacy attainment and workforce and citizenship preparation.

Globalization provides not only awareness of the possibilities of these processes, but socioeconomic responses to them as well. Norway's Regional Colleges "fill undemocratic gaps between districts, generations and sexes" (Kintzer, 1979, p. 73). Likewise, the Czech Republic developed community college models, because existing "education programs are presently restricted to a small percentage of the population able to meet university entrance requirements" (CCID, 1999b, p. 1). The proposed World Community College, however, while seeking to "link far-flung community colleges together into a single worldwide college . . . [which will] open their doors to students from any nation and community in the network," (Eskow, 1975, p. 1), raises new concerns regarding equity for those with no Internet technology access.

Globalization hastened various degrees of mirroring the U.S. model, because local education may "not have the same market value, social prestige or general reception in the society as other degrees or diplomas. This may be the reason why models are made along the lines of the U.S. model" (Kintzer, 1979 p. 75; echoed in Eskow, 1999; Kintzer, 1998; Strydom and Lategan, 1998). At one extreme, programs, curriculum, and philosophical discourses are transplanted from the United States to another country, such as Yong-In Technical College in Yogin City, Korea, and the First Global Community College Nong Khai-Udon Thani in Thailand, where short-term courses in business, tourism, and technical subjects are offered to largely rural poor populations. For others, a concerted adoption of specific characteristics highlights an American-style institution, while still asserting local individualism, such as South African Community Colleges, Regional Colleges in Israel, and the Community College in Yemen. For others, a purposeful seeking of help reinforces imitations, such as the pairing of Madras Community College with Sinclair Community College in Ohio to create and support workforce skills courses, or the recent Middlesex Community College, Massachusetts, project in Cambodia, which teaches conflict resolution training (CCID, 1999a). The next century will illustrate that community college models abroad not only react to globalization tendencies, but reinforce them in the form of new, stand-alone institutions.

Community College Models

Community college models move toward convergence as four homogenizing characteristics are evident. Tables 8.1 and 8.2 delineate the variations discussed in endnote one, to which community college models conform. First, all models are postsecondary and postcompulsory, and although they are included in national educational plans, they have a curriculum, budget, and mission that expresses localized connections. As many provide accredited pre-university curricula and thus are accountable to local universities, they also must relate programs

Table 8.1 Community College Models: Program Variations

Country	Specialized Technical/ Vocational Programs	Public Support	Multi-purpose Short-Cycle Programs	Binary Short-Cycle Programs: Bridge College Secondary and University	Technical University/ Polytechnic Branches	Lifelong Learning: Literacy/ Cultural Attainment	Expanded-Postsecondary and Adult Education	Limited University Transfer
Argentina	X		X	X		X		
Australia	X	X	X					
Austria			X					
Bahamas		X	X					
Belarus		X	X		X			
Belize		X	X	X		X	X	
Britain			X	X				
Bulgaria		X					X	
Canada		X	X		X	X		regionally
China	X		X	X				
Colombia	X	X	X	X		X		
Czech Republic	X	X						
Denmark	X	X		X		X	X	
Egypt	X			X				X
El Salvador	X			X		X		
France	X	X		X		X	X	
Germany	X	X			X		X	
Greece	X	X		X				
Guyana	X			X	X			
Hungary	X		X		X			
Iceland	X	X		X				
India	X	X						
Indonesia	X					X	X	
Inner Mongolia	X							
Iran	X					X		

Country						
Ireland	X	X				
Israel	X	X				
Japan	X	X		X	X	X
Kazakhstan	X	X		X		
Kenya	X	X				
Korea	X	X				
Libya	X	X	X	X	X	X
Malaysia	X	X	X		X	
Mexico	X	X	X	X	X	X
Mauritius	X			X		
New Zealand	X	X	X	X	X	X
Norway	X	X	X	X	X	X
Pakistan	X		X	X	X	X
Russia	X (also private)		X	X		
Slovak Federal Republic	X	X	X	X	X	
Slovenia	X	X	X	X	X	
Spain	X	X	X			
Sri Lanka	X	X				
Surinam Republic	X	X	X			
Sweden	X	X	X	X	X	X
Taiwan	X	X	X	X		
Tatarstan	X	X	X	X		
Thailand	X	X		X		
Ukraine	X (also private)		X	X		
United States	X	X	X	potential	X	X
Yemen, Republic	X	X	X			

Sources: Arthur Cohen, Accommodating Postcompulsory Education Seekers around the World. *Community College Review*, vol. 21, no. 2 (1995), pp. 13–18; Frederick C. Kintzer, Higher Education Approaches the Twenty-first Century: New Perspectives on Nonuniversities. Unpublished presentation to the Nova Southeastern University, 1994, pp. 6–16; and Rosalind Latiner Raby and Norma Tarrow (eds.), *Dimensions of the Community College: International, Intercultural, and Multicultural Perspectives.* (New York: Garland, 1996), pp. 197–203.

Table 8.2 Community College Models: Model Variations

Country	Model Type	Descriptions
Argentina	7	1,500 Terciarios
Australia	2	College of Advanced Education of Victoria (CAE); Technical & Further Education Colleges (TAFEs) (120 in New South Wales)
Austria	6	Fachhochschulen
Bahamas	2;7	
Belarus	2	
Belize	2;4;7	Community College of Belize; Muffles Junior College in Belize
Britain	1;5	682 Colleges of Further Education (CFE)—part of reform move to create free postcompulsory education
Bulgaria	2;9	40 community colleges
Canada	2;4;8	Colleges of Applied Arts and Technology College. Quebec—560 d'Enseignment General et Professionnel (CEGEP), offer first-year university courses and technical-oriented courses; Alberta, influenced by U.S. model; Ontario, little emphasis on general education; British Columbia, some confer degrees with university status.
Chile	6;7;8	Collegios universitarios regionales
China	8	Vocational University; Worker's College
Colombia	7;8	Association of Colombian Universities
Czech Republic	2	Dutch Model. Czech Technical University in Prague
Denmark	3;8	
Egypt	2	Ma'had
El Salvador	7;8	Technical Institutes of Don Bosco University
France	8	Instituts Universersitaires Technologiques (IUTs)
Germany	3;5;8	20 Fachhochschulen (technical education); 900 Volkhochschulen (lifelong education)
Greece	8	
Guyana	2	
Hungary	2;8;9	Technical University of Bucharest
Iceland	5;8	
Indonesia	8	
India	2;4;6	United States Education Foundation of India; Madras Community College; Stella Maris College
Japan	2;4;8	561 Junior Colleges and 62 Technical Colleges. Nagasaka Community College—majority of students are women—major in humanities, home economics, and education; 3,152 Special Training Schools (i.e., Osaka College of Medical and High Technology; Tokyo Wild Life College)—men are majority of students—major in foreign languages, business, technology, or paramedical. 3,000 Misc. postsecondary private schools
Inner Mongolia	8	
Iran	6;8	
Ireland	6;8	
Israel	2;6	

Kazakhstan	5;8;9	
Kenya	8	15 Harambee
Korea	8	130 Technical Colleges
Libya	6;8	
Malaysia	2;4;8	Institut Tecknologi; Kolej Damansara Utama (KDU); Maktab Sains MARA community college in Kuantan
Mauritius	6;8	Colegio Nacional de Educacion Profesional Tecnica (CONALEP) (254); Central de Estudios Tecnologicos Leon, Guanajuato; Mexican Centros de Ensenanza y Superior (CETYS); Universidad Iberoamericana; Mexico City Instituto Tecnologio y de Estudios Superiores de Monterrey (ITESM); Universidad Nacional Autonoma de Mexico (UNAM)
Mexico	5;7;8	
New Zealand	2;5;8	20 Technical Colleges
Norway	3;6	
Pakistan	2;6;8	
Russia	2;5;8;9	Neva College
Slovak Republic	2;5;9	Community College based on Fachhochschulen model
Slovenia	2;9	
Spain	6;8	Columbo International College (Seville & Marabella); American Community College of Asturias
South Africa	2;8	
Sri Lanka	4	
Surinam Republic	2	
Sweden	3;8	
Taiwan	4;8	National Taiwan Institute of Technology
Tatarstan	2	Community College of Kazan (associated with Kazan Pedagogical Institute)
Thailand	2;8	Phuket Community College of Prince of Songkla University; First Global Community College
Ukraine	6;8;9	15 Regional Colleges
United States	2;4;8	1,200 community colleges
Yemen, Republic	2	Community Colleges in Sana and Aden

Legend:
1) Colleges of Further Education
2) Community College
3) Folkhighschool
4) Junior College
5) Polytechnic
6) Regional College
7) Regional Technical Institutes of Latin America
8) Technical College/Institute
9) Vishe Skhole

Sources: Arthur Cohen, Accommodating Postcompulsory Education Seekers around the World. *Community College Review,* vol. 21, no. 2 (1995), pp. 13–18; Frederick C. Kintzer, Higher Education Approaches the Twenty-first Century; New Perspectives on Nonuniversities. Unpublished presentation to the Nova Southeastern University, 1994, pp. 6–16; and Rosalind Latiner Raby and Norma Tarrow (eds.), *Dimensions of the Community College: International, Intercultural, and Multicultural Perspectives.* (New York: Garland, 1996), pp. 197–203.

to serve economic and sociopolitical needs of the business community. Ural (1998) notes that distinct organizational patterns exist that are managed nationally in Germany; regionally in Israel; by states in the United States; by individual districts in Norway; by secondary school systems in Austria, Denmark, Indonesia, and Sweden; by polytechnic and technical colleges in Colombia and New Zealand; and by their own system in Canada. Cohen (1995) postulates that in nations where compulsory education ends early, community college models are four to five years in duration and serve upper secondary, undergraduate collegiate, and paraprofessional functions. In countries where students attend school for ten or more years, community college models accentuate pre-baccalaureate, occupational, and recurrent education studies often less than two years in duration.

Secondly, each model has a specific purpose that advocates a singular element (technical or occupational) or combines pre-university academic, technical, vocational, occupational training/retraining with sociocultural and adult education. All models provide certificates and/or diplomas that provide entry to continuing education (lifelong learning) and/or employment. The unifying commonality is that all emphasize short-term career/personal advancement education.

The third characteristic is a worldwide phenomenon: community college models are not highly regarded by governments, university scholars, or the populace. Often community colleges are located in rural or in urban lower-class areas and frequently are poorly supported in both finance and social status. Government support can foster growth, for example, Argentinean *terciarios*, or facilitate demise due to lack of support, as with consolidation of Chilean technical institutes within the university hierarchy (Kintzer, 1998). Due to uncertain status, tuition is consistently lower than the university, yet out of reach for the majority of the poor. Complicating this situation is their immense popularity, which is increasing enrollments faster than support services, which, in turn, multiplies overall costs. This results in a situation where "wherever short-cycle colleges are found, financing is the primary dilemma" (Ishumi, 1988, p. 163–74).

Finally, community college models embody an ideal that low tuition accentuates open access, which in turn perpetuates alternative routes for postsecondary education that can build and maintain democratic overtures in relation to societal change. The U.S. model is specifically emulated by developing countries because lower socioeconomic class and subordinate minority ethnic groups students do attend U.S. community colleges in such large numbers. Many assert that since this ideal is realized in the United States, it can also be realized in their own country (Strydom, Bitzer, and Lategan, 1995; Mellander and Mellander, 1994). However, while community college models do provide a viable access to higher education, the ideal that equitable access leads to opportunities, and that these opportunities provide a foundation for economic/political reform, is dubious at best. Economic globalization has raised living costs and altered accessibility for models in Japan, Great Britain, Eastern Europe, Latin America, New Zealand,

and Russia, while increased student tuition in the United States has actually eliminated "open access" for thousands of students (Raby, 1996).

GLOBALIZATION TO PROMOTE LOCAL IDENTITY

The impact of individualized connections positions the local as a significant actor in the globalization process. Thus, "unlike the promoting of globalization for sameness, the advent of the local cannot be ignored" (Eagleton, quoted in McLaren, 1999, p. 11). Consideration of the local in the context of globalization correlates to what Eskow (1999) refers to as global paradox—when the polity and economy grow larger, the needs of the local become more manifest. A paradox emerges, in that rhetoric, vision, and structure of community college models affiliate with the local and the communal in preparing local students for citizenship and work. Yet, due to globalization, they can no longer serve their communities well if they do not effectively link to the global.

Robins describes globalization as the "compression of time and space horizons and the creation of a new global space. . . . [Space is] a space of flows, and electronic space, a decentered space, a space in which frontiers and boundaries have become permeable" (Robins, 1992, p. 318). Accordingly, connections are not only within this new global space, but become a predominant feature of it as well. Individualized connections made by community college models not only defines them as unique entities, but also serves as a self-maintaining mechanism. The question of what is the meaning of community in a global space and how it affects community college models becomes an issue.

The sameness that is promoted through the proliferation process has not erased local adaptations. Rather, numerous variations echo local needs in many forms. Japanese junior colleges, developed during the occupation period by U.S. community college educators, currently bear little resemblance to the U.S. model, as they are now 84 percent privately controlled and service primarily women. The Hawke's Bay Community College in New Zealand, initially aimed to provide lifelong education, but refocused its efforts to tailor its programs to the needs of its major ethnic minority, the Maori community (Kintzer, 1979). These and other variations highlight promotion of local identities that provides (1) a need to link beyond the local; (2) appreciation of diversity that connections provide; and (3) interdependent relationships that result from such connections.

First, local connections are made with local communities, local universities, community college models abroad, local governments, and local/global industries. All connections affect the economic, technological, and philosophical direction of the college. Some connections have negative repercussions, such as when local community college models clash with international colleges, global business, or local university agendas that undermine local autonomy. As a result, weakened programmatic relevancy and insecure future job placement can cause difficulties in implementing many community college model goals. Nonetheless, positive examples exist as the local takes control of their destinies, such as Madras Community College's work with Sinclair (SCC) (Ohio) and Eastern Iowa Community Colleges to translate small business curriculum into Tamil and develop a text for semiliterate and illiterate students. SCC also works with Stella Maris College (Chennai, India) to develop a Tamil functional literacy curriculum for primary school teachers, targeted at women in rural villages surrounding Chennai. Another example is the International Consortium for Economic and Educational Development (ICEED), which links community colleges in Arizona, California, New Mexico, and Texas to those in Mexico to ease postsecondary educational problems. These programs exemplify responsiveness to local needs and adaptations of the community college model.

Secondly, through policy borrowing, technology transfer, and knowledge diffusion (Taylor, Lingard, and Rizvi, 1997), academic, technical, and occupational programs' connections proliferate. In many, the value of an American-style education transverses the world as entire courses, complete with syllabus and textbooks, are adopted. Balanced connections also exist, such as a co-taught theater art program by Los Angeles Harbor Community College and Barnsley College in England in which students participate in, learn together, and put on plays via telecommunicating and video-conferencing. At the other extreme, globalization creates unique conditions whereby connections circulate from other models to U.S. models. Holistic reform policies of community college models in Australia, Canada, New Zealand, and western Europe have influenced U.S. community college models with concepts of decentralization, merging occupational education with university certification into a new configuration of a B.A. degree, and competency-based curriculum revision (Raby and Tarrow, 1996). Expanding access to global telecommunications technologies continues to facilitate future unlimited and multidimensional educational connections.

A third connection occurs in sharing philosophies, images, and dissemination of knowledge that affects cultural diffusion. In 1975, community college educators from fourteen countries met to design resolutions for ongoing international collaboration, much of which is adhered to today (Eskow and Caffrey, 1974). In the 1990s, dissemination of the community college model itself persists as these institutions are increasingly being introduced into the community and are becoming "learning centers for the whole community . . . [that] weave together people and projects that reach beyond traditional educational boundaries" (Gordon, 1999, p. 1).

Finally, connections occur through personal exchanges (student, faculty, staff, etc.); through Internet, e-mail, and telecommunications (individual or programmatic); and through dissemination within the international scholarly community, all of which have long-lasting effects. Educators from diverse locations communicate, plan, and learn from one another cost-efficiently and effectively, making distance between countries no longer an obstacle and giving the Internet considerable power to evoke social change. The emphasis on connections illustrates that many responses to globalization are not merely economic in nature.

Much emphasis placed on connections refers to diversity potential rather than to unified cultural components (Strydom and Lategan, 1998). Critics, however, contend that globalization does not produce interdependent relationships nor diversity, but rather dependent relationships that support "western imperialism, whether economic political, technological or broadly cultural" in orientation (Mosa, 1996, p. 1). As a result, community college models stress values and norms that predominantly reflect mainstream Western culture, which, by default, makes them a feature of Westernization that diminishes individual (local) initiatives and legitimates nondemocratic choice. At the extreme, deterritorialized diversity results from the destruction of the local. The question, Does this global culture become one of repression or liberation? thus arises. The questions of who controls what is defined as knowledge, what gets taught and acted upon in a global culture, therefore, is of extreme importance.[4] Finally, Shorish (1998, p.1) acknowledges that the "parallel of the 'Global Person' with the 'Soviet Man' and globalization with colonialization can hardly be lost on comparative education." The impact of this process on the community college model must also be realized.

REPERCUSSIONS OF GLOBALIZATION

While globalization impacted symbiotic relationships between U.S. community college models and those abroad, globalization also provoked five repercussions, which, when combined, altered financial, academic, cultural, applied, and philosophical foundations of these institutions. Strydom (1998, p. 98) suggests that these repercussions heighten "disadvantage(s) to [those] whom the community college model should serve."

On the financial level, substantial difficulties exist in executing these models in economically strained periods. Lack of substantial and secure backing, logistical costs, hidden costs, and local and global economic conditions can undermine efforts. Financial competition can result in a "for-profit philosophy" that affects academic mission, curriculum, professional relationships, and funding (Yamano and Hawkins, 1996). Furthermore, financial, ethical, and philosophical dilemmas of tuition-based instruction undermine open access and reveal a plethora of questions regarding the mission of the community college model. Notable similarities exist between community college models in developing countries and those in California, as both reinvented themselves as a result of dealing with diminishing financial resources in the face of increasing enrollments. A dichotomy exists in maintaining low-cost and open access in fiscally difficult times that can undermine the core open-access philosophy and place these much desired programs at risk (Dolye and Trombley, 1997). Perhaps the most ominous trend, however, is that even with low tuition, for some community college models—like Darwin Community College in Australia, which serves Aborigines and migrant residents, 81 percent of whom have only reached the ninth grade; the Malaysian community college; or the Egyptian Mahad—the cost is still out of reach for the poorest population, the people they were initially intended to serve. Thus, although the models do increase access to postsecondary education, they merely perpetuate an already unequal higher educational system (El Mallah et al. 1996; Kintzer, 1979).

On the academic level, it is difficult to define standards that are acceptable both locally and globally, and as a result, the global is frequently highlighted over the local. Various factors influencing educational decisions are removed from the local. Difficulty exists in community college models maintaining academic autonomy in a system that incorporates local university, local and global business, and an international college's agendas. While U.S. college models include governing boards, accreditation, and labor unions, these networks may not exist nor be appropriate in a foreign setting (Alleyne, 1978). In addition, exportation of specialized curricula may be irrelevant if graduates succumb to chronic unemployment. In some international development programs, maintenance of global academic standards and uniform performance standards becomes difficult and may conflict with the reality of the local environment. In addition, privatization emphasis can result in community colleges cooperating with, and at times becoming subordinate to, the interests of international enterprises. Finally, although Eskow (1989, p. 4) claims that "instruction originating in those countries can move to the United States and to our students who want to learn about other countries and cultures," such patterns have yet to become realized. Instead, a neocolonial American-centric curriculum has circumvented the world.

On the cultural level, local sociopolitical, economic and environmental issues, that are culture-bound, can counter basic tenets of the community college. Cultural misconceptions of community, international developmental assistance, or academic standards make adoption of U.S. characteristics puzzling at best. Cultural intolerance arises from strained relationships between indigenous staff, counterparts abroad, and indigenous financial backers, all of whom have their own, oftentimes conflicting, agendas. Poor faculty preparation to adapt to culture shock further negates relationships and can place programs in jeopardy. While revolutionary changes in travel, mass media, and communications technology facilitate massive diffusion of this model, they further complicate this cultural variable. The availability and usability of fax machines, e-mail, and the ability to reciprocate travel visits are not always guaranteed, especially in developing countries. Furthermore, even when a communication infrastructure is available, it remains subject to culturally defined patterns of behavior. The manner in which the local responds to globalization forces that emphasize unification underscores a basic conflict of building global identities while trying to preserve and maintain their own identities (Currie, 1996). Finally, sociocultural neocolonialism that results from Western interaction and dominance has positive as well as negative consequences, the latter of which must not be discounted. It is still too early to discern whether or not community college models will promote social reconstruction or social fragmentation.

On the applied level, "the most crucial function of community colleges then has been to provide students with training and retraining programmes which help them to achieve social mobility and contribute to the economic well-being of a country" (Cohen, 1995, p 65–75; see Ratcliff and Gibson-Berninger, 1998; *Introduction*, 1996). Actualization of socioeconomic reform, however, depends upon the type of education exported (technical/vocational, personal development, professional, or academic), the type of student targeted, the relationship of the type of education to the college's mission, and what students actually do with this education, (i.e., transfer to a university, work, or drop out). The vocational school fallacy (Selvarathuam, 1998) insinuates that two-year technical/vocational colleges that ignore a general education foundation may not be an optimal means for solving manpower needs. These colleges are often cost-ineffective and have courses that are short-sighted, out-of-date, and oftentimes irrelevant. Since many community college models, especially in developing countries, are victims of this fallacy, they are placed at risk. Furthermore, in many countries, due to both internal links, such as with poor national planning, and external links, such as with transnational corporations, appropriate jobs may be lacking upon graduation. As a result, implementation of a community college model does not always evoke social reform as suggested by Cohen (1995). Similarly, an international development fallacy exists in that exported community college ideals may not lead to career/academic opportunities and such training often does not provide the foundation for economic/political reform (Raby, 1999; Strydom and Lategan, 1998).

Finally, on the philosophical level, many community colleges take pride in considering themselves a significant form of "community education in the context of redressing inequalities" (Ural, 1998, p. 199). There is evidence that community college models can be effective in reducing cultural conflict in multicultural societies as well as in increasing access to higher education as exemplified in Australia, Bulgaria, China, India, Japan, Malaysia, and the United States (Van der Linde, 1996; Mellander and Mellander, 1994). For the past two decades globalization tendencies portended the U.S. model as having the "resources and expertise, especially in applied technology, that could serve well . . . in sustainable development" (Elsner, Tsunoda, and Korbel, 1995, p. 1). The ubiquitous ideal that community college models can utilize postsecondary education to counter socioeconomic inequities, while not proven in academia, has nonetheless been sufficient enough to encourage educators abroad to enter into agreements that facilitate transplanting community college models to their own countries (Strydom and Lategan, 1998; Elsner, Tsunoda, and Korbel, 1995; Koltai, 1993).

The U.S. community college model continues to grow in popularity, and students who attend these institutions do so in ever increasing numbers, especially in developing countries. Future development and support of these institutions persists because they are (1) less expensive and more accessible than universities; (2) adaptable to providing product-oriented, as well as transferable, curricula; (3) flexible in providing short-term programs that address varying interests of the community; and (4) able to meet the demands of emerging local population and regional needs. Above all, community college models are designed to serve both the people and their communities as "the most crucial function of the community colleges then has been to provide students with training and retraining programmes which help them to achieve social mobility and contribute to the economic well-being of a country" (Ural, 1998, p. 119).

However, it must be noted that consequences of globalization have reinforced realities of linguistic, cultural, and moral Westernization that reinforces economic and cultural dependency. As the global collides with the local, it hinders attempts to maintain cultural identity and autonomy in the face of world homogenization. Exporting U.S. community college characteristics is complicated by the ethics of aid, trade, and neocolonialism, which maintain nonacademic ulterior motives. In efforts to maintain local control, new restrictions have made it increasingly difficult to import U.S. community college characteristics through contract education programs in Australia, Indonesia, Japan, Korea, and the Philippines. In that globalization of the community college model affects educational reform, the aforementioned repercussions remain of crucial importance.

Consequences of exporting U.S.-based characteristics range from a benign provocation for educational reform to transference as a form of neocolonialism. Implementation becomes an interesting blend of full acceptance (as in community college models in Alberta, Hungary, India, Israel, Kazakhstan, Malaysia, Singapore, Sri Lanka, Thailand, and Mexico), to partial acceptance (as in community college models in Egypt, Indonesia, Ontario, and South Africa), to rejection (as in the Japanese branch colleges) (Raby and Tarrow, 1996). At a time when basic community college ideals are being compromised and sometimes abandoned, questioning the extent of emulation becomes all the more critical.

CONCLUSION

Proliferation of the community college model has impacted educational systems as it continues to attract those who respond to demands to break out of traditional university patterns and to promote nontraditional educational access. In a continuous effort to emulate specific and sometimes idealized elements of U. S. community colleges, a symbiotic relationship is maintained between various models, supported through international development and distance education programs. Kintzer (1998, p. 2) maintains that U.S. educators "are more likely to act as consulting members of teams interested in the knowledge and technology that other nations produce. Especially in developing nations, these collaborations contribute to expand secondary or higher education systems into new, flexible, stand-alone institutions." The marketing of the U.S. community college model as the singular means by which to accomplish this task, in part, maintains the U.S. model's dominance.

Social change is cultivated at both global and local levels. The process of introducing a community college model into a society encourages local educational change. This change can provide some access for the general population, help achieve career/personal advancement opportunities, provoke reduction of culture-conflict in multicultural societies resulting from the education of the underprivileged, and impact local business and industry by introducing new curricular emphasis and a newly trained workforce. Global links are cultivated by international students who attend colleges abroad, by individual exchanges abroad, and by internationalization of campus and curriculum. Initial contacts can emerge into business relationships that then help local business concerns. These relationships are dynamic and further establish bonds between individuals on campus, the local neighborhood, and the global community.

Despite the popularity of the community college model, implications for developing countries interested in creating, revising, or endorsing characteristics of this model are clear. It is critical to understand community college realities as well as highlight their ideals. Reverberations from globalization can force countries to abandon a basic and most emulated tenet of the community college, that of open access. Suggestions that community college models can no longer sustain the educational ideals envisioned and expected by diverse sections of society are of significant consequence worldwide. The variations of the community college model may be a reaction to this process as each country is attempting to conform an ideal into its own workable model.

Nonetheless, the impact of heightened community college model growth will not diminish in the next century. Indeed, it is more likely that community college models will become further ingrained in postsecondary educational structures. In that our world is increasingly multiethnic, multicultural, and multilingual, a higher educational structure, such as the community college model, that acknowledges, endorses, and respects that diversity becomes most desired.

NOTES

1. See Raby 1996 for a discussion of these terms that include college of further education, community college, folkhighschool, junior college, open universities, regional college, short-cycle program, technical institute, tecknicums, vishe skhole, and village polytechnics. The term *community college model* is utilized throughout this article.

2. Homogenization is also evident in assimilation components of International Student Programs (Altbach 1998), ethnocentric experiences of some Student Study Abroad and Administrative/Faculty Exchange Programs that reinforce distinct similarities, and Global Curricula Programs that underscore cultural similarities rather than local concerns and differences.

3. In 1998, 90 CCID member colleges, ran projects with 150 faculty working in 43 countries, 1,411 students in study/work abroad programs in 24 countries, and 925 international trainees on CCID campuses. In addition, 23 percent of the 62 member colleges of the California-based consortium California Colleges for International Education conducted similar projects (Raby 1999).

4. Mosa (1996, p. 6) elegantly describes this issue:

In this rush toward globalization, scarce time is given to ponder not what is gained by the concept of conformity, the globalism basic agenda. What is lost in the globalists' putsch? A rain forest here, parts of the ozone layer there, a localized language here, a first nations culture there. At a more personal level: doesn't globalization strike not only at the local, but also at the individual? Does it not require the inquiring mind to become the conforming mind, for individual insight to give way to committee consensus? Is it not time to modify the globalist dictatorial agenda to allow for diversity and localization?

REFERENCES

ACIIE/Stanley Foundation. 1996. Education for the Global Community: A Framework for Community Colleges. Muscatine, IA: Stanley Foundation Publications.

Alleyne, Michael H. 1978 (February). Educational Objectives in Latin American and the Caribbean and the Role of Community Colleges. Paper presented at the Conference of Postsecondary Education in the International Community, Orlando, Florida.

Altbach, Philip. 1998. Internationalization and Multinationalization in Higher Education—The Melding of Academic Culture Worldwide. Paper presented at the Comparative and International Education Society National Conference, Buffalo.

Cerych, Ladislav. 1993. The Return to Europe: Issues in Post-Community Higher Education. In Arthur Levine (ed.), *Higher Learning in America: 1980–2000*. Baltimore: John Hopkins University Press, pp. 5–27.

Cohen, Arthur. 1995. Accommodating Postcompulsory Education Seekers around the World. *Community College Review*, vol. 21, no. 2, pp. 65–75.

CCID. 1998. *1997 Annual Report and Capabilities Statement*. Cocoa, Florida: Brevard Community Colleges Publications.

———. 1999a. Homepage. Exemplary Programs. <http://ccid.kirkwood.cc.ia.us/exemp.html>.

———. 1999b. Homepage. Exemplary Projects. <http://ccid.kirkwood.cc.ia.us/projects.htm>.

Cook, Jean. 1996. Community Self-Help International Development Projects: A Humanistic Perspective. In Rosalind Latiner Raby and Norma Tarrow (eds.), *Dimensions of the Community College: International, Intercultural, and Multicultural Perspectives*. New York: Garland, pp. 37–53.

CSU Report to the TASK FORCE on CSU Globalization (March 18, 1998). California State University System on International Education.

Currie, Jan. 1996. Globalisation Practices and Universities: Some Examples from American and Australian Universities. Paper presented at the Ninth International Congress of Comparative Education Societies, Sydney.

Doyle, William, and William Trombley. 1997. Closed Doors? *Crosstalk*, vol. 5, no. 1, pp. 1–14.

Eagleton, Terry. 1996. *The Illusions of Postmodernism*. Oxford: Blackwell.

El Mallah, A. Amin, Kal Gezi, and Hassan Abdel Hamid Soliman. 1996. Egyptian Community Colleges: A Case Study. In Rosalind Latiner Raby and Norma Tarrow (eds.), *Dimensions of the Community College: International, Intercultural, and Multicultural Perspectives*. New York: Garland, pp. 273–91.

Elsner, Paul, Joyce Tsunoda, and Linda Korbel. 1995 (May). *United States Agency for International Development. Seeking a New Partnership: Task Force Report on U.S. Community Colleges*. Washington, D.C.: United States Agency for International Development.

Eskow, Steven. 1975 (November). Resolution on the Development of World Community College: A College of Colleges Devoted to the Exchange of Information and Assistance on Community-Based, Short-Cycle Education. Resolution from World Community College Conference. Vancouver, British Columbia.

———. 1989, Fall. Toward Telecommunity College: From Open Admissions to Open Learning. In Ervin Harlacher (ed.), *Cutting Edge Technologies in Community*. Washington, D.C.: American Association of Community and Junior Colleges, pp. 32–50.

———. 1999. Pangea Network Homepage. World Community College: Has Its Time Come? <http://www.pangea.network.com>.

———, and John Caffrey. 1974 (Autumn). World Community College: A 2020 Vision. In William Birenbaum (ed.), *Class to Mass Learning: New Directions for Community Colleges*, vol. 4, no. 7. San Francisco: Jossey-Bass, pp. 17–26.

Gordon, Michelle. 1999. International Programs at Middlesex Community College. Pioneering Leadership Exemplary Programs Occasional Papers Series. CCID Web Page. <http://www.ccid.kirkwood.cc.ia.us/exemp.htm>.

Humphrys, James G., and Albert M. Koller, Jr. (eds.). 1994. *Community Colleges for International Development, Inc.: The Vision and the History, 1976–1994*. Brevard, Florida: Community Colleges for International Development, Inc.

An Introduction to Community Colleges: A Guide for South Africa. 1996 (March). Cape Town: Salty Print, pp. 6–8.

Ishumi, Abel G. M. 1998. Vocational Training as an Educational and Development Strategy: Conceptual and Practical Issues. *International Journal of Educational Development*, vol. 83, pp. 163–74.

Keer, Clark. 1996 (October). Preserving the Master Plan. Occasional Paper. Sacramento: California Higher Education Policy Center.

King, Maxwell C., and Seymour H. Fersh. 1992. *Integrating the International/Intercultural Dimension in the Community College*. Cocoa, Florida: Association of Community College Trustees and Community Colleges for International Development, Inc.

Kintzer, Frederick C. 1979. World Adaptations to the Community College Concept. In Arthur Cohen (ed.), *Advancing International Education: New Directions for Community Colleges*, no. 26. Jossey-Bass: San Francisco, pp. 65–79.

———. 1993. Higher Education beyond the United States: A Glimpse of Short-Cycle Higher Education in Other Countries. *Community/Junior Community College Quarterly*, vol. 16, no. 1, pp. 1–8.

———. 1994 (August). Higher Education Approaches the Twenty-first Century: New Perspectives on Nonuniversities. Unpublished Presentation to the Nova Southeastern University, pp. 6–16.

————. 1998 (June). Community Colleges Go International: Short-Cycle Education around the World. *Leadership Abstracts World Wide Web Edition*, vol. 11, no. 6, pp. 1–4.

Koltai, Leslie. 1993 (November). Are There Challenges and Opportunities for American Community Colleges on the International Scene? Keynote Address at the Comparative and International Education Society Western Region Conference, Los Angeles, California.

Larin, Nancy. 1999 (Winter). Humber Established Another Link with China. *Community Colleges for International Development International News*, pp. 7–8.

McLaren, Peter. 1999. Introduction: Traumatizing Capital: Oppositional Pedagogies in the Age of Consent. In Manuel Castells, Ramon Flecha, Paulo Freire, Henry Giroux, Donald Macedo, and Paul Willis. *Critical Education in the New Information Age*. Boulder, CO: Rowman & Littlefield, pp. 1–37.

Mellander, Gustavo A., and Nelly Mellander (eds.). 1994 (August). Towards an Hungarian Community College System. ERIC Document Reproduction Service No. ED 375870.

Mosa, Ali A. 1996. Why Globalization? Paper presented given at the Ninth World Congress of Comparative Education Societies (WCCES), Sydney.

OECD. 1971. *Short Cycle Education: Search for Identity*. Paris: OECD Publications.

Raby, Rosalind Latiner. 1996. International, Intercultural, and Multicultural Dimensions of Community Colleges in the United States. In Rosalind Latiner Raby and Norma Tarrow (eds.), *Dimensions of the Community College: International, Intercultural, and Multicultural Perspectives*. New York: Garland, pp. 9–36.

————. 1999. *Looking to the Future: Report on International and Global Education in California Community Colleges*. Sacramento: State Chancellor, California Community Colleges Publications.

Raby, Rosalind Latiner, and Norma Tarrow (eds.). 1996. *Dimensions of the Community College: International, Intercultural, and Multicultural Perspectives*. New York: Garland.

Ratcliff, James L., and Barbara Gibson-Berninger. 1998. Community Colleges in a Global Context. In A. H. Strydom and L. O. K. Lategan (eds.). *Introducing Community Colleges to South Africa*. Bloemfontein, South Africa: University of the Free State Publications, pp. 2–36.

Robertson, Roland. 1992. *Globalization Social Theory and Global Culture*. London: Sage.

Robins, Kevin. 1992. Reading a Global Culture. In Stuart Hall, David Held, and Tony McGrew (eds.), *Modernity and Its Futures*. Cambridge, UK: Polity, pp. 318.

Schugurensky, Daniel, and Kathy Higgins. 1996. From Aid to Trade: New Trends in International Education in Canada. In Rosalind Latiner Raby and Norma Tarrow (eds.), *Dimensions of the Community College: International, Intercultural, and Multicultural Perspectives*. New York: Garland, pp. 53–79.

Selvarathuam, V. 1998. Limits to Vocationally-Oriented Education in the Third World. *International Journal of Educational Development*, vol. 8, pp. 8–14.

Shorish, Mobin. 1998. Globalization and the Standardization of Culture. Paper presented at the Comparative and International Education Society national conference, Buffalo.

Strydom, A. H. 1998. A Regional Model for Community Colleges in More Rural Provinces of South Africa. In A. H. Strydom, and L. O. K. Lategan (eds.), *Introducing Community Colleges to South Africa*. Bloemfontein, South Africa: University of the Free State Publications.

Strydom, A. H., E. M. Bitzer, and L. O. K. Lategan. 1995. *Community Colleges for South Africa*. Bloemfontein, South Africa: Academic Development Bureau.

Strydom, A. H., and L. O. K. Lategan (eds.). 1998. *Introducing Community Colleges to South Africa*. Bloemfontein, South Africa: University of the Free State Publications.

Taylor, Sandra, Miriam Henry, Bob Lingard, and Fazal Rizvi. 1997. *Policy and the Politics of Education*. St. Leonards, New South Wales, Australia: Allen and Unwin.

Ural, Ipek. 1998. International Community College Models: A South African Perspective. In A. H. Strydom and L. O. K. Lategan (eds.), *Introducing Community Colleges to South Africa*. Bloemfontein, South Africa: University of the Free State Publications, pp. 106–19.

Van der Linde, Cornelia H. 1996. The Role of the Community College in Countering Conflict in Multicultural Societies. In Rosalind Latiner Raby and Norma Tarrow (eds.), *Dimensions of the Community College: International, Intercultural, and Multicultural Perspectives*. New York: Garland, pp. 239–59.

Willis, David, Yasuko Minoura, and Walter Enloe. 1998. Transculturals, Transnationals, and International Education: Future Visions for Education. Paper presented at the Ninth World Congress of Comparative Education Societies, Sydney.

Yamano, Tina, and Hawkins, John. 1996. Assessing the Relevance of American Community College Models in Japan. In Rosalind Latiner Raby and Norma Tarrow (eds.), *Dimensions of the Community College: International, Intercultural, and Multicultural Perspectives*. New York: Garland, pp. 259–73.

9

Local/Global Labor Markets and the Restructuring of Gender, Schooling, and Work

Jane Kenway and Peter Kelly

The 1990s have been characterized by dramatic and confusing economic, social, and cultural change. In response to these changes, globalization has become a popular concept among vocational education and training (VET) policymakers in Australia. However, their understanding of this term is largely associated with economics and "global competitive markets." VET's prime purposes are then reduced to and read off from such foci. However, it is our view that such a reading of globalization is too thin. It does not adequately explain contemporary times. It does not attend to social and cultural globalizing influences or to the relationship of the big material and structural shifts to everyday life and to changed structures of feeling. This chapter is informed by a view of globalization that attends to the changing relationships between globalizing economic and cultural influences, place, institutions, and personal relationships and identities. Its focus is on masculinities, femininities, and VET in Australia's schools in their globalized local and institutional contexts.

Restructuring is a local expression of global trends and forces. This chapter identifies four important processes of restructuring. These processes are key components of the ways in which globalization is impacting on the lived experiences of VET in Australian schools. These intersecting and overlapping processes are (i) the restructuring of the labor market, (ii) the associated restructuring of the family and of transitions from child to adulthood, (iii) the restructuring of schooling and the transitions from school to work, and (iv) the restructuring of locality. Each involves and evokes enduring gender issues, new gender issues, and new manifestations of old issues.

Our purpose in this chapter is to offer both an eagle's and, to a lesser extent, a worm's eye view of these processes of restructuring. Clearly each restructuring modality requires considerably more attention than we are able to give it here, as do the intersections between them. However, we do not seek to offer a definitive data-based account of the issues involved but rather to be suggestive, to clarify the concepts and directions of analysis that inform our research. In our view these have the potential to open up this sort of inquiry in a more holistic and grounded manner.

THEORETICAL FRAMEWORKS

This chapter and the research that it discusses draw conceptual inspiration from the work of British sociologists Giddens (1991 and 1994), Lash and Urry (1994), and Urry (1995) and the complementary feminist research of Massey (1994) and Walby (1997) in particular. Together, their work offers a conceptual framework that allows for a layered analysis of large-scale economic and cultural shifts and influences, their social and cultural manifestations in place and space, their implications for identity and biography, and the role of gender and other axes of power such as class and ethnicity.

Theories of Contemporary Times and Economies of Place

Rather than draw on the concept *globalization*, Giddens largely addresses what he calls the "altered context of political life" (see Giddens, 1994). He argues that there are three key overarching processes at work in this altered context: (i) the re-organization of space and time, (ii) the move to a "post-traditional social order," and (iii) the increasing centrality in our lives of "social reflexivity." He also argues that these are associated with changes in broad structures of feeling—with a generalized sense of tension and emotional and moral disquiet. Urry (1995) is concerned with the "sociology of place," and, working with and developing Giddens's and others' ideas, he explores the ways in which place and its dynamic articulations with wider global forces shape the ways local people live and change their lives. His work points to the sociological and cultural issues associated with the restructuring of local economies and public services and the localization of the global. It is concerned with the rapidly changing "economic base of place" and draws particular attention to the tourism, holiday, and leisure culture industries, which have become increasingly important in the regeneration of certain regional economies. Although his concern is with place, it is interested too in that which flows through and influences place—for instance, the flow of tourists, workers, information, and screen images. He attends to cultural constructions of place and to the ways in which place and identity intersect. Here memories and traditions often collide with the present.

These ideas have been applied in this research project as follows. Conventionally in terms of broad structural analysis, ideas associated with the reorganization of space and time are assisting us to come to grips with local articulations of the global with regard to changing local economies and local youth labor markets. But such ideas have also prompted us to consider how space and time are being reorganized in young people's lives and the implications of such reorganization for socially and spatially situated young people. The notion of the increasing centrality of social reflexivity is helping us to (i) explore the knowledge that schools draw on to understand social and economic change and to assist young people to deal with it and (ii) the significance of certain knowledge and authority in vocational education and training and the ways in which they connect with the "gendered biographies" of young women and men. A consideration of changes in broad structures of feeling enables us to understand young people's responses to new vocational agendas, in the context of their biographical projects. Giddens's argument that in a globalizing world we have moved to a post-traditional social order has provoked an examination of the changing manifestations of gender in localities, with regard to the implications of changing local labor markets for families and the rise and role of gender fundamentalism.

In Giddens's view, we have moved to a "post-traditional order." This order is a result of the many challenges to traditional ways of doing things, organizing our lives, and interacting with nature. This "post-traditional order" is brought about by a range of factors. These include the declining influence of traditional agencies of socialization (the church, the family, and the school) and the rise of other major influences (e.g., the media, popular culture). They also include new scientific and technical knowledge and its applications to nature and our bodies, new social movements and their challenges to convention and habit, the clash of values brought about by the rise of global differences, and the spread of different cultures around the globe. As Giddens (1994, p. 83) argues, such changes and challenges have forced traditions into the open, they have been "called to account," required to justify themselves. As a result of the changing nature of tradition we now have what Giddens calls "a runaway world of dislocation and uncertainty"; a world of "manufactured uncertainty" (Giddens, 1994, pp. 93–95). In this world we now often have to decide upon many of the things that once were taken for granted or regarded as simply natural. And, as he indicates, this often results in calls for a return to particular traditions. Here he makes particular mention of the rise of both religious and "secular" fundamentalism, which he argues are a defense of tradition based on the tradition it defends. Fundamentalisms tend to sentimentalize, romanticize, oversimplify, and misrepresent the past. Christian, Islamic, ethnic (nationalist), gender, and family fundamentalism can be seen as manifestations of a post-traditional social order in globalizing contexts. Mackay's (1993, pp. 24–55) account of new women and old men is very telling in this regard. So too is Adkin's (1995) discussion of the ways in which women's work is being de-traditionalized and re-traditionalized simultaneously.

Gender and Place

Most recent feminist work on globalization is particularly conscious of the "uneven and fractured" (Bakker, 1996, p. 19) process of both globalization and of identity formation within the webs of power that constitute what Grewal and Kaplan (1994) call "scattered hegemonies." This work points to the importance of what Haraway (1991) calls "partial and situated knowledges," and to matters of place, embodiment, and experience. Further, social class, gender, and ethnicity are currently being considered "through the prism of space" (Urry, 1995, p. 14). Inequality is understood as spatial as well as social. In particular this feminist literature identifies the geography of gender. It explores the changing gendered discourses, identities, and relations of local-cultural space/places, pointing to place-based variations in the construction and reconstruction of gender. Studies of the changing economic base of place are assisting us to see how gender is being reshaped accordingly (Bagguley et al., 1990). As Massey (1994, p. 178) says for example, "What it means to be masculine in the Fens is not the same as what it means in Lancashire." This literature also looks at how changing economic forms and regional policies are differentiated by locality and by gender and how such changes can bring about changes in gender relations at work and home and in the overall gender order of the locality (Walby, 1997). Further consideration is also given to the gendered symbolic meanings and use of various spaces and the implications of such meanings for experience and identity. Given that growth and development are uneven, it is also the case that social inequalities exist between as well as within localities (e.g., between suburbs and between rural areas).

Biographical Projects

According to Giddens (1991, pp. 187–201), the altered context of political life has provided "new mechanisms for self identity." Narratives of self are shaped by the rapidly changing circumstances of social life on a local, national, and global scale and by associated new forms of fragmentation and integration. Current times have brought a confusing array of new "choices" of education, work, family, and leisure as many traditional anchors of identity are challenged and changed. While freedom from old constraints offers more apparent choice and autonomy it also generates new uncertainties and fragmentations around gender, family, work, knowledge, and authority—"Who am I? Who do I believe? What is my place in this world, my future? Will I survive, how?" Central to the contemporary biographical project of identity formation then are new issues of risk, trust, and ontological security. In this context, says Giddens (1991, pp. 187–201), individuals must resolve many "dilemmas of the self" and these are particularly consequential at key points or "fateful moments" (Giddens, 1991, p. 203). However, and very importantly, Giddens observes that "survival values" can play an integrating role. These are most strongly related to the "high consequence risks" associated, for example, with the economic uncertainty and risks generated by the global economy.

We are interested in the ways in which the young people in our study construct their narratives of self identity in contemporary times and places; how they deal with increased choice and autonomy; the dilemmas of the self that they address, their fateful moments; and the ways in which risk, trust, and ontological security are inscribed in their lives and the survival values that they and their peers and communities draw on to sustain themselves. Males and females and different groups among them experience these matters differently: some experience more risk and uncertainty than others and have different ways of maximizing choice, minimizing risk, and searching for certainty in their distinctive localities. The extent to and ways in which schools understand and address students' biographical projects is of particular consequence to this study.

Methods

This research considers VET in schools in changing economic, technological, and institutional contexts in Australia with particular reference to masculinities, femininities, and localities. The emphasis is on the contexts that impact on VET but are too often ignored in analysis. The focus is particularly on issues of gender, social class, and location and the de- and re-traditionalization of gender in contemporary globalized/localized times and spaces. This three-year empirical study is being conducted in twelve schools in two states of Australia and in several different types of local labor markets, all of which have been reconstituted in one way or another as a result of changes in global markets, transnational business practices, the globalization of the market metanarrative, and the privatization and downsizing of the provision of state services. In the following pages the schools and the companies are anonymized but the localities are not.

Through an examination of various aspects of localities (labor markets, local government policies, local information, and communication networks) the project studies the schools' and the local workplaces' reconstruction of themselves as suppliers of various forms of vocational education. And, through a series of interviews with students and teachers, it identifies teachers' methods of managing the risks the students now confront and students' reconstructions of themselves as worker/citizens in the uncertain labor markets of globalization. The male and female students of this study come from different sociocultural backgrounds, but many are in localities that offer them a risky employment future.

THE ALTERED CONTEXTS OF EDUCATIONAL LIFE

There are four important restructuring dynamics to the "altered context of educational life" pertinent to this study.

The Restructuring of Gender and Work

In Australia as in other advanced Western economies, a feature of globalizing labor processes and labor markets is what Bakker (1996, p.7) calls the "gender paradox of restructuring." This involves the "contradictory effects of the dual process of gender erosion and intensification" and demonstrates that arguments about the feminization of restructured globalized/local labor markets are inadequate.

Here we see the decline of heavy (male-dominated) manufacturing and the rise of the retail and service sector (dominated numerically by females). Further, we see the gendered polarization of labor markets. Certain core, traditionally male, labor markets are shrinking. Masculinity is intensifying in such core labor markets, and women are thus finding it more difficult to be part of them. There is a generalized backlash against the advancement of women and against the "political correctness" of Equal Employment Policies (EEP). Further, work in the core is intensifying, thus making it more difficult for those who care for households and children to participate fully. Masculinist ideologies are intensifying too as in hard-nosed management doctrine. Hence, gender differences and inequalities in some aspects of work are intensifying.

In contrast, certain peripheral, traditionally female, labor markets are expanding. Here we see the gendered convergence of labor market experiences. More workers, both male and female, are in poorly paid, part-time, nonunionized casual work. Beck (1992, p.143) calls this the "generalization of employment insecurity." Jobs traditionally filled by men are being downgraded and filled by women, but also, for want of something better, males are moving into traditionally female jobs. This expanding periphery then has seen the generalization of employment insecurity from women to men, and from the working class to middle class. Some call this the feminization of the labor market. They see this as a major swing in the labor market in favor of women, but as indicated this is not an accurate or indeed a nuanced reading.

Further, the labor market is dominated by flexibility agendas and notions of the fluid firm, which can outsource and downsize at will. While training agendas stress the flexibility for workers in terms of skills and movement through employment and education systems, this is not what is stressed by employers. Employers stress numerical, spatial, and financial flexibility. In other words, workers can be dropped, have their hours regularly reduced and changed, or can be relocated at the whim of the employer. This insecurity has extended to core markets too in the professions and in employees of the state such as teachers. Unions' influence is declining, and more workers now adopt an individualistic approach to their work in the search for some certainty. It is common now to talk of the overworked; the underworked and the out-of-work (Probert, 1995). There is also much discussion of the changing psychology of the workplace—angry organizations; cultures of anxiety and distrust; and, more broadly, a changing cultural psychology represented by decreasing expectations. All of this destabilizes class and gender identities and relationships to the extent that masculinity and femininity are being reconceived in a post-traditional social order. These identity processes are, indeed, being de-traditionalized and re-traditionalized at the same time.

It is possible to argue that these changes are having particular implications for the broad structures of feeling associated with masculinity. Indeed, in our schools there is a generalized sense of tension and emotional disquiet about boys' education and more subtly masculine identity (Kenway et al., 1998). There has always been a strong historical identification between masculinity, potency, and paid work. Now as further research into masculinity is demonstrating (Kenway et al., 1987/8), as males lose power in one sphere they try to regain it in another; they search for new ways of expressing it in order to reclaim their sense of manhood. Changes in employment may thus have contributed to the rise of gender fundamentalism.

The shifts noted above have had particularly destructive implications for manual trades, long associated with apprenticeship opportunities for young men. These "trades" no longer guarantee employment. For those men whose manual labor is an important source of their masculinity these shifts have cut deeply into the foundations of their identity. This places in question those masculinities formed through manual work. Mac an Ghaill's (1996) research from the United Kingdom shows how certain traditional conceptions of working-class masculinity seem to be at risk and how others are emerging. His work also sheds some light on the implications of this for vocational education in schools.

Mac an Ghaill (1996) shows that new hierarchies between high- and low-status vocational fields are developing in the United Kingdom and leading, particularly, to the restratification of working-class male students. The emerging high-status technological and commercial subject areas such as business studies, technology, and computer studies are providing some such boys with what he calls an "ascending and modernizing version of working-class masculinity" with an associated disposition toward an instrumental, rationalized, forward planning of career and life options. Those are the subjects and programs that they believe will get them into the new world work order. Other working-class boys, he argues, are maintaining a traditional and "descending" mode of masculinity based on low-level, practically based subject areas that reflect the tough masculinity of the disappearing shop floor. These boys stick to manual labor and refuse to consider "girls' jobs."

It is our view that these boys have a three-way relationship to risk. Subscribing to this mode of masculinity places them "at risk" of unemployment. Further, perhaps perversely, they are not prepared to put their masculinity at risk by adopting other ways of working. Perhaps also they put others at risk if, in their search for new identity props, they resort to dangerous risk-taking behavior. We have come across both types of boy in our research, but we have also come across boys who are flexible about their masculinity. Such boys are prepared to go into traditionally female areas such as the service industry. Indeed, they will take whatever is available and be whatever they have to be.

The themes of de-traditionalization and re-traditionalization apply somewhat differently to girls. Many girls now adopt what might be called a nontraditional approach to work. They expect to do paid work *and* to share household work. Further, the feminist movement has led many to hope for work in the core labor market. For those who gain such work this will be nontraditional in the terms of the history of women's work. But, on the other hand, in the context of the intensified masculine core it will take on many traditional elements. Further, due to overwork, many will contract out much of their household and caring work. This too is nontraditional for them, but in the creation of a new home service class, it re-traditionalizes class relations between women. Most girls, however, will move into peripheral labor markets and particularly into the service sector. With regard to VET, our observations indicate that girls who are undertaking vocational education programs tend to still be clustered in programs associated with retail, hospitality, service, and secretarial work. This is quite a traditional pattern. Many in our study express a keen interest in hospitality (see also Teese et al., 1995), and, as Adkin's (1995) research demonstrates, hospitality and tourism represent both de-traditionalizing and re-traditionalizing moments for women and men, particularly in the context of family relations. She points, for example, to the increasing importance of "married teams" to tourist organizations and shows how women work as wives for manager husbands.

> Wives—with no wage labor contract—are not working as employees. . . . [R]ather they are working as wives. In other words their contract may be regarded not as an employment contract but as a family-marriage contract. . . . [W]ives do not own their own labor; they cannot exchange family work with their employers, it is only manager husbands who can perform this exchange.

It is also worthwhile noting here an intensifying aestheticization of work evidenced by the rise of the importance of "the look," of style in our image-conscious culture. Many employers are looking for what could be called "designer employees"—those whose clothes and indeed bodies look right for the job and the firm. In many ways this traditionalizes girls and de-traditionalizes boys. The feminist movement has long taught girls that they are more than their looks and that they should not obsess about appearances; however, certain employers are teaching them otherwise. We found constant examples of this for girls. Certain boys are also becoming more concerned with their image. Those who are flexible about their masculinity believe they enhance their chances of employment. Meet Max:

> Every time I've gone for an interview I've got a hair cut, I've made sure I've got the right clothes on, you know, made myself look presentable because as soon as you

walk in you know you don't have five pages of resume spread out in front of you, you have what's here and that's first thing they're going to notice. You know you can be the most qualified person in the world but if nowadays, if you're not a people person, if you don't have presentation you've got buckleys.

So you would change your image then according to the different job interviews that you went to?

Certainly, certainly, as a matter of personal expression and that sort of thing, I can do that outside of my work, I can do that outside of school. While I'm in a company or a job or any situation, I'm there for them, they're not here for me, I conform to what they want, as soon as I leave I can be whoever, whatever I want, I can wear whatever I want. But you don't go to a corporation in dog collars and dreadlocks and that sort of thing. It's just, if you think you're going to get a job like that, then you are bloody stupid.

I'm just looking at like, your hair color changes though, every time I see you.

Yeah. Every time I've gone for job interviews it's back to brown.

It is interesting to consider the "aestheticization of work" (Lash and Urry, 1994) in terms of particularly disaffected young people. Many adopt rather an outrageous style to affirm for themselves some sort of identity in a world that denies them a sense of their worth. To insist that they rearrange their look is to attack their sense of who they are. The work of Wexler (1992) on young people "becoming somebody" explains the important connections between style and identity, particularly for disaffected young people. Our research points to the deep resentment they feel when expected to change their style for work. It suggests that they may feel naked without their identity props. Of course some young people simply cannot afford the "right look" or simply can't accomplish it easily—"style" is acquired; it has a class and a locational habitus. However, as the case of Max indicates, some others can be more flexible about their style and possibly their identities.

Much feminist scholarship on globalization points out that global economic imperatives and processes have an important impact on the household and home (e.g., Unterhalter, 1996). Clearly, the changing character of work has implications for the family, but usually these are factored out of consideration in discussions of VET and young people's responses to VET in schools. In our view, to do so is to offer a most incomplete picture of the young worker/citizen who emerges from the new world work order.

Restructuring the Family and "Transitions" from Childhood to Adulthood

Over the last few decades, there have been massive changes in family forms: dual parent, sole parent, divorced, blended, de-facto "serial" and same-sex family groupings. In addition, changing patterns of work and unemployment are having a big impact on household dynamics (Probert and Mackie, 1996). We are now seeing all sorts of different patterns beyond the traditional family and the traditional use of household space. These include young people in work and parents not, mothers in work and not fathers, parents never home due to overwork in one or multiple jobs, parents away frequently due to more and more travel associated with jobs, parents at home all the time due to outworking or an office at home, telecommuting, and possibly all the family at home all of the time due to them having no paid work at all. In our research, we have met young people across this range, including those who do not live at home and those who bring in the family income while at school.

These changes are bound to have an impact on the gender dynamics of households. There is not enough research being done on this topic, but there is some that indicates first that despite such changes women continue to carry most of the burden of emotional and caring work. Secondly, it indicates that such emotional and caring work is increasing due to the decline in welfare provision as governments withdraw more and more social services and as this places more and more strain on families (Bakker, 1996; Brodie, 1995; Edwards and Magarey, 1995). In this sense it is argued that women are "nurturing globalization" (Delhi, 1998).

All of this is having an impact on traditional transitions from childhood to adulthood. One aspect of such traditional transitions was the move into the paid labor market; paid employment was often seen to mark the onset of adulthood. But now young people's patterns of work are de-traditionalizing this transition process. More young people are in part-time work while at school, and more are continuing with their education at and after school. More are unemployed, underemployed, or in multiple jobs. More are staying at home longer, or they are part of the working poor, living independently. What we see then are changing patterns of independence and dependence between parents and children and again more potential for increased stress and tension in households (Sweet, 1995).

The gender implications of all of this are not yet clear, but here are some suggestions in our research. They may well re-traditionalize girls, particularly those who spend more time at home and who live at home longer. The private sphere is a traditional space for girls and women. They may thus be expected to carry more of the burden of the household work. Indeed, the following remark is not at all unusual among the young women in our study:

> I do a lot of the stuff now that my mum works. I'd come home from school and I'd cook dinner and for my brothers and then have to cook a different meal for my dad who just won't eat what my brothers eat and then I'd clean up and then I'd do my homework after that.

While we are not aware of any research on the topic, the extent to which such changes also place girls more at risk of various forms of abuse in the home is worth exploring. As we suggest below and have expanded at length elsewhere, when masculinity is under siege it may seek to reassert itself through various forms of violent and abusive behavior (Kenway and Fitzclarence, 1997).

On the other hand, if the girls are in work and contributing to the household income it may have the opposite effect. For example, one girl in a school vocational program is the primary income earner in her household now that her father has lost his job. She says she now feels more adult, and less is expected of her in terms of household work:

And so we've only got my mum who's working a part-time job, like three or four hours a day she works and then that's it and my brother's looking for a job. So it's really hard right now. . . . I think it's when I've got, now actually because I've got more responsibility then ever. Like before I used to work when I wanted, but now I sort of have to you know, save my money and think of what I'm going to do with it. . . . I have to think where the money's going.

Gender identity issues arise here for boys too. Take the case of unemployed boys. Having no work, no income, and much additional time in the traditional female space of the home may well place their sense of their masculinity at risk. This may have implications for the ways they behave in public spaces and lead them to search for risks that are dangerous to themselves and to others in order to prove their masculinity to themselves and their friends. It may also lead them to try to assert additional power in the household and in relationships in traditionally gendered ways. These are matters that we are currently considering.

Restructuring Schools and the Transitions from School to Work

De- and re-centralizing the institutions of the state is a feature of globalization and Australian schools, and VET programs are feeling the effects of such influences. On the decentralizing side of this agenda are school management, funding on a per capita basis, and the interschool competition that arises from both. On the re-centralizing side are curriculum and, ironically, market ideologies. VET for school students is part of this dynamic (see further, Kenway et al., 1997).

VET is centralized through the reflexively ordered National Training Reform Agenda (Kenway and Willis, 1995). Indeed, it represents what Giddens (1994) calls "burgeoning institutional reflexivity." Over time and in various ways, an avalanche of reports has led to VET curricula that promote workplace competencies, enterprise education, and new apprenticeship and traineeship schemes. While such documents appear to represent a sense of certainty in the field, in fact "radical doubt" (Giddens, 1994) about their effects has led to their constant revision (see Kenway, 1999; Kelly, 1999). In contrast, VET is decentralized through another avalanche of imperatives that cluster under the master narrative of the market. These include school/industry partnerships and the introduction of the training market with its stress on a level playing field between public and private providers and user choice and user pays. Schools now compete for clients (students and industry partners for work placement).

The schools in our study have all developed different orientations to the government imperatives for the vocationalization of education. Some have adopted a narrow competency or a broad competency agenda, others an enterprise curriculum, others a whole-school enterprise model, and others have vocationalized the entire curriculum. Most have entered some sorts of partnerships with local businesses and with private and public further education providers. In this context we see the rise of the entrepreneurial school, which uses vocational education to market itself and to gain a competitive edge against its competitors—other schools. Students recognize the benefits of a well-marketed school: "Even my last job that I had . . . when they said oh you go to St Mary's College, we've heard that's a good school, you know and they knew about it, they'd heard of it, so I guess it's got a good reputation, so."

We also see the rise of the school that reorganizes itself mainly as a VET school. These processes also promote the emergence of the entrepreneurial, "networked" VET coordinator, who hustles for work placements, partnerships, sponsors, and grants.

These shifts generate new gender and power issues for schools, teachers, and students. In the field of vocational education, entrepreneurial males seem to be taking over from more pastoral females. Networking with local business and industry and local service organizations such as the Rotary Club seems to be easier for the males. Some schools are becoming private providers and are making demands that certain of their teachers retrain. Such demands are usually made on those teachers whose subjects are attracting less student numbers. These are the humanities and such social sciences as history and geography. Traditionally, female teachers predominate in these areas, and thus it is females who are under the most pressure to reinvent themselves in line with the new vocational agenda.

New vocational agendas require the reorganization of students' use of space and time. Without going into all the details, VET students in schools are now dispersed across quite complicated multicredentialing and multisite arrangements. For example, they must move between the school, a Technical and Further Education (TAFE) college or private providers (PP) of VET and the workplaces where they do their work placement programs. In this context the school timetable becomes either a source of liberation or constraint. The capacity to move with ease and to use time efficiently is essential.

Currently VET in schools is contending with both new and old gender and class issues. Old traditions die hard. VET is still on the margins of most schools, although some try to adopt a whole-school approach—invoking the head, the hand, and the heart. VET, however, still remains lower in status than general education. It is still seen to be for the "less bright" students or for working-class kids, mainly boys. It is still dominated numerically and psychically by boys. It is still very gender segmented in terms of subject and vocational choices. In addition, students crossing the borders between school, TAFE/private provider, and workplaces usually travel across three different gendered and adult/child cultures. Schools sometimes feel the weaker partner—unable to negotiate gender issues for fear of risking the partnership.

In this research we commonly hear old gender stories of very sexist trainers and teachers in TAFEs and workplaces, most often in fields that are nontraditional for girls. We also hear stories of sexual harassment of girls and some boys. Students now have to negotiate across these different cultures, and their transitions can be quite difficult. They face extra workload and extra psychic load. In addition, TAFE and PP courses can be costly; they may involve fees, travel, equipment, and uniform. These extra costs can cause additional difficulties for some young people and some schools. The question is, are the "at risk" kids the ones who are doing these courses? There is some evidence to suggest that it is the "can-do" girls and boys that are involved in these programs and that all of this is too much for those students most at risk (Angwin et al., 1998).

There are some new and old class and gender issues around the ways in which VET is caught up in the marketing agendas of schools, and matters of risk, trust, and ontological security are intertwined here. Getting students jobs becomes part of the marketing strategies of schools, and unfortunately some schools make promises they cannot keep, raising issues of trust between school and students. Getting sponsors and partnerships becomes an important part of programs, thus schools want to put their best students forward. Some potential students are seen to be bad for the school's image with their partners and if not exactly encouraged out of VET programs, then are not exactly encouraged to stay in them either. Other, high achieving, highly motivated students from other districts are encouraged into the school, displacing opportunities for the students normally at the school. Neglect, ill treatment, and harassment in the workplace may not necessarily be addressed due to worries about the viability of partnerships and programs or to teachers' lack of time in schools under stress. We have evidence of girls being asked, "Do you want to risk the program for other girls?"

The institutional reflexivity and manufactured uncertainty (Giddens, 1994) that characterizes the emergence of VET policy and practices, and the de- and re-traditionalizing class and gender identities that emerge in a post-traditional social order have profound effects in the schools in our study. These processes unsettle some basic (traditional) understandings of schooling, education, and young people for teachers in our schools. Many teachers face enormous difficulties keeping up to date with the reflexively monitored VET system and must increasingly rely on expert advise to assist them. However, reflexivity is not necessarily a feature of most vocational education curricula; competency-based curricula is hegemonic with unreflexive workers the object. While students are certainly the subject and object of various expert systems, not all schools have a World of Work component. In these circumstances students can be exposed to a curriculum that does not require them to know anything at all about the politics of workplaces, industrial relations, the changing nature of work, unemployment, and so on. In such cases, students are implicitly encouraged to be compliant workers without a sense of themselves as worker-citizens with a critical and creative approach to the workplace. This does not bode well for future workers in the world of enterprise bargaining, workplace agreements, and so forth. Minimal survival values guide many programs and students' engagements with them.

Of course some schools do teach students about the gendered and other politics of work, and even some private providers do too. Take the case of Alison:

> I learnt a lot [from the Retail Course] because it actually helped while I was working. I picked up things like customer service and about knowing what rights I have as well. Like with my job when I first started there, they didn't pay me for about six weeks. . . . Something went wrong with my files and at first I was just like oh, you know, they'll pay me and I didn't say nothing. I just sort of sat back and waited but I noticed that they weren't doing anything unless I rang constantly to nag them about it. Anyway I talked to someone at the Retail Course and they told me that I have to constantly go back. They called up for me and everything and they organized it and they came down with me so I could actually get my pay. Apparently my name wasn't even on the payroll at all and that's why I didn't get paid. No one had even bothered to put it on there. So that helps cause I didn't know what to do. I was sort of like thinking oh you know they'll pay me, I work here.
>
> It's not only useful at work. When I go out and I buy things a lot of places say no refunds, no this, no that. But we learnt a lot of things like, everywhere you're allowed to have a refund and people can't say that you're not allowed to. You're entitled to your money back and if things are falsely advertised you're entitled to it for free. Some people say no refund on it or you can't bring it back if it's been reduced but according to the law you can. Yeah, so there was a lot of things like that.

Where questions of worker and consumer citizenship are addressed we see much richer survival values and narratives of self among the students. Indeed, for many of the students, vocational education programs, even in their most reductionist competency modality, have provided them with new mechanisms for self-identity. For many the choice to do such programs has indeed been a "fateful moment." Outside the school, they feel treated more like adults; we hear stories of very positive relationships with private providers of retail courses for example. They feel they are doing something worthwhile—something that will really improve their life chances and life choices. Indeed, they place a great deal of faith and trust in their program's capacity to give them the competitive edge. These students trust the school to do the best thing by them and to help them to understand what it means to work in the age of uncertainty.

We are yet to see how effective these programs will be, if they will fulfill their promises. Youth unemployment still looms large, and clearly schools cannot compensate for that. However, some schools and students are much better "placed" than others on this matter.

Restructuring Locality

Our research demonstrates that an appreciation of the changing economic base of place and the associated sociology and culture of place is vital to understanding the directions of vocational education in schools and in considering the suitability of schools' approaches. Each locality under scrutiny in our research is somewhat distinctive with regard to its economic, demographic, geographic, and climatic features. Each place is dynamically and differently articulated with wider forces, and these are clearly shaping the ways local people in schools and households live and change their lives. All the patterns noted above are manifest differently in different localities. Each has its particular patterns with regard to the labor market, the family, school to work patterns, and gender and class relations and identities.

The localities we are studying include depressed, "traditional" rural, entrepreneurial/tourist rural, provincial manufacturing cities in decline, inner-city localities empty of most possibilities of employment except in some service industries, and a post-Fordist boom city. Each of these different localities is differently affected by the localization of the global order of work. Many have also been affected by processes of national, state, and local government restructuring with regard to the privatization and downsizing of public services. Together with industry restructuring the demise of the public sector and reductions in public services have had a severe impact on people's capacity to find and travel to work.

Most of our localities have high levels of general unemployment, youth unemployment, and "working poor." Indeed, in some, social welfare is an important part of local economies. These localities are of special concern due to the economic and social difficulties and associated cultural changes they are experiencing. School students must contend with particular problems because of the instability and uncertainty of their locations and thus require specific educational interventions.

Many regional economies in Australia are presently exploring various forms of renewal and restructuring (McKinsey and Company, 1994). This is the case in our studies, too. Our localities have their own particular responses to globalizing processes and have mobilized their resources in particular ways. In some localities the marketing of place, tourism, and hospitality have developed as part of the locality's growth strategy. Schools, industries, and local councils have responded in a range of ways.

Economic restructuring has often led to the displacement of manufacturing in regional areas as these industries move from rust bucket to sunbelt (if they are lucky). However, restructuring has also led to the "manufacturing of place" by local government councils. Local councils have taken on the job not only of developing regional economic plans but also of promoting the region to prospective industries (employers) and residents. They are now in the business of branding the local—of giving it an image, a personality. This is done through such things as the use of glossy brochures and stickers and posters.

Our research project includes two schools in the Geelong region of the Australian state of Victoria. Here the City of Greater Geelong has just re-"badged" itself as a "great place to live" through the slogan "Geelong: Smart Move." In brochures, posters, and booklets, much is made of the waterfront and access to nature (nearby beaches and mountains). Colorful flags line the entrance to the city, and incentives are made available to potential homebuyers, including free membership in the Geelong Australian Rules Football Club—the Cats. One of the city's main industries and employers is the multinational car manufacturing company Ford. Decisions made at a distance constantly threaten the future of this company in the town. The locals are urged to buy Ford via this slogan: "Ford: Live It." Think local is a driving imperative (excuse the pun).

Two of our other schools are in the western suburbs of the city of Melbourne, a region historically reliant on the employment opportunities offered by large-scale manufacturing enterprises. It is to these parts of Melbourne that successive waves of postwar unskilled migrant labor have been attracted. Consequently this region now boasts an incredible diversity of ethnic, religious, and language groups. These groups have generated extensive community networks during the postwar boom years and in the last three decades of industrial decline. One young Maltese Australian woman in our study boasted of, and also lamented, her connection to a large family network of uncles, aunts, and seventy-eight cousins.

In this region the same processes of manufacturing place are occurring. The brochures and websites developed by various local and regional government agencies now emphasize the lifestyle benefits of multicultural diversity as the economy attempts to restructure and build on its "iron age" infrastructure. The Western Region Economic Development Organization (WREDO), for instance, sees itself "as a facilitator of change within the region—a promoter of the region's competitive benefits of world class infrastructure (Australia's best port, best road system, and best airport) within a dynamic, multicultural living environment. WREDO and its stakeholder groups in local government and the private sector have repositioned the region to emerge once again as one of the powerhouses of Australia's economy." One of these "stakeholders," the City of Maribynong in its 1996/97 Annual Report argues that the city "is the cultural, business and retail centre of Mebourne's western region. The west is Australia's premier industrial zone." Industrial land is ten times less expensive than in Sydney and fifty-six times less expensive than in Osaka.

> 60% of all industrial land sales in Victoria last year were in Melborne's west. . . . 41% of all Victoria's exports are from the west. . . . Over the next four years there will be

$7 billion worth of projects in Melbourne's west. . . . [This region] has the best accessibility to road, rail and sea transport in Melbourne. It is 5 minutes from Melbourne's ports and national rail freight centre. It is 10 minutes from the Central Business District. It is 15 minutes from Melbourne Airport. It has quick and easy access by road and rail to all parts of Victoria.

This accessibility to various important nodes in transport networks figures prominently in the promotional material put out by WREDO and the various local government authorities. It appears that if you intend to promote the region for its manufacturing industrial base, then you have to be able to demonstrate its connections to transport networks that can move manufactured products into global markets. This is a different process to promoting an information age economy because then you only need to demonstrate your access to information networks. In the context of three decades of de-industrialization, there is an attempt to reposition the region as an industrial zone that has access to global transport networks (for export/import activities) and compares favorably to other industrial zones in global manufacturing economies/markets.

Our studies include localities that have degenerated and then regenerated. For example we have one region where the work opportunities abound. In the 1960s and early 1970s this was a traditional agricultural (wheat, cows) area in trouble. However, in the 1970s and early 1980s there was an inward migration of alternative lifestylers ("hippies"), often disaffected middle-class professionals. At the time there was much local consternation and policing of the boundaries with regard to who was and was not entitled to live in the region and claim it as home. The hippies were seen as invaders, disrupting others' sense of self and its connection to their sense of place. Over the subsequent two decades these hippies led an economic recovery based on new forms of primary production and the de-traditionalization of older forms of primary production—gourmet beef (lightly marinated). The region's wineries now produce very fashionable table wines. The new arrivals were also instrumental in generating new nonrural industries in what Lash and Urry (1994) have called global "economies of signs and spaces." In these globalizing economies, tradition and nature become commodities. In this region we witness the emergence of various art and craft cottage industries, "new antiques," tourism (city to coast; inland to coast), leisure, holidays, weekenders (surfing), and nature-based enterprises. The area is now well known for its connections to the culture industries. It holds cultural spectacles. Its annual festival flies in international superstars such as Elton John. This move reflects an international trend toward the expansion of the service and tourist sector, and this area has clearly (cleverly) anticipated the rise of the tourist industry and the culture industries (see further Willis and McLelland, 1997).

This locality is also rich in a sense of community, and this flows into the school's vocational programs. It is a middle-class school, rich in cultural and other resources. Teachers only have to say what they want with regard to work placement and they get it locally and more widely. The school will take students all over the state for work placement. It has integrated the VET with the state's High School Certificate (HSC) and students do both, "adding value" to their HSC. They trust their school to know how to help them. Many go away to university but usually come home to summer work: seasonal work in a village where employers who are neighbors and friends know them. Flow across space is easy, normal, and natural for the young people of this region (see further Willis and McLelland, 1997).

In contrast though and in the main, the localities under scrutiny have degenerated and stagnated in the face of processes of globalization and are now struggling to reinvent themselves. Take the case of another rural area. This is a one-industry town: the dairy industry and the local dairy factory, which we will call Corbetts, is the major "player."

What we see in this area are the ways in which the nature of both business organization and dairy production are changing. Corbetts was originally a farmers' cooperative, embedded in the community. It became a public company then joined up with other similar companies to become a global operator in the expanding dairy industry. (It has its own webpage.) Once Corbetts had strong connections to the locality, but these connections are changing. The manager used to be "a big man" in the community: he belonged to local service organizations, the Rotary, and the like. Now Corbetts is managed from a distance with global as well as local markets in mind. In order to be competitive in these new spaces, and to win and maintain a distant, "trusting" customer base, it needs to conform to International Best Practice (IBP)—ISO-100 (a standardized, internationally recognized schedule of quality assurance practices).

Here we see the global in the local in very direct way. A leading local employer now operates at arm's length from the local schools and does not even have work placement for students due to the particular management, work, health, and safety practices necessary to maintain IBP. The path from school and farm to factory and back to the farm for local boys has been disrupted. Family connections into the factory are irrelevant for employment purposes. IBP demands certain hygiene and quality control practices that require new forms of work skills and expertise. In the context of globalizing markets and "best practices," dairy production and the processing and manufacturing of dairy products are being transformed by new production technologies and products; processes of rationalization at the company level and at the farm level—larger farms, larger herds, new milking technologies, new herd-gene technologies that have increased farm output, and a movement into global food-products markets. What we observe here is the way in which the locality is opened up and restructured by regional/ global markets and networks and flows (Lash and Urry, 1994). The industry and the economic base of the region are increasingly regulated by processes and flows quite distant from the places where students at the local school live and might hope to gain a job.

Geography is always gendered as gender relations in this region show. Indeed, they reflect the deeply gendered patterns of behavior in rural areas that Dempsey (1990 and 1992) elaborated upon in the early 1990s. Many of the boys subscribe to traditional masculinities associated with farming and mechanics and sport. Farms are passed down from fathers to sons, but boys "back up with a trade" just in case. Their views of gender are also spatially organized with girls doing the inside work and boys the outside.

The girls' work chances are limited by the local labor markets that are both very restricted and highly gendered. There are limited jobs for girls, most of which pay poorly. Typically, the girls have two types of response: absorption in local cultures of femininity or migration. Some girls plan to stay in the district and take whatever casual jobs are available. They celebrate their locality. They construct their femininity very much the way their mothers did around notions of home, community building, and women's rural role. They also become involved in the informal and reproductive economy of activities such as childcare (baby-sitting). One gets the sense in talking to these girls that they are preparing to become guardians of the local moral order. Already they are constructing the city as a dangerous space of drugs and crime and, in contrast, the rural as safe.

The migrating girls from the area have a deficit view of their locality and sometimes a fantasy view of elsewhere. Again the city may be configured as alien, and so their ambitions may be to go to a neighboring provincial city. Meet Mary: "I am from the country and I've grown up here all my life. I just want to get out. Not just to the city. Maybe just out of this area where everyone knows everyone, out where there's chances of better jobs in bigger places." "I just want to get out" is a common refrain of many country girls.

Our research also includes some city suburbs that are empty of industry and work opportunities for young adults. Indeed they are increasingly empty of many useful public services (Lash and Urry, 1994). Sometimes, the schools have to provide work placement themselves or the students have to go out of the area to find it, a long way out. This can be very expensive in money and time terms for those who can ill afford it. Poor public transport may mean students leaving for work placement at five o'clock in the morning to make all the bus connections.

Crossing locational borders may also mean crossing stylistic boarders too. Some girls in particular have found it hard to match the style demands of workplaces on the up-side of town. Indeed, the style demands of the up-side of town are increasingly migrating into their home locations.

I applied for a job around this area and the guy just took my resume but apparently said to one of the workers that I looked really sus(pect), I looked like the type to rip off his store and I thought I've never done a wrong thing in my life, like I've never ripped off stores, I'm just not like that, nah. So I was really cut up about that, I haven't been to his shop for ages now. Yeah he didn't want to employ anyone local. He goes because they'll get into a scam. He doesn't have a high opinion of this area.

Living in this area sort of stigmatizes you a bit. . . . I was stunned, I thought oh my God. I thought you can't judge me just by looking at me. I'm able to sell and everything and he just went on about the area that I lived and everything. So, now I don't go there and it's actually quite a good shop.

In some localities there is one industry only, and schools have had to work hard to build relationships with that industry in the interest of local students. In one such case the industry refused to employ local students, believing them to be "rat bags." The school has spent several years showing that industry's management that "the kids are not monsters." In contrast, another school, despite very poor tertiary entrance results, refuses to "make kids fodder for industry" and sticks rigidly to the modernist notion that the general academic curriculum fits all. We have other localities where local industry has taken the initiative and actively sought to support local youth in the area as part of their corporate citizenship responsibilities. Some local councils are considering schools as part of the regeneration of regional economies.

Clearly some of the locations in this study are geographies of trust, hope, and security; others are geographies of risk, uncertainty, and "future panic." Overall, in location, gender, and class terms our research suggests that different localities need different approaches to vocational education (see Kenway, 1999). We are anxious that some of the "best practice" VET models we see offered simply don't fit many localities. One size does not fit all.

CONCLUSION

In this chapter we have offered both an eagle's and a worm's eye-view of the implications of globalization for the social and cultural contexts of VET in schools in Australia. We have shown how the restructuring of the labor market, the family, schooling, and locality can be understood as expressions of global trends and forces. We have also shown how each involves and evokes the de- and re-traditionalizing of gender. In so doing we paid particular attention to the intersections between gender, class, and locality. In discussing globalization in this manner we have both drawn on and to some extent problematized sociological ideas associated with the post-traditional social order, the changing relationships between space and time, and the rise of social reflexivity. We have also drawn on ideas associated with cultural geography. In deploying such ideas we hope to enrich the somewhat sterile discussions of globalization that abound in studies of VET. While we have not sought to evaluate globalization in either positive or negative terms, we have pointed to some of the problems that arise as a consequence of it.

These are times of great upheaval; risks and uncertainty abound. Gender and class are being shaken up in ways that are both challenging some traditions of inequality and reinscribing others. In preparing young people for this new world of work orders, old solutions may not fit new problems. New solutions will also bring problems and possibilities of their own. Researchers have a responsibility to help tease these out. Schools have an enormous responsibility to understand these changes and their implications for the particular students in their care. Through our research we seek to document the complexities of the altered contexts of educational life and to assist schools to prepare their students for the life of work and the work of life.

REFERENCES

Adkins, Lisa. 1995. *Gendered Work: Sexuality, Family and the Labor Market*. Buckingham, UK: Open University Press.

———. 1997 (July 17–19). Community and Economy: The Retraditionalisation of Gender. Paper presented at "Transformations: Thinking through Feminism," Institute for Women's Studies, University of Lancaster.

Angwin, Jennifer, Colin Henry, Louise Laskey, Robin McTaggart, Nicola Picken. 1998. Paths to Pathways: Vocational Education and Training for Educationally Disadvantaged Groups of Young People. Deakin University, Geelong, Deakin Centre for Education and Change.

Bagguley, Paul, Jane Mark-Lawson, Don Shapiro, John Urry, Sylvia Walby, and Alan Warde. 1990. *Restructuring: Place, Class and Gender*. London: Sage.

Bakker, Isabella (ed.). 1996. *Rethinking Restructuring: Gender and Change in Canada*. Toronto: University of Toronto Press.

Beck, Ulrich. 1992. *Risk Society—Towards a New Modernity*. London: Sage.

Brodie, Janine. 1995. *Politics on the Margins: Restructuring and the Canadian Women's Movement*. Halifax: Fernwood Publishing.

Delhi, Kari. 1998. Nurturing Globalisation. International symposium on *Gender, Education and Globalization*. Paper presented at the American Education Research Association (AERA) Conference, San Diego.

Dempsey, Ken. 1990. *Smalltown: A Study of Social Inequality, Cohesion and Belonging*. Melbourne: Oxford University Press.

———. 1992. *A Man's Town: Inequality between Women and Men in Rural Australia*. Melbourne: Oxford University Press.

Edwards, Anne, and Susan Magarey. 1995. *Women in a Restructuring Australia: Work and Welfare*. St. Leonards, New South Wales: Allen and Unwin.

Giddens, Anthony. 1991. *Modernity and Self Identity: Self and Society in the Late Modern Age*. Cambridge: Polity Press.

———. 1994. *Beyond Left and Right: The Future of Radical Politics*. Stanford, CA: Stanford University Press.

Grewal, Inderpal, and Caren Kaplan. 1994. *Scattered Hegemonies: Postmodernity and Transnational Feminist Practice*. Minneapolis: University of Minnesota Press.

Haraway, Donna. 1991. *Simians, Cyborgs, and Women: The Reinvention of Nature*. London: Free Association Press.

Kelly, Peter. 1999. Wild and Tame Zones: Regulating the Transitions of Youth at Risk. *Journal of Youth Studies*, vol. 2, no. 2, pp. 193–211.

Kenway, Jane. 1999. *In and Out of Place: Girls, Localities and Work*. Paper presented at the annual conference of the Network of Women in Further Education, Northern Sydney, Institute of TAFE, Sydney.

———. 1999. Change of Address? Educating Economics and Vocational Education and Training. *International Journal of Work and the Economy* (UK).

Kenway, Jane, and Lindsay Fitzclarence. 1997. Masculinity, Violence and Schooling Challenging Poisonous Pedagogies. *Gender and Education*, Special Issue on Boys' Education, (UK), vol. 9, no.1, pp. 117–33.

Kenway, Jane, Peter Watkins, and Karen Tregenza. 1998. Vocational Education Policies: Are Boys at Risk? In Sheena Erskine and Maggie Wilson (eds.), *Gender Issues in International Education*, New York: Garland, pp. 71–91.

Kenway, Jane, and Sue Willis, with Jill Blackmore and Leonie Rennie. 1997/8. *Answering Back: Girls, Boys and Feminism in Schools*. London: Routledge (1998); and Sydney: Allen and Unwin (1997).

Kenway, Jane, Karen Tregenza, and Peter Watkins (eds.). 1997. Vocational Education Today: Topical Issues. Deakin Centre for Education and Change, Geelong, Victoria.

Kenway, Jane and Sue Willis. 1995. *Critical Visions: Policy and Curriculum Rewriting the Future of Education, Gender and Work*. Canberra: Australian Government Publishing Service.

Lash, Scott, and John Urry. 1994. *Economies of Signs and Space*. London: Sage.

Mac an Ghaill, Mairtian. 1994. *The Making of Men: Masculinities, Sexualities and Schooling*. Buckingham, UK: Open University Press.

———. 1996. "What about the Boys?": Schooling, Class and Crisis Masculinity. *Sociological Review*, vol. 44, no. 3, pp.381–97.

Mackay, Hugh. 1993. *Reinventing Australia: The Mind and Mood of Australia in the 90s*. Pymble, New South Wales: Angus and Robertson.

Massey, Doreen. 1984. *Spatial Divisions of Labour: Social Structures and the Geography of Production*. Macmillan: London.

———. 1994. *Space, Place and Gender*. Cambridge: Polity Press.

McKinsey and Company. 1994. *Lead Local, Compete Global: Unlocking the Growth Potential of Australia's Regions*. Sydney: McKinsey and Co.

Pocock, Barbara. 1995. Women's Work and Wages. In Anne Edwards and Susan Magarey (eds.), *Women in a Restructuring Australia: Work and Welfare*. St Leonards, New South Wales: Allen and Unwin, pp. 95–120.

Probert, Belinda. 1995. The Transformation of Work: Social, Cultural and Political Contexts. In J. Spierings, I. Voorendt, and J. Spoehr (eds.), *Jobs for Young Australians*. Adelaide: Jobs for Young Australians Conference Organising Committee in association with Social Justice Research Foundation Inc., pp. 25–31.

Probert, Belinda, and Mackie, Fiona. 1996. *The Work Generation: Work and Identity in the Nineties*. Melbourne: Brotherhood of St Laurence.

Sweet, Richard. 1995. All of Their Talents? Policies and Programs for Fragmented and Interrupted Transitions. Dusseldorp Skills Forum, October.

Teese, Richard, Merryn Davies, Margaret Charlton, and John Polesel. 1995. *Who Wins at School? Boys and Girls in Australian Secondary Education*. Melbourne: Department of Education Policy and Management, the University of Melbourne.

Unterhalter, Elaine. 1996. States, Households and the Market in World Bank Discourse, 1985–1995: A Feminist Critique. *Discourse: Studies in the Cultural Politics of Education*, vol. 17, no. 3, pp. 389–402.

Urry, John. 1995. *Consuming Places*. London: Routledge.

Walby, Silvia. 1997. *Gender Transformations*. London: Routledge.

Wexler, Philip. 1992. *Becoming Somebody: Toward a Social Psychology of School*. London: Falmer Press.

Willis, Sue, and McLelland, Peter. 1997. Reading the Region. Paper presented at the Australian Association for Educational Research conference, Brisbane, 1997.

10

Globalization, Adult Education, and Development

Shirley Walters

The processes of globalization reconfigure the international and local contexts in which the practices and policies of adult education are being debated and redesigned. Adult education, as used here, can be informal, nonformal, or formal and is integral to social processes. It includes (1) educational strategies that help people to survive the harsh conditions in which they live (examples include education relating to basic needs such as health care, nutrition, family planning, and literacy); (2) skilling for the informal sector of the economy; (3) skilling for the formal labor market, including training for the unemployed worker, and re-skilling people already engaged in the labor market at all levels; and (4) political and cultural education that addresses civic issues, social justice, and people's participation in civil society (Wolpe, 1994). In attempting to rethink adult education in the context of globalization, we enter vast, largely uncharted, waters that are swirling with contradictory currents.

GLOBALIZATION

Globalization is shorthand for describing the current global capitalist economy. It reflects processes in which social relations are not only linked at the economic level but also permeate the political, social, cultural, and environmental spheres to impact on everyday life. The following illustrations of the cultural, economic, and political dimensions of globalization are provided by an adult education nongovernmental organization (NGO) in Cape Town, South Africa (International Labour Research and Information Group, ILRIG, 1998, p. 1). They describe graphically some commonsense understandings of globalization and how global forces are seen to impact on local realities and vice versa.

An activist told how he woke up one morning and found the body of a dead man in his front garden. Apparently the man had been murdered during the night. The murder took place on the same day that Princess Diana was killed in a car crash in Paris, France. For many days thereafter, every time he switched on his television or radio he heard every detail about the life, death and family of Princess Diana. During this same period he kept going to the police, to neighbors, to many people in his community trying to find out the details of the man who had been murdered in his front garden. It was two weeks before he was able to find out the name of the man. He never found out why the man was killed. This he said is what globalization is doing to our lives, making it easier to find out what is happening to famous people far away than to ordinary people on our own doorsteps.

In 1997, [South African] Minister of Health Nkosazana Zuma put forward a plan to restrict the buying or importing of expensive, brand name drugs, and to promote the production and importation of cheaper, generic drugs. These generic drugs, she said, would offer patients exactly the same medicine at a much cheaper price. Progressive health practitioners and community activists praised the plan. But others opposed it. International pharmaceutical companies threatened to sue the South African government for restricting trade, saying that the proposal from Minister Zuma violated international regulations on free trade. Some South African chemical workers, employed by international pharmaceutical companies also questioned the wisdom of Zuma's policy. They claimed that generic drugs were cheaper because they were being made in India by child labor. The workers argued that globalization was threatening their jobs.

On New Year's Eve 1993, guerrillas from the Zapatista National Liberation Front occupied several towns in southern Mexico. They were demanding land and democracy. Since their actions were given no attention by the local media, they put news of their struggle and their political program onto the Internet computer network. Across the world, activists got information about the Zapatistas from their computers and took action to lend support. Today there are Zapatista solidarity groups and computer networks in dozens of countries. Some people say that globalization was crucial in terms of building international solidarity for the freedom struggle of the Zapatistas.

Each of the above examples demonstrates the multilayered and complex impact of globalization on the local and, in the latter two, the impact of the local on the global. The first example highlights the cultural dimension of globalization, in particular how the mass media influences local realities. The second illustrates the economic dimension and, as Harris (1997, p. 125) states, the economic dimension is the centrifugal force of globalization, "a force sufficiently powerful that other dimensions of globalization are subsidiary." This example shows the powerful role of transnational corporations (TNCs) and "free trade" economic policies. It highlights the contradictory position of workers within the TNCs who express both concern about their jobs and about the exploitation of child labor in India. It is also an example of local resistance to the control of a national market by a TNC. The third example illustrates the political and cultural dimensions of globalization. It shows how a local political struggle can be taken up globally through the use of new communication and information technologies. It demonstrates a form of globalization that is referred to as "globalization from below" (Marshall, 1997, p. 57).

Giddens (1994, p. 4) states, "Globalization is really about the transformation of space and time." Globalization diminishes space and time dimensions of physical geography, thereby permitting, encouraging, and sometimes requiring new kinds of human interaction. In the above illustrations it is clear that these new possibilities can be used for multiple purposes and for different social and political ends. It is important therefore to qualify the different perspectives of globalization that are under discussion. There is an argument from people on the Left who describe at least two perspectives of globalization (Arruda, 1996; Gindin, 1998; DAWN, 1997). One is "competitive globalization," which is the dominant form. Its internal logic is the accumulation of capital. It is top-down in its approach to development; it is shaped by the corporate interests of TNCs and the geopolitical interests of the rich and powerful corporations and countries. Then there is "cooperative globalization." Its internal logic is accumulation of human capacities, with human development as its primary motivating force. It has a bottom-up approach to development that is shaped by the basic needs of the planet's inhabitants and by citizen action. The proponents of this perspective argue that it is imperative for the very survival of the planet to find development alternatives to the neoliberal, competitive, and environmentally destructive economic and sociopolitical policies and practices that are dominating the world.

Debates about globalization are also debates about development. As many intellectuals, development workers, activists, and educators analyze the last five decades of international development, there is growing agreement that the dominant top-down ways of doing things have been wrong. There are still very large numbers of people on the never-ending treadmill of poverty, deprivation, and marginalization. Some 2.5 billion people live in abysmal poverty. At the same time the environmental resource base on which people depend is degrading— forests, rivers, and productive soils are gradually disappearing. Given that the aim of the last five decades of development have been to eradicate poverty, regenerate the environment, and influence the demographics, the five decades, Khosla (1998, p. 12) believes, can be seen as lost. As he says, "for those who have traveled the 50 years down this road with their windows open, it has become obvious that the future belongs to smaller, more decentralized initiatives that involve the active participation of people affected."

To be successful from human development perspectives, actions must be designed from the bottom up. They have to be much more sensitive than before to issues of gender, social justice, environment, community, and local culture; and they need to lead to financially and ecologically sustainable institutions. The argument is that goals of development need to be redefined to achieve "the accumulation of human capacities" rather than the "accumulation of capital." The interests of the majority of women and men will be served only through forms of "cooperative globalization."

The contestation over what forms of development are necessary and possible within local, national, regional, or global contexts is at the heart of discussions about globalization and adult education. It influences the multiple, competing, often contradictory adult education policies and practices.

SOME TRENDS AND ISSUES FOR ADULT EDUCATION

The debates and redesign of adult education policies in South Africa since the early 1990s manifest the competing needs for economic development and simultaneous achievement of redress and equity for black women and men excluded from the education and training system by apartheid.

In 1994 the first democratic government, employing the rhetoric of basic needs and provision of opportunities to the previously disenfranchised, was elected, which provided a moment of social restructuring and democratic possibility. But this was a moment framed by a phase of capitalist development that demanded that South Africa plug into the highly competitive globalized economy. The debates around adult education and training have encapsulated the at times competing interests of the business sector, the revolutionary trade union movement, and elements within the state and civil society. The issues have related to how adult education can address the simultaneous needs of competitiveness within the global economy and the meeting of basic needs among the 70 percent of the population who are impoverished.

Historically, a vibrant democratic civil society set the stage for adult education as integral to cultural and political activities. The international anti-apartheid movement was an excellent example of "cooperative globalization." The apartheid government and the business sector invested minimally in adult education and training. With the political change the expectation from civil society activists was that adult education for survival and for cultural, community, and economic development would be expanded rapidly. This has not happened except in relation to the economy, where levers to ensure greater investment in vocational training by employers are being put in place. The South African case places in sharp relief the questions about the social purposes and the provision of adult education within "competitive" and "cooperative" perspectives globally.

Adult Education, Adult Learning, or Lifelong Learning?

In 1997 the Fifth International Conference on Adult Education (CONFINTEA V) was held under the auspices of the United Nations in Hamburg, Germany. These conferences take place every ten years and reflect the major trends in the field. In the Hamburg Declaration and the Agenda for the Future (UNESCO, 1997) the discourse of *adult education* changed to *adult learning*. This shift is significant as it holds within it enormous challenges in terms of both pedagogy and organization of adult education.

The shift in discourse to adult learning reflects the influence of information and communication technologies such as the Internet on adult education and adult learning processes, particularly in the powerful industrialized countries. The technologies are enabling individuals to access information without formal enrollment in courses, without a "teacher." Learning rather than teaching is being accentuated with the shift to the needs of learners rather than educators. Learning and teaching strategies are being fundamentally rethought as technologies revolutionize conceptions of time and space and enable different learning and teaching possibilities (Bishop, 1998).

Perhaps the shift also reflects the trend to privatize education and training and organize it primarily in relation to market needs. It is not entirely clear how far the change in language usage is rhetorical or indicative of deeper educational philosophical shifts, but, increasingly, individuals are required to take responsibility for their own learning. As the state retreats from responsibility for provision the onus is on individuals to engage in lifelong learning to keep abreast of developments in the marketplace.

The use of different terms is still fairly unstable. The shift to adult learning holds both promise and concern. Talk of adult learning is inclined to reflect a process of individualization rather than mobilization of groups of learners. It also does not speak to the organization of the field of practice. *Education* conveys some institutional structures to support provision whereas *learning* does not. At the same time, perhaps because it does not reflect structural arrangements, adult learning can be more easily understood as legitimate forms of practice within a wide range of sectors. It is, for example, easier for people in agriculture, health, or land affairs to recognize that adult learning is an integral and essential part of their development work rather than adult education.

While the shift in discourse is apparent at the global level, it has not necessarily taken root in local situations. For example, in South Africa there is the simultaneous use of a range of terms whose meanings have not necessarily settled. *Adult learning* is not in general use although it has begun to be used increasingly by those most clearly located within the field of adult educational practice and influenced by the Hamburg Conference.

There has been a range of terms used to describe adult education, including *continuing education, nonformal education*, and *popular education*, each with its own history and meanings. More recently in South Africa there has been the adoption within government of the term *Adult Basic Education and Training* (ABET) to denote "the second chance to learn" provision by the state, business, and NGOs and to register the need to integrate education and training. It includes adult education up until the equivalent of nine years of schooling and is strongly linked to formalizing processes within the field. But even within the government domain, where ABET language has dominated policy documents, shifts continue to be visible as adult education and training, lifelong learning, and ABET jostle with one another for ascendancy. An illustration of this is that the National Directorate was recently renamed the Adult Education and Training Directorate from being the ABET Directorate. This signifies at least a recognition of the need for adult education to relate to the next band of provision within the Further Education.

The use of adult learning as opposed to adult education has begun to infiltrate South African policy documents and general discourse. It links to the adoption of the framework of *lifelong learning* by the new government in 1994, which mirrors trends internationally. Lifelong learning itself is still to be given substantive content and at the present signals the need for individuals who have been disadvantaged by apartheid to have opportunities for "second chance learning" and for the workforce to be skilled to compete globally. Within policy documents lifelong learning hinges mainly on the construction of a National Qualifications Framework (NQF), which is to provide a central framework in which all qualifications are registered and to which providers are accountable. NFQ is to enable learners to access the education and training system more easily and to move more agilely across institutions and learning pathways. It focuses on qualification of learners and therefore emphasizes the individualization of learning. The NQF mirrors developments in several other countries and will enable greater transferability of qualifications across national boundaries as well. The trend toward greater compatibility of qualifications reflects the globalization of economies.

The notion of adult learning or lifelong learning tends to de-emphasize government responsibility for learning. It fits more closely with a market-driven approach to adult education and training, which is concerned mainly with developing the economy. In South Africa the neoliberal economic imperatives of workers to achieve global competitiveness appear to have gained ascendancy over demands of social movements for social justice, redress, and equity. In line with these developments we can anticipate that the language of adult learning and lifelong learning will grow in prominence.

Demarcation of the Field

As suggested above, the contestation over language is not just a semantic concern. It reflects complex strands of different histories and different priorities. In South Africa the government's initial support of adult education in the form of ABET is already beginning to weaken. It has established small directorates or subdirectorates nationally and in provinces to manage its adult education centers. While this has been an advance on the previous apartheid government, which had actively suppressed adult educational activity among the black majority, it does not show the political will to sustain and expand its involvement.

Since 1994 the government has invested time and effort in orchestrating a collaborative policy development process for all stakeholders. This culminated in a policy launch of a new "National Multi-Year Implementation Plan for Adult Education and Training: Provision and Accreditation" in February 1998. At the same time as the plan was being launched at least three of the nine provinces had decided to temporarily close their adult education centers because of lack of financial resources. These contradictory practices result in growing disillusionment and disappointment at the lack of investment by the government in the field. While it had identified ABET as a lead project within the reconstruction and development processes, it has relied heavily on external donors to support the work. Donors are beginning to withdraw their levels of support as the gloss of the new South Africa fades as does the enthusiasm for adult education generally among the donor agencies.

While government at national and provincial levels through the Departments of Education has already begun to retreat from their financial support of adult education, there is a wide range of adult learning opportunities being made available. These are, for example, through the health, welfare, water, prisons, and labor sectors and through the media, where there has been a proliferation of thirty new community radio stations in the last four years. This then begs the question when asked to describe adult education—Where do you look and what do you look for?

As Paul Belanger (1994) has argued previously, "lifelong learning is not a norm to prescribe but an empirical reality to analyze and reconstruct." The same can be said for adult education or adult learning. Lifelong learning inevitably exists in all societies in different forms as people move through life's stages. Belanger argues that there are many "lifelong educations" as in each society lifelong learning refers to the totality of learning activities, which can be broken down into three specific constituent elements: (1) initial education, which refers to schooling and tertiary education; (2) adult education, which refers to organized adult learning; and (3) the diffuse learning environments, which refer to the informal learning events and processes that take place throughout life.

With these categories in mind, the conceptual framework of lifelong learning becomes increasingly important to capture the multilayers and diverse spectrum of adult learning that takes place despite limited government support. If adult education is to be equated with government activity through the Departments of Education in South Africa, then the outlook is bleak. But if a wider framework is adopted, the picture changes quite significantly.

The extent of adult learning through the various state departments, business, and civil society is unknown. There are some indications that in the Departments of Prisons, Labor, Health, and Water Affairs there are a number of active programs. The major new initiative is that of the Department of Labor, which has launched a national skills strategy that aims to boost expenditure on training and drive a wide-ranging human resource development program. It is trying to realize a vision of an "integrated skills development system which promotes economic and employment growth and social development through a focus on education, training and employment services." It is creating a national training fund through a levy on the payrolls of mainly private-sector companies. It is a mechanism to ensure that the private sector does invest in training. Eighty percent of the levy collected will be earmarked for enterprise-based training as well as for entry-level skills training in that particular industry. The remaining 20 percent of the total levy will go to a National Skills Fund to support training targeted at priority skill needs within industry. The Skills Development Strategy affords the government significant leverage over the development of a systematic and comprehensive skills development strategy while relying on enterprise funding (Soobrayan, 1997, p. 255). The impact of this new initiative will increasingly tilt adult education toward the needs of the economy and the market.

In South Africa there is a danger of equating adult education with ABET and with narrow Department of Education initiatives. As a result there is an urgent need to broaden this perspective and to undertake empirical research in order to be able to quantify the scale of adult education and learning provision and activity. The use of Wolpe's classification, which includes Belanger's last two categories, would be a useful starting point. This would be more in line with the definition of adult education within the Hamburg Declaration on Adult Learning (UNESCO, 1997, p.1):

Adult education denotes the entire body of ongoing learning processes, formal or otherwise, whereby people regarded as adults by the society to which they belong, develop their abilities, enrich their knowledge, and improve their technical or professional qualifications or turn them in a new direction to meet their own needs and those of their society. Adult learning encompasses both formal and continuing education, nonformal learning and the spectrum of informal and incidental learning available in a multicultural learning society, where theory- and practice-based approaches are recognized.

Integrating Adult Education and Training

Gustavsson (1997) points out that there are historically two different and important theoretical and ideological strands that argue for lifelong education and training. The dominant trend in the Western world is the human capital school mostly supported by neoliberal ideology. The theory of human capital expresses a view concerning the economic reasons for education and training, but says nothing about the learning process. It is most concerned with the needs of people located within the industrialized urban centers. The other trend is the humanistic school, which is concerned with a democratic and holistic approach to people's education and training. These two ideological strands are also reflected in the discourses of *education*, *training*, and *development*. As Gamble and Walters (1997, p. 123) point out, while there are many similarities of form at the level of activity, they have different social functions and purposes; they are subject to different pressures and constraints; and they are embedded in different philosophical traditions.

In South Africa adult education has traditionally been concerned more with social, political, personal, and cultural development than with economic development. It has been very closely tied in the last fifty years to the political struggle against apartheid. This, as Gumede (1997) argues, has been a major limitation for many adults whose primary concern is economic survival. About 50 percent of South Africans are unemployed. Not surprisingly, a recent survey rated the need for jobs as the top priority. For the rural poor, piped water was almost as high a priority.

A key initiative in the movement toward a new adult education and training system in South Africa came from the formal economic sector, where different stakeholder groups (business, labor, and government) negotiated a new policy. Given the particular moment, it was necessary that any new training strategy should address the twin concerns of economic reconstruction and growth within globally competitive markets, while at the same time correcting past injustices and inequities in the provision of training. The unions realized that even radical improvement of the existing industrial training system would still leave their members in a second-class position. They needed to improve their own skills and knowledge to get better jobs. They also needed to improve conditions in their own communities.

The various sets of concerns among the various stakeholders interacted in both complementary and contradictory ways to shift the debate first from a concern about vocational training, to a broader conception about vocational education and training, and finally to an integrated approach to all activities and systems currently classified as education and training. The NQF was proposed as the regulatory mechanism that would bring cohesion to current learning systems and practices and simultaneously transform them. A broad competency model was adopted to define and access learning outcomes at all levels of the NQF. This model was strongly influenced by developments within Australia and New Zealand, and some commentators believe those to be strongly driven by the interests of the business sector. The seeming contradictions in the adoption of an outcomes based, formalized system, which is seen to reflect primarily the interests of the business sector, by a revolutionary trade union movement concerned with socialism has been the subject of widespread discussion. A key debate is whether the NQF can simultaneously contribute to economic development and to the achievement of redress (Lugg, 1997; Kell, 1996).

The question of integration of adult education and training is an important notion, which has opened up spaces to engage different traditions and potentially to challenge the human capital notion. As Lugg (1997) and Gamble and Walters (1997) point out, in the structures of the NQF, the designing of outcomes-based curricula, the teaching methodologies, and all aspects of the teaching and learning processes there need to be struggles to ensure that the human capital and technicist views do not necessarily predominate. Many of the concepts can be interpreted in conservative or progressive ways, for example, recognition of prior learning has transformative and conservative possibilities (Michelson, 1997). At present, the power of the concept of integration lies in the fact that opportunities are being created for practitioners to "live in the gaps" between sectors and traditions of adult education and training. It is, for example, forcing community adult educators to take the needs of economic development seriously and workplace trainers to remember the needs of a democratic civil society. At a time of rapid change in South Africa, and the world more generally, it is important to rethink adult education and training theories and practices in radical ways. Living in the gaps between adult education and vocational training traditions, even if this is sustained only briefly, can contribute to this happening.

In South Africa, as in many other parts of the world, the human capital paradigm seems to hold sway. There is concern among adult educators that the integration debate is being driven by interests of large corporations in the formal economic sector, by both organized labor and employers. But with 70 percent of people living in poverty, it is in the informal sector that most of the people live and work. Since policies are developed with only the formal sector in mind, by definition the majority of people will not benefit.

Flexibility across boundaries of established knowledge domains is increasingly being accepted globally as necessary as new economic and social problems are addressed. Global competitiveness is driving a growing number of corporations around the world to adopt approaches to "risk management" that require them to have more holistic and integrated approaches to adult education and training. For example, in remote new mining areas in Canada and Chile, companies are "managing risks," and these include working with indigenous people and managing the environmental impact, in order that there be social and environmental sustainability. This leads to agreements with local populations, which build on indigenous knowledge and incorporate some of the best participatory practices of community adult education to engage in an integrated approach to community development. These corporations recognize the need to work closely with the local populations in order most effectively to succeed in maximizing profits.

While there are some excellent examples of an integrated approach to education and training where social and economic development are brought together and participatory methodologies are used by a corporation in a local context, the overriding concern is with maximizing profit, not with accountability to the citizens. Economic rather than human values predominate (Marshall, 1998).

Everyday Learning and Education

The relation between everyday learning and education (organized learning) is one of the most fundamental questions in educational discourse. Larsson (1997) states that adult education must be understood as something that can change the results or the character of everyday learning. He points to research that demonstrates the important connection between stimulation in work and openness to learn. The more you are stimulated, the more you are challenged intellectually. It is also the case that the more education people have, the more they want, hence the profile of the majority of learners in adult education in many parts of the world are middle class and highly educated.

In recent years in some countries like Great Britain, Australia, and the United States, skills learned in the home or in the community are being recognized toward further educational qualifications or for employment. This has been particularly important for poorly educated women entering or returning to work after raising children. In the last ten years there has been an explosion of access courses to facilitate entry into higher education. It is mainly women who have used these. Coats (in Michelson, 1997) points out that it is very important to question what knowledge is being accredited by whom. She shows that there are sexist, Eurocentric biases built into assessment practices internationally. Key questions are whose knowledge is affirmed, how is that knowledge constructed, and does it challenge the subordination of marginalized sectors.

This critical stance to the affirmation of everyday knowledge is adopted by many people concerned with marginalized knowledges (Holt et al., 1997). They argue for the importance of affirming indigenous knowledge, as, in many instances, it affirms human and environmentally sustainable values. The resurgence of the arguments for the valorization of indigenous knowledge from indigenous people around the world, which has strong echoes in the women's movements, is an important critique of the human capital paradigm. They support an argument that humanity must work toward a renewed consciousness about future human existence rather than being dominated by narrow economic imperatives. Cooperative global movements have formed to further these perspectives.

The essential role that social movements play in the production of knowledge and in informal and nonformal adult learning processes has been highlighted by several writers (Eyerman and Jamison, 1991; Welton, 1997). Many people have, as their starting point, the learning processes from studies and experiences in social movements. Social movements are considered carriers of historical projects of importance to all people. They address universal questions such as the relations between men and women as highlighted through the women's movements and nascent men's movements, between nature and people through the environmental movements, and between master and slave through liberation and civil rights movements. In their search for knowledge through their actions, people produce culture and new knowledge. A social movement can therefore be characterized by its cognitive praxis.

Globally, the majority of people manifestly engage with learning for their own purposes and interest when it is to meet a social, economic, political, or technical need. Through the liberation movement in South Africa, innovative, creative learning took place. The political organizing processes were educational (Walters, 1989). As part of the movement for democracy, thousands of NGOs and community-based organizations participated in educational and organizational activities within, for example, health, work, media, culture, child care, human rights, and adult literacy.

The significant role of NGOs as expressions of the relationship between local action and globally significant social movements on the one hand, and between local communities and governments on the other, has been critical both to adult education and to building civil society. In the last decade the United Nations conferences on such topics as adult education, housing, women, and the environment are all excellent examples of global organizing by social movements and NGOs, which ensure that citizen's voices were heard by governments. These efforts, among others, have been used to highlight the critical importance of developing a global civil society in order to engage with global governance structures and globalizing economic forces.

At the workplace there are also examples of the building of international solidarity among workers in order to connect their very local struggles to the global struggles against domination by the market. Marshall (1997), for example, describes how steelworkers in Canada and Chile have developed joint strategies to ensure that employers do not play Canadian workers off against Chilean workers. They are consciously developing strategies to engage in the global economy to negotiate with employers more effectively. A form of cooperative globalization among workers is developing within a rampantly competitive environment.

A very significant development in the discussion of the relationship between everyday learning and education is the emphasis being placed on *learning*. As mentioned earlier, the concept of learning has emerged as one of the keys to the future. It has helped to put the learner, rather than the educator or practitioner, at the center of policy and implementation. It also draws attention to the ways in which adults learn at different points in their lives outside recognized educational institutions. While a centering on the needs of learners is positive, the pressures placed on people to continue learning while existing in vulnerable work situations can create other problems.

Emphasis on learning also challenges the traditional roles of the adult educators and trainers. They are mediators of learning, which often takes place through technological software and hardware. In that instance, the role of materials designers then becomes key. The roles and professional identities of the adult educators may be changing quite fundamentally in response to these developments (Gamble and Walters, 1997).

Participation: Problems and Possibilities

A central theme in adult education is that of participation. It can relate to systemic, substantive, cultural, or personal dimensions. Questions about participation are posed in different ways in the literature as to the form, purpose, interests, beneficiaries, possibilities, and constraints. Participation at the interpersonal, classroom, organizational, and broader societal levels often address issues of power relations. These can be in relation to ethnicity, social class, gender, age, physical ability, or geography. The debates about participation point to the two essential aspects of adult education—the pedagogical and the political (Walters and Manicom, 1996). At their root are questions about vision and social purpose.

SOCIAL PURPOSES OF ADULT EDUCATION

Competitive globalization requires adult education and training to be concerned primarily with economic development. It is concerned with developing human capital that will contribute to productive labor and economic competitiveness. Cooperative globalization is concerned with human values and the development of human capacities. Adult learning is central to the missions of both. The social purposes and underlying logics are very different.

The different notions of globalization have different understandings of democracy and different views of people's participation in society. Democracy within the competitive framework is limited to representative forms, while full, participatory democracy is the goal within the cooperative framework. But globalization challenges understandings of democracy, as democracy has been closely related to nation-states. The future of nation-states is being questioned as the world is reorganized into regional economic blocs and TNCs push ever harder to be able to traverse the planet doing business free of any constraints. An example of this was the attempts to have the Multilateral Agreement on Investment passed, which was to remove restrictions on the movement of investments between nations, giving TNCs free reign and diminishing the economic controls of nations and, by implication, their citizens. An international network of civil society organizations mobilized opposition to this and stalled its introduction (Jackson and Sanger, 1998). A central arena of development and contestation is therefore the future of democracy and citizenship.

The "Mumbai Statement on Lifelong Learning, Active Citizenship, and the Reform of Higher Education" (UNESCO, 1998, p. 1) captures succinctly some of the critical concerns. It states:

> We see the purpose of lifelong learning as democratic citizenship, recognizing that democratic citizenship depends on such factors as effective economic development, attention to the demands of the least powerful in our societies, and on the impact of industrial processes on the caring capacity of our common home, the planet. The

notion of citizenship is important in terms of connecting individuals and groups to the structures of social, political and economic activity in both local and global contexts. Democratic citizenship highlights the importance of women and men as agents of history in all aspects of their lives.

The notion of citizenship is a concept that is undergoing radical redefinition under pressure from globalizing economies on the one hand and social movements of environmentalists and feminists on the other. Korsgaard (1997) presents a useful synopsis of some of the major pressures on the notion of "citizenship." He states that the emergence of the modern understanding of citizenship in the West was associated with the advent of capitalism and of centralized nation states in the sixteenth and seventeenth centuries. Citizenship was finally given voice as a massively influential political concept in the seventeenth and eighteenth centuries by the historical events of the English, American, and French Revolutions. The "natural rights" and "Rights of Man" announced by these revolutions; their concepts of "liberty, equality, fraternity"; and their attempts to found the modern nation-state constitutionally on the will of the people helped construct the modern Western concept of citizenship. However, globalization of the economy and the creation of economic blocs are beginning to challenge national sovereignty and citizenship. The emergence of a strong European Union (EU) is one good example of this: the citizenship of the EU and one of the member countries may be in tension at different times, for example, around monetary policy or military actions.

In addition, feminism in modern society challenges the masculine structures of the state, the market, and civil society; feminists challenge men in modern society to recognize the existence of a patriarchal order and of the manifold ways in which they both dominate women's lives and benefit from doing so. In effect, feminist discussions about citizenship challenge men to accept a duty to act against the patriarchal order in which women are second-class citizens and to act for a society of equal citizenship.

The environmental movements are also concerned with rights—the rights of nonhumans (animals, the environment, nature, etc). Of course nature's rights imply duties for humans. Environmentalists also champion nature and the environment on behalf of posterity. Thus generations of humans as yet unborn are assumed to have the right to an environment at least as resource-rich and as undegraded and undamaged as the one the present generation inherited. The "rights of future generations" are thus deemed to impose duties of environmental "stewardship" on all individuals, communities, organizations, and nations. Thus, environmental concerns challenge the dominant paradigm of citizenship in two ways: they expand its sphere beyond the nation-state to the global level and vice versa; also, they expand it beyond the present generation and require us to consider the intergenerational dimension of our sociability and our moral and citizenship duties.

In South Africa, the notion of citizenship is also hotly contested. It is only recently that South African citizenship has been deracialized; economic status, however, is still highly racialized with nearly 95 percent of the poor being black, 5 percent colored, and less than 1 percent Indian or white. South Africa is forging a new national identity after the previous government sought to systematically fragment the population by declaring that there were "many nations in one." Simultaneously, South Africa's political and economic position in the southern African region is being emphasized as the imperative to forge a strong economic bloc in the region is stressed. There are some calls for a wider identification of citizens with the region. On a local level though, there is growing xenophobia as unemployment, poor housing, and crime are being blamed, for example, on Mozambicans, Malawians, and Zambians. Thus, South Africa is both building a nation at a time when the nation-state is being de-emphasized in many parts of the world and simultaneously building a consciousness of being a citizen of the region and the continent at a time when economic hardships and the legacies of apartheid spur on xenophobia among the citizens.

Clearly the notion of citizenship is a "site of struggle" where global and local interests try to influence its meaning within specific contexts. Therefore, education for citizenship will also be an area of contestation. According to Paulo Freire,

> Citizenship is the exercise of being oneself in the context of the state. It is a social construction; it doesn't appear by chance. Either the masses impose themselves through struggle or citizenship doesn't exist. The dominated classes need to democratize citizenship. A literacy program must include political aims to build citizenship; the capacity to understand the world, to establish relations between fact and problems demands the politicization of persons, the political comprehension of the world, permanent curiosity, the right to participate, mobilize, and organize grass-roots groups. It demands going beyond common sense to change reality, to overcome domination, and to invent solidarity (quoted in Stromquist, 1997, p. 217).

In the South African context while there is formal democracy there most certainly is not equality. There is still a long trek, under conditions that by no means guarantee a happy outcome, to achieve a truly democratic, nonracist, nonsexist society. In a context where discourses of the market and business are becoming increasingly hegemonic, all educational institutions in South Africa have an important role to play in ensuring that people, particularly poor, black people and women, are supported in their attainment of active citizenship. But how can this be done?

Adult education for active citizenship is a debate about curriculum. As Muller (1997, p. 181) states, "nothing is more urgent than a clear and dispassionate view of who or what the South African citizen is, or could be. This in turn focuses the question: what kind of curriculum do we therefore need in order best to foster this citizen-to-be?"

Education for citizenship has a long history. As Comeliau (1997, p. 33) says, "Torrents of ink have flowed on the new imperatives for education in the context of globalization: we need to know how to manage and calculate, we must develop advanced technological knowledge, we must acquire 'flexibility,' learn foreign languages and be receptive to 'intercultural dialogue,' and so forth." But that is not enough. He, like many others, argues that alternatives must be found to the crucial conditions for survival, equilibrium, and full development of human societies. While it is essential to train good engineers, financiers, technicians, and specialists in many fields, it is important that a dominant view of economic globalization "that there is no alternative" must be changed to "there must be an alternative" (DAWN, 1997, p.1).

This search for alternatives is not seen as a disembodied intellectual exercise, but one which is the collective work of social groups and institutions, which is both an intellectual and a political task. As Comeliau (1997, p. 34) argues, "the requirements of this new education [are] a collective awareness of the real issues involved in long-term development (which are very different from those of growth) and progressive training for the many tasks needed to respond to them." Adult education institutions have to make hard political and economic choices that will either reinforce the status quo or challenge it.

As long as adult education, for survival and skilling for the informal sector and for the cultural and political development, is unlikely to be adequately funded by governments within the current climate, alternative sources of support have to be found. One source could be, for example, mainstream institutions like universities, which could be urged to provide diverse adult learning opportunities for a wide range of constituencies.

As adult educators we do not work in isolated national contexts. As Muller (1997, p. 199) argues, "The importance of not losing sight of the local can never be minimized." He continues:

> Citizenship in a plural and diverse world consists in mastering the various skills of autonomy, but retaining, or constructing, some or other local home to actually live in, in a meaningful and fulfilling way. Autonomy without a home lacks relevance, one might say, but this time a personal relevance not easily reducible to group or national relevance. It is at the juncture of cosmopolitan and local, of autonomy and relevance, that a new sense of citizenship for a runaway world will be constructed.

Developments within education reflect the impact of globalization on the curricula, teaching and learning processes, and employment practices (e.g., the increasing casualization of employment). Lifelong learning for active citizenship requires all educators to work collaboratively across regions in order to take on the pedagogical and political challenges of creating alternatives that can build on the positive aspects of globalization. As Buchbinder and Rajagopal (1996) urge, we need to be working to ensure that we are not moving uncritically to the tune of global capital. Educators and learners would need to engage along with other activists with issues like those described by Arruda (1996, p. 30): "We are seeking to connect critically the micro with the macro and, in the search for a vision of the world which will be both utopic and viable, point to an horizon of a cooperative globalization, built by individuals and societies that have become active and conscious subjects, personally and collectively, of their own development."

The struggle over economic, political, and social priorities that are raging in South Africa, and elsewhere, becomes a crucial curriculum issue for learners and educators. Adult learning for active citizenship is therefore both about pedagogy and politics, which requires local and global cooperative actions of solidarity to build alternatives that emphasize human development. It seems that the potential of adult learning for human development will only be fully realized through collective struggles across national and regional boundaries, where some of the benefits of globalization, like the new communications technologies, can be used to forge new visions of a world that are both utopic and viable. Active citizens need to come to understand in a profound way what it means to think, feel, and act both globally and locally on an everyday basis.

REFERENCES

Arruda, Marcos. 1996 (Dec.). Globalization and Civil Society: Rethinking Cooperativism in the Context of Active Citizenship. A paper of the Institute of Alternative Policies for the Southern Cone of Latin America, Rio de Janeiro, Brazil.

Belanger, Paul. 1994. Lifelong Learning: The Dialectics of "Lifelong Education." *International Review of Education*, vol. 40, nos. 3–5, pp. 353–81.

Bishop, Ann. 1998 (July 12). The Agonies of Online Learning. Unpublished paper, University of British Columbia, Vancouver.

Buchbinder, Howard, and Pinayur Rajagopal. 1996. Canadian Universities: The Impact of Free Trade and Globalization. *Higher Education*, vol. 31, pp. 283–99.

Comeliau, Christian. 1997 (March). The Challenges of Globalization. *Prospects*, vol. XXVII, no. 1, pp. 29–34.

DAWN. 1997. From "There Is No Alternative" to "There Must Be an Alternative." University of Western Cape, Bellville.

Eyerman, Ron, and Andrew Jamison. 1991. *Social Movements: A Cognitive Approach*. Cambridge: Polity Press

Gamble, Jeanne, and Shirley Walters. 1997. ETDP: Passing Fad or New Identity? In Shirley Walters (ed.), *Globalization, Adult Education and Training: Impacts and Issues*. London: ZED, pp. 120–27.

Giddens, Anthony. 1994. *Beyond Left and Right*. London: Polity Press.

Gindin, Sam. 1998. Socialism "With Sober Senses": Developing Workers' Capacities. *The Socialist Register*, pp. 75–101 (United Kingdom).

Gumede, Ellen. 1997. On the Periphery: The Needs of Rural Women. In Shirley Walters (ed.), *Globalization, Adult Education and Training: Impacts and Issues*. London: ZED, pp. 233–36.

Gustavsson, Berndt. 1997. Lifelong Learning Re-considered. In Shirley Walters (ed.), *Globalization, Adult Education and Training: Impacts and Issues*. London: ZED, pp. 237–49.

Harris, Elayne. 1997. Home Thoughts on Globalization: Wagging the Dog. Casae Proceedings, Canada, pp. 124–28.

Holt, Lillian, Michael Christie, and Norman Fry. 1997. Aboriginal Education: A Case for Self-Determination. In Shirley Walters (ed.), *Globalization, Adult Education and Training: Impacts and Issues*. London: ZED, pp. 188–95.

International Labour Research and Information Group (ILRIG). 1998. *An Alternative View of Globalization*. Cape Town: ILRIG.

Jackson, Andrew, and Matthew Sanger. 1998. Dismantling Democracy. Canadian Centre for Policy Alternatives. Toronto: James Lorimer Publishers.

Kell, Catherine. 1996. Getting the 15 Million onto the NQF Jungle Gym: Towards a Critique of Current ABET Policy and Practice from the Social Uses of Literacy Perspective. In Pursuit of Equality, Kenton Education Association, Juta, Kenwyn, South Africa.

Khosla, Ashok. 1998. Development Alternatives—Action from the Bottom Up. *Alliance*, vol. 3, no. 3. pp. 12–15.

Korsgaard, Ove. 1997. Adult Learning between Global Economy and National Democracy. In Ove Korsgaard (ed.), *Adult Learning and the Challenges for the Twenty-first Century*. Copenhagen: Association for World Education, pp. 113–27.

Larsson, Staffan. 1997. The Meaning of Lifelong Learning. In Shirley Walters (ed.), *Globalization, Adult Education and Training: Impacts and Issues*. London: ZED, pp. 250–61.

Lugg, Rosemary. 1997. The NQF, Reconstruction and Development. In Shirley Walters (ed.), *Globalization, Adult Education and Training: Impacts and Issues*. London: ZED, pp. 128–40.

Marshall, Judith. 1997. Globalization from Below: The Trade Union Connections. In Shirley Walters (ed.), *Globalization, Adult Education and Training: Impacts and Issues*. London: ZED, pp. 57–68.

———. 1998 (July 29). Globalization, Adult Education and Training from Workers' Perspectives. A lecture presented at University of British Columbia, Vancouver, Canada.

Michelson, Elana. 1997. The Politics of Memory: The Recognition of Experiential Learning. In Shirley Walters (ed.), *Globalization, Adult Education and Training: Impacts and Issues*. London: ZED, pp. 141–53.

Muller, Johan. 1997. Citizenship and Curriculum. In Nico Cloete, Johan Muller, Malegapuru W. Makgoba, Donald Ekong (eds.), *Knowledge, Identity and Curriculum Transformation in Africa*. Cape Town: Maskew Miller Longman, pp. 181–201.

Soobrayan, Bobby. 1997 (July). From Apartheid Education to Lifelong Learning: Assessing the Ameliorative Potential of Emerging Education Policy in South Africa. A paper presented at the Lifelong Learning Conference, University of Surrey, Guildford, England.

Stromquist, Nelly P. 1997. *Literacy for Citizenship: Gender and Grassroots Dynamics in Brazil*. Albany: State University of New York Press.

Tedesco, Juan Carlos. 1997 (March). Editorial. *Prospects*, vol. XXV11, no. 1, pp. 3–4.

UNESCO Institute of Education. 1997 (July). The Hamburg Declaration and the

Agenda for the Future. Fifth International Conference on Adult Education, Hamburg, Germany.

———. 1998 (April). The Mumbai Statement on Lifelong Learning, Active Citizenship, and the Reform of Higher Education. Hamburg, Germany.

Walters, Shirley. 1989. *Education for Democratic Participation.* Bellville, South Africa: CACE Publications.

———, (ed.) 1997. *Globalization, Adult Education and Training: Impacts and Issues.* London: ZED.

Walters, Shirley, and Linzi Manicom (eds.). 1996. *Gender in Popular Education: Methods for Empowerment.* London: ZED Books.

Welton, Michael. 1997. In Defence of Civil Society: Canadian Adult Education in Neo-Conservative Times. In Shirley Walters (ed.), *Globalization, Adult Education and Training: Impacts and Issues.* London: ZED, pp. 27–38.

Wolpe, AnnMarie. 1994. *Adult Education and Women's Needs.* Bellville, South Africa: CACE Publications.

Part 3

National Case Studies of
Globalization Impacts

11

Globalization and Universities in the Commonwealth Caribbean

Anne Hickling-Hudson

We hover on the brink of a Global Age in which the globe rather than the nation-state will be the point of reference for sociopolitical movements, economic patterns, and expressive culture. The contours of this future can only be imagined/extrapolated from present trends, but we can more clearly perceive the features of globalization, the process of moving toward the global age. At the current stage of globalization, two particular features have significant implications for universities in developing countries. One is the world economic trend toward intensifying and expanding capitalism globally by means of increasing privatization, rapid flows of finance, the removal of trade barriers, and the search for sophisticated "niche markets," all of which are making it less and less possible for societies to live adequately on the neocolonial economic foundations of relying mainly on raw material production and underdeveloped enterprises (Farrell, 1993a and 1993b; Hoogveldt, 1997).

The second is the increasing power and reach of communications technologies. Global capitalism and global communication technology combined have led to the trend for universities and colleges from wealthy countries to expand their "offshore" education activities in developing countries, through sophisticated distance education and "twinning" arrangements. Many impoverished countries are caught in the dilemma of being faced with this competition when they have been unable to develop their own tertiary education sectors sufficiently to meet burgeoning local demand. There is a higher education vacuum, and the universities of wealthy countries are rushing in to fill it.

This chapter will examine how these issues apply to higher education in the English-speaking Caribbean. The attention to this small region of some five million people stems from my deep attachment to it as the region of my birth and upbringing, and from my view that the Caribbean warrants deeper educational policy analysis than it has hitherto received. It demonstrates the intersection of education with postcolonialism in all its complexity—the continuing attempts of the newly independent nations to pursue deep needs for cultural self-definition, the constraining of these attempts by the consequences of Euro-American colonialism and imperialism, and the new threats and opportunities of a globalizing environment.

The region is characterized by the uneasy coexistence of pockets of wealth and privilege with poverty that cannot depend on alleviation by unemployment benefits from the state, and by various degrees of international indebtedness and dependence on international structures. In the formerly British-owned Caribbean, which calls itself the "Commonwealth" Caribbean, annual per capita income is below the equivalent of US$2,000 for most of the independent countries, except Trinidad and the Bahamas, which means that most Caribbean governments do not have the resources to fund significant new developments in the education system. However, higher education at the end of the twentieth century has taken the first steps to respond to the challenges of globalization.

GLOBALIZATION AND DEVELOPING COUNTRIES

Globalization is currently a deeply flawed process to the extent that it is intensifying the global spread of the overconsuming capitalism of modernity with its framework of totalizing assumptions—for example the triumphalist post–Cold War belief that "free" market ideology and prescriptions should shape all societies (see Samoff, 1999, pp. 56–57). However globalization has a strong impact, not necessarily negative, as a process of social change in the sphere of culture. Global flows of thought, cultural expression, and practice center around spheres posited by Appadurai (1990) as ethnoscapes, mediascapes, technoscapes, financescapes, and ideoscapes. These in turn are shaped by the de-territorialization brought about by migration, travel, and the global division of labor.

A research agenda for postmodern radical development theory calls for deconstructing modernist assumptions that equate nonsustainable development with "progress" and replacing these with new ways of understanding and tackling poverty and social dualism. The new practices would be based on ecological and people-centered thinking, the critical use of appropriate technologies, the recognition and fostering of local and traditional knowledge, the strengthening of social movements for community empowerment, and research grounded in practice. Such theory rethinks the relationship between structure, agency, and social change in the Caribbean (see Ramphall, 1997, pp. 19–26; Meeks, 1993, pp. 1–6) and addresses the need to restructure economies and knowledge systems to cope with the challenges of global change (Farrell, 1993b). Postmodern radical development theory oriented to Caribbean circumstances would sit easily within the ideals of "globalism," seen as "all those values which focus on the condition of the globe and the well-being of people within it" (Albrow, 1994, p. 166). This would include a trend that Falk (1992) calls "globalization from below," comprising the global civic movements gathered around issues such as environmental, feminist, and other social justice concerns. Globalism introduces a significant new dimension of post-Eurocentric thinking that challenges and rethinks the values of Western-shaped universality, which are rhetorically grand but in reality limited and constrained by ethnocentric assumptions and flawed scientific, technological, and economic practice.

Can higher education restructure itself to prepare people for these features and trends of globalization and for new ideologies of globalism? In most developing countries, the universities and colleges established during the twentieth century were built in the image of the knowledge systems and institutional structures left by formerly colonial powers. In spite of some attempts to change, they may have outlived their suitability for the challenges of the postindustrial era, in which knowledge-based production and services hold the key to economic and social improvement. The importance of preparing for a global, knowledge-based economy is so frequently invoked that it is almost a truism; but what does it mean? The meaning needs to be expressed in a way that is relevant to higher education, which has the responsibility for producing the producers of knowledge-based improvement. Farrell (1993) points out the following aspects of the crisis of globalization for the Commonwealth Caribbean:

- The Caribbean is stuck with a set of export specializations, most of which have lost their growth dynamic. All of the key export sectors of the region are in deep trouble—sugar, bauxite, oil, bananas, and tourism—they are at the end of their "product life-cycle."
- The political systems based on the British Westminster model of government are inherently flawed, since they do not permit the people, through organizations and institutions which reflect their life, to participate in an organic and ongoing fashion in the conduct of public policy.
- The institutions of the state, such as the public service bureaucracies, are anachronistic, using management, administration, and seniority systems that allow inefficiency and are simply inconsonant with the kind of administration that transformation requires.
- The education system is weak and inadequate as an engine of transformation, with poor mechanisms for science and mathematics training, insufficient attention to creativity and values development, poor articulation between the tertiary education sector and the productive sectors of the economy, and weak research and development (R&D) capacity.

Against this background, the region must find a way of restructuring in order to survive and respond to the challenges of globalization. It must develop an economic system characterized by anticipation of trends on a global scale; by a high speed of response to local and global opportunities; by a "highly developed cerebral apparatus" in the public service and state sectors; and by social articulation between the governmental system, the education and R&D institutions, and the productive sector. Without wanting to slip into the problematic assumptions of human capital theory that improved education alone will bring about such outcomes (see Hickling-Hudson, 1997, pp. 110–11), I concur with the widely held view that education reform would be a major component of these changes. Since "a small region with limited manpower must pit David against Goliath on a daily basis," the educational institutions have to produce people who are cosmopolitan, have a highly developed sense of self, are "great generalists as opposed to narrow specialists," can move rapidly between specializations as need dictates, and can be efficient managers (Farrell, 1993a, p. 341).

The sense of self that Caribbean people must nurture can find space within the processes of globalization. Robertson's famous statement that "globalisation as a concept refers both to the compression of the world and the intensification of consciousness of the world as a whole" (1992, p. 8) provides the setting for his argument that local cultures now, more than ever, can potentially use the power of the new information technologies to seize spaces to express and develop local cultural and political expression with a global audience. Caribbean scholars passionately express the need for the region's cultures to preserve and develop their unique features more determinedly than ever to resist the homogenization trends within globalization. Although "the Caribbean is itself the product of globalization," argues Stuart Hall, yet globalization in its modern form is a very puzzling phenomenon presenting, "all kinds of difficulties which seem . . . to threaten the fragile cultures which we have developed" with homogenization, commodification, and massive discrepancies in power. Yet we cannot pull down the hatches and climb back into the bunker of tradition. What is necessary is for us to use our diasporic cultural strengths to construct a culture of a different kind; to live with dissemination; to draw from other cultures; to know that "unless we have made the return to our symbolic home in our hearts and minds we will never know who we are"; but to know, at the same time, that we can't go home again (Hall, 1996, pp. 25–33).

Rex Nettleford, a famous Caribbean choreographer and cultural studies scholar, inaugurated in 1999 as the vice-chancellor of the University of the West Indies (UWI), talks of the Caribbean quest for authenticity rooted in action, asserting that "We are right to persist in the search for modes of reintegration, reaffirmation, as well as of the relationships between the micro and the macro, the terrestrial and the celestial, the relationship between the inner space of the mind and heart and the outer physical space which we tenant" (1997, pp. 91–92).

HIGHER EDUCATION IN THE COMMONWEALTH CARIBBEAN: CURRENT REFORMS AND CONTINUING PROBLEMS

It is a tall order for higher education in the Commonwealth Caribbean to respond to the multiple challenges of globalization and globalism, producing scholars, students, and structures that meet the region's needs for creative new ways of operating rooted in both global and local consciousness. In spite of current reforms in the higher education sector, many of its features, stemming from the traditions of the past, are problematic for taking it into the globalizing future.

The British did not pay their Caribbean colonies the compliment of establishing universities in the early years of colonization, as the Spanish did in Hispaniola and Cuba in the sixteenth century. British Caribbean colonies, treated as sources of exploitation for metropolitan enrichment for over three hundred years, from the seventeenth to the mid-twentieth century, had to wait until 1948 for a university or college. A few West Indians, who could afford to travel overseas or who won a handful of scholarships, received their higher education in England. At last, the University College of the West Indies, a college of London University, was established in 1948 at the Mona campus in Jamaica to serve all the countries of the region. In the 1960s and 1970s, most of the Caribbean countries gained their political independence. In 1962 the university college metamorphosed into the University of the West Indies (UWI), independent of London. A second UWI campus was established in Trinidad and a third in Barbados. UWI continues to flourish as a successful federal university, serving over sixteen Caribbean countries. Other universities in the region are the University of Guyana (UG); the University College of Belize; and, in Jamaica, the University of Technology (UTech, formerly the College of Arts, Science and Technology); and the Northern Caribbean University. Higher education takes place at twenty-eight university sites across the Caribbean (World Bank 1993, p. 153), but its expansion has been numerically inadequate, resulting in a labor force of which fewer than 3 percent hold a university degree. Caribbean universities, with only about 25,000 students among them, are far from being adequate to serve the higher education needs of a region of some five million. In 1996 UWI had about 15,500 students in three island campuses and centers in several islands, UTech had about 7,000, and the University of Guyana had approximately 3,000. Additionally, there are some 45,000 students across the region in colleges that offer sub-degree diplomas and certificates in technical and vocational fields (World Bank 1993, p. 154), and some of these are starting to add degree programs to their range.

The late start for higher education in the Commonwealth Caribbean means that the difficult process of building an infrastructure and learning regional cooperation dominated the second half of the twentieth century. As is characteristic of decolonization processes, problems that bear the stamp of the British colonial origin have been embedded in this newly developed higher education sector in the Caribbean. The small size of the sector stems from an elitist tradition that drastically restricts broad access and equity in a deeply stratified educational system closely modeled on the traditional British one. Universities and colleges produce too few graduates for the labor needs of the region. Curricula have been criticized as being too specialist too early and pedagogy for being didactic and insufficiently student-oriented. There is a shortage of postgraduate education, and undergraduate education shows low system efficiency internally in terms of high dropout and repetition rates (between 12 and 42 percent), indicating substantial student wastage and contrasting negatively with the current British university system where 94 percent of all first-year students graduate after three years (World Bank, 1993, pp. 167–68). Such problems severely constrain the ability of the region to meet the challenges of globalization, despite the fact that the universities have played a vital role in creating and disseminating a new knowledge base relevant to the cultural, scientific, and economic needs of the region, with outstanding Caribbean-focused scholarship and innovations in many fields (Adams, 1999). The recognition by Caribbean educational leaders of the inadequacies of the tertiary education sector has led to a ferment of change: as Miller (1997) puts it, "tertiary education is the new frontier in Caribbean education." Over the past decade, Caribbean governments and educators have made tremendous efforts to expand tertiary education capacity by implementing or supporting the strategies discussed below (see Peters, 1993; Miller, 1997a and 1997b; Hall, 1998; University of Guyana, 1993; Ministry of Education, Jamaica, 1995; University of the West Indies, 1997).

Financial Strategies

Governments have expanded scholarship and loan schemes and encouraged private sector involvement in providing scholarships, loans, and workplace training schemes. They have instituted "cost-sharing," which requires university students to pay a portion of their tuition fees. Starting from the mid-1980s, UWI has substantially improved its ability to raise a part of its own finance, and other universities are also following that path. But the higher education sector is persistently faced with a shortage of resources (Hall 1998, p. 121), with the drastic consequences in 1999 of UWI having to turn away many qualified applicants because of the large sums owed by the Jamaican and other contributing governments (Fine, 1999). This illustrates the problem of being faced with having to expand the education needed for preparing the "highly developed cerebral apparatus," yet being thwarted by financial crises that threaten existing levels of achievement (Miller, 1997b, p. 34).

Establishment of Coordination and Accreditation Bodies

New coordinating bodies are working to facilitate the rationalization and standardization of the whole system of tertiary level programs and qualifications. The Association of Caribbean Tertiary Institutions (ACTI) was established in 1990 as a voluntary advisory body, which, by developing equivalency classifications and systems of quality control, helps tertiary institutions all over the region to streamline the system of links and pathways between institutions. The region has adopted the U.S. idea of the associate degree (AD), which students earn for passing college-based courses, sometimes in combination with Advanced Level examination subjects (Cambridge, UK), which can gain them entry to UWI (see Peters, 1993). The contentious issue yet to be settled is whether the AD should be equivalent to the first year of a university degree rather than to a pre-university qualification. Since many U.S. universities accept an AD as being equivalent to their first year, this encourages students to seek places in the second year of U.S. programs rather than in the first year of UWI ones. In Jamaica, the University Council of Jamaica has been set up to accredit and register tertiary institutions and programs and to help network them. The Joint Commission for Tertiary Education seeks to promote interaction between Jamaican tertiary educators from different institutions by holding conferences and other meetings.

Expansion of the Capacity of Nonuniversity Tertiary Institutions

Colleges, institutes, and other postsecondary institutions are being reorganized to (a) qualify increasing numbers of midlevel professionals; (b) become multidisciplinary rather than single disciplinary, offering a wider range of nationally accredited courses and qualifications, particularly the new community colleges being designed along the lines of the North American model (Alleyne, 1995, pp. 148–49); (c) work within ACTI, the regional accreditation body, to ensure that specific courses are accredited toward enabling their graduates to enter UWI, U-Tech, or UG and complete a degree; and (d) develop so that they themselves can offer degrees in some fields independent of UWI if so desired.

Governments have allowed the increasing availability of degree programs of foreign universities offered through offshore sites, distance education, or partnership with national institutions.

Expanding the Relationship of the Universities with Other Tertiary Institutions

The three major universities all work with the tertiary colleges to decide on how their programs are to be linked and to upgrade and accredit courses and qualifications in order to expand links. At present, the tertiary institutions have many types of relationships with UWI and UTech and between themselves, and these are being systematized by the work of ACTI. Miller (1997a, p. 65) specifies six types of UWI relationships with colleges, ranging from affiliate relationships in which colleges offer degrees linked to UWI, to the franchised curriculum, to the validation relationship. UWI plays an important role in linking institutions through its Office of University Services (OUS). This body assists national and community colleges all over the region to systematize their courses and upgrade them to the accreditation level of the associate degree, which permits entry into the first or second year of selected UWI degrees. Both UWI and UTech play pivotal roles in the Association of Caribbean Tertiary Institutions.

University Expansion

University enrollment is increasing, though not fast enough to meet the demand. The majority of new enrollments, however, are not for degree programs; rather, they are for shorter subprofessional certificates and diplomas. Distance education and part-time programs are also being increased. At the Mona campus of UWI, 20 percent of the enrollment is part time, at the Cave Hill campus 36 percent, at the St. Augustine campus 13 percent, at UG 41 percent (World Bank, 1993, p. 160), and at UTech 58 percent. Nearly all degree programs need further expansion of enrollment to meet the demand, especially in law, management, and communications technology. UWI and UG have changed from a three-term to a two-semester system, and courses are being modularized to facilitate easier transfer of credits.

In spite of policy efforts to develop the universities, the annual output of graduates from them remains so small that, according to World Bank estimates, it would take years, at present levels, to increase the proportion of university graduates in the population by just 1 percent. In Barbados it would take six years; in Dominica, St. Lucia, and St. Vincent it would take seventeen years; in Grenada twenty-five years; and in Belize, one hundred years (World Bank, 1993, pp. 162–63). UG graduates represent only 0.9 percent of the Guyana population. This starkly summarizes the high level of external inefficiency of the Commonwealth Caribbean higher education sector. It provides skilled professionals, but too few of them for the needs of the societies. There are substantial shortages of graduates across the public and private sectors in science, engineering, computing, teaching, and management. The Caribbean produces only 198 graduates per 100,000 population, a small proportion compared to Latin America, with 1,250 per hundred thousand (World Bank, 1993, p. 154). Numbers of postgraduate students have increased but remain low at only 6 percent of total enrollment (World Bank, 1993, p. 156). The shortage of professionals is exacerbated by the fact that several thousand West Indians are overseas, mainly in North America, studying for undergraduate and postgraduate degrees (World Bank, 1993, p. 153), and many of them do not return.

Expanding Graduate Schools

All of the Commonwealth Caribbean universities, particularly the smaller ones, have low numbers of postgraduate programs and students. They would like to find a way of retaining more of their best graduates for research rather than losing them to graduate schools abroad. UWI has been discussing the establishment of a graduate school that would have responsibility for all university research centers and programs, for assisting academic departments to maintain and develop coherent research programs, and for developing a research strategy for UWI based on the needs of the region and internal research strengths. The view is frequently advanced that UWI should have a large proportion of its capacity devoted to graduate work and research and that much of the undergraduate education that it carries out, and all of the sub-degree programs, should be spread out among other tertiary learning institutions in the region.

Staff development facilities have traditionally consisted mainly of paid study leave and conference leave for lecturers to undertake research and other professional activity. Because of inadequate funding, these privileges are not widely or regularly accessible to all staff. Student evaluation of their professors' teaching is being introduced on a voluntary basis, and UWI and UTech are experimenting with employing full-time staff members to assist the professional development of academics in pedagogical skills. But it is clear that fully equipped and staffed professional development units are needed to systematize such programs.

Caribbean policies and trends in higher education, though they take some factors of globalization into account, are not shaped by a discourse that sees globalization and futures planning as central. Universities and colleges are responding to a limited extent to the necessity of expanding places to meet the need for more graduates in the region. But there is no regional planning process for restructuring the entire education system, including the universities, along the lines of lifelong learning supported by sophisticated technology. It has to be asked whether the reforms in Caribbean higher education are comprehensive enough in scale, or deep enough, to respond effectively to rapid change in the environment.

Overseas Universities: Wooing Our Students or Globalizing Them?

As UWI lecturer Ermina Osoba (1998) puts it, the trend is for "the persistent and highly organized wooing of our students by foreign colleges, universities, and even private high schools." The high level of Caribbean study at overseas universities, as well as the burgeoning offshore campuses and programs in the Caribbean, illustrates the potential for these universities to fill the vacuum that has been left by the inadequate policy of Caribbean governments toward developing the tertiary sector. Caribbean higher education policy documents and papers appear to view the expansion of overseas "foreign" universities as a distinct threat in terms of the competition that they pose. For example, the UWI Governance Report (1994, p. 35) states that "the ever more aggressive competition offered by off-shore institutions (largely emanating from the United States) . . . currently threatens the effectiveness of the University's outreach in the region."

Overseas universities located in the Caribbean include St. Georges University (USA), which started in Grenada as an offshore school of medicine. (President Reagan used the excuse of "saving American lives" at this university as one of his reasons for sending U.S. troops to invade tiny Grenada in 1983 to put an end to its revolutionary experiment.) St. Georges University has expanded its operations in the past decade. It now recruits not only U.S. students, but also Grenadian and other Caribbean students for undergraduate programs in the liberal arts and sciences as well as medicine. Other universities offering programs in the Caribbean include the Universities of Wales and of Manchester (UK), which provide a master's degree in business administration in Jamaica for full fees; Barry University and Nova University (Canada); and Florida International University and the University of New Orleans (USA). With the tremendous increase in distance education programs, some Caribbean nationals are finding it more convenient, and cheaper, to remain at home and buy an overseas distance or offshore degree, rather than go overseas to study. This exacerbates a drain of foreign exchange out of countries that can ill afford it. There are questions here that clearly should be pursued and researched by Caribbean governments. Is this cost worth the product in terms of professionals being well prepared and willing to work for the region and relate creatively to regional and global issues? Should overseas university activity be regarded positively, since existing Caribbean national and regional universities can only provide a drop in the proverbial bucket of the region's need for graduates? Analysis of the nature of this competition, and its role in the region, might lead to expanded collaboration or other positive outcomes.

In Jamaica there is an increasing demand for degrees in business. Some are offered in the national tertiary education system, but overseas universities have been making significant inroads into that student market. These universities "woo" Jamaican students by offering them an attractive product, for example MBAs by distance education, which is not easily available at home and holds the promise of increasing the global portability of the graduates. These MBAs, offered by the UK Universities of Wales and Manchester, are examples of "first generation distance education," according to categories used by Utsumi and Villarroel (1992). They see distance education as going through six stages or "generations," five of which currently exist. The sixth is a goal of the Global Systems Analysis and Simulation Project (GLOSAS), headquartered in the United States and aiming to develop a Global University (GU). The six stages are (1) correspondence education by postal service; (2) a combination of correspondence education with instructional TV (one-way broadcasting); (3) a combination of (2) with an audio line for discussion between individual students and an instructor, and later with audio teleconferencing among all; (4) a combination of (3) with computer conferencing to facilitate interaction; (5) global extension of (4); and (6) a combination of (5) with globally cooperative database and simulation models.

Global communications technology has the potential to intensify greatly the activities of overseas universities in developing countries. UTech now offers its own degrees in business, but many graduates both from there and from UWI still find it desirable to earn overseas MBAs at great personal expense (for example, the thirty-month degree from the University of Wales/Manchester costs a minimum of 8,250 pounds (US$12,885). The Commonwealth of Learning is a distance education university project subscribed to by some universities in the British Commonwealth, and there is a globally operating United Nations

Educational, Scientific, and Cultural Organization (UNESCO) university. It is the proposed GU, however, which has potentially the most far-reaching implications for developing countries.

The Global University Consortium is a worldwide, nonprofit telecommunications and electronic network. Still in an embryonic stage, its core is GLOSAS, which has played a major role in extending the U.S. data communications network to other countries. It has also assisted the deregulation and cost-reduction of telecommunications in some countries, such as Japan, and has organized and implemented university teleconferencing through a project called the Global Lecture Hall (GLH), linking more than twenty-four universities in Japan, South Korea, Venezuela, Australia, Europe, and the United States. GLOSAS showed how 1,500 people could actively participate through interactive multimedia on a problem-solving exercise during the "Crisis Management and Conflict Resolution" conference of the World Future Society in New York in 1986. It assisted over 1,200 Latin American distance educators from some fifty countries at the Fifteenth World Conference of the International Council of Distance Education in Venezuela in 1990. The work of the GU has been extensive in Latin America, where it is helping several distance education institutions to improve their telecommunications capability. Such GLOSAS projects have demonstrated

> how people can be linked across political and geographic boundaries for joint study, discussion, debate, research, planetary problem-solving and political action. In so doing they have also helped foster a participatory spirit and a sense of transnational identity among participants (Utsumi and Villarroel, 1992).

GLOSAS invites international membership and cooperation in setting up a GU that would exchange education internationally through interactive multimedia. The university is to be a nonprofit, worldwide educational network: a collaborative partnership of universities and businesses; governmental, nongovernmental, and community organizations; students; and workers. It seeks to provide on a global scale a variety of educational and cultural knowledge and activities, including course exchange through an educational telecommunications network that will span the globe and will not be confined to traditional educational offerings. Each participating country will have a GU consortium, which will facilitate and train its members for distance education by offering telelearning, transferring technologies, preparing projects or programs, locating and approaching funding agencies, and supporting research and development. GLOSAS is attempting to help various countries and regions, determined "partly by geography, cultural history and the footprints of communication satellites," to create the Global Pacific University, the Global Latin American University, the Global Indian University, and the Global European University. These can then become part of a GU, consisting of a federation of consortia linked in a cooperative network. Each would be invited to have an "authorized, cooperative, and collaborative relationship with the GU/USA, a divisional activity of GLOSAS/USA. Similar consortia are being created in Canada, Japan, Australia, Sri Lanka, Brazil and other countries" (Utsumi and Villarroel, 1992).

This kind of development could sweep the small Commonwealth Caribbean universities into their organizational fold. Just as overseas universities are individually wooing Caribbean students, so could university consortia woo Caribbean universities into joining them with a promise of expanding their capacities and enhancing the quality of their programs. This might be a viable structural framework for Caribbean universities to consider in order to overcome the disadvantage of their late start in the tertiary education field. The question becomes one of how far Caribbean higher education leaders are prepared to make decisions about these imminent possibilities. Are they positioning themselves to meet the inevitable future of the globalizing university on their own terms, terms that suit the imperatives of Caribbean development?

RESTRUCTURING CARIBBEAN UNIVERSITIES: SOME SCENARIOS FOR THE TWENTY-FIRST CENTURY

Organized in the old ways, the higher education sector in the Commonwealth Caribbean is unlikely to be able to provide the sophisticated cultural and technological education necessary to create a less stratified society in the twenty-first century. These developing countries will find it difficult to strengthen their unique cultural industries so that they do not become swamped and displaced by the power and reach of media and information technology from North America and Europe. Broader discussion is needed of the globalizing cultural field within which education operates. It is useful to inform this discussion not only by the traditional historically based situational analysis, but also by futures studies techniques that utilize scenario planning. As Nettleford puts it, "a sense of daring is badly needed in any plan of strategy for the way forward" (1997, p. 93), and bolder, futures-oriented strategic thinking and planning might provide that sense of daring. Compared to the short-term planning found in traditional policy documents, the futures approach is, as Inayatullah (188–89) points out, longer term, creating scenarios for up to fifty years hence (instead of one to five years). It is less likely to be institutionally or theoretically restricted, since it scrutinizes basic assumptions in a way that could call into question the viability of the entire framework of traditional planning. It aims at creating a range of possible futures—not just a series of wish lists, but informed orientations that can clarify management decisions, help create new organizational directions, and combine the features of a social movement with those of an academic field. To achieve this, scenario planning should be more participatory, including all types of stakeholders instead of only powerbrokers less technical; and more vision-oriented, inspiring ideas of what is possible.

As a contribution to the idea of "visioning," I sketch below a futures-oriented vision as one of many possible scenarios for tertiary education in the Caribbean. It is designed not only to put forward broader pictures of possible futures than the traditional five-year plan can do, but also to raise questions that may expose some taken-for-granted assumptions of current planning.

Think Tanks, Visioning, and Fifty-Year Orientations

A foundational scenario for the twenty-first century is that Caribbean societies will collaborate in creating socioeconomic and educational "visioning" for the region for the next fifty years. This regional collaboration resonates with the lead of the national visioning exercises engaged in by several African countries, including Nigeria, Tanzania, and Uganda (Adesida and Oteh, 1998, pp. 569–70). In my scenario, an Organization for the Development of Higher Education in the Caribbean (ODHEC) is established to coordinate this "visioning" and to advise governments and institutions how to plan for the expansion and restructuring of Caribbean higher education in a way that will bring benefits to the region as well as to each country. The ODHEC will include existing agencies, such as the important ACTI; educational representatives from across the spectrum of political parties; representatives from community organizations and business; and observers from universities in the Spanish-, French- and Dutch-speaking Caribbean and in the United Kingdom, North America, Australia, and New Zealand. Input into the visioning process is invited from localities all over the Caribbean as well as from the thriving Caribbean diasporas worldwide, and this input is facilitated, stored, analyzed, and publicized electronically using the Internet, as well as radio and television.

Expanding Capacity and Access

The hypothetical ODHEC advises Commonwealth Caribbean governments on strategic options for higher education. Given the urgency of rapidly expanding knowledge-based enterprises and industries that can counter Caribbean poverty and underdevelopment, it debates how the region can move toward achieving the tertiary education profile of about 30 percent of the eighteen to twenty-eight age cohort that characterizes developed countries and in what time frame this might be possible, given the starting point of under 3 percent in most Caribbean countries. The overall goal for the twenty-first century is to achieve a substantial increase in student numbers. The ODHEC argues for planning to have at least 100,000 students (including some 20,000 pursuing postgraduate degrees) in universities located in the Caribbean by the end of the twenty-first century, quadrupling capacity compared to the small number of 25,000 students in 1999. A second goal is to increase the 1999 number of 45,000 students in sub-degree programs (certificates and diplomas) to 300,000 by 2099. A third goal is to establish a carefully articulated system whereby one level of study is accredited to lead into another across all institutions. The scenarios that follow are developed to concretize strategies toward this vision of an expanded, thriving higher education sector.

Internationalizing Higher Education

At present, Commonwealth Caribbean universities have a national or regional emphasis: they are not competing in the process of internationalization being undertaken by many of the universities in the wealthy countries. Having been involved in internationalizing activities in the Australian university sector, I have come to recognize the complexity and difficulty of the process, which is at an incipient stage compared to its greater development in some universities in the United States and Europe (van der Wende, 1996). Internationalization involves the goals of incorporating a comparative, multicultural, and global perspective into every discipline while retaining a national focus in many, bidding for and engaging in international higher education projects on a broad and systematic level, selling higher education programs to substantial numbers of international fee-paying students, developing twinning and offshore programs, and upgrading the skills and knowledge of staff and administrators to facilitate this process.

An important scenario that Commonwealth Caribbean universities and colleges could choose is to take the path of developing themselves to engage in such an internationalization process. Yet, since their product has to be unique to succeed, it must continue to offer many courses specializing in the study of issues relevant to developing countries and in Caribbean affairs and culture. The combination of global, local, and regional emphases would bring immense benefits to the higher education sector in terms of greater sophistication of the curriculum and pedagogy, greater attractiveness of courses and programs for both national and overseas students, and a broader and deeper range of skills for academic and administrative staff. In the internationalization scenario, many types of universities and colleges would proliferate. UWI would continue as the flagship regional university; UTech Jamaica would become UTech Caribbean, with federated campuses throughout the region; and national, state-supported universities would expand (perhaps absorbing many of the small colleges) in countries or groups of countries that have a large enough resource and population base to support them. There would be an expansion of the numbers of private universities and colleges. The new universities will not have as high infrastructural costs as universities of the old twentieth-century style, since they utilize the open learning, high-tech facilities that will be made available through local Ministries of Education.

Most Caribbean universities and colleges in the twenty-first century would choose to operate within global consortia of universities such as the one envisaged by GLOSAS. This pulls them into the globalizing higher education process of developing courses of unified standards and aids students who wish to do some of their study programs overseas at partner universities. With the expansion of an internationalized culture as a context for a unique specialization in Caribbean and developing country issues, Caribbean universities and colleges in this scenario would aim at attracting annually over six thousand overseas fee-paying students. Many would come from the French-, Dutch- and Spanish-speaking Caribbean, from the Caribbean diasporas in North America and the United Kingdom, and from Africa. Some would do the full undergraduate and postgraduate degrees, others would enroll in lively, dynamic short programs of Caribbean Studies for academic credit, or sometimes simply for leisure enrichment.

Infrastructure and Open Learning

In order to meet the challenge of delivering an internationally excellent tertiary education product, the Caribbean has to provide a suitable infrastructure of up-to-date learning resources and technology and academics who deliver superb pedagogy and research. My scenario sees the twenty-first-century OHDEC advising governments to hire consultants from the world's best Open Universities to help Caribbean universities and colleges improve the delivery of programs using an open learning, flexible delivery approach that makes interactive university programs accessible to every rural and urban locality in the Caribbean and to a wider audience overseas. This utilizes a combination of the Internet, computer programs, teleconferencing, radio, television, postal correspondence, and on-campus classes to bring lectures, readings, graphics, email, chat rooms, and exercises to students all over the Caribbean. In this system, people can study from home at times convenient to them, coming into their nearest university campus or center occasionally for special week-long workshops, which would allow them to interact with other students and enjoy those features of campus life that are a necessary complement to "virtuality" in education (Gibson and Hatherell, 1997, p. 134). Special departments with peripatetic task forces would be set up to help university academics develop skills in organizing and implementing open learning. Computer expertise, pedagogical skills, and audio-visual and electronic equipment are concentrated in these departments and put at the service of regional educational development. When this system is established, it becomes possible to reduce the costs of financing university education (Schugurensky, 1999, pp. 291–92).

Financial Strategies

The expansion of universities is predicated on acceptance of the commercial model (see Schugurensky, 1999, p. 297) since governments cannot afford to underwrite it, although they continue to provided a portion of the costs through annual subventions. There is cost-saving through a reduction in student/teacher ratios once the infrastructure for sophisticated open learning and flexible delivery has been established. Universities and colleges are partnered by business and public enterprises, and though some ugly features of this may need to be challenged, such as the monopoly of campus food or products by sponsors, it might usefully include the employment of students at some points in their educational career. User-pays education is expanded (the student loan scheme grows, and there are scholarships for those from very poor families). Governments and institutions develop closer links with Caribbean nationals abroad, drawing on their fundraising skills, knowledge, and networks. Universities improve in their capacity to raise a substantial proportion of their own funds through activities such as winning research grants, the sale of publications including multimedia, providing research consultancies, the sale of professional development programs, and providing fee-paying short courses for overseas students. Some of the universities make money by running radio and TV stations and operating extra-academic enterprises such as organic supermarkets.

CONCLUSION

A new context for culture in all societies has been created by globalization and the possibilities of globalism. The Caribbean and other regions of the "South" are at a disadvantage in the drive to restructure higher education. These regions, constrained by resource shortages and by the traditions and embeddedness of neocolonial institutions, are now tackling the daunting task of moving them beyond decolonization to the goals of a postcolonial, globalizing society.

If it is true, as Albrow (1994, p. 113) points out, that "the discourse for the Global Age can no longer rely on an idea of a society which provides an all-embracing frame in theory and practice," intellectuals may need to de-link themselves from many of the modernist ideas of the twentieth century to be in a better position to appreciate the potential, tackle the challenges, and pursue the possibilities of the Global Age. This does not mean a quest for novelty. We can retrieve what is relevant from the traditional and the modern and proceed from the non-Western as much as from the Western. This will enable us to perceive how the Global Age "sets the old elements of modernity in new relations with each other and introduces new elements which have transformed the total configuration" (Albrow, 1994, p. 114). De-linked from the Fordist- and Taylorist-type organization and the Eurocentric assumptions characteristic of modernity, spheres such as the state, education systems, social relations, the traditional academic "disciplines," all face reconstitution unconfined by boundaries in time or space. No guarantees comfort us as to their suitability. What is clear is that universities and colleges in developing countries must work even harder than their counterparts in the wealthy world to reinvent themselves on their own terms. Otherwise, in the inevitable decline of the traditional university, they will be swallowed up, on terms dictated by other societies instead of on terms negotiated equally, into the virtual knowledge systems that are an emerging feature of a globalizing world.

REFERENCES

Adams, Winston. 1999 (February 21). UWI Compiles Index of Research. *Sunday Gleaner.*

Adesida, Olugbenga, and Arunma Oteh. 1998. Envisioning the Future of Nigeria. *Futures*, vol. 30, no. 6, pp. 569–72.

Albrow, Martin. 1994. *The Global Age: State and Society beyond Modernity.* Cambridge, UK: Polity Press.

Alleyne, Michael. 1995. The Community College in the Commonwealth Caribbean: Focus on Trinidad and Tobago. *Caribbean Journal of Education*, vol. 17, no. 1, pp. 137–50.

Appadurai, Martin. 1990. Disjuncture and Difference in the Global Cultural Economy. In Mike Featherstone (ed.), *Global Culture: Nationalism, Globalization and Modernity.* London: Sage, pp. 295–310.

Currie, Jan. 1998. Globalization Practices and the Professoriate in Anglo-Pacific and North American Universities. *Comparative Education Review*, vol. 42, no. 1, pp. 15–29.

Escobar, Arturo. 1995. Imagining a Post-Development Era. In Jonathan Crush (ed.), *Power of Development.* London: Routledge, pp. 211–27.

Falk, Richard. 1992. *Explorations at the Edge of Time: The Prospects for World Order.* Philadelphia: Temple University Press.

Farrell, Trevor. 1993a. The Caribbean State and Its Role in Economic Management. In Stanley Lalta and Marie Freckleton (eds.), *Caribbean Economic Development: The First Generation.* Kingston: Ian Randle Publishers, pp. 200–14.

———. 1993b. Some Notes towards a Strategy for Economic Transformation. In Stanley Lalta and Marie Freckleton (eds.), *Caribbean Economic Development: The First Generation.* Kingston: Ian Randle Publishers, pp. 330–42.

Fine, Philip. 1999 (May 28). Caribbean V-C [vice-chancellor] Faces Struggle for Funds. *Times Higher Education Supplement*, no. 1, p. 386.

Gibson, Dennis, and William Hatherell. 1997. Reflections on Stability and Change in Australian Higher Education. In John Sharpham and Grant Harman (eds.), *Australia's Future Universities.* Hanover, NH: University Press of New England, pp. 121–36.

Hall, Douglas. 1998. *The University of the West Indies: A Quinqagenary Calendar 1948–1998.* Kingston: The Press, University of the West Indies.

Hall, Stuart. 1996. Caribbean Culture: Future Trends. *Caribbean Quarterly*, vol. 43, nos. 1–2, pp. 25–33.

Hickling-Hudson, Anne. 1997. Cuba's University Scholarships to Its Neighbours and National Development in the Caribbean. *Centro* (Journal of the Center for Puerto Rican Studies, City University of New York), vol. IX, no. 9, pp. 95–117.

Hoogvelt, Ankie. 1997. *Globalisation and the Postcolonial World: The New Political Economy of Development.* Basingstoke, UK: Macmillan.

Meeks, Brian. 1993. *Caribbean Revolutions and Revolutionary Theory: An Assessment of Cuba, Nicaragua and Grenada.* London: Macmillan.

Miller, Errol. 1997a. Colleges Training Teachers and the School of Education, UWI. *Journal of Education and Development in the Caribbean*, vol. 1, no. 1, pp. 61–82.

———. 1997b. Education for All in the Caribbean. *Caribbean Journal of Education*, vol. 19, no. 1, pp. 1–35.

Ministry of Education, Jamaica. 1995. 1995–2000 Draft Education Plan: Tertiary Education. Jamaica: Ministry of Education, Youth and Culture. Unpublished typescript.

Nettleford, Rex. 1997. The Continuing Battle for Space—The Caribbean Challenge. *Caribbean Quarterly*, vol. 43, nos. 1–2, pp. 90–95.

Osoba, Ermina. 1998 (July 22). The Future of the University of the West Indies and the Non-Campus Countries: Growth, Stagnation or Decay? In Marlene Hamilton (ed.), *The University of the West Indies: Celebrating the Past, Charting the Future: A View from Within*. Proceedings of the fiftieth anniversary symposium, 22 July 1998. UWI Mona: *Caribbean Quarterly*, pp. 66–75.

Peters, Bevis. 1993. The Emergence of Community, State and National Colleges in the OECS Member Countries and Institutional Analysis. Barbados: Institute of Social and Economic Research, University of the West Indies.

Privateer, Paul. 1999. Academic Technology and the Future of Higher Education: Strategic Paths Taken and Not Taken. *The Journal of Higher Education*, vol. 70, no. 1, pp. 60–79.

Ramphall, David. 1997 (March). Postmodernism and the Rewriting of Caribbean Radical Development Thinking. *Social and Economic Studies*, vol. 46, no. 1, pp. 1–30.

Robertson, Roland. 1992. *Globalization*. London: Sage.

Samoff, Joel. 1999. Institutionalizing International Influence. In Robert Arnove and Carlos A. Torres (eds.), *Comparative Education: The Dialectic of the Global and the Local*. Lanham, MD: Rowman & Littlefield, pp. 51–90.

Schugurensky, Daniel. 1999. Higher Education Restructuring in the Era of Globalization: Towards a Heteronomous Model? In Robert Arnove and Carlos A. Torres (eds.), *Comparative Education: The Dialectic of the Global and the Local*. Lanham, MD: Rowman & Littlefield, pp. 283–304.

University of Guyana. 1993. *Vice Chancellor's Development Plan*. Georgetown: Guyana.

University of the West Indies. 1994. A New Structure: The Regional University in the 1990s and Beyond. Report of the Chancellor's Commission on the Governance of UWI [unpublished].

———. 1997. *Strategic Plan, 1997–2002*. Kingston: Canoe Press.

Utsumi, Takeshi, and Armando Villarroel. 1992. Towards Establishing a Global/Latin American Electronic University. Internet: <axv@psuvm.psu.edu>.

Van der Wende, Maria. 1996. Internationalising the Curriculum in Dutch Higher Education: An International Comparative Perspective. Ph.D. dissertation: University of Utrecht, Netherlands.

World Bank. 1993. *Caribbean Region: Access, Quality and Efficiency in Education*. Washington, D.C.: World Bank.

12

Internationalization in Japanese Education: Current Issues and Future Prospects

Lynne Parmenter

Although internationalization and globalization are worldwide phenomena, their interpretation and realization are significantly influenced by the political, social, economic, and cultural context of any particular nation or region. In this chapter, Japan is used as a case study to explore how internationalization and globalization are interpreted in one particular national context of education policy.

GLOBALIZATION AND INTERNATIONALIZATION IN JAPAN

Worldwide Forces

The first point to be made with regard to globalization and internationalization is that a multiplicity of interpretations of these forces has to be acknowledged and accepted. As Jameson (1998, p. xi) observes, "globalization is the intellectual property of no specific field." The phenomena of globalization and internationalization are being approached from within many established fields. Scholars working against the background of these fields bring with them, as a form of "cultural baggage," certain understandings, definitions, and interpretations of globalization and internationalization constructed from different knowledge bases and different methodologies. These interpretations from a wide range of sources provide a rich fund of perspectives from which to embark on the exploration of these phenomena. In this section, therefore, I do not assume to provide a definitive account of what globalization and internationalization are or should be. Instead, I introduce various perspectives, focusing especially on discussions of the distinction between the terms *globalization* and *internationalization*, as this distinction is relevant to an analysis of Japanese education policy.

Broadly speaking, there are three approaches to defining globalization and internationalization in relation to each other. As a first approach, some researchers clearly divide globalization and internationalization. For example, Kress (1996) distinguishes internationalization and globalization by their territorial spheres, with internationalization operating within a narrower territorial domain. Other researchers use different criteria. For instance, Jones (this volume) distinguishes globalization and internationalization primarily according to their spheres of action. Whatever the criteria, the significant feature of this approach is that internationalization and globalization are conceptualized as qualitatively distinct phenomena.

A second approach is to adopt a "stage model" way of thinking. This approach is apparent in the work of those researchers who conceptualize internationalization as a progression from nationalism and globalization as a progression from internationalization. Using parallel concepts, for example, Taylor (1996, p. 106) argues we are in the process of transition from inter-stateness (internationalization) to trans-stateness (globalization). A similar way of thinking, but on a micro- rather than macro-scale, is evident in Meyer's (1991) work on levels of intercultural performance. Meyer (p. 142) argues that students progress from an "intercultural level," where "the learner stands between the cultures" to a "transcultural level" (p. 143), where "the learner stands above both his own and the foreign culture." In stage models like these, such "trans-stateness" or "transculturalism" (globalization) is perceived to be somehow more advanced than internationalization (inter-stateness, interculturalism).

A third approach is to see internationalization and globalization not as distinct phenomena or as stages of the same phenomenon, but as different perspectives. In this way of thinking, I would argue that internationalization is the process of constructing and seeing the world from the perspective of a particular nation or nations. This meaning is inherent in the term *inter-nationalization* itself, where the nation is still the dominant concept. Internationalization usually begins with the perspective of looking out at the world from one's own native country and culture, but also involves the realization that there are other perspectives on the world and on one's own country and culture. In internationalization, then, a multiplicity of perspectives is accepted and understood, but the conceptualization of the world is dominated by specific nations and cultures. To put it metaphorically, the view of the world is from the inside out. Specific nations/cultures (native or otherwise) provide the standpoint from which to look out to the world. By contrast, the alternative perspective is to view the world from the outside in. Nations and cultures still exist in their own right, but are no longer the dominant unit. They exist as parts of a whole but are superseded as the unit of reference by that whole, which is the globe. The world provides the standpoint from which to look in at individual nations and cultures, groups of nations and cultures, and the relationships between them. According to such a definition, unlike the stage model interpretations, globalization is not "better" or "more advanced" than internationalization. Internationalization and globalization, in this way of thinking, are complementary rather than conflicting or progressive. They are alternative perspectives that are appropriate to different situations and circumstances.

Further interpretations of internationalization and globalization abound, but those outlined here should serve to introduce some of the issues relevant to this chapter. To claim that one interpretation is somehow "better" than the others would be presumptuous. As Ball (1994, p. 14) observes, "In the analysis of complex social issues . . . two theories are probably better than one."

All three groups of theories of internationalization/globalization will be used in this chapter to try to understand internationalization in Japanese education. At the same time, it should be kept in mind that all theories of globalization and internationalization are subject to interpretation, negotiation, and reconstruction at various levels.

National Interpretations

Globalization and internationalization, by their very definition, extend beyond national boundaries. The routine everyday lifestyle of people all over the world is affected by what happens in other parts of the world. To a certain extent, commodities, knowledge, and principles have become common currency, shared by people in Asia, America, Africa, Australasia, and Europe. This is not to say that globalization and "global culture" necessarily threaten national and local cultures. Although commodities, knowledge, and principles may be shared worldwide, the interpretation and use of those same commodities, knowledge, and principles are often culture- and nation-specific. As Featherstone (1990, p. 1) notes, "It is . . . misleading to conceive a global culture as necessarily entailing a weakening of the sovereignty of nation-states which . . . will necessarily become absorbed into larger units and eventually a world state which produces cultural homogeneity and integration."

It is true that nation states can no longer "opt out" of the internationalization and globalization processes. A return to moves such as the "closed country" policy of Tokugawa Japan is hardly feasible, as it would lead most countries to political isolation and economic starvation. While opting out is no longer possible, individual nation-states are not obliged to accept without question the dominant discourses of internationalization and globalization. Nation-states can embrace the processes of internationalization and globalization without surrendering their national autonomy or character. Differing worldviews, based on different cultural, religious, and social traditions, and different histories, are bound to color the individual's and the national interpretation of internationalization and globalization. Featherstone (1995, p. 113) phrases this concept as "a plurality of national responses to the process of globalization." In Robertson's (1992, p. 99) definition of globalization as "the interpenetration of the universalization of particularism and the particularization of universalism," the universal (the processes of internationalization and globalization) and the particular (national interpretations of internationalization and globalization) continuously construct and reconstruct each other. Globalization and internationalization are not fixed entities, but are constantly self-renewing, two-way processes in which national interpretations play an important role.

Individual Identities

If nations are significant in the interpretation and construction of the processes of internationalization and globalization, so too are individuals. Spybey (1996, p. 5) argues that the influences of globalization can only exist if people "take them into their lives." Of course, the influences of globalization (mass media, commodities, etc.) exist independently of individuals, but they can exist only as influences if people are conscious of them.

This leads to the question of identities. Globalization as "the intensification of consciousness of the world as a whole" (Robertson, 1992, p. 8) affects the individual's ways of seeing and thinking about the world and consequently the individual's identities in the world. Identities are constructed throughout life as the individual seeks to situate him/herself in particular social and cultural groups, which extend to the "imagined communities" (Anderson, 1983) of the nation and the world. Internationalization and globalization are thus just as much individual as transnational processes. It is only through engagement on the part of the individual that globalization and internationalization as "a state of mind" or as an integral part of people's identities can be achieved.

In making this statement, two points need to be emphasized. The first is that identities are not fixed, but are constantly being modified and reconstructed (Larrain, 1994, p. 163). The second point is that the individual has many identities. Sometimes these identities may clash, but it is more often the case that the individual is at ease with a variety of identities. As Hobsbawm (1996, p. 1067) remarks, "The concept of a single, exclusive, and unchanging ethnic or cultural or other identity is a dangerous piece of brainwashing. Human mental identities are not like shoes, of which we can only wear one pair at a time."

This is a particularly important point in discussions of internationalization and globalization, as these forces are often seen to threaten existing national, cultural, and ethnic identities. The implication of this point is that it is quite possible for the individual to construct identity as a member of the world—a likely outcome of globalization as "a state of mind"—without "losing" any existing identities.

Japanese Education

The term *globalization* (in Japanese, *guroubaruka*, or *chikyuuka*) is problematic in a Japanese context. This is because, until the late 1990s, its use was confined almost exclusively to discussions of environmental issues or the economy. Still now, the term *globalization* is overshadowed by *internationalization* (*kokusaika*), which has been in common usage since the 1960s and is now omnipresent in Japanese society. In fact, Katou (1992, p. 310) goes so far as to make the following claim: "Encouraged over the past decade by the government, *kokusaika* has become the latest in a series of all-embracing slogans. . . . *kokusaika* has come to mean all things to all men."

Since about 1996, however, globalization has begun to appear in discussions of education. Some researchers (e.g., Yoshino, 1998) accept the theories outlined earlier in this chapter of internationalization and globalization as qualitatively different phenomena. For other researchers (e.g., Umakoshi, 1998, p. 178), *globalization* has replaced *internationalization* as a general term. Implicit in this idea is the view described earlier of a stage model, where globalization progresses from and replaces internationalization. Still others (e.g., Tada, 1997) seem to subscribe to the view that internationalization incorporates globalization. This definition of internationalization subsuming globalization (or vice versa) did not form part of the interpretations discussed previously, but is perhaps the most common interpretation among Japanese education researchers.

As education is part of society, and as education systems are increasingly perceived and structured as part of the economic and political capital of the society (Brown and Lauder, 1997), it naturally follows that internationalization has become an issue of education in Japan as in many countries. In some countries, such as Japan, internationalization has been officially adopted as a national education policy. In these cases, internationalization typically involves such measures as the development of an appropriate national curriculum and the establishment of exchange programs and activities. It may be necessary to delve further than face-value to understand the significance of such measures, as Robertson (1992, p. 186) cautions:

> On the one hand, the increasing concern with "other cultures" and with global trends is to be greatly welcomed. . . . On the other hand, we must realize that in considerable part that step is predicated on the proposition that countries which do not promote "international education" will suffer in economic and political terms in an increasingly interdependent world. In other words, much of the drive to "internationalize" the curriculum is based on, or at least legitimized in terms of, national or regional politico-economic self-interest.

ANALYSIS OF INTERNATIONALIZATION IN JAPANESE EDUCATION POLICY

Analysis of policy involves more than just examination of the text of a document. As Taylor et al. (1997, p. 25) remark, "policy involves the production of the text, the text itself, ongoing modifications to the text and processes of implementation into practice." Just as internationalization and globalization as forces are negotiated and reconstructed at various levels by various people, so policies of internationalization and globalization are not set in stone. Rather, the policy is subject to interpretation, reconstruction, and re-creation by the people and institutions it affects.

With this caveat in mind, the focus in this chapter is on the text of reforms announced in 1998 by the Japanese Ministry of Education (hereafter referred to by its Japanese name, Monbusho) and on the implications of these policies in the context of reform. The 1998 policies, which are due to be implemented in schools from the year 2002, will be compared with the previous set of Japanese education policy reforms, announced in 1989 and implemented from 1992 onward. In general, Monbusho implements education reforms once a decade. A committee is appointed by Monbusho to discuss and propose education reforms. The committee, which comprises school educators, university professors, business leaders, and others, deliberates for one to two years and then presents a report to Monbusho. On the basis of this report, Monbusho develops policy for the following decade and publishes the relevant documents. There is usually a gap of three to five years between publication of policy documents and implementation of policy in schools.

As the 1998 reforms have not been implemented at the time of writing, discussion will have to be limited to ideological statements of what the government thinks education should be. This is the *tatemae* (outside face) of education policy, which will need to be balanced by examination of the *honne* (inner face) of what is actually happening in schools once the policies are implemented. Although these ideological statements are only one facet of policy, they are undeniably important. In Japan, Monbusho exercises a great deal of power in deciding the school curriculum. Monbusho policies specify in detail the aims and content of each subject, as well as the number of hours each subject should be taught each year. In addition, textbooks, on which most teaching is based, have to be authorized by Monbusho before they can be used in schools. In order to be authorized, they have to adhere closely to Monbusho policy. Transmission of Monbusho policy to individual students in school classrooms is thus assured.

Knowledge

In terms of knowledge, the overriding concern of Monbusho in the 1998 reforms is to reduce the mass of factual information being memorized by students at all levels of education. The number of school hours will be reduced from the year 2002, with the adoption of a full five-day week (at present, children attend school two or three Saturday mornings each month). Throughout the 1998 policy documents, emphasis is placed on students understanding the main ideas of the curriculum content, rather than memorizing the details, facts, and figures. Consequently, subject content will be cut, reduced, or postponed to later years in all areas of the curriculum, including those that relate to internationalization.

Knowledge of Other Countries

At present, Japanese children learn virtually nothing about other countries until their fifth or sixth year of elementary school (ages ten to twelve). Even at this stage, most subjects contain no reference to internationalization in their aims or content. The two exceptions are social studies and moral education, with most knowledge concentrated in social studies. Although pupils begin to learn social studies in their third year, it is not until the sixth year that the international sphere becomes a significant part of the social studies curriculum. The 1989 and 1998 Monbusho guidelines state that sixth-year students should understand something of the countries that have strong relationships with Japan and should understand the role of Japan in international society (Monbusho, 1989a, p. 33; 1998a, p. 28). The knowledge of other countries gained at elementary school is almost exclusively filtered through the national lens of that country's relationship with Japan.

At junior high school, knowledge of other countries becomes a greater part of the curriculum. In the 1989 policies, which are currently in practice in Japanese schools, the geography section of the social studies curriculum is divided into three themes: "the world and its regions," "Japan and its regions," and "Japan in an international society" (Monbusho, 1989c, p. 18). In "the world and its regions," students study the countries of the world and ways of life and environments in various countries. In contrast to elementary school, these countries are not presented purely in terms of their relation to Japan, but also in their own right. Topics covered within the study of these regions include physical geography, industry, political issues, and the relationship of the region to the world.

In the 1998 reforms, the structure of the geography curriculum is changed. "Japan" and "the world" are no longer studied separately, but are combined into the following themes: "the regional structure of the world and Japan," "investigations appropriate to the regional scale," and "Japan seen through comparison to the world" (Monbusho, 1998b, p. 16). It remains to be seen whether this structural change in the social studies curriculum will make a significant difference to the amount and nature of knowledge of other countries taught and learned in junior high school. One possibility is that the new policy, by treating Japan and the world together, will encourage greater emphasis on relationships between Japan and other countries, which is the next aspect of international knowledge.

Knowledge of Relationships between One's Own and Other Countries

As mentioned above, under the 1998 revisions a large proportion of the international knowledge gained in elementary and junior high school concerns relations between Japan and other countries. In the sixth year of elementary school, students' study of Japanese history includes international aspects, such as the Chinese and Korean influences from the sixth century, encounters with the West and Christianity in the sixteenth century, Japan's opening to the world in the mid-nineteenth century, the war in Asia, and Japan's postwar international involvement. Students also study something about life and people in other countries for the first time. The countries selected for study are to be chosen because of their close ties with Japan. For example, one textbook currently in use presents the United States because of its importance for trade, Saudi Arabia because it provides most of Japan's oil, and China because of its historical links (Mitsumura Tosho, 1996). In spite of the emphasis on relationships between Japan and other countries in the curriculum, many elementary school students seem to have little notion of Japan in the world. In a questionnaire undertaken with fourth and sixth-grade elementary school pupils in several schools in rural Japan, when asked to select from a list which countries are in Asia, only 26 percent of Japanese fourth-grade and 35 percent of sixth-grade students correctly identified Japan as being in Asia. In contrast, answering the same question, 89 percent of fourth graders and 93 percent of sixth graders in elementary schools in Hong Kong correctly identified Japan as part of Asia (Parmenter and Tomita, 1998). One explanation for this limited knowledge on the part of the Japanese children has to be the late introduction of international knowledge into the elementary school curriculum, but the 1998 policies promise few changes in this area of the curriculum.

In junior high school, students study international relations in the theme "Japan in an international society." For example, one textbook (Tokyo Shoseki, 1996, pp. 260–85) introduces trade links between Japan and the world. It then goes on to case studies of relations between Japan and Korea, Japan and Brazil, and Japan and Australia. Finally, students study Japan's economic aid to developing countries. In junior high school history, too, students are exposed to a significant amount of world knowledge, particularly Japan's historical links with other countries. It seems likely that the 1998 reforms, which lay even greater emphasis on "Japan in the world" will lead to a strengthening of this relational approach. For example, a section of the 1998 guidelines on history (Monbusho, 1998b, p. 25) states that "The teaching of world history should be limited to the context necessary for understanding matters directly related to our country's history."

Of course, it is important that students recognize links and relations between their own and other countries. The risk of this approach, however, is that all world knowledge is filtered through a particular national interpretation, and the world is understood from only one perspective, and that is as it relates to Japan.

Knowledge of International and Global Issues

Knowledge of international and global issues is not introduced in any systematic way in elementary or junior high school. In various areas and at various stages of the curriculum, however, there is some reference to such issues. For example, in the 1998 reforms, environmental education is advocated at all stages of school (Kyouiku Katei Shingikai, 1998, p. 14). Students are also introduced to the activities of transnational organizations. In particular, they study the role, activities, and structure of the United Nations, first in elementary school and then in more detail in junior high school (Monbusho, 1998a, p. 30; 1998b, p. 31). The greatest consistent emphasis in the area of global issues, however, is, and will remain in the 1998 reforms, knowledge about and commitment to peace education. From elementary school onward, children learn about the effects of the nuclear bombs dropped on Hiroshima and Nagasaki. In junior high school, they learn about the Japanese Constitution and principles of pacifism (Monbusho, 1998b, p. 30). At all stages, this knowledge is explicitly value-led, with teachers instructed by Monbusho to develop in students a commitment to strive for world peace.

Competencies

Compared to previous Japanese education policy, the 1998 curriculum emphasizes the development of students' competencies or skills over the acquisition of factual knowledge. The shift in emphasis is particularly apparent with the introduction from 2002 of a completely new area of the curriculum—the so-called *sougoutekina gakushuu no jikan* or "integrated study time." From the third year of elementary school to the third year of junior high school, students will spend between seventy and 130 hours per year on integrated study time. The aim of this area of the curriculum is to develop students' ability and competence to respond independently to the changes of society, such as internationalization, by developing their abilities to transcend subject boundaries and think and learn by themselves (Kyouiku Katei Shingikai, 1998, p. 15). The 1998 policies are peppered with references to the development of "the ability to think and learn of one's own accord"; "problem-creation and problem-solving skills"; "skills of independent learning and judgment"; "skills of synthesizing and applying knowledge to real life"; and, more specifically, information technology skills. These particular skills are newly emphasized and occupy a prominent place in the 1998 reforms. All these general skills have some bearing on internationalization, but the focus in this section will be on the skills that are directly necessary for internationalization.

Language

It goes without saying that language competence is an essential element of the skills required in internationalization. Language competence is a broad concept, and the discussion here will be limited to language awareness and foreign language competence.

Neither the current Monbusho policies nor the proposed 1998 reforms contain any explicit reference to language awareness other than Japanese at elementary school level. Within the curriculum, although the greatest proportion of school time in every year of elementary school is devoted to language, there is never any mention in the Monbusho guidelines of awareness of languages other than Japanese. Japanese children's contact with and awareness of foreign languages is thus coincidental, and a possible, and often observed, result is that foreign languages are perceived as "exotic," "impossible," and "strange."

This lack of awareness of other languages is compounded by the assumption that all children in Japanese schools are, or should be, monolingual Japanese speakers. Although programs have been established to teach Japanese to returnees or to foreign children in Japanese schools, Monbusho does not support any bilingual education or minority language maintenance programs.

For most students, then, the first contact with foreign languages comes at the age of twelve. At junior high school level, foreign language is currently an optional subject but, in practice, almost all junior high schools teach a foreign language. In the 1998 policies, foreign language becomes a compulsory subject in junior high school. At present, schools are allowed to teach any foreign language, and guidelines are given for English, French, and German. In practice, in junior high school, English is the only foreign language available, and the only foreign language for which textbooks are authorized. In the 1998 reforms, Monbusho imposes English as the foreign language for junior high school (Monbusho, 1998b, p. 96).

The situation in practice will change little in junior high schools, but greater attention is focused on what will happen in elementary schools. In the years of debate preceding the publication of reforms, there was a great deal of discussion about whether to introduce English as a subject into elementary schools. The final compromise is that foreign languages will become an optional element of the integrated study time (Monbusho, 1998a, p. 3). It remains to be seen how many schools will interpret this policy as the opportunity to give their students a "head-start" in the English currently taught at junior high school. A more optimistic view is that this policy will enable elementary schools to introduce other areas of language competence that are lacking in the current curriculum. In this respect, integrated study time has the potential to enable children to develop a wider language competence, rather than merely develop the same narrow English language skills at an earlier age.

Culture

In terms of competencies, language competence alone is insufficient for internationalization. Students also need to develop intercultural competence. As Fennes and Hapgood (1997) argue, "not only should intercultural learning involve those who are directly confronted with or affected by multicultural settings, but, because of the complexity of modern societies, intercultural learning has to involve everyone."

Cultural competence includes the ability to recognize differences as well as similarities (Kramsch, 1993), the ability to decenter and see one's own culture from an outside perspective (Byram, 1989), the ability to accept and understand different ways of acting and thinking, and the ability to negotiate a range of meanings and interpretations (Byram, 1997).

The ability to recognize the similarities and differences between Japan and other countries is encouraged by Monbusho in both the 1989 and 1998 reforms. In the international sphere, greater weight is given to differences than to similarities. For example, in the 1989 guidelines for foreign languages (Monbusho, 1989d, p. 88), the following statement appears in a section on materials: "In the study of foreign languages, it is necessary to arouse even greater interest in the differences of foreign people's way of life, customs and habits, and to draw attention to the variety of cultures."

The ability to decenter is a competence accorded importance by Monbusho. As noted above, a third of the geography section of the social studies curriculum for junior high school is devoted to the theme "Japan seen through comparison with the world." Each subsection takes a theme (for example, natural environment, population, resources, or industry) and looks at the distinctive features of Japan from a world perspective (Monbusho, 1998b, p. 18). Similar approaches are also apparent in the history and civics sections of the junior high school social studies curriculum. Interestingly, though, in the guidelines for foreign language and moral education, this approach does not feature.

The ability to accept and understand different ways of acting and thinking, together with the ability to negotiate a range of meanings and interpretations, is closely connected with ways of seeing and thinking, which will be discussed shortly. In the 1989 and 1998 policies, the development of such abilities in the international sphere is not addressed directly by Monbusho.

Communication

In addition to language and cultural competence, communication competence is also essential for the practice of internationalization. Two aspects of communication that are of significance for internationalization are interpersonal communication skills and information technology skills.

Interpersonal communication skills—the ability to establish and maintain relationships with others—are as important in internationalization as in everyday life. Although this competence rarely appears in Monbusho guidelines in the international sphere, it is often referred to in discussions of the immediate environment. In the curriculum for Japanese language for six- to eight-year-olds, for example, children are expected to develop skills of expressing their ideas in an orderly way and listening with interest (Monbusho, 1998a, p. 6). By junior high school, they should be able to summarize their opinions according to the subject and then listen and speak while showing respect for their interlocutor's perspective and ideas (Monbusho, 1998b, p. 10). Evidently, such interpersonal skills are premised on the assumption that children have certain cognitive abilities (e.g., to be able to summarize and express ideas) and also certain ways of seeing other people. The desired "ways of seeing other people"—with respect, gratitude, and concern—are explicitly laid out in the moral education curriculum, and will be returned to in the next section. Although Monbusho rarely refers to interpersonal skills in the international sphere, these skills are generic and can easily be applied to the international context.

The development of information technology (IT) skills as a means of communication is one of the major themes of the 1998 Monbusho reforms. At present, computers are little used in Japanese schools, and many students leave school with extremely limited IT skills. As a subject in itself, IT forms a small part of the Industrial Arts curriculum in junior high school, in most cases amounting to less than twenty hours of class time over three years, and this situation will not change in the 1998 reforms. However, the aim is to install computers in every school and link every school to the Internet by 2003 (Kyouiku Katei Shingikai, 1998, p. 13). Teachers are then expected to use computers across the curriculum, beginning with integrated study time and extending to other subjects. The aim is for students to develop the skills to live in an information-oriented society, a society that obviously transcends national boundaries. It will be interesting to see how this measure of "bringing the world" into every Japanese school will affect internationalization in Japanese education. If current teaching methods continue, it is likely that students' access to information will be entirely controlled by the teacher, and the degree of internationalization/globalization (or otherwise) will effectively be decided by the teacher. If the students are given a greater degree of freedom in access to information (a measure that would be highly innovative in the current education system), the outcomes are less predictable. The issue then would be one of students' abilities to locate, understand, evaluate, and use relevant information. These would be determined not only by foreign language abilities, but also by the more general abilities of interpretation, judgment, and so on, precisely the kinds of abilities newly advocated by Monbusho in the 1998 reforms.

Ways of Seeing and Thinking

The guidelines published by Monbusho are not limited to policies on curriculum content and competencies to be developed, but also specify the qualities, values, and attitudes that should be encouraged in young people. The prominent and explicit place of values in the Japanese classroom has been well documented by researchers of Japanese education (e.g., Hendry, 1986; White, 1987; Rohlen and LeTendre, 1996). Lewis (1995, p. 212) stresses the point that "Japanese education . . . focuses on children's long-term internalization of values rather than on their immediate compliance."

In the immediate sphere, a wide spectrum of desired values, attitudes, and qualities is specified. These are most explicitly advanced in the guidelines for moral education. For example, the guidelines for junior high school moral education (Monbusho, 1998b, p. 98) consist of a list of aims, which include "deepening the spirit of warm love for humanity," "having a heart of gratitude towards and concern for other people," "understanding the value of friendship," "respecting individuality," "understanding that there are various ways of seeing and thinking about things," "having an open heart which humbly learns from others," "being aware of one's role and responsibility," and "striving for the realization of a society without discrimination or prejudice." These values permeate the daily life of the school (for detailed description, see Lewis, 1995; and Benjamin, 1997). Although these aims are not put forward in the context of the international sphere by Monbusho, it is evident that the empathy, respect, love for humans, gratitude, caring, trust, humility, sense of responsibility, and justice that are advocated in the immediate sphere could all be conceived as appropriate values/qualities in the development of internationalization.

In the international sphere, the values and attitudes expected in the individual student are more limited, restricted to interest, respect, understanding, and lack of prejudice. Interest comes first, appearing in the moral education guidelines for third- and fourth-grade elementary school students (Monbusho, 1998a, p. 91). This is a development from the 1989 guidelines, where the first mention of the international sphere in moral education did not come until the fifth/sixth grade. In the 1998 guidelines, fifth- and sixth-grade students are expected "to have self-awareness as a Japanese person and to strive for friendship with people of the world" (Monbusho, 1998a, p. 93). In this aim, the tension and balance between national and international elements is already apparent. Familiarity and love for Japan, as well as self-awareness as a Japanese person, are prerequisites for any encounter with the "outside" world. In junior high school, the moral education aim that relates to this sphere is more abstract and is virtually unchanged from the 1989 policy (Monbusho, 1989b, p. 119; 1998b, p. 99): "To have self-awareness as a Japanese person in the world, to take an international perspective, and to contribute to the peace of the world and the happiness of humankind."

These statements all result from the recommendations made by the Curriculum Council regarding internationalization:

> As internationalization is progressing rapidly, it is from now even more important to develop education with the viewpoint of raising Japanese people who live in international society. The aim of education to cope with the progress of internationalization is to try to develop the qualities and abilities of understanding other cultures from a wide perspective, not being prejudiced against, but interacting naturally and living with, people who have different cultures or habits. In order to do that, we think it is important first to have education which cultivates understanding, love and pride in our own country's history, culture and traditions (Kyouiku Katei Shingikai, 1998, p. 12).

The phrase about "interacting naturally and living with" people of different cultures is new in the 1998 reforms, and is a significant addition, but the rest is familiar from the 1989 policies. Again, there is a perceived tension here between internationalization and national identity, with an underlying assumption that internationalization threatens national identity.

Implications of the 1998 Reforms for Internationalization in Japanese Education

Bias toward the West, which is evident in foreign language policy and curriculum content, is still apparent in the 1998 reforms. The only foreign language junior high school students can learn is English. The vast majority of foreigners who are employed in Japanese schools are native-English-speaking Westerners, and approximately half are Americans. Japanese students' contact with foreigners, therefore, is almost entirely with Westerners, in spite of the fact that the vast majority of foreigners in Japan are actually other Asians. Under such circumstances, it is hardly surprising that many Japanese elementary school students are unaware that Japan is part of Asia, as mentioned previously. Recently, there is a growing awareness of this situation in Japan, and the reform committee specifically mentions the problem of bias toward the West (Kyouiku Katei Shingikai, 1998, p. 13). However, no recommendations are made as to how this bias should be dealt with, and the same committee advocates English as the sole foreign language and foreign language as the core of internationalization, so their report is self-contradictory.

This is not the only ambiguity in the reforms. The term *kokusaika* (internationalization) itself, used as it is as an "all-embracing slogan," is highly ambiguous. Monbusho's statements do little to clarify the concept. The greatest potential for dealing with such ambiguity, and indeed for tackling the problem of bias to the West, seems to lie in the new integrated study time of the 1998 reforms. It is recognized that "education for international understanding" will be a significant component of integrated study time (Kyouiku Katei Shingikai, 1998, p. 16). The curriculum for integrated study time is not determined by Monbusho, but is left for schools to develop according to the characteristics of their locality and region. In theory, this will allow schools to determine their own interpretations of "education for international understanding" and may lead to a reduction in institutional bias toward the West, especially in regions where many non-Japanese Asians live and work. In practice, it remains to be seen what degree of awareness of and interest in this issue will be shown in schools. In this respect, the ambiguity of internationalization remains, but the ambiguity leaves a "discursive space" (Lincicome, 1993, p. 123), within which schools, teachers, and students have freedom to construct their own interpretations.

In terms of competencies, the 1998 reforms offer little promise of change in the areas of language and cultural competence. Language competence is still perceived narrowly as "English language skills" and is almost completely divorced from cultural competence. In spite of the inclusion in the general aim of foreign language education of "understanding culture" (Monbusho, 1998b, p. 88), there is no reference in the content guidelines as to how this could be approached. In fact, cultural competence is tackled only in the social studies curriculum, where it bears little relation to other aspects of intercultural communication. The major development contributing to intercultural communicative competence (ICC) is the emphasis on the use of information technology in schools in the 1998 policies. The potential for developing ICC in this area will depend to a large extent on the teaching methods employed in classrooms. Overall, though, the competencies involved in internationalization, and especially the links between these various competencies, remain underaddressed in the 1998 policies.

In what is perhaps the central issue of internationalization in education, the basic principles of the 1989 policy on internationalization remain unchanged. The basic rationale for and aim of internationalization in Japanese education remains the development of "Japanese people living in international society" (Monbusho, 1989b, p. 7; Kyouiku Katei Shingikai, 1998, p. 12), not the development of international people. National identity is prioritized over individual, international, and global identities. At no point does Monbusho advocate any attachment to the world group or international society. Instead, it uses the international context to reinforce attachment to the national group, thus strengthening national group boundaries.

Although the general picture is the same in the 1998 reforms, with Monbusho guidelines for junior high school Japanese (1998b, p. 15), foreign languages (1998b, p. 95), and moral education (1998b, p. 99) repeating the same aim of developing "Japanese people who can live in international society," there are a few signs of change. For example, the aim for elementary school sixth-grade social studies has changed from "[students] should have self-awareness as a Japanese person in the world" (1989a, p. 33) to "[students] should be conscious of the importance of living with the people of the world as a peace-seeking Japanese" (Monbusho, 1998a, p. 28). The same theme of "interacting naturally and living together with people who have different cultures" reappears in the recommendations of the curriculum committee, as quoted earlier (Kyouiku Katei Shingikai, 1998, p. 12). The concept of "living with" rather than "them and us" is a significant development in Monbusho policy, as it paves the way for the addition of global identity as a member of the world to the currently dominant national identity of being Japanese in the world.

CONCLUSION

Returning to the interpretations of internationalization/globalization outlined early in this chapter, there is little evidence in Japanese education policy of any attention to globalization in any of its definitions. Instead, Monbusho focuses exclusively on internationalization, where the main unit of reference is still "the nation." On the one hand, Monbusho welcomes internationalization, advocating it as a national policy for the twenty-first century. On the other hand, there seems to be a constant tension between internationalization and national identity and culture in the policy documents. In this respect, Robertson's (1992, p. 186) comment, quoted earlier, is especially pertinent to the Japanese situation. The underlying cause of the tension seems to be the fact that Monbusho does not recognize the possibility of students constructing multiple identities in the world. Rather than being seen as alternative or additional identities, international and global identities seem to be perceived by Monbusho as threats to national identity. Monbusho's response is to use internationalization in large part to reinforce the development of national identity. Differences are emphasized over similarities, knowledge of the world is constructed as it relates to Japan, and the explicit aim is to develop "Japanese people who live in international society." However, small but significant changes are visible in the 1998 reforms. Growing awareness of the world—facilitated by multimedia access, recommendations to take notice of Asia, and more concrete activities in the context of integrated study time—may help in the development of a new generation of Japanese who have "greater consciousness of the world as a whole" (Robertson, 1992, p. 8). At the same time, the general values that Monbusho advocates in the immediate sphere—values such as empathy, a sense of responsibility, lack of prejudice, and trust—would, if extended to the international sphere, provide a solid foundation for the construction of world citizenship as well as national citizenship. In this way, although Monbusho may not directly promote or even wish for the development of global identity as a result of its internationalization policy, this may be one of the unintended consequences of the 1998 reforms. As Taylor et al. (1997, p. 15) observe, "Policies are . . . dynamic and interactive, and not merely a set of instructions or intentions."

Globalization and internationalization have to be filtered not only through the national lens, but also through the school and teacher lens, before they can be used by the individual to create his/her "identities in the world." The ambiguity of internationalization in Japan, together with the leeway given to schools and teachers in introducing internationalization in integrated study time, and the influences of other factors such as media and increased contact with foreign people, means that Monbusho's guidelines in this sphere may be subjected to a wide variety of interpretations. It remains to be seen what will actually happen when the 1998 policies are implemented in schools in 2002.

REFERENCES

Anderson, Benedict. 1983. *Imagined Communities: Reflections on the Origin and Spread of Nationalism*. London: Verso.

Ball, Stephen. 1994. *Educational Reform: A Critical and Post-Structured Approach.* Buckingham, England: Open University Press.

Benjamin, Gail. 1997. *Japanese Lessons: A Year in a Japanese School through the Eyes of an American Anthropologist and Her Children.* New York: New York University Press.

Brown, Phillip, and Hugh Lauder. 1997. Education, Globalization, and Economic Development. In A. H. Halsey, Hugh Lauder, Phillip Brown, and Amy Stuart Wells (eds.), *Education: Culture, Economy, and Society.* Oxford: Oxford University Press, pp.172–92.

Byram, Michael. 1989. *Cultural Studies in Foreign Language Education.* Clevedon, England: Multilingual Matters.

———. 1997. *Teaching and Assessing Intercultural Communicative Competence.* Clevedon, England: Multilingual Matters.

Featherstone, Mike. 1990. Global Culture(s): An Introduction. In Mike Featherstone (ed.), *Global Culture: Nationalism, Globalization and Modernity.* London: Sage, pp. 1–13.

———. 1995. *Undoing Culture: Globalization, Postmodernism and Identity.* London: Sage.

Fennes, Helmut, and Karen Hapgood. 1997. *Intercultural Learning in the Classroom: Crossing Borders.* London: Cassell.

Hendry, Joy. 1986. *Becoming Japanese: The World of the Pre-School Child.* Manchester: Manchester University Press.

Hobsbawm, Eric. 1996. Language, Culture and National Identity. *Social Research*, vol. 63, no. 4, pp. 1065–80.

Jameson, Fredric. 1998. Preface. In Fredric Jameson and Masao Miyoshi (eds.), *The Cultures of Globalization.* Durham, NC: Duke University Press, pp. xi–xvii.

Katou, Shuichi. 1992. The Internationalization of Japan. In Glenn D. Hook and Michael A. Weiner (eds.), *The Internationalization of Japan.* London: Routledge, pp. 310–16.

Kramsch, Claire. 1993. *Context and Culture in Language Teaching.* Oxford: Oxford University Press.

Kress, Gunther. 1996. Internationalisation and Globalisation: Rethinking a Curriculum of Communication. *Comparative Education*, vol. 32, no. 2, pp. 185–96.

Kyouiku Katei Shingikai. 1998. (National curriculum standards reform for kindergarten, elementary school, lower and upper secondary school and schools for the visually disabled, the hearing impaired and the otherwise disabled). <http://www.monbu.go.jp. singi/Katei/00000216>.

Larrain, Jorge. 1994. *Ideology and Cultural Identity: Modernity and the Third World Presence.* Cambridge: Polity.

Lewis, Catherine. 1995. *Educating Hearts and Minds: Reflections on Japanese Preschool and Elementary Education.* Cambridge: Cambridge University Press.

Lincicome, Mark. 1993. Focus on Internationalization of Japanese Education: Nationalism, Internationalization, and the Dilemma of Educational Reform in Japan. *Comparative Education Review*, vol. 37, no. 2, pp. 123–51.

Meyer, Meinert. 1991. Developing Transcultural Competence: Case Studies of Advanced Foreign Language Learners. In Dieter Buttjes and Michael Byram (eds.), *Mediating Languages and Cultures: Towards a Theory of Foreign Language Education.* Clevedon, England: Multilingual Matters, pp. 136–58.

Mitsumura Tosho. 1996. *Shakai 6 Jou* (Social studies sixth grade part 1). Tokyo: Mitsumura Tosho.

Monbusho. 1989a. *Shougakkou Gakushuu Shidou Youryou* (The course of study for elementary school). Tokyo: Monbusho.

————. 1989b. *Chuugakkou Shidousho: Kyouiku Katei Ippan Hen* (Junior high school guidelines: General education curriculum). Tokyo: Monbusho.

————. 1989c. *Chuugakkou Gakushuu Shidou Youryou* (The course of study for junior high school). Tokyo: Monbusho.

————. 1989d. *Chuugakkou Shidousho: Gaikokugo* (Junior high school guidelines: Foreign languages). Tokyo: Monbusho.

————. 1998a. *Shougakkou Gakushuu Shidou Youryou* (The course of study for elementary school). Tokyo: Monbusho.

————. 1998b. *Chuugakkou Gakushuu Shidou Youryou* (The course of study for junior high school). Tokyo: Monbusho.

Parmenter, Lynne, and Yuichi Tomita. 1998. Elementary School Students' Perceptions of Internationalisation in Four East Asian Regions. Paper presented at JASTEC conference, Akita, Japan, September 1998.

Robertson, Roland. 1992. *Globalization: Social Theory and Global Culture*. London: Sage.

Rohlen, Thomas, and Gerald LeTendre (eds.). 1996. *Teaching and Learning in Japan*. Cambridge: Cambridge University Press.

Spybey, Tony. 1996. *Globalization and World Society*. Cambridge: Polity.

Tada, Takashi. 1997. *Kokusai Rikai Kyouiku* (Education for international understanding). Tokyo: Touyoukan shuppansha.

Taylor, Peter. 1996. The Modern Multiplicity of States. In Eleonore Kofman and Gillian Youngs (eds.), *Globalization: Theory and Practice*. London: Pinter, pp. 99–108.

Taylor, Sandra, Fazal Rizvi, Bob Lingard, and Miriam Henry. 1997. *Educational Policy and the Politics of Change*. London: Routledge.

Tokyo Shoseki. 1996. *Atarashii Shakai: Chiri* (New social studies: Geography). Tokyo: Tokyo Shoseki.

Umakoshi, Tooru. 1998. (The changing face of Asia and Japanese people's internationalization). In Yutaka Saeki, Isao Kurosaki, Manabu Sato, Takahiko Tanaka, Sumio Hamada, and Hidenori Fujita (eds.), *Kokusaika Jidai No Kyouiku* (Education in the age of internationalization). Tokyo: Iwanami Shoten, pp. 167–86.

White, Merry. 1987. *The Japanese Educational Challenge: A Commitment to Children*. Tokyo: Kodansha International.

Yoshino, Kosaku. 1998. [Globalisation and nationalism]. In Yutaka Saeki, Isao Kurosaki, Manabu Sato, Takahiko Tanaka, Sumio Hamada, and Hidenori Fujita (eds.), *Kokusaika Jidai No Kyouiku* (Education in the age of internationalization). Tokyo: Iwanami Shoten, pp. 31– 49.

13

Globalization and Decentralization in Sub-Saharan Africa: Focus Lesotho

William M. Rideout, Jr.

As globalization is becoming an increasingly permeating phenomenon, so too is decentralization being acknowledged as one of its major and most pervasive affiliates in Sub-Saharan Africa. The extent of this relationship is difficult to determine because globalization, global education, decentralization, and educational decentralization are still evolving with an ultimate definition of globalization in relation to the three other terms being especially difficult to delimit. In his chapter (herein) Jones has defined globalization as "economic integration achieved in particular through the establishment of a global marketplace marked by free trade and a minimum of regulation." He further specifies that its most fundamental feature is "the organization and integration of economic activity at levels which transcend national borders and jurisdictions" (1997, p. 1). Although maintaining the dominance of economic globalization, Waters has also added political globalization and cultural globalization, which powerfully expand the concept of globalization (1995, p. 15). A third definition frequently used, as outlined by Sweeting, considers it to be

> relatively simple, if quite dramatic and comprehensive . . . clearly a process—of making or becoming "global," where "global" must be assumed to refer to the whole world, or "mother earth" or "our home planet." Most commonly, the expression "globalization" (or one of its derivatives) is used in contradistinction to "local" and "parochial." Certainly in modern journalistic and laymen's parlance, a positive value tends to be accorded to globalization, whereas limitations of view and insufficiencies of vision are frequently associated with the local and parochial (1996, pp. 379–80).

In one of the conceptual chapters of this volume, Carnoy focuses on the "finance driven" reforms associated with decentralization but notes that "educational decentralization is a major manifestation, if not of globalization itself, certainly of an ideology closely identified with, and pushing the development of, the global economy in a particular direction. So we need to ask how this larger ideological package, that includes, but is not limited to, decentralization, affects education."

In addition to the economic factors, decentralization has also been defined to mean "any change in the organization of government which involves the transfer of powers or functions from the national level to any subnational level(s), or from one subnational level to another, lower one" (Conyers, 1984, pp. 97–109). Decentralization "is further clarified as the transfer of legal, administrative and political authority [functional authorities] to make decisions and manage public functions from the central government to field organizations of those agencies, subordinate units of government, semi-autonomous public corporations, area-wide development authorities, functional authorities, autonomous local governments, communities, or nongovernmental organizations" (Whitacre, 1997, p. 3).

These functional authorities might include ecological, cultural, political, technological, and health sectors/factors and/or combinations thereof, most of which, as noted above, are also often affiliated with the expanded definition of globalization. Educational decentralization, however, also places special emphasis on the "bottom-up" approach to governance rather than the "top-down." Ideally, a nation's school system should be structured to assure the most appropriate school governance by a shared ownership between the school sites' populations and national officials. Without this integrated involvement the sustainability of expanded schooling, and especially the achievement of compulsory schooling and national literacy, are extremely difficult development goals for many nations, especially those with limited national incomes. However, throughout the developing world there are often inadequate or inappropriate bottom-up policies as well as inadequate participation. The World Bank has noted in its recent publication *Knowledge for Development* that first among four factors that governments should consider in focusing on policy reforms, to promote people's capabilities to absorb knowledge is to "Decentralize education to give more power to those with the most information about educational needs and how to meet them: students, parents, teachers, and local school administrators" (World Bank, 1998/99, p. 147). Thus, in conjunction with its growing emphasis on primary education as a priority human resources development approach, the World Bank has, with several other donors, also been emphasizing greater school-site governance.

While the globalization concept has been developing over roughly the last twenty years, so too has the concept of decentralization become increasingly pervasive, and especially educational decentralization, in the developing world. The latter concept has been evolving from a spectrum of decentralized educational efforts in the postindependence years ranging from "adult education, continuing education, on-the-job training, [to] extension services" and "ruralization" (Coombs, 1968, p. 139); it also implies that "responsibility for their management and funding [has been] scattered across dozens of public and private agencies.

They spring up spontaneously, come and go, at times succeed brilliantly but just as often die unnoticed and unmourned" (Coombs, 1968, p. 139). Thus, Coombs in the 1960s recommended that development be based on the assignment of suitable roles not only for formal education (schooling) but also for nonformal education in order to successfully meet the vast array of human resource development needs in developing countries. This was considered part of decentralization since the knowledge and learning components were to be substantially influenced by the environment in which they occurred and would be practiced. There was a new emphasis on community participation and community-based development.

> This [has] entailed a wrenching departure from the prevailing top-down approach. The problem there was not so much one of resistance to the idea; no one could deny its obvious good sense. The problem was rather the lack of know-how in going about it, for these top-down organizations, including not least of all most ministries of education, had little previous experience with working in equal partnership with individual communities and groups within them (Coombs, 1985, p. 176).

Coombs's preliminary research and recommendations coincided with Robert McNamara's being named president of the World Bank in 1968. McNamara was committed to expanding educational lending, which

> he linked both to individual productivity and to social stability. Philip Coombs was hired to undertake an analysis of the relationship between education and rural poverty, which resulted in a broadening of the Bank's education sector work. A 1974 sector paper announced a new Bank interest in primary and nonformal education (Mundy, 1998, p. 466).

Thus, a key factor in educational development became relevance, which was enhanced by the link between decentralization and community participation and community-based development. Reflecting his research findings, some of which were sponsored by the World Bank, Coombs emphasized that this new community emphasis

> entailed a wrenching departure from the prevailing top-down approach. The problem there was not so much one of resistance to the idea; no one could deny its obvious good sense. The problem was rather the lack of know-how in going about it, for these top-down organizations, including not least of all most ministries of education, had little previous experience with working in equal partnership with individual communities and groups within them (Coombs, 1985, p. 302).

A further result of this decentralization/relevance research was the publication of Coombs and Ahmed's *Attacking Rural Poverty: How Nonformal Education Can Help* (1974). Recommendations for Sub-Saharan Africa in line with those of Coombs and Ahmed subsequently highlighted the prevailing disparities related to planning and programming; they maintained that improved performance by enabled local authorities would result in improved management and promote "economies of scale and lead to more appropriate responsiveness to particular needs and situations of different regions and groups; and by engaging active involvement of the community and private sector groups in local schooling, decentralization [would] generate more representativeness and equity in educational decision making, and thus foster greater local commitment to public education" (Maclure as quoted in Whitacre, 1997, p. 4). An increasing capability would therefore exist for addressing more effectively gender, rural/urban, geographic, and ethnic discrepancies and other cultural, technical, health, environmental, and socioeconomic inequalities.

In summary, globalization, as reflected in the definitions quoted above, and congruent with Carnoy's description of globalization's evolution mentioned earlier, has shared a remarkably similar developmental process with decentralization, especially regarding educational decentralization and development, in Sub-Saharan Africa over the past thirty years. Researchers and scholars in the field, such as Coombs, have emphasized the need for vastly improved relevance between education—formal and nonformal—and the local environments/economies. The World Bank has been significantly involved both in helping to fund such research and in subsequently changing its own developmental priorities, in this case increasing support for education and modifying the conditions under which such support is made available. A standard loan practice, prevalent in World Bank–supported assistance, has evolved, which often includes a "set of pre-conditions aimed at assuring successful educational policy and practice" in support of views about educational processes that the World Bank might wish to promote. "In painting a picture of the pre-conditions for successful educational development, the Bank is in effect depicting its view of the ideal economy" (Jones, 1997, p. 10) and complaining that where the management of education in an economy is "by central or state governments little room [is allowed] for the flexibility that leads to effective learning" (World Bank, 1995, pp. 3–6). And educational priorities, including effective learning, should be designed and evaluated in terms of outcomes (World Bank, 1995, p. 9).

A global approach to educational development and decentralization has historically been actively supported by other United Nations (UN) agencies, with UNESCO and UNICEF playing leading and pioneering roles. However, given the World Bank's position as the major UN source of financial resources to support planning and implementation, the Bank has had a major impact on promoting and achieving decentralization. This emphasis has been congruent with the policies and practices of some of the major bilateral donors too, such as the United States and Germany, which also have supported decentralization outcomes, especially in educational development programs. America's promotion of decentralization is exemplified by the case study of Lesotho reviewed below. Germany's support of decentralization is illustrated by Germany's economic assistance organization DSE (Deutsche Stiftung fur internationale Entwicklung), which recently published the statement that "The globalisation of world trade and information technology opens up new chances for worldwide educational processes [aimed at] counter[ing] environmental destruction, poverty in large parts of the world, population growth and regional and ethnic wars" (cited in Peters, 1998, p. 8).

As Carnoy (herein) indicated, and as reinforced by Jones (herein) and Waters (1995), globalization does have a foundational base in economics that subsequently supports interaction and involvement with other developmental sectors (Whitacre, 1997, p. 4). Although like globalization the term *decentralization* still lacks a precise definition (Whitacre, 1997, p. 4), the decentralization occurring in Sub-Saharan Africa appears increasingly to be affiliated with the globalization endorsed by the World Bank and some major bilateral donors since decentralization policies and programs are among the most widely sponsored and implemented.

THE DICHOTOMY BETWEEN POLICY AND PRACTICE

In Sub-Saharan Africa, where the majority of nations are desperately poor, it is often the case that bottom-up participation, even where occurring, is not recognized. Such recognition by a central government apparently would acknowledge its failure to provide the educational resources to which the government has, invariably, committed itself nationally and internationally and for which it very often inaccurately persists in claiming full credit in terms of whatever achievements occur. The communities' building and maintenance of schools; construction of protective fences around the schools; procurement of school books and classroom furniture; less often teachers' salaries, but more often "income subsidies" and housing for teachers; plus pencils, paper, etc., for the students all occur repeatedly because of parental support throughout Sub-Saharan Africa. These community/parental contributions are, for the most part, never acknowledged nor even included in official national and/or international reports of national expenditures for education. It has been estimated that these contributions may constitute one-fourth of the educational budget in some Sub-Saharan African countries. But admission of this impressive level of popular support appears to be perceived by some governments as reflecting negatively on their own status, prestige, and performance. This decentralization, although very frequently unacknowledged, has been pervasive and expanding.

Our analysis of decentralization will focus briefly on three Sub-Saharan Africa countries, the Democratic Republic of Congo (Congo/K, formerly Zaire), Senegal, and Cameroon.[1] Thereafter, a more detailed case study analysis will be presented on Lesotho, a quite unique instance of "decentralizing decentralization." In each subject country the centralization–decentralization factors will constitute the major foci under consideration. Both de jure and de facto components will be considered; de jure representing the governmental creation of policies related to decentralization and de facto including what is actually implemented. The de facto implementation may or may not have been sanctioned by de jure policies. And because decentralization is being considered and/or implemented so pervasively throughout Africa it will be considered as a component of the globalization phenomenon.

Thus, our study is fundamentally comparative, starting with an effort to ascertain what *is* and what *is not* in each of the four subject countries. What appears to be a common process of decentralizing vis-à-vis implementation may be quite profoundly different in terms of procedures and outcomes—the four cases below have unique characteristics and the outcomes are distinct, even though each moves toward planned decentralization within its respective educational system.

Congo/K

One of the most enduring models of de facto decentralization has been the case of Congo/K. For nearly two decades the central government has provided insignificant, if any, financial assistance to schools outside of the urban areas, thus violating its de jure policies and official financial responsibilities. Among the Congo/K's cities, Kinshasa, the capital, has had considerably more success in securing at least minimal financial assistance, although still inadequate, than have other cities. For all schools in Congo/K, but especially for those in the interior and in rural areas (except, under Joseph Mobuto's regime, his home region in the north), survival has been based on the ability of schools to obtain the finances, goods, and services required from noncentral government sources—most especially from the schools' communities. The situation has, at present, reached a point where many schools and educators in the interior have even sought to block post-Mobutu reforms if such reforms reassert a commanding central government administrative role based on promises of financial support. Post-Mobutu reforms, such as those that were under discussion immediately following the installation of Laurent Kabila's government, which ostensibly addressed correcting the existing abuses within the financial system, tended to be refuted by the previously disenfranchised population. From an historical perspective most Congolese educators and school site committees have little reason to respect central government commitments and/or performance. Before the international focus on globalization and decentralization, the educational system in Congo/K was assessed as experiencing profound "diversity" in terms of practices, inputs, and outcomes, especially in education. Assessing these phenomena in the late 1990s based on the evolving international concepts of globalization and decentralization, we find that what the Congolese people have endured may not be unique, but their case was certainly extreme in terms of de jure demise and de facto dominance.

Planning and implementation are, in addition to other requirements, supposed to improve national well-being. What has occurred in Congo/K has caused a popular reaction of wanting nothing to do with policies and practices that might stimulate the revival of undependable central government participation, which ultimately would only result in a breakdown of their existing self-sufficient, albeit penurious, financing. Thus, what they have achieved—the survival of their decentralized education system—would be jeopardized by reassertion of central control without a *guarantee* of dependable financial support. In short, de facto decentralization has occurred and is being defended and preserved irrespective of existing de jure policy or de jure reform commitments by the post-Mobutu government, which do not equate with de facto implementation.

Senegal

A novel interaction between de jure and de facto decentralization is being carried out in Senegal, where a de jure policy approach is to be created based on findings derived from experimental school models. A most impressive new national education decentralization law—which attempts to combine or double-stream nonformal and formal education in the same classrooms—has been passed and provides national policy guidelines, although the final design will not be determined for several years. In this case the ultimate policy and reform model(s) will be based on the evaluations of over fifty school-site experimental models, which have been authorized pursuant to the new policy guidelines. Evaluations of these experimental schools will ultimately determine what Senegal's policy (or de jure model—and perhaps even models) will look like based on the de facto findings required by the decentralization bill (Rideout, 1998, pp. 1–3). This could result either in a two-tracked (formal and nonformal) basic primary school structure aimed at providing equal academic outcomes for graduates of each track or in a single combined formal/nonformal track. In Senegal's case there is very substantial international nongovernmental organization (NGO) and World Bank/donor support promoting this globalization objective of efficient decentralization. While local populations are being solicited to participate actively in this process, it should also be noted that Senegal has one of the most centralized governmental structures in the world (Rideout and Ural, 1993, pp. 60–65). In effect, this policy development endeavor responds to the formal/nonformal models, discussed previously, which were proposed for global application in developing countries by the World Bank and some other major donors over twenty years ago.

Cameroon

In Cameroon, where 22 percent of the population is classified as Anglophone and 78 percent as Francophone, the government has endorsed decentralization but violated previous de jure policies and practices, especially by reneging on its financial commitments while failing to identify financial alternatives for the existing authorized and operating system. Thus, it has seriously eroded its de facto and functioning educational system, which was initially created to conform with the approved centralized de jure structure. In this instance, as central government failed to supply the funds historically authorized for the national system, Western (or Anglophone) Cameroon sought, with considerable success, means within its own region to help compensate for this reduction of central government support. A critically important asset inherited as part of its British colonial heritage was a dynamic Parent–Teacher Association (PTA), which had historically played a major role in school site management, including fundraising and financial accountability, and was also a key factor stimulating the development of private schools.

In the Francophone region there was also the French surrogate model in operation—the Association of Parents of Students (APE—*Association des Parents d'Elèves*) (Maclure, 1997, pp. 17–23). The two models (APE and PTA) are often considered synonymous, but their missions and modus operandi have been profoundly different. Reflecting the centralized French system from which it was derived, the APE's historical functions had traditionally been limited to advisement; direct operational involvement in the school-site system was never practiced, fully understood, nor transmitted. This was congruent with the traditional French Cartesian approach: top-down. On the other hand, PTAs had been influenced by the logical approach of Francis Bacon, which reflected a bottom-up emphasis. The bottom-up approach, derived from the British colonial heritage, subsequently enhanced the ability of the PTA to promote local involvement, commitment, mobilization of school-site populations, and accountability for the control of funds. School-site committees of parents, teachers, and principals, often with student representatives, worked together to consider and resolve their schools' needs. As a result, the Government of Cameroon (GOC) has periodically restricted the operations of the PTA in the Anglophone zone to attempt to reduce the growing disparity between the two educational systems. The PTA's ability to perform in a decentralized framework has exacerbated the growing difference between the educational outcomes in the Anglophone and Francophone zones.

In this instance the growing de jure support of the government for increased decentralization since the 1980s was de facto deliberately violated by the GOC operationally in the Anglophone zone to prevent the latter's successful maintenance of the decentralized system. It has been acknowledged in Cameroon that the West Cameroon educational system has, subsequently, provided noticeably better education than is offered in Francophone (East) Cameroon from primary through university levels (Rideout and Usman, 1999, pp. 13–18). The obvious and growing disparity in education between the two formerly distinct colonial zones does little to promote national unity. In this case de facto decentralization equated to the reduction of central government financial support with, as noted, neither the identification of adequate alternative sources of funding nor the provision of leadership for the development of alternatives. Not having a "PTA model" to fall back on for effective decentralization, the Francophone region's educational system has experienced educational deterioration substantiated by increasing enrollments of Francophone students in Anglophone schools. Cameroon's case clearly indicates the diversity of outcomes from decentralization's application—both positive and negative even in the same nation. For Cameroon the serious imbalance between Francophone and Anglophone regions in achieving decentralization, compounded by diverse colonial heritages and lack of external assistance, has produced a decentralization model further exacerbating contentions between East and West Cameroon. The Francophone-dominated central government seeking equal educational outcomes for the Francophone region has promoted a de jure/de facto model that blatantly is most detrimental to the Francophone educational system—ergo, a politically debilitating enigmatic conundrum for the GOC.

LESOTHO'S EDUCATIONAL DECENTRALIZATION

Formerly the British Protectorate of Basutoland, Lesotho, with a population of 2,076,628 (1996), has classified its population as being 49 percent poor and 26 percent ultra-poor; the national per capita income is US$720. Christians constitute 70.5 percent of the population, and the adult literacy rate is also 70.5 percent. Life expectancy increased from 42.9 years in 1960 to 57.9 years in 1994. Lesotho is one of the very few developing countries where women's average educational attainment is higher than that of men, although the fertility rate for Basotho women remains at 4.9 children and the population growth rate between 2.6 and 2.9 per annum. Lesotho's ranking on the human development index (HDI) stands at 137 out of 175 countries in the Human Development Report—thirteen of the Sub-Saharan countries performed better (Kingdom of Lesotho, 1997, pp. 1–2).

Given the existing poverty level, the sparsity of natural resources, and the rapidly growing population, the Government of Lesotho (GOL) is politically aware of the critical need to mobilize its human resources to address the pervasive national problems threatening the present and future well-being of its people. This will require the understanding, participation, and commitment of the country's citizens, and the GOL has clearly selected decentralization with a special focus on education and, increasingly, health and environment, as critical content components, as well as stressing privatization, which in this case would also reduce management and funding costs by the government (Kingdom of Lesotho, 1997, p. 2). For Lesotho its people constitute, with its surplus water, its natural resources.

A critical and unique factor vis-à-vis Lesotho's educational system is that it is approximately 97 percent owned and operated by Christian religious denominations—the remaining schools are governmentally or privately owned. Therefore, any changes or modifications in the system obviously impact the vast majority of church-owned schools. Three churches—Catholic, Evangelical (Presbyterian), and Anglican—have over two hundred schools each, which is the minimum number required by the GOL to grant them recognition as "proprietors." With the "proprietor" classification a church is authorized to have its own educational hierarchy, including an educational secretary and secretariat recognized by, and in partnership with, the Ministry of Education's (MOE) bureaucracy. When the GOL established this de jure decentralized model in 1971, it did not sanction the de facto school-site committees already operational throughout most of Lesotho prior to 1971. This school-site model has a great deal in common with that in West Cameroon in terms of an efficient and participatory PTA.

Article 7 of the Education Order of 1971 was supposed to have provided for local participation (MOE, 1971, pp. 207–17). It specified that proprietary schools, if not directly run by the proprietor, should be managed by some person who was connected with the school; a resident of Lesotho; and appointed by the proprietor, a committee, or board of governors to be manager of the school. The appointment of every manager, committee, or board of governors of any school was subject to approval by the minister of education. Apparently it was initially contemplated that this provision, whether in the form of an individual, a committee, or board of governors, would result in the creation of a "management committee" for each school. However, given (a) the potential complexity of this proposal, (b) its vagueness, (c) the likelihood that it would disrupt the existing proprietorial establishments' operations, and (d) the lack of commitment by both the proprietors and the MOE to ascertain that these committees were established and operating, the provision remained essentially unimplemented. Thus, while some de jure management committees were approved, they did not function as school-site committees; the unapproved school-site committees that were already in operation prior to the Education Order of 1971 continued to function de facto and quite dynamically at the school-site level.

During the late 1970s the MOE became increasingly concerned about the "distance" and the "lack of interaction" between itself and proprietary schools. In effect the decentralization model in operation provided national decentralization for the church (denominational) owners but not for the clientele directly involved in schooling. The only direct link between the MOE and the proprietory schools was the school inspector. While theoretically an inspector is supposed to visit every school at least once a year, in fact this rarely happens, and many, especially primary schools, are not inspected even once every six years. Thus all reporting and operations have occurred through the proprietors—most through their own mini-MOEs. The MOE began to seek ways to remedy the situation, but it did not, at the same time, wish to alienate the proprietors who were running a quite effective and economically viable national school system. Nevertheless, decentralization based on ownership became an increasingly contentious issue, and the

GOL began to push for a decentralization reform that would empower the population being "schooled" and also benefit the GOL by providing direct access to the school-site populations.

Thus, in 1983, an amendment was enacted and Section 7 of the 1971 bill was modified. Now it was specified that unless the proprietor ran the school directly the proprietor would appoint persons (no longer an individual) "connected with the school and resident in Lesotho, or a committee member or board of governors to be the manager of the school" (MOE, 1983, pp. 221–25). The appointment of every manager, committee, or board of governors continued to be subject to the approval of the minister of education. However, there were no specifications as to the qualifications of those who were to constitute the committees or the board of governors—whether or not parents were to be involved was not addressed. There was some indication that these committees might have been intended to replace the proprietary parish level administrative structure, which functioned somewhat like a school district office and provided direct governance over a specific geographical area of schools.[2] The proprietors did agree to accept the management committee in place of parish supervision, but in so doing they captured the management committee by then placing it under the supervision of the parish administrative structure. The national attempt at popular decentralization (empowerment of local site populations) was recaptured by religious centralization.

After nearly another decade the Education Order of 1992 was enacted, and the management committee was recognized as being a parish level committee. Now a subordinate school-site committee, named the advisory school committee (ASC), was to be created at each school. This was to provide direct interaction between the communities and their schools without proprietors controlling the processes. It must be noted, however, that the Education Order of 1992, though enacted, did not go into effect until it was subsequently integrated into the 1995 Education (Amendment) Bill. The reason was that the 1992 order contained as an opening statement, "This Order . . . shall come into operation on a date to be fixed by the Minister by Notice in the Gazette." No date was ever specified by the minister regarding the order's coming into operation. Therefore, it was activated only when its "amendment" the 1995 bill, was passed (MOE, 1992, p. 18). This combined bill and order are now being implemented and constitute the essence of the new decentralization reform. The GOL has not been seeking a means of "displacing" the proprietors in their educational roles but, through decentralization reforms within their national democratic structure, to gain access to direct interaction with their constituents—the schools and their communities. The GOL did not want to have to reach its education clientele uniquely through church-controlled bureaucracies; it also wanted to provide de jure support for the de facto school operations. While there was collaboration at the school sites between the de jure school managers and the de facto parent/community communities, basically the churches benefited from de jure recognition—they got the credit and recognition.

In summary, the management committee never really operated at the school-site level. Although originally conceived as the school-site committee, it was not needed since those committees already existed. As time passed the existing committees gradually became parish-level committees serving clusters of schools in proprietary catchment areas, and they were totally controlled by the proprietors. Their catchments varied substantially—from fewer than eight schools per management committee to nearly thirty. In 1971 the schools had, or were already establishing, school committees that provided the context within which head-teachers (principals), teachers, and parents could work together to solve the problems related to school fees, especially fees for teachers, new school buildings, maintenance of existing buildings, etc. Addressing such issues when the proprietors could not supply the capital needed to support such investments meant that it was the parents who ultimately "filled the gap" in providing funds, labor, or materials needed to tackle and solve the array of problems concerning their children's schools. Consequently, school-site committees, as noted, functioned de facto because of sheer necessity throughout most of Lesotho by 1970 and continued until 1996.

Decentralizing Decentralization

Decentralization by religious denomination had certainly empowered their respective school systems, but it did not provide "popular decentralization" whereby the school-site committees could exercise at least limited "home rule" free of religious domination. Religious decentralization had been the initial step, and powerfully enhanced the formal education system through its links with major Christian churches in Lesotho. Not only did the churches do their utmost to expand their schools, they have traditionally put at the disposal of the schools whatever church properties were needed to augment enrollments and retention. The church buildings themselves were in fact very often schools six days out of the week. Those with children attending the schools were overwhelmingly members of the church running the school, and, to the extent possible, the teachers and administrators would also be members of the same denomination. However, children from other denominations, or non-Christians, had access to all schools, and the enrollment of children, if desired, in schools operated by another denomination has not created difficulties.

The problem that existed was that if one were critical of the school or its staff it was likely that one was being critical of his or her church. Thus, it was very difficult for church members to raise issues related to their denomination's schools without losing status as a member of the church and perhaps even as a Christian. By the late 1970s this problem, as noted above, was recognized by the GOL, but efforts to begin to modify the system were not effective until 1995 and

1996. Earlier reform efforts were farcical, since control by the churches was never reduced; it was usually enhanced. As their country is a small one, Lesotho's leaders—government, business, religious, etc.—know each other well, and it was difficult in terms of status, prestige, and reputation for a governmental leader to criticize the churches' educational systems without personal embarrassment.[3] At school-site levels the parents serving the schools of their denominations were, at the same time, serving their churches. How does one criticize the church's school but not the church? Criticizing one's church school when one is a member of the church involved was an exercise in self-criticism. The union between churches and schools has been a powerful and dynamic linkage—with pluses as well as minuses.

In explaining the educational system in Lesotho, especially the primary level, the GOL and MOE invariably use as an analogy the "three-legged pot," with one leg representing the government, another the churches, and a third the parents/communities (MOE, 1995, pp. 960–62). These "legs," however, differed profoundly, as did their reactions to "popular decentralization" proposed by GOL.

Leg 1

The GOL sought an on-going direct relationship and involvement with the schools. Obviously the unique mechanism for achieving this, visits by the inspectors, did not even marginally serve this purpose. While the churches owned the schools, the MOE provided salaries for the bulk of teachers in church schools and also contributed in terms of books and learning materials. Moreover, the denominational schools, as noted, regardless of their direct linkages with the churches, constituted over 97 percent of Lesotho's national educational system, and the GOL wanted its affiliations strengthened and direct. However, prior to 1995 the government's leg could best be described as shrunken and shrinking.

Leg 2

From the Churches' position the "status quo" was generally preferred. In terms of management and administration, the MOE has depended upon the management committee, which serves groups of denominational schools, reports directly to the educational secretary of the churches, and provides daily supervision. If, for example, the school principal has problems, the management committee is expected to help resolve them—not the inspector. Consequently, the church leg has, in terms of management and administration, been the "super leg." The churches have obviously been satisfied with the pre-1995 management structure since they were almost fully in control of their own schools while still being subsidized by the MOE and school-site committees. "Local" management of the schools was under the parish (regional church control), which oversaw the management committee—a body, as noted, reporting to the church secretariat and composed of members of the church. The MOE was basically cut off from "its" own schools.

Leg 3

With growing responsibilities for education, parents and local communities wanted their roles redefined to reflect their historical and enhanced involvement. Although, also as noted, the school committees enjoyed active parental and community participation throughout Lesotho from the late 1960s on, they still lacked official status and have had no formally acknowledged de jure functions or responsibilities. The parent/community leg of the pot, although well-known for its contributions, has not officially received the recognition it deserves—in short the parent/community leg has been dwarfed and eroding since it was "illegal" and thus inarticulate and ignored. Its functions were acknowledged as being different from those of the churches only if the latter agreed to such recognition. And from the perspective of the churches the parent/community and church legs were one and the same. Nevertheless, parents have been doing more and more to support the education of their children, and one study found that "poor families can spend up to 50 percent of their incomes on education in fees, uniforms, etc." (Kingdom of Lesotho, 1997, p. 26).

The GOL Sector Development Plan for the period 1991–92 to 1995–96 committed the MOE to five "broad goals and policies for the system." Two of these were expressly related to the role of the family and community. First: "Education programmes should incorporate cultural values and activities that enhance individual and social development, in particular, the role of the family and communities in school activities should be expanded." Second: "There should be an active, co-operative partnership in education administration and management and the provision of education services between and among the churches, the government, the community and other non-governmental organizations." And the strategies for implementing these objectives were specified and included:

1) "revision of education legislation in order to improve administration and management of education;
2) decentralization of educational management to the districts and strengthening of the inspectorate; and
3) improving management and resource use at the school level" (MOE, 1996, pp. 5–6).
4) The Primary Education Strategy for achieving the above listed general education strategies, policies, and goals included a commitment to "improving educational and local-level school management by decentralising the MOE, establishing a strong field inspectorate, and providing management training to school head-teachers and school committees" (MOE, 1996, p. 43).

Yet in spite of these development and planning goals, the law finally providing for school-site committees was not enacted until January 17, 1996. The delay in the final approval of the 1995 bill until 1996 was due to the lack of specificity regarding the role, structure, and function of the school-site committees. Many MOE officials were disappointed that a clear decentralization mandate was not being specified. The inference being transmitted was that the proprietors were going to succeed in maintaining the historical "three leg" imbalance in their favor. In addition, the empowerment of the school committees was also considered a critical factor in view of the fact that the GOL was faced with a key decentralization condition contained in the United States Agency for International Development (USAID)–GOL Primary Education Project (PEP) agreement. USAID/ Lesotho (the mission office in Maseru) advised the MOE that, if the school committees were not empowered, future USAID disbursements in excess of US$1 million to the project would be blocked. Given these two factors—and the fact that this issue had been pending in Lesotho for over twenty years—Parliament returned the bill initially proposed, which was assessed as not meeting the decentralization requirement, to the MOE for modifications. A completely revised bill, fully empowering school-site committees (designated in the bill as advisory school committees—ASCs), was then passed into law and signed by the king the day before he was killed in an automobile accident.

In preparing what became the final version of the bill, the GOL quite simply stated the powerful mandate of the ASC as "The function of the Advisory School Committee is to advise the management committee on all matters related to education in the relevant school" (Lesotho Government Gazette Extraordinary, 1996, p. 961). In addition, as requested by the MOE, the reform bill meaningfully altered the composition of the two committees involved with primary education. The ASC has four parent members (out of a total of nine), who are elected by school parents at a traditional "pitso" (very similar to a town meeting). Other members will be provided by the proprietor (2) and elected by each school's teachers (1), the school's principal (1), and the local chief (1) (Lesotho Government Gazette Extraordinary, 1996, pp. 960–61). The ASC will elect its chairperson and vice chairperson. Thus, the ASC can be controlled by parents, assuming they attend the meetings. Since the local chief is inevitably expected to support the parents, together the parents and chief can constitute a committee quorum of five members.

Also, an extremely important provision in the bill is a completely revised future management committee (MC), made up of eight members who will be selected or elected from the ASCs that belong to a given MC's region. The MC's members are two elected by representatives of the proprietor, one of whom will be chairperson; three elected by representatives of the parents; one teacher elected by representatives of teachers; a principal elected by principals from the schools in the MC area; and a representative of the chiefs who will be a member of one of the ASCs in the MC (Lesotho Government Gazette, 1996, pp. 957–59). The

MC is limited to eight schools per committee, and MCs cannot be created until the ASCs are formed since all MC members must come from the ASCs in their respective MC zones. Again five members constitute a quorum in the MC, but here, unlike the ASCs, the parents and the chief will not be a quorum by themselves; with four members they could prevent a majority vote from occurring on any issue they oppose.

Implementation of the Educational Decentralization Mandate

The law enacting these development plan goals became effective on January 17, 1997. However, such laws subsequently require "regulations" that specify how the laws will be implemented. These regulations must also be approved by the Parliament before the enacted law is actually enforced; such regulations are considered somewhat pro forma but they must, theoretically, be approved before the law legally can go into effect. As of September 1999, these pro forma regulations had not yet been approved for the Education Law reform. It is anticipated that this process will be completed by the end of 1999. Nevertheless, and extraordinarily commendable on the part of the MOE officials responsible, implementation of the law has progressed irrespective of the failure to enact the law's regulations. Moreover, the GOL has made available from 1997 to 1999 over $7 million to provide training for the ASCs. In short, by August of 1999, a three-day training program had been conducted for 1,100 of Lesotho's 1,300 primary school ASCs.[4] It is planned that before the end of 1999 all ASC members will have received training to prepare them to perform their committee functions effectively. In addition, preparations are underway to replicate the same committee structure at Lesotho's secondary schools.

GOL officials have consistently affirmed that they were increasingly aware of the need for direct involvement in the operations of the national school system not, as some of the churches perceived, to displace or disinvest the churches, but to make certain that issues of governance, content, and pedagogy were dealt with equally, fairly, and democratically. Governance, whether religiously based or not, had to be monitored bottom-up to ascertain that the basic well-being of the entire population was being served effectively. Churches and schools were and are linked, but they simply were not and are not synonymous. The creation and empowerment of ASCs reflected the structures of the denominations involved—hierarchical versus democratic structures: the Catholic proprietors, the most hierarchical and top-down were most reluctant, while the Evangelicals (Presbyterians), the most democratic and bottom-up, were most accommodating; the Anglicans were in between. However, all have actively participated in the ASC training programs, and the GOL is preparing to extend the ASC model to secondary education in the near future. It should also be noted that while USAID's "conditionality" played a key role in this reform, decentralization reform was something the GOL had been seeking for over two decades; conditionality was ultimately the final straw that made the difference between implementation and further delay. And in this case decentralization empowered not only the school-site population but also the MOE by establishing a direct operational link to the schools in addition to the indirect link through the existing proprietary structure.

Although the reform is not yet fully "legal" (i.e., the regulations have not yet been passed by Parliament), nor have all ASCs yet received training and begun to perform their new school-site management functions, the initial reaction to the reform is very positive in the GOL. The government is considering in the near future sending its annual financial support for each school directly to the respective school where its ASC will be responsible for management, administration, disbursement, and accountability of its own budget. At the same time the World Bank, impressed by what has been accomplished, is considering funding an educational project in excess of $20 million, which will further enhance the decentralization process and provide special allocations for rural schools in mountainous and impoverished regions. Lesotho's initial decentralization provided a structural arrangement that permitted the state and the churches to collaborate in promoting the national educational system—the state was acknowledged as dominant, while the churches were managers. The reform now being implemented acknowledges the power of the state and the contribution of the churches and provides for the empowerment of the school-site population. All three legs are now becoming more equal and fully operational, and the most common reaction from those in ASC training sessions has been their expressions of amazement regarding their empowerment and the responsibilities that they and their ASCs now have. While this model in its entirety may not be generalizable to other African states, at the very least elements may prove as beneficial to other states as they appear to be in the evolution of Lesotho's educational system. It is potentially a powerful globalization-related model for a continent targeting decentralization, and it may also benefit other parts of the world.

CONCLUSION

Globalization tends to focus on what humans share, or predominantly agree that they should share, in common—it is oriented toward centralization and "commonalities." It is submitted that this has tended to have a top-down bias. In our four cases, the only profound exception is Congo/K, which, fundamentally, has only experienced bottom-up development; top-down is dominant in Senegal and Cameroon, although there is serious noncompliance from West Cameroon. An exceptionally collaborative blend of top-down and bottom-up occurs in Lesotho between donors, central government, religious organizations, and school sites. The overall theme for all four countries reviewed is that there is a global endorsement of decentralization, but how this is and is not occurring is profoundly diverse.

Decentralization appears increasingly to be concerned not only with what objectives may be held in common and how to promote them, but also with what humans at the base of the globalization pyramid want to retain and practice that may be unique, indeed, idiosyncratic—and perhaps non-global—for restricted application, not generalization. When decentralization is emphasized there appears to be a definite concern for serving unique needs, wants, and behaviors even though they may be exceedingly marginal, or just slightly inconsistent, with the predominant global mode. Thus, while globalization has a tendency to reflect a top-down logical approach, decentralization, reflecting a bottom-up logical emphasis, is less predictable; it may reinforce globalization, but it may also support common, limited bottom up beliefs and practices of diverse communities and populations often in specific, even restricted, areas. Particular forms of globalization are influenced by socioeconomic status; first and third world perspectives; and cultural, racial, and religious differences. It is also very evident that those basically committed to a globalization position may, given certain issues, opt for non-globalization options within a decentralization mode although they do not seek to impair or jeopardize desired globalization outcomes.

Basic needs across humanity are indeed fundamentally the same for the preservation of the species. How each culture goes about meeting its basic needs, plus those "nonessential needs" that may have come to be considered as also being basic as they have evolved within specific cultural groups, provides a range of very diverse behaviors, beliefs, practices, and processes. Thus, it is often in the process of satisfying even the most basic global needs that values, behaviors, and beliefs have evolved to become most profoundly different. (The global divergencies involved in dealing with rites of passage at puberty are illustrative of the lack of consistency in dealing with a common biological phenomenon.) Decentralization can provide a bottom-up range of options that may, may not, or partially support the prevailing global mode but nevertheless be constructive, functional, and economically viable in promoting specific educational skills and unique practices attractive to others—even the dominant majorities. In the education case studies we have reviewed in Sub-Saharan Africa we have seen decentralization being promoted as a potential remedy for failures found in human resources development efforts since independence, and the procedures/practices that have been employed have been profoundly different, based on the realities existing in the countries involved. These realities cannot be ignored.

It should be noted that as greater efforts are made in educational systems to achieve nonformal and informal outcomes, which seek to prepare people to improve their well-being in their home regions, the options being incorporated at the base of the educational structures may be increasingly different—and thus increasingly nonglobal. However, improving educational outcomes would still be an overriding global outcome. Thus a productive union blending the best bottom-up and top-down results could enhance the productivity of the relationship between globalization and decentralization.

NOTES

1. The author served as a member of the World Bank teams participating in the États Généraux de l'Éducation for Zaire (1996) and for Cameroon (1996). Data acquired during these missions contributed to the two brief case studies.

2. A parish is a cluster of schools (officially up to a maximum of eight in number pursuant to the Education Order Amendment of 1995) that form proprietors' geographical catchment areas. These catchment areas have historically coincided with a given church's parish boundaries. At most parishes there is a management committee for that proprietor's school.

3. In August 1998, Lesotho suffered a damaging attempted coup, which destroyed an estimated 150 buildings in Maseru. It also seems to have severely damaged the former collegiality that previously seemed to have prevailed among Lesotho's leaders.

4. The training program content for ASC members reflects the responsibilities identified in the MOE's justification for the creation and empowerment of the ASCs: (a) background information on the Education Act of 1995; (b) the Education Act of 1995 (elections of ASCs, functions of ASCs, governing regulations—once they are approved); (c) leadership (qualities of leadership, styles of leadership, duties of a leader); (d) communication (communication channels, problems encountered in communication, how to improve communication, parts of a message); (e) meetings (types of meetings, duties of portfolio holders, writing minutes and reporting); (f) planning; (g) collecting, using, and reporting on school funds; (h) partnership of the "three-legged pot" in education; and (i) evaluation.

REFERENCES

Conyers, Diana, 1984. Decentralization: The Latest Fashion in Development Administration. *Public Administration and Development*, vol. 4, no. 2, pp. 187–98.

Coombs, Philip H. 1968. *The World Educational Crisis: A Systems Analysis.* New York: Oxford University Press.

———. 1985. *The World Educational Crisis.* New York: Oxford University Press.

———, and Manzoor Ahmed. 1974. *Attacking Rural Poverty: How Nonformal Education Can Help.* Baltimore: Johns Hopkins University Press.

Jones, Phillip W. 1997. From Internationalism to Globalisation: The Multilateral Dilemma for Education. CIES Western Regional Conference, University of Southern California.

Kingdom of Lesotho. 1997 (November). *Eighth Round Table Conference on Poverty Reduction within the Context of Good Governance.* Document presented to the Round Table Conference, Geneva.

Lesotho Government Gazette Extraordinary. 1996. *Education Act 1995.* Maseru: Government Printer.

Maclure, Richard (ed.). 1997. *Overlooked and Undervalued: A Synthesis of ERNWACA Re-*

views on the State of Educational Research in West and Central Africa (1997). Support for Analysis and Research in Africa (SARA)/Health and Human Resources Analysis in Africa (HHRAA), Africa Bureau, USAID, Office of Sustainable Development.

Ministry of Education. 1971 (August 27). The Education Order 1971: Order No. 32 of 1971. *Supplement No. 1, to Gazette No. 32.* Maseru: Government Printer.

————. 1983 (December 9). The Education Order (Amendment) Act 1983: Act No. 17 of 1983. *Supplement No. 5 to Gazette No. 58.* Maseru: Government Printer.

————. 1992. Education (Amendment) Bill 1995: A Bill for an Act to Amend the Education Order 1992. Maseru: Government Printer.

————. 1995 (November 1). *Criteria for Inspection and Self-Evaluation: A Manual for Inspectors, Headteachers and School Managers.* Maseru: Printed by the Lesotho Distance Teaching Centre.

————. 1996. *Education Sector Development Plan, 1991/92–1995/96.* Maseru: Government Printer.

Mundy, Karen. 1998 (November). Educational Multilateralism and World (Dis)Order. *Comparative Education Review,* vol. 42, no. 4, pp. 448–78.

Peters, Heidrun (ed.). 1998. *Learning for a Common Future.* Deutsche Stiftung fur internationale Entwicklung (DSE). Bonn: Germany.

Rideout, William. 1998 (October). Educational Reform in Senegal: It's Policy, Not Practice. Presented at the Western Regional Comparative International Education Society Conference, Sacramento, California.

————, and Ipek Ural. 1993. *Centralised and Decentralised Models of Education: Comparative Studies.* Policy Working Papers No.1, Development Bank of Southern Africa Centre for Policy Analysis. Pretoria, South Africa.

Rideout, William, and Abraham Usman. 1999 (April). Evaluation of the Sustainability of the Support to Primary Education Project in Cameroon. Technical Paper No. 106. Washington, D.C.: USAID.

Sweeting, Anthony. 1996. The Globalization of Learning: Paradigm or Paradox? *International Journal of Educational Development,* vol. 16, no. 4, pp. 379–80.

Tye, Barbara, and Kenneth Tye. 1992. *Global Education: A Study of School Change.* Albany: State University of New York Press.

Waters, Malcolm. 1995. *Globalization.* London: Routledge.

Whitacre, Paula. 1997. *Education Decentralization in Africa: As Viewed through the Literature and USAID Projects.* Washington, D.C.: SARA Project/HHRAA Project, USAID, Africa Bureau, Office of Sustainable Development.

World Bank. 1995. *Policies and Strategies for Education: A World Bank Review.* Washington, D.C.: World Bank.

————. 1998/99. *World Bank Development Report: Knowledge for Development.* Washington, D.C.: Oxford University Press.

14

Globalization and Educational Policies in Mexico, 1988–1994: A Meeting of the Universal and the Particular

Rosa Nidia Buenfil

KEY FEATURES OF GLOBALISM[1] IN EDUCATION AND INTERNATIONAL AGENCIES

To some extent, interconnectedness among nations is not new, nor is the influence international agencies exercise upon particular countries.[2] One can trace back to the sixties, for instance, the inclusion of the Multinational Project of Educational Technology Transference[3] in the overall developmental strategy sponsored by the Organization of American States (OAS) and the Inter-American Development Bank,[4] whose influence in Latin America cannot be overlooked. Two publications by the Organization for Economic Cooperation and Development (OECD, 1971) and United Nations Educational, Scientific, and Cultural Organization (UNESCO, 1968)[5] can be considered the ancestors of what today is viewed as the globalization of educational policies.[6] The World Conference on Education for All in Jomtien (1990), the United Nations Development Programme (UNDP)–UNESCO meeting of 1991, and the two key meetings hosted by the Economic Commission for Latin America and Caribbean (ECLAC in English; Spanish acronym, CEPAL)–UNESCO (on "Education and Knowledge: Basis for Productive Transformation with Equity," held in 1992), and the Fifth Regional Inter-Governmental Meeting on the Principal Education Project for Latin America [PPEALC] (held in 1993) are the new versions of those old global links. Those were links whereby academic trends, financial agreements, exchange of scholars, and administrative strategies came visibly from international agencies to the Latin American region, and so on, which thirty years ago were conceptualized as an outcome of domination and dependency.

Perhaps what distinguishes contemporary globalization from the connections in the 1960s is, on the one hand, that they take place in a world politically, economically, and culturally reorganized (i.e., from "East and West" to "North and South"). On the other hand, today we are more aware of what is happening elsewhere, of the increasing presence of previously silenced "minorities" emerging in the political arena, and of conflictive encounters between opposite tendencies.

Globalization is not a mere tendency to homogenization and universalism, but the condition produced by the clash between universalism and particularism, homogenization and heterogeneity. However, the tendency to homogeneity cannot be overlooked, as there are some educational features that can be verified throughout the world, for example, an expansion of the school system and a demand for schooling and the acceptance of a model of schooling for which six basic features can be distinguished:

- An administrative structure generally created, controlled, and financed by the state;
- A school system internally differentiated according to successive levels, each with its syllabi and examinations;
- Teaching and learning processes being organized according to uniform age groups and time units;
- Governmental regulation of such processes through more or less detailed requirements incorporated in curricula, guides, and exams;
- Specification of teacher and student roles and teaching methods, together with the teacher's professionalization; and
- The use of certificates, diplomas, and credentials linking school and professional curricula and connecting schooling with social stratification (Boli and Ramirez, 1992, cited in Schriewer, 1996, p. 27).

Some would say that a global narrative of educational progress has emerged and operates as an educational ideology (Fiala and Landford, 1987) contributing to the globalizing process. The evidence of policies of restriction and adjustment in universities, both in industrialized and in "Third World" countries, and the internal measures permeated by marketing dictates, are increasing. The tendency to impose the thinning of financial support for public school can be linked with a neoliberal influence and a global procedure.

In Mexico the main global influence on educational policies does not come from a particular country (e.g., Spain), but from international agencies such as the World Bank, OECD, UNESCO, and through the Regional Office for Education for Latin America and the Caribbean (OREALC) and the CEPAL. Global influences can be detected in national educational policies. However, these features are resignified,[7] or given a different meaning, in their very implementation in each particular site.

CONCEPTUAL ASSUMPTIONS INFORMING THIS ANALYSIS

Before I present my analysis of the traces of globalization in a Mexican educational policy, let me make explicit my own standpoint. I will discuss here the concept of globalization and some assumptions upon which I support my analysis and interpretation of the resignification of global educational policies in a particular instance, specifically, Mexico. To summarize some key aspects of the variety of meanings, I will highlight some crucial points that will later support my argument. In the literature specializing in education, for instance, the relationship between globalization and capitalism, the idea of its historical tendency, its presumed necessity, the idea of universalization and homogeneity, and the links between globalization and a promising or a catastrophic horizon are frequently found.

Even from a progressive culture-oriented perspective, economic issues are put forward:

> The global flow of merchandise and capital depends on a fragmentation or reparochialization—of sovereign territories. Education processes both in the larger social community and in schooling sites are inextricably linked to the politics of neoliberalism driven by an expanding capitalism (McLaren and Gutiérrez, 1997, p. 196).

While some have described globalization as a mere historical tendency involving the universalization of market economy, others emphasize how naive it is to believe that globalization guarantees a better distribution of wealth in the world economy, since in the last instance it is a hierarchical market system organized by just one pole of the world capitalist structure. This involves the prevalence of a central point of view—a Western, modern outlook permeating cultural and educational tendencies in an "area of influence," for instance, U.S. views will prevail throughout the entire American continent. In its early stages globalizing university curricula was viewed as a means to produce such educational innovation that students would develop world cognitive maps for better understanding everyday local events (Perlmutter, 1991).

Still some others construe globalization as an inevitable tendency in contemporary history that should be met, regardless of the guarantee of equity and welfare that it may or may not provide (Buchbinder, 1994) since it poses challenges to educational strategies that cannot be ignored (Del Valle, 1992; Barabtarlo Zedanski, 1992; Casillas, 1993; Del Valle and Taborga, 1992; Marum, 1993; Weiss, 1994). A group of scholars considers it an opportunity to substantiate the creation of new research centers (Garibay and de la Torre, 1992), while others just state the changes it has brought about in education (Sosa, 1994) without further judgment or qualification of these changes; yet others take it as something against which educational strategies have to contend (Abreu, 1993).

This review could be quite lengthy because of the great quantity of writing that has been produced covering the debates on such related topics as integration versus fragmentation, centralization versus decentralization, juxtaposition versus syncretism, and so on. However, at this point it is time to set some analytical grounds for their examination.

Elsewhere I have presented the wide area of dispersion of meanings of globalization.[8] On the one hand, in a genealogical gesture, one can trace back and find that it has become a key signifier in the late 1980s and the 1990s, albeit, as a process of planetary interconnection, it can be found much earlier. The works by Wallerstein (1989), Braudel (1991), and McLuhan and Powers (1989)[9] pioneered the proliferation of writing on the subject. On the other hand, in an organizing gesture I have grouped this area of dispersion into a family resemblance (Wittgenstein, 1963) aggregation of three elements:

1. The view of an intrinsic connection between globalization, modernity, and neoliberal capitalism can be observed, though there might be some differences in terms of how their "benefits" are anticipated. Through either the laws of history or the course of economies, it seems that there is a necessary link among these three signifiers. The connection between globalization and homogenization seems to be taken for granted.

2. An association is asserted between globalization and a neoliberal, postmodern, postsocialist global capitalist society that can be superseded by progressive anticapitalist global perspectives. In this enterprise, rationalism and Habermas's "non-distorted communicative action" (1987) would play a key role. In this case, the links between globalization and capitalism can be broken; nonetheless, there are still residues of a logic of necessity retroactively operating as the condition of possibility for a "non capitalist global village" (Archer's [1991] "new object of sociology"). According to this perspective we can have "bad" capitalist globalization as a necessary condition for the emergence of the "good" global village.

3. The dissociation of globalization from a universal, necessary tendency of history, and from mere cultural, economic, ethical, or political imperialization (either capitalist or postcapitalist), can be observed. Cultural clash and integration, postsocialist political world repositioning, and economic world reorganization, among other forces, are considered as historical conditions for globalization. Emphasizing the heterogeneous and differential character of social communities in the planet, globalization can be understood as a condition for contact between what is different. Or as Puiggrós (forthcoming) put it: a horizon characterized by a dense and intense production of signification.[10]

If one conceptualizes globalization as contact and interconnectedness, an important dimension for understanding the resignification of global policies in their particular manifestations can be grasped. However, two more assumptions have to be discussed before one can fully recognize this process.

Social reality is constructed and can be accessible as meaning. This means that the existence of the world-outside is taken for granted, but its social meaning is not derived from the mere existence; its meaning is socially constructed in time and space—in history. This enables us to deal with globalization as a process that has been constructed through the variety of meanings previously sketched and also permits us to handle these significations not as some being true and others being false, but as discursive constructions entangled with power relations among international agencies, national states, governmental institutions, and local authorities—within different levels of generality and specificity of social relations. Thinking of the relations between different levels of generality and specificity brings us to the question concerning the extent to which it is possible that international global policies may consider local conditions. This is, of course, an important dilemma that has to be faced by any policymaker and by all policy administrators and puts forward the very question of the universality and particularity of globalization. Some have dealt with the idea of glocalization—living locally and thinking globally, thinking globally and acting locally (González, 1998, p. 5). However, further consideration of the relationship between particular and universal is convenient to approach globalization in a deeper way.

The universal and the particular cannot be thought of apart from each other.[11] From here I derive two ideas: globalization cannot be understood as mere homogenization of the planet under a universal direction, and global educational policies—which are already an outcome of the contact between universalism and particularism—are resignified when they reach particular sites of educational practices and agents. The universal is frequently understood as "something common to all particulars," but one seldom asks how these universals came to be: they derive either from a metaphysical entity or from a social agreement. From Rousseau's social contract onward, universal values have been increasingly interrogated, and the relationship between universality and particularity has become an issue and can no longer be taken for granted; today many consider them to be an outcome of negotiations historically and geographically situated and no longer transcendental a priori. This should not be misunderstood as "the abyss of relativism," as foundationalists call it. The lack of an ultimate-positive foundation[12] of morals, science, the community, and so on, does not amount to saying that "anything goes."[13] The relationalist position[14] I am sustaining holds that all foundations, including "our universal values," are historically established, ergo, context-dependent, which means that there is no atemporal essence; all universal values once were particular values that came to reach some universality. However, they have to be defined in each specific context (be it within a wider or narrower scope), and on our planet these contexts are heterogeneous and unequal.[15] They may, of course, expand their area of influence as long as they either persuade and articulate other particulars or dominate other particulars and impose their particular as "the universal" (both imply, of course, political relations).

Accordingly, if one understands globalization as mere universalization then one must, at least, account for the construction of a particular as the universal. Universalization cannot be understood apart from its counterpart, the presence of particulars, and each application of the universalized value will be "contaminated," so to speak, by the particular context of each implementation.

The position I assume associates globalization neither with a universal, necessary tendency of history, nor with a cultural, economic, ethical, or political impending imperialization, the ruling of a single homogeneous view over the planet (not even if it were noncapitalist). Rather, drawing upon arguments displayed by Giddens (1990, p. 175), Robertson (1990, p. 22), Perlmutter (1991, p. 911), and Kawame and Gates (1997, p. xi), I adhere to the idea that globalization can also be understood as interconnectedness. We have interpenetration of economic tendencies, contact of cultural diversity, intertwining of many traditions, and interdependence of political trends. This means acknowledging our contemporary existential situation as a multidirected conditioning of the universal and the particular, the homogeneous and the heterogeneous, with the understanding that opposed tendencies such as fragmentation and integration, centralization and decentralization interact with each other.

Indeed, it involves the production of syncretic and hybrid economic, cultural, educational and political schema as well as contention by assorted fundamentalist positions fostering a mythical pure and uncontaminated identity. Interconnectedness, contact, and interlacing of the diverse does not occur without conflict since our planet has unequal development in each realm and geopolitical area. Tension, encounter, friction, clash, and conflict[16] are part of the process and this can hardly be overlooked or concealed by wishful Enlightenment thinking. However, this does not amount to a pessimistic outlook.

Globalization can be associated with the prospect of some commensurability between the heterogeneous, contact between the different. Lyotard's metaphor on the archipelago is appropriate to visualize this possibility, since it involves the "different islands" (e.g., cultures and values), which are separate and yet connected by the sea (i.e., language in his metaphor, discourse in ours).[17]

GLOBAL EDUCATIONAL TRENDS AND NATIONAL POLICIES

In Mexico, global educational policies can be traced throughout the whole schooling system: from the basic level to higher education. One topic in recent discussion concerns the links and distance between strategies and means issued by policies and "what really happens in schools." To cite the extreme views, some are convinced that policies are discourses that remain at a general level and never have contact with what really happens in the classroom. Therefore, if one conducts research on education, one should study the particularity of local actions in the classroom. Others would claim that policies determine, as an overarching apparatus, all corners of educational practices. Therefore, one should study the goals and strategies of state apparatuses and see how they affect specific institutions. My position is that no matter where one starts the search, one has to look for the circulation of certain meanings throughout different levels since causality is never unidirectional, but is rather a multi-way conditioning.

Consider Giddens's approach to this issue:

> People live in circumstances in which disembedded institutions, linking local practices with globalized social relations, organize major aspects of day-to-day life. Globalization articulates in a most dramatic way this conflation of presence and absence through its systemic interlocking of the local and the global (Giddens, 1990, p. 79).

From a critical perspective, McLaren and Gutiérrez[18] have produced interesting research showing how "recent local antagonisms, evident both in the larger social community and in the educational arena, are inextricably linked to the politics of neoliberalism driven by an expanding global capitalism" (1997, pp. 195–96). They argue for the development of a framework "for better understanding the ways in which the micropolitics of the urban classroom are in fact the local instantiations of the sociopolitical and economic consequences of a rapidly expanding global marketplace" (p. 196). They propose that critical ethnography and pedagogy become the vehicles for connecting the local and the global in school sites and for pushing the boundaries of educational and social reform. With many years of ethnographic classroom observation in both urban and suburban schools, they can today show that the social architecture of the classroom, and its normative and other discursive practices, is permeated by global educational policies.

A different approach to these issues is undertaken by Popkewitz, who, drawing from a Foucauldian perspective, approaches educational reforms as specific forms of governing practices, namely, "the administration of the soul" (1991, p. 7). He considers that moral and political rhetoric of educational struggles have shifted through the languages of neoliberalism and analyses of neoliberalism (markets, choice, privatization). He considers what is called "neoliberalism" and the dismantling of the welfare state to be more appropriately a reconstruction of the governing practices that do not start with recent policies but are part of more profound social, cultural, and economic habits that occurred well before Margaret Thatcher in Great Britain or Ronald Reagan in the United States (see the discussion in Popkewitz, 1991 and 1999).[19] He objects to one current association between globalization and neoliberalism.

The discursive representation of time, according to some postcolonial theorists, for example, leaves unscrutinized the Western narrative of progress and enables the management and surveillance of "the Third World" in the guise of some notion of "development" (see, e.g., Chakrabarty, 1992, and Gupta, 1996, both cited in Popkewitz, 1999). Further, discourses of and about neoliberalism re-inscribe the state/civil society distinction that was undermined with the construction of the liberal welfare state itself (Popkewitz, 1999, p. 7).

His interest being the registers of social administration and freedom in the practices of reform, he concludes, "If the modern school is a governing practice, then contemporary reform strategies need to be examined in relation to changes in its governing principles" (p. 8). In previous work, Popkewitz (1997) also showed us how an educational reform permeates and is re-signified in its actualization in the classroom. The point here is that in the microphysics of each space, even in the classroom, traces can be found of what the national policy sought to foster. Global policies have also been studied in tertiary education (Peters, 1999), stressing the British and the Australian cases and many others. However, what I wanted to emphasize in the previous cases of U.S. research (McLaren and Gutiérrez 1997; Popkewitz, 1997 and 1999) is the circulation of the signifiers incarnating these policies and their displacement throughout different levels or social strata.[20]

Let me mention now some examples of research carried out in Mexico illustrating how globalization displaces itself throughout different social scopes ranging from the international recommendation, to the national policy, to the school-specific program (curriculum and syllabi), and finally to the classroom. One example is work dealing with two specific features that these national policies take or retrieve[21] from international agreements; one concerns professional identity, the other refers to training schemes for industrial workers. Another will provide a closer glance at research dealing with a recent Mexican national policy.

Research has been conducted on Mexican policies on higher education and their impact on the professional identification of sociology students in the early 1980s. These policies indeed retrieve international standards and ideals for the region. Fuentes (1998) shows that policies do not determine but certainly do set conditions for the changes in professional identification of those sociology students. These national policies filter down throughout diverse institutional levels: from the vice-chancellor of the four hundred thousand-student Universidad Nacional Autonóma de México (UNAM), to the director of the Escuela Nacional de Estudios Profesionales, to the head of the Department of Sociology, to the Lecturer Board, and to the students. Consider, for instance, the model of "a university for the development," a "technocratic" university where the administrative dimension articulates the political and academic tasks of higher education leading it toward higher level of efficiency. In moving to different institutional scales, these policies are combined with the advances of disciplinary knowledge, micropolitics, and other dimensions of the local site, thus being re-signified (Fuentes, 1997, chapter 2; 1998).

Another example is that of the very concept of "basic academic skills" that today in Mexico is part of the discursive fabric concerning preparatory school (upper secondary school, before college) and can be traced back as an effect of a global educational policy stated by the OECD (Organización de Cooperación y Desarrollo Económico, OCDE, 1986; OECD, 1993) and also by the College Board (1983) (Medina, 1995). This concept can be found later in the *Programa de Modernización Educativa* (Secretaría de Educación Pública, SEP, 1989) and the *Curriculum Básico Nacional* (SEP, 1994), and of course, it works in textbooks, syllabi, and didactic strategies in the classroom as a general guide defining their features.

Another example concerns training schemes for industrial workers focusing on the need to operate with a foreign language (be it English, in the case of Mexicans who work in Mexico, or be it elementary computational languages). Papacostas (1996) offers us some highlights of how "technological literacy" involves these skills that now are a piece of global training that would allow industrial workers to be competitive in different national settings. He studies how the idea of a "universal technician" orientates the curricula for industrial workers in a Mexican company. Highly diversified technical abilities tend to be homologized by the abstract and functional operations involved in digital technologies (Papacostas, 1996, chapter 3). The point here is that industrial workers tend to be trained in competencies that may not be of immediate use and still have become important due to the globalization of economy, technology, and productive equipment. So the traces of globalization, in the sense of preparing a "universal technician" may be found in these training schemes even if the reason is not directly present in the company's basic scheme of activities.

In these examples one can see that globalization operates as a key signifier articulating "neoliberalism," "basic academic skills," and "language competence" and is re-semantized from the most particular context to the most general one. Indeed the concept in the classroom is not the same as in the "recommendations" made by the OECD and yet the signifier is exactly the same, and some traces may be found in the classroom although with part of its previous or "original" meaning excluded. As an effect of the very process of globalization, an intense displacement of signifiers from one context to another takes place, and—as in the case of "language competence"—indeed changes its meaning and yet preserves some commonalities in both interpretations.

The example I will develop in more detail here concerns a recent educational policy in Mexico: *Modernización Educativa* (Educational Modernization), which was issued in 1989. Recent research exploring the conditions of its production (Cruz, 1998) shows, among other things, how domestic educational policies retrieve their main issues from recommendations made by the World Bank, UNESCO, and the International Monetary Fund (IMF). This research by Cruz reveals how these recommendations sometimes are taken literally, sometimes are subtly changed, and sometimes are massively re-signified in the very process of their appropriation.

CONDITIONS OF PRODUCTION OF THE EDUCATIONAL MODERNIZATION DISCOURSE

Modernización Educativa is the name of a Mexican educational policy in force during 1988–96, although as a trend modernization had been fostered much earlier by national policies and international agencies such as IMF, World Trade Organization, the World Bank, and the Inter-American Development Bank for the Latin American region.

The Mexican government assumes "social liberalism" (a euphemism for neoliberalism[22]) as the philosophical axis of this reform, thus subordinating education to economic views (e.g., education as investment), economic needs (e.g., schooling as unemployed depot), and rate of movement (e.g., education paced as training), thus inscribing on education a managerial administration. Neoliberalism in Mexico is articulated with a traditional moral and institutional conservatism and with the contingent effects of a political reform.[23]

Some considerations must be advanced concerning the relationship between political and civil societies and the specific way in which neoliberalism is appropriated in a society such as Mexico's. Although neoliberalism entails the thinning of the state, the reduction of the institutional apparatuses and the opening of "social participation," in Mexico it is the conservative forces that are more organized and have the means to occupy those spaces deserted by state control. By conservative I mean (a) the Roman Catholic Church through its different branches, (e.g. the political ecclesiastic hierarchy, civilian associations headed by religious interests, the majority of parents' associations); (b) the Accion Nacional Party (PAN); and (c) religiously based private interests. On the other hand, both nationalist and pro-U.S., and both laic and pro-religious business associations, have increased the number of private schools—at all levels—the competitiveness of which is increasingly stronger and legitimized since they meet a demand that the official system cannot.

The point here is that globalization will emerge as a nodal signifier in *Modernización Educativa* in a peculiar articulation with neoliberalism and neoconservatism. It interlaces the various threads of the international educational policies and the Mexican context, temporarily fixing the meaning of the modernization educational policy and permeating diverse official measures to actualize it. Thus, from curricula to "incentives" for schoolteachers, from school administration to finance, from programs to textbooks, this meaning circulates acquiring specific features in each level and yet keeping the promise of a future of "a more competitive national integration into the new world concert."

THE SYSTEM OF SIGNIFICATIONS OF THE EDUCATIONAL MODERNIZATION PROGRAM

The three main documents where this policy is condensed are: the *Programa de Modernización Educativa* (National Program on Educational Modernization,

SEP, 1989), the *Acuerdo Nacional para la Modernización de la Educación Básica* (National Agreement on the Modernization of Public Education, SEP, 1992), and the *Ley General de Educación* (General Education Law, 1993). I will stress only that the *Acuerdo* does not present any substantial change if compared with the *Programa*, but the political insertion of the former, as an agreement allegedly achieved as the product of consensus, makes some difference between them. (There was a "consultation" with schoolteachers and their proposals were said to have been incorporated in the *Acuerdo*.[24])

Within this framework, the meaning of educational modernization is displayed in values (e.g., "quality," "equity," "productivity"), institutions, rituals, and budgets orientating educational policies and incarnating their values. The *Programa* is structured in ten chapters, the first of which displays the values and reasons for this policy. Before the first chapter, one will find the president's speech in which he introduced the program, beginning with a review of the history of the Mexican school system. This review operates as a device to link the new program with the nationalist value, with the idea of a process that has a course whose almost natural, needed, or logical consequence is educational modernization. The main proposals of the policy document are organized in the other nine chapters devoted to school levels (primary, secondary, and higher education) and to specific areas such as schoolteacher qualifications; adult education; training schemes; open education; educational evaluation; and a final chapter devoted to premises, equipment, and building maintenance.

The first chapter condenses the orientation of the policy. After establishing links between the policy and the Mexican Constitution, reinforcing them with a reference to the Mexican Revolution, the *Programa* seems to be sufficiently legitimized in advance. However, it stresses seven challenges or goals, among which decentralization occupies a key position, and later it proposes the policy in items and sub-items where the model, its goals, and civic values are presented. Quality, coverage (of the demand for schooling), and decentralization are the strategic axes of this reform. Five key items are said to guarantee the much-needed quality: content, teaching and learning methods, teacher qualifications and in-service training, links between school levels, and links with science and technology.

Each chapter starts with a diagnosis of the then current schooling system,[25] indicating its main failures and consequently establishing the main challenges for the plan (see SEP, 1988). The *Acuerdo* (SEP, 1992) puts forward the following deficiencies: insufficient coverage and quality, lack of articulation among school levels, high proportion of repetition in primary and high school, excessive concentration of administration, poor teacher conditions. The orientation to be stressed by the new policy follows from this diagnosis. The similarities between these two documents of the Mexican policy, in terms of values, strategies, orientation, and ways to legitimize the program, are remarkable.

One can see both in the *Programa* and the *Acuerdo* that globalization operates as the cause of *Modernización Educativa*, but also as the consequence this policy will bring about. Globalization is signified as the goal of the policy but also as that which confers meaning to other discrete components of the general policy (e.g. basic competencies, didactic material, content and methods, curricula and syllabi). It is constructed as a means to further an end (i.e., the insertion of Mexico in the international market) and also as an end in itself. And in reading the different chapters of both official documents one can observe how globalization circulates throughout the different items involved in the general strategy.

THE WORLD BANK AND THE *ACUERDO:*
IS IT MERE COINCIDENCE?

Some of the specific items stressed in the Mexican educational policy are almost a literal translation of international recommendations: widening access, redistributing places, and improving quality and enhancing pertinence and relevance, level integration, administrative de-concentration, and teachers' conditions.

The official documents offer the solutions: equity; reform of plans and syllabi; integration of the former kindergarten, primary, and secondary into a "basic cycle"; administrative decentralization; and the revaluing of schoolteachers (Buenfil, 1996). Below I present some relevant examples, using an exercise made by Medina in her research (1996, p. 52 and ff.).

The World Bank maintains that:

> Education is the cornerstone of economic growth and social development as well as one of the main means of people welfare. Primary teaching is the basis, therefore there are three fields where it is necessary to introduce improvements: the teaching environment, teacher training and motivation, and the administration of educational systems (1990, p. 2).

Modernización Educativa proposes

> More resources, more effective teaching time, and adequate programs, better textbooks and teachers properly stimulated might have poor effects on educational quality and access if they cannot get beyond the obstacles and inefficiency of centralism and excessive bureaucracy damaging the national educational system. This is why it is important that the other axis of our strategy is the reorganization of the national educational system (SEP, 1992, p. 7).

No sophisticated analysis is needed to see the similarity between these two pieces: the emphasis on the environment in the former is translated into teaching time, programs, textbooks; improvement in teaching motivation and training is translated into teachers properly stimulated (which in the Mexican document occupies one of the five central positions); and "the improvements in the administration of educational systems" are translated into "overtaking centralism and excessive bureaucracy and the general re-organization of the national educational system."

Another example. The World Bank states,

Research undertaken in diverse countries has shown that the amount of time devoted to academic studies is systematically related to learning levels in children at school. In general, the more time teachers devote to actual teaching, the more the children learn. Three factors determine the annual number of hours dedicated to study any subject at school: the duration of the school year in hours, the proportion of these hours assigned to the subject and the amount of time lost due to school stoppage, absence of teachers or students, and other interruptions (1990, p. 21).

The Mexican educational policy echoes:

It is of great importance to rectify an evident tendency in recent years to reduce the number of effective class-days in the school year. As a first step, beginning with the next school term, an increase of at least ten percent in effective school days will be encouraged, and this can be achieved [strictly following the official school calendar] (SEP, 1992, p. 7).

More examples could be given of this "translation" of key World Bank aspects retrieved by the Mexican policy. Medina (1996) compared the 1990 World Bank document and the 1992 Mexican *Acuerdo* in an accurate localization of paragraphs: motivation toward teachers' qualifications improvement (World Bank 1990, pp. 5 and 26–30; SEP, 1992, pp. 8 and 22) and opportunities for professional advancement (World Bank, 1990, p. 28; SEP, 1992, p. 20). Even the timing for updating teachers' guides shows a surprising similarity between the two documents.

This may sound quite reasonable until one becomes aware that contemporary conditions for Mexican schoolteachers are overlooked, since many of these "non-effective days" are used for teacher training, in-service seminars, or simply as a break in an exhausting double school shift job. This points to the clash between global homogeneity and particularity.

DIFFUSION OF THE MEANING OF EDUCATIONAL MODERNIZATION

While in previous pages one could witness the similarity between international educational policies and the literal text of the Mexican Educational Modernization, this does not amount to seeing globalism as pure homogenization. I will present the way in which this Mexican policy is resignified at the point of implementation, showing the side of heterogeneity in a global process.

I draw on another recent piece of research dealing with how this educational policy, *Modernización Educativa*, provides models of identification for school-teachers and how these models are resignified in the very process of their appro-priation by the schoolteachers. López (1998) concentrates on the different inter-pretations it acquires in the official sector, in the dominant teacher (white) union, in its "dissident" faction,[26] and from the classroom teacher. The proliferation of meanings (of the model of identification proposed in the *Programa* and the *Acuerdo*) is conceptualized as dissemination (Derrida, 1982).

As was mentioned above, the question of schoolteachers occupies one of the central positions of the *Acuerdo*. This issue—the teacher's role—is unfolded into six points: basic qualification, in-service programs, wages (equal to three and four minimum wages), housing, *carrera magisterial* (involving a new promotion sys-tem,[27] which takes into account qualifications, productivity, and so on), and fi-nally, social recognition and acknowledgment of the teachers' work.

In his research López (1998) deals with four main groups of protagonists in this policy—the Ministry of Education (SEP) and its administrators, the domi-nant teacher's (white) union (Sindicato Nacional de Trabajadores de la Educa-ción, SNTE), its dissident leftist faction (Coordinadora Nacional de Trabajadores de la Educación, CNTE), and classroom teachers—showing how in each site the policy is disseminated. Taking one item for this exercise, the "revaluation of the schoolteachers' role,"[28] he shows that in spite of its being a nodal point articulat-ing the whole discursive edifice, its meaning is resignified in each level of appro-priation. So where the policy, in the words of President Salinas, stated, "We need to forge the right mechanisms for the acknowledgment of their work, we must strengthen their role, and reconcile their sense of service and improve their living conditions" (SEP, 1989, p. xii), it proposed the following strategy: a system con-ferring honors, awards, prizes, distinctions, and economic incentives to school-teacher productivity and achievement.

The SNTE understood the "revaluation of the schoolteachers' role" as an op-portunity to revitalize the historic heritage of schoolteachers; to rescue and strengthen the "tradition of the normal school"; and to link these two aspects to solve their problems of isolation and "immobility" (lack of promotion), thus improving their economic and labor conditions (López, 1998, p. 152). The leftist CNTE resignified this nodal point as mere demagogy and a failed attempt. In their view this was just a government product that did not permit the achieve-ment or recuperation of the highly valued image the schoolteachers had lost (López, 1998, p. 137).

Finally, the classroom teachers, confessing they had not studied the policy, re-signified the "revaluation of the schoolteachers role" as a policy that proved inca-pable of resolving their labor and economic conditions. They support their opin-ion in daily experience. One teacher said,

The *Programa Modernizador* states that a critical and self-reflective teacher is needed but the society and the pupils no longer respect us. We have lost today our human values. They used to respect us, support from the government used to arrive, but today it is no longer like that. We could fail a pupil [in an exam] but with the new evaluation forms we have to pass them all (López, 1998, p. 137).

Following López's research on the dissemination of several nodal points of the educational modernization, it can be said that this educational policy is re-signified by the protagonists according to their position:

SEP administrators reproduce it, legitimizing and magnifying it. SNTE unionists introduce nuances supplementing, criticizing and deconstructing it. CNTE unionists antagonize it fissuring, negating, criticizing and deconstructing it. Classroom teachers fissure it, antagonizing, deconstructing, disseminating, threatening, and, paradoxically, reproducing it (López, 1998, p. 154).

This research shows that each position of appropriation and dissemination of the official program does not operate in a unidirectional way, but rather in different and even contradictory ways. For instance, the CNTE teachers fissure it, expanding the gaps of the official discourse, showing its inner incoherence and to what extent it denies the very existence of actual teachers behind grandiose goals, wishful thinking, and demagogic strategies (e.g., retrieving the very consultation results).

Further research has to be done to state in a systematic way what we have already visualized: how the "revaluation of the schoolteachers role" is also re-signified as a "compulsory way to study and update their skills"; as a way to "bargain with certificates and diplomas"; as a way to "simulate"; as a way to "produce low academic quality pupils"; and even the opposite, as a way to improve the schoolteachers qualifications and living conditions, especially for those who, following the new rules, aim to succeed in their trajectory of *carrera magisterial*. Further research has also to be conducted to understand how, apart from schoolteachers, other schooling practices (e.g., teaching and learning, new curricula, and so on) are permeated by this global view and yet resignified in educational policies. Nonetheless, what has been presented above gives clear indications of the multifarious convergence between global and national policies.

THE GLOBAL MEETS THE PARTICULAR: AMBIGUITY AND DISSEMINATION OF THE GLOBAL

Global policies in education involving some uniformization of neoliberal criteria, measures, values, and strategies are well known both in industrialized and poor countries. However, the way in which their implementation is produced in each particular site produces their resignification or reinterpretation. The encounter between the global policy and the specific conditions of each case brings to the fore the complex tension between universality and particularity when one conceptualizes globalization and produces an interpretation of its effects on education.

I mentioned at the beginning of this chapter the old existence of international agencies producing educational policies. In the 1960s more attention was given to the impact these agencies, namely the OAS and the World Bank, were having in Latin American countries. The traces of that famous trend on educational technology fostered in the 1960s, when learning seemed guaranteed by organizing teaching through behavioral objectives, can still be found in some contemporary curricula.

We have witnessed the increasing presence achieved by UNESCO in the 1970s and 1980s through its regional office (OREALC) and project (PPEALC) and by OECD, the World Bank, and the Inter-American Development Bank in the last decade. This financial, political, administrative, and academic presence by no means amounts to saying it has achieved its idealized goals. Rather, it means that domestic policies cannot ignore academic trends, administrative patterns, and other recommendations issued by these agencies. The different conditions in which the links between national and international, "central and peripheral," "advanced and developing" countries were observed in the 1960s and today cannot be overlooked. The economic interdependence, raising of minority voices, end of the Cold War, noticeable environmental decay, and increasing presence of critical perspectives and intellectual trends undermining our enlightened faith in progress are among the most evident conditions that show this transformation. However, and even considering these differences, a tendency toward an interconnection at a planetary scope must be acknowledged.

The previous discussion demonstrates that even if globalization is a term we have been using with frequency recently, the tendency toward internationalization is not that new. Considering this and the fact that globalization is signified according to many different disciplinary approaches, political views, economic perspectives, and long-term or short-term historical considerations, what we have is a wide area of dispersion of its meaning.

For analytical purposes I distinguish three scenarios condensing the area of dispersion of the meanings of globalization:

1. The polarization of two discursive fields where the signified of "globalization" has been temporarily fixed either as a good value or as an evil threat, and—in spite of their opposition—they share the view of an intrinsic connection between globalization, modernity, and neoliberal capitalism.
2. Globalization is seen as a necessary universal process involving the real exploitation of the planet as a single unity that organizes production, market, and competitiveness and whose effects are economic, military, cultural, and global political formations.
3. Globalization is neither a universal, necessary tendency of history, nor a cultural, economic, ethical, or political impending imperialization, specifically,

the ruling of a single homogeneous view over the planet (not even if it were noncapitalist). As we saw, globalization can also be understood as interconnectedness.

This third position means:

1. assuming our contemporary existential situation as a multidirected conditioning of the universal and the particular, the homogeneous and the heterogeneous; and the product of the interaction of opposed tendencies such as fragmentation and integration, centralization and decentralization;
2. the production of syncretic and hybrid economic, cultural, educational, and political schema bringing about positions against fundamentalist nostalgia for a mythical uncontaminated identity;
3. the existence of conflict, generated by the interconnectedness and contact of the diverse, since our planet has unequal development in each realm and geopolitical area. Tension, encounter, friction, clash, and conflict are part of globalization and this can hardly be overlooked or concealed by wishful Enlightenment thinking. However, this does not amount to a pessimistic outlook; rather, this challenges us to invent different forms of plural utopias, which are not to be taken as a new transcendental universal.

In analyzing the impact of Educational Modernization on teachers' identity (Medina, 1996), we can see the encounter of the universal and the particular. On the one hand World Bank recommendations are almost literally copied in the Mexican educational policy *Modernización Educativa* (1988-1994).[29] On the other, a study about the different ways in which authorities, white unionists, leftist unionists and classroom teachers shows how they understand, signify, interpret and react to the item "revaluation of the schoolteachers' role" (López, 1998). Some ignored, others rejected, some resignified and some others even reproduced its meaning showing the proliferation of meanings that emerged in the implementation of the policy.

Beyond the ethical and political value of including particular views in any global policy, a value which may or may not be considered by "universal" policymakers in international agencies, there is another dimension where the encounter between universality and particularity operates. This dimension has been the axis of this chapter. It refers to the particularity (local) overflowing and contaminating the universal (global). This particularity is derived from the specific instantiations of the policy and cannot be anticipated by policy designers but operates precisely in the realization of educational policies; in so doing, it produces a surplus of meaning, an excess of signification. I maintain that this surplus is a discursive space for ethical and political intervention.

NOTES

1. In this chapter I will use the signifier *education* as synonymous with schooling, though in general terms I adhere to a more comprehensive meaning.

2. Different international agencies have been producing educational programs for Latin America. See, for instance, UNESCO (1965) where a managerial view of education was proposed as the view to be held. See UNESCO (1968), prescribing how research in universities had to be conducted. See also Pan American Union (c. 1967).

3. Concerning the general course of educational technology in Mexico as a paradigm prevailing in the curriculum during the early seventies, I thank Dr. Alicia de Alba for her advice on this issue. Official information about the OAS concerning education can be consulted in Fernando Chaves (1962) and OAS (1996). The Inter-American Development Bank and its projects for Latin America can be consulted in Davis (1950).

4. See for instance the Chilean journal *Tecnología Educativa* during the 1970s. In its pages one can find a precise model of schooling structures, contents, teaching, methods, expected learning, and other practices that allegedly guarantee good results for primary school children.

5. See, for instance, UNESCO's *World Survey of Education* (1971), where the importance of planning overruled other aspects of educational issues, research included. The OECD's *Educational Policies for the 1970s Conferences on Policies for Educational Growth* (1971) also recommends educational planning as the center for articulating educational policies.

6. Consult also UNESCO (1981).

7. Resignification will be understood here as an operation by means of which a different signified (meaning) is attached to a signifier. It does not imply that the first signification is truer than the second, it only involves their difference while referring to the same word. The point is to see if there are differences when a notion such as "productivity" is inscribed in the context of an UNESCO document; when it is inscribed, for instance, in a Mexican syllabus; and when it is uttered by the teacher before his or her pupils.

8. In Buenfil (2000), I present a deeper consideration of the enormous variety of meanings linked to globalization, their genealogy, and implications.

9. According to the preface, this work was actually written between 1976 and 1984.

10. Puiggrós (forthcoming) made this characterization in the seminar "política educativa, alternativas pedagógicas y nuevas fronteras político culturales" organized by APPEAL, in the Faculty of Philosophy at the UNAM, México, in December 7–9, 1998.

11. This idea is fully developed by Laclau (1996) and has deep implications in the way we think of ethical and political utopias.

12. In this sense I would agree with the idea that relativism is a false problem posed by foundationalists. Excellent work has been done on this issue. See Bernstein (1983), Margolis (1991), and Rorty (1989), among others.

13. Or, as Habermas (1987) bitterly accused the postmodern thinking, the difference between repression and emancipation is blurred.

14. This has an obvious family resemblance with postfoundationalism (Arditi, 1996).

15. For a lost Third World village a literacy campaign may be introduced as a progressive and liberating strategy, while for a neighbor village the very same campaign could become a repressive and colonizing practice (if their language is different from that which

is fostered in the literacy campaign). There is no privileged position from which our "senior brother" will pre-define how this literacy campaign will be appropriated in each particular site (I discuss more examples in Buenfil, 1997).

16. Insightful considerations about this contact have been made by De Alba (1995), who proposes the idea of cultural contact that inevitably is unequal and conflictive.

17. This presupposes a painful assumption: that there is no distortion-free communication, no transparent society, no final resolution of antagonisms: in short, no final suture of the social. Accordingly, once the necessary tendencies of history and a quasitranscendental reason are conceptually rejected, one has to face the responsibility of one's own decisions.

18. McLaren and Gutiérrez consider that "the materialist and nondiscursive dimensions of social life have become cavalierly dismissed in a research climate that seems to have become infatuated with the primacy of textual exegesis (as in the practice of postmodern ethnography or curriculum studies)." Their aim is to "rethink from a more materialist global perspective the links between the local and the broad educational practices." There is an evident difference between McLaren's view and the one I defend here concerning the concept of the nondiscursive. Actually, McLaren reproduces either a colloquial notion of discourse or he retrieves it from Foucault, who based on a rather substantialist concept of discourse, reduces it to linguistic actions. But if we follow either Wittgenstein's concept of language game or the Saussurean semiological project, or Barthes, Derrida, Lacan, Eco, Laclau, and many others, we will realize that signification is not conveyed by linguistic signifiers alone (e.g., the text, in Derridean terms, is not reduced to the printed matter between the two book covers). Therefore to analyze the discursive features of education by no means indicates dismissing objects; action; architecture; practices; or, in McLaren's words, the materialist nondiscursive. I would in turn ask McLaren, if he analyzes the material features of schooling, does he scrutinize the quality of mixture of concrete and liquid in the walls, or precisely their meaning in a social practice?

19. Citing Rose and Miller (1992, p. 201), Popkewitz continues:

At one level is the breakdown of the Fordist compromise in post-war Europe and the United States, a compromise among workers, industrialists and the state which produced a division of labor and mechanization in exchange for a favorable wage formula and the implementation of a state welfare system, as Fordism lost its efficiency with technologies and markets. The organizations of work that we are now witnessing is in part a response to the lack of efficiency of Fordist mass production. But at a different layer, there is a range of other challenges to the mechanism of social government that emerged during these same decades from civil libertarians, feminists, radicals, socialists, sociologists and others. These reorganized programs of government utilize and instrumentalize the multitude of experts of management, of family life, of lifestyle who have proliferated at the points of intersection of sociopolitical aspirations and private desires for self-advancement.

20. This opens new theoretical questions as to the traditional idea of determination, teleology, and the Hegelian expressive totality that I will not discuss in this paper.

21. I will use the verb *retrieve* to mean that a word is recovered, rescued, recuperated, taken from a discursive context and inscribed in a different one. For instance, the signified *equity* can be recuperated from a global recommendation and inscribed in a local program. The point is that in this retrieval a different association between signifier and signified may occur.

22. I assume neoliberalism as the contemporary logic that has been displaced from economics to other social fields such as education, namely, the marketing strategies pervading educational policies.

23. Political reform has opened state governments and municipal positions to representatives of political parties. This was unthinkable back in 1980. Now it is possible, for instance, to find a PAN governor legitimately establishing educational orientations undoubtedly regressive in moral and intellectual terms. For instance, in Guanajuato, a PANista governor, authorized by the local representative of the minister of education, published a "Guide for the Good Schoolteacher" recommending attitudes, clothing, and rituals combining a strong authoritarianism (as for discipline) and puritan values (for dressing, speech, teaching subjects, etc.). This is easily identifiable with a prerevolutionary ethical imaginary (i.e., the so-called "Porfirista morals").

24. The *Programa* was issued in 1988; there was a consultation to teachers, and later the *Acuerdo* was issued. There are some modifications and precisions in the latter, but some analysts claim that the *Acuerdo* had already been written before the consultation, that the consultation had been a farce and its results were "oriented" beforehand. The official sector can show the insertion of the consultation results; however, in my view this does not prove that the consultation was not manipulated. As we can see this is not a matter of "true or false" but rather of how this process took place.

25. Basic schooling; schoolteachers' qualifications and in-service training; adult education; occupational training; secondary education; higher education; graduate studies; and scientific, humanistic, and technological research.

26. Strange as it may seem, there is a national union of education workers SNTE, founded in the 1940s as a compromise between the SEP and the numerous teacher unions, which has had successive internal dissident factions and movements. The CNTE is a contemporary leftist faction inside the SNTE, also known as the "Democratic Tendency."

27. There is a strong coincidence in the way in which this point is developed in the *Acuerdo* and the way in which the World Bank recommends it (1992, pp. 5, 28, and ff.).

28. The normalist tradition refers to the high academic and professional value that teacher education used to have since it was created emulating the French *Ecole Normale*, and later, the *Ecole Normale Superieure*. Up to the Mexican Revolution and the first half of the twentieth century, this tradition was preserved.

29. México educational policies tend to be officially installed and removed in terms of political timing, e.g., the changes of administration. Thus, every six years with a change of president and cabinet, the possibility of having a new educational policy is opened, regardless of the benefits or damage of the previous one. Sometimes the previous is "evaluated" in order to prove the importance of the coming policy. In the case of *Modernización Educativa* the president elected in 1994, Ernesto Zedillo, had previously been the head of the Ministry of Education. His educational program may have not been really different from the former, but whatever difference had to be patent in order to set his own legitimacy.

REFERENCES

Abreu, Luis. 1993. La Modernización de la Educación Médica. *Revista de la Facultad de Medicina*, vol. 36. no. 2, pp. 89–96.

Archer, Margaret. 1991. Sociology for One World: Unity and Diversity. *International Sociology*, vol. 6, no. 2, pp. 131–47.

Arditi, Benjamin. 1996 (April). The Underside of Difference. Working Papers, No 12. Essex: Centre for Theoretical Studies in the Humanities and the Social Sciences.

Barabtarlo Zedanski, Anita. 1992. Apuntes de un modelo de formación de recursos humanos en salud. *Revista Mexicana de Educación Médica*. vol. 3, no. 3. pp. 12–17.

Bernstein, Richard J. 1983. *Beyond Objectivism and Relativism: Science, Hermeneutics, and Praxis*. Oxford: Blackwell; and Philadelphia: University of Pennsylvania Press.

Braudel, Fernand. 1991. *Escritos sobre la historia*. México: Fondo de Cultura Económica.

Buchbinder, Howard. 1994. Tiempos difíciles, falta de financiamiento, corporaciones, globalización y gobierno en las universidades canadienses. *Perfiles Educativos*, no. 64, pp. 27–31.

Buenfil, Rosa. 1996. Globalización: Significante nodal en la modernización educativa. *Cuadernos Pedagógicos*, nos. 26–27.

———. 1997. Education in a Postmodern Horizon: Voices from Latin America. *British Educational Research Journal*, vol. 23, no. 1, pp. 97–107.

———. 2000. Globalization, Education, and Discourse Political–Analysis: Ambiguity and Accountability in Research. *International Journal of Qualitative Studies in Education*, vol. 13, no. 1, pp. 1–24.

Casillas, Miguel. 1993. Los retos de globalización y políticas de ciencia y tecnología en Brasil. *Universidad Futura*, vol. 4, no. 13, pp. 36–46.

CEPAL-UNESCO. 1992. Educación y conocimiento: Eje de la transformación productiva con equidad. Santiago, Chile: Comision Economica para la America Latina y el Caribe and UNESCO.

Chaves, Fernando. 1962. *La educación cooperativa en América Latina*. Washington, D.C.: OAS.

Chomsky, Noam, and Heinz Dietrich. 1995. *La sociedad global*. México: Joaquín Mortiz.

College Board. 1983. *Academic Preparation for College: What Students Need to Know and Be Able to Do*. New York: The College Board.

Cruz, Ofélia. 1998. El discurso modernizador: Proyecto político del estado mexicano para la formación de docentes, 1988–1994. Master's thesis, Universidad Nacional Autónoma de México.

Davis, Harold. 1950. *Social Science Trends in Latin America*. Washington, D.C.: Issued in co-operation with the Inter-American Bibliographical and Library Association, American University Press.

De Alba, Alicia. 1995. Postmodernidad y Educación: Implicaciones epistémicas y conceptuales en los discursos educativos. In Alicia De Alba (ed.), *Educación y postmodernidad*. México: CESU/UNAM and M. A. Porrua, pp. 129–75.

Del Valle, Jorge. 1992. Tres oleadas de desafíos a las Universidades de México. *Reforma y Utopía: Reflexiones sobre Educación Superior*, no. 6, pp. 75–92.

De Alba, Alicia, and Huascar Taborga. 1992. Formación de los ingenieros frente a la globalización. *Revista de la Educación Superior*, vol. 20, no. 2, pp. 37–45.

Derrida, Jacques. 1982. *Margins of Philosophy*. Brighton: Harvester Press.

Fiala, Robert, and Audri Gordon Langford. 1987. Educational Ideology and the World Educational Revolution, 1950–1970. *Comparative Education Review*, vol. 31, no. 3, pp. 315–32.

Fuentes, Silvia. 1997. Identificación y constitución de sujectos: El discurso Marxista como articulador hegemónico del processo identificatorio de los estudiantes de sociología de la ENEP Aragón, gen 79–83. Master's thesis, Departamento de Investigaciones Educativas–Centro de Investigación y Estudios Avanzados, México.

———. 1998. Análisis de un proceso identificatorio: Los sociólogos de la ENEP Aragón, 1979–1983. *Revista Mexicana de Investigación Educativa*, vol. 3, no. 5, pp. 77–100.

Garibay, Luis, and Fernando de la Torre. 1992. Papel de la educación en el desarrollo de recursos humanos para la Cuenca del Pacífico: El caso de México. *Docencia*, vol. 20, no.1, pp. 107–19.

Giddens, Anthony. 1990. *The Consequences of Modernity*. Cambridge: Polity Press.

González, Edgar. 1998. *Un enfoque antiesencialista: Centro y periferia de la educación ambiental*. Mexico: Mundi Prensa.

Habermas, Jurgen. 1987. *Teoría de la acción comunicativa*. Buenos Aires: Taurus.

———. 1989. *El discurso filosófico de la modernidad*. Buenos Aires: Taurus.

Kawame, Anthony Appiah, and Henry Louis Gates, Jr. 1997. *The Dictionary of Global Culture*. New York: Knopf.

Laclau, Ernesto. 1996. *Emancipation(s)*. London: Verso.

López, José. 1998. Modernización educativa: Resignificaciones por cuatro protagonistas. Master's thesis, Departamento de Investigaciones Educativas-Centro de Investigación y Estudios Avanzados, México.

Margolis, Joseph. 1991. *The Truth about Relativism*. Oxford: Blackwell.

Marum Espinosa, Elia. 1993. Globalización e integración económica: Nuevas premisas para el Posgrado. *Reforma y Utopía: Reflexiones sobre Educación Superior*, no. 8, pp. 7–21.

McLaren, Peter, and Kris Gutiérrez. 1997. Global Politics and Local Antagonisms. In Peter McLaren (ed.), *Revolutionary Multiculturalism: Pedagogies of Dissent for the New Millennium*. Boulder, CO: Westview.

McLuhan, Marshall C., and Bruce R. Powers. 1989. *The Global Village: Transformations in World Life and Media in the Twenty-first Century*. Oxford: Oxford University Press.

Medina, Patricia. 1996. Impacto de la modernización educativa en la identidad de los maestros de primaria: Reporte final de investigación. México: Universidad Pedagógica Nacional.

Medina, Sara. 1995. Educación y modernidad: El bachillerato en México ante los desafíos del tercer milenio. Doctoral dissertation, Universidad Nacional Autonoma de México.

OAS. 1996. *Yearbook of Educational, Scientific and Cultural Development in Latin America*. Washington, D.C.: OAS.

OCDE. 1986. *La naturaleza del desempleo de los jóvenes: Informes de la Organización de Cooperación y Desarrollo Económico*. Madrid: OCDE.

OECD. 1971. *Educational Policies for the 1970s Conferences on Policies for Educational Growth*. Paris: OECD.

———. 1993. *Education at a Glance: Indicators*. Paris: OECD.

Pan American Union. 1967. *The Alliance for Progress and Latin American Development Prospects: A Five-Year Review 1961–1965*. Baltimore: Published for OAS by Johns Hopkins University Press.

Papacostas, Alcibiades. 1996. Alfabetización tecnológica: Un enfoque constructivista. Master's thesis, Departamento de Investigacion Educativas–Centro de Investigacion y Estúdios Avanzados, México.

Perlmutter, Howard V. 1991. On the Rocky Road to the First Global Civilization. *Human Relations*, vol. 44, no. 9, pp. 897–1010.

Peters, Michael. 1999. The Post-Historical University? Prospects for Alternative Globalisations. In *Jahrbuch für Bildings und Erziehungphilosophie*, vol. 2. Special issue on Globalisierung: Perspektiven, Paradocien, Verwerfundgen (Globalization: Prospects, paradoxes, and ruptures), W. Bauer, W. Lippitz, W. Marotzki, J. Ruhloff, A. Schafer, and C. Wulf (eds.) Schneider Verlag Hohengeren, pp. 105–24.

Popkewitz, Thomas. 1991. *A Political Sociology of Educational Reform: Power/Knowledge in Teaching, Teacher Education, and Research*. New York: Teachers College Press.

———. 1997 (Oct.–Nov.). Lecture delivered at the V Congreso Nacional de Investigación Educativa, Mérida, México.

———. 1999. Reform as the Social Administration of the Child: Globalization of Knowledge and Power. In Nicholas Burbules and Carlos Alberto Torres (eds.), *Globalization and Education: Critical Perspectives*. New York: Routledge. Puiggrós, Adriana. Forthcoming. Proceedings of the Conference at the Jornadas Academicas de APPEAL 1998, México: UNAM.

Robertson, Roland. 1990. Mapping the Global Condition. In Mike Featherstone (ed.), *Global Culture*. London: Sage (Reprinted from *Theory, Culture and Society*, vol. 7, nos. 2–3, pp. 15–30.)

Rorty, Richard. 1989. *Contingency, Irony and Solidarity*. Cambridge: Cambridge University Press.

Schriewer, Jurgen. 1996. Sistema mundial y redes de interrelación: La internacionalización de la educación y el papel de la educación comparada. In Miguel A. Pereyra (ed.), Jesús García Mínguez (trans.), *Globalización y descentralización de los sistemas educativos*. Barcelona: Pomares-Corredor, pp. 17–58.

SEP (Secretaría de Educación Pública). 1989. *Programa de Modernización Educativa*. México: SEP.

SEP. 1992. *Acuerdo Nacional para la Modernización de la Educación Básica*. México: SEP.

SEP. 1994. *Curriculum Básico Nacional*. México: SEP.

Sosa, Magdalena. 1994. El intercambio académico en América Latina. *Universidades*, vol. 44, no. 8, pp. 10–13.

UNESCO/Lyons (ed.). 1965. *Problems and Strategies of Educational Planning*. Belgium: UNESCO and IIEP.

———. 1968. *Education, Human Resources and Development in Latin America*. New York: UNESCO-ECLA.

———. 1971. *World Survey of Education*. Geneva: UNESCO.

———. 1981. *Curricula and Lifelong Education*. Geneva: UNESCO.

Wallerstein, Immanuel. 1989. *El capitalismo tardío*. México: Siglo XXI.

Weiss, Edward. 1994 (Enero–Abril). Situación y perspectiva de la investigación educativa. *Avance y Perspectiva* (México), vol. 13, pp. 33–41.

Wittgenstein, Ludwig. 1963. *Philosophical Investigations*. Oxford: Blackwell.

World Bank. 1990. *Educación Primaria*. Documento de Política del Banco Mundial. Washington, D.C.: World Bank.

15

South African Higher Education in Transition: Global Discourses and National Priorities

Crain Soudien and Carol Corneilse

The South African higher education system, like many others elsewhere in the world (see Currie, 1998), is in the throes of far-reaching changes. These changes, the conjunctural product of a number of complex national and international forces, have seen the universities, technikons, and other colleges[1] that make up the system having to restructure what they do; how they relate to each other; and, fundamentally, how they position themselves in relation to the state and the wider economy. Most notably, the changes have precipitated the emergence of institutions that are in a stronger dialogue with a world that traditionally has been their object of study as opposed to being a site for their engagement. The meaning and significance of these developments have been the subject of some debate both in South Africa and in the rest of the world (see Cooper, 1997; Orr, 1997; Subotzky, 1997).

As the higher education sector is forced to look both inward and outward, and to account for itself, several questions suggest themselves in terms of what the new university ought to be about. Among these are broad sociopolitical questions such as the role of the higher education sector in the process of social renewal in South Africa. How ought the sector to represent itself vis-à-vis contentious issues such as the "national good?" How, more to the point, do universities in particular relate to currently fashionable injunctions of "building the nation?" With respect to economic relevance, the question arises of what priority institutions place on training and sharpening the vocational edge of their qualifications. Should the sector be concerned with the government's economic strategies, and should it gear its program offerings to the needs of the marketplace? Further, as the sector grapples with the seemingly contradictory demands of cosmopolitanism and indigenization, what epistemological imperatives shape the nature of its discourse? And then there is a more complex question: How do the epistemological nuances of cosmopolitan versus indigenous knowledges relate to what Scott (1997, p. 21) has identified as "the challenge from inside"—the erosion of the dominance of small elite producers of knowledge and the entry of a diversity of knowledge brokers, producers, and users "ming(ling) promiscuously" and leaning toward a concern for knowledge application, accountability to the market, and transdisciplinarity (Scott, 1997, pp. 35–36). These and other questions suggest that the turning point that has been reached in higher education is possibly more far-reaching than anything else experienced this century.

While recognition of this turning point is often cause for considerable alarm and disquiet in the sector, particularly among faculty members who see only the specter of diminishing job security, this chapter will argue that the complexity of the social terrain in which higher education is located resists the teleological prefigurement of, say, the simple marketization of higher education, or, at the other extreme, and admittedly an increasingly more unlikely prospect, the detachment of the sector from the everyday world. In seeking to make this argument, and to posit a somewhat more complex perspective of the possibilities that are inherent in the new developments in the sector in South Africa, the chapter looks at curricula reforms within the university community of the higher education sector. Special reference is made to the developments that have taken place in the area of program development. In this analysis particular attention is given to the struggle, at the University of Cape Town, around an introductory program in the Humanities with an African Studies focus.

THE SOUTH AFRICAN HIGHER EDUCATION SECTOR: A FOCUS ON UNIVERSITIES' GLOBALIZATION

During its long period of isolation, South Africa, officially at least, stood outside of the world system. Because of the odor of its apartheid policies, the country was deliberately excluded from the international terrain. Its scholars, athletes, trade representatives, inter alia, were shut out of those arenas where they would have interacted with their international peers. As a result of the dismantling of apartheid, the country has been rapidly reassimilated into the international community. This has meant, in some instances, intensifying long-standing connections to the wider world, and in others, establishing new linkages to and association with institutions, practices, norms, and standards from which apartheid deliberately sought to shield the country.

SOUTH AFRICA AND THE WORLD: A MULTIPLICITY OF INFLUENCES

A consequence of the isolation that South Africa experienced has been an inclination, evident particularly in political analysis and discussion about social identity (see Mamdani, 1998c, p. 14), toward a South African exceptionalism. A hallmark of this exceptionalism has been a reluctance within South African scholarship to see the country as part of Africa and, instead, to locate its politics, culture, and history in the vocabulary of an internationalism frameworked in the syntax and orthography of Europe, particularly that of the British colonial tradition. Even this exceptionalism, however, has not been without its complexities and is represented by a range of constructs that are themselves the intellectual and political products of liberal, socialist, religious, philosophical, and social influences that derive from a wide range of non–South African influences. Examples include the complex notions of Afrikaner *volkdom* (group identity), which have been profoundly influenced by a medley of Calvinistic and Germanic-Dutch philosophical traditions. The radical tradition, which achieved a hegemony in the universities for a period of time in the eighties and permeated the political and labor movement, is a borrowed Anglo-European tradition with strong links to Antonio Gramsci, Louis Althusser, Ernest Mandel, and the Frankfurt School. It is only very recently that a public interest in Africanist notions that invoke the ideals of a supposedly authentic African social and cultural practice has emerged. This is mediated through the currently fashionable guise of what is called *ubuntu*—a sense of humanity—which is as yet only vaguely adumbrated. The importance of these illustrations is only to emphasize what the process of democratization has done for South Africa in showing how much South Africa is, and has always been, in complex connection with the wider world.

The complexity and significance of South Africa's relationship with the wider world are particularly visible as the process of education reform gathers pace. The markers of this relationship are evident and might be seen in the extent and the pervasiveness of the internationalized *talk* that has permeated educational discourse in South Africa. Nowhere is this more apparent than in the curriculum restructuring process that is currently underway in South Africa's schools. *Curriculum 2005*, awaiting phased implementation in primary and secondary schools, is underscored by innovations that are currently the subject of much debate in Scotland, New Zealand, and in certain parts of the United States. Interestingly, in confronting the apartheid past and in developing the principles of the new curriculum, school reformers in South Africa have come to the conclusion that it is in re-skilling their young people through an outcomes-based curriculum that the road to progress and development is to be reached and not through, specifically, the infusion of a new anti-apartheid content. This debate itself has borrowed strongly from previous international debates, particularly in the United Kingdom, around the question of skills versus content.

In seeking to understand South Africa's relationship with the world, it would, however, be a mistake to see South Africa as simply being a site upon which an internationalized discourse has been inscribed. It is important, in making sense of this relationship, to recognize how complex processes of globalization are.

The approach that is adopted in this chapter builds on Giddens's (1990) work, which stresses that globalization by no means signifies the inexorable march of the world toward a homogeneous and uniform universality. Instead, it is a process marked by contingency and the iterative and pervasive presence of discourse and interaction. Giddens (1990, p. 64) talks of globalization being realized in what he calls mutually opposite tendencies or binary oppositions. These oppositions include the tensions between universalization and particularization, homogenization versus differentiation, integration as opposed to fragmentation, centralization against decentralization, and juxtaposition versus syncretization. What these oppositions make possible is a world inflected in hegemonic global discourses; the space and time through which these discourses are articulated, however, produce a world characterized by unevenness. Some regions of the world and even regions within countries are more "deeply implicated in global processes than others. Within nation-states, some communities (e.g., financial ones) are tightly enmeshed in global networks while others (e.g., the urban homeless) are totally excluded (but not unaffected) by them" (McGrew, 1992, p. 76).

This unevenness presents a world where asymmetries of power are intense and where inequalities and injustices are exacerbated through the privileged access of the elite to information, new sources of wealth, and power. At the same time, however, that this power finds new mediums and modalities, so too do new centers of resistance emerge—new challenges to new hegemonies. As power blocs are reconfigured so too are nodes of resistance. Therefore, far from taking communities and polities in a single direction, globalization suggests the movement of the world into a fractured and often discontinuous space where multiple logics are at work.

The significance of this discussion for higher education in South Africa is profound where globalization pressures have been intense but have been insistently challenged by demands for what Kraak (1997, p. 62) has called massification.[2] These developments have been analyzed in a number of different ways by South African scholars: there is on the one hand a community that emphasizes the emergence of new knowledge production regimes. These new regimes offer opportunities for developing a higher education system that is both more responsive to the needs of an emergent economy and those of a previously excluded majority; in contrast, there is the perspective of those who see the current restructuring as the denouement of the capitalist hold on the South African political economy and the assimilation of higher education into a marketized and commodified world.

A key perspective within the first group is offered by Kraak (1997). He argues that social transformation in South Africa has been characterized by the demand for equality and the opening up of elite institutions to disadvantaged students. These processes have led to the expansion of program offerings in universities. Evident, as the product of almost half a decade's innovation, is a movement in the universities toward programs that have moved beyond the traditional disciplines and in the direction of "recurrent, continuing and professional education and training" (Kraak, 1997, p. 64).

Since 1996, most South African universities have gone through processes of restructuring of one kind or another. In several institutions this has involved a fundamental revision of the academic frame and a move toward a program-based approach to learning and teaching. Programs, following the model at the University of Cape Town (UCT), are "a planned and coherent (not necessarily uniform) set of teaching and learning activities, pursued [in] depth in one or more specialization fields, at one or more qualification levels" (Academic Planning Framework, Interim Report for Discussion, 1996, p. 3). In the UCT version of this experience, and perhaps similarly at other institutions, the institution of programs involves a shift

> from a disciplinary point of view to a perspective which places the overall experience of individual students at the centre-stage in the philosophy of academic planning. . . . A student-oriented point of view . . . will emphasize the totality of the curriculum, including its coherence, opportunities for disciplinary specialization, quality, educational outcomes, and its provision of development opportunities for *all* students. (Programme Planning and Implementation within UCT's Academic Planning Framework, 1998, p. 4, emphasis in the original).

The movement toward programs in South African universities has been partly shaped by requirements of the National Qualifications Framework (NQF), which defines the higher education system as program based, specifically, it is conceived of as comprising instructional programs at various levels to which access can be gained (by virtue of prior learning—formal and nonformal—being recognized) or from which the individual can exit having the desired qualification. The aim of the NQF is to develop a national accreditation and qualifications system that allows for lifelong learning. This type of "qualification acquisition" is best achieved in a system envisaged as "a range of institutions offering qualifications at particular levels, and of particular institutions offering qualifications at multiple levels" (National Commission on Higher Education, NCHE, 1996, pp. 106–7). All programs offered in the sector would be registered with the NQF, at least at exit level of whole qualifications. The South African Qualifications Authority coordinates the task of ensuring that the ladder of qualifications is coherent and that it will facilitate articulation between institutions and qualifications. Central to this is the notion that all learning programs should articulate with one another through their emphasis on generic skills and outcomes.

FACTORS INFLUENCING CHANGE IN HIGHER EDUCATION

Kraak makes the point that the changes in the system have, in the first instance, been motivated by globalizing economic factors. He argues that the "informational economy has required a more educated and trained workforce, and this has been reflected in the massive expansion of para-professional and professional recurrent and continuing education" (1997, p. 64). The growth in the system is also attributable to the needs of learners. Learning has had to be delivered, therefore, in "open learning" systems. A key feature of these new developments is the growth of partnerships between industry, higher education, and the state. These, Kraak argues, are both a response to a precondition of the informational economy, namely, the need to develop and strengthen innovation in the interests of national economic competitiveness, and a social response by a more educated and empowered citizenry who are using their knowledge in the struggles against a range of social problems.

Bertelsen (1998) reads the setting somewhat differently from Kraak. Following Jameson (1991), and in focusing on higher education, she takes the contesting imperatives of globalization and massification and recasts them as a contest between the university's traditional social democratic discourse and the neoliberal culture of the market. The new culture of the market, she says, is presented as a cultural revolution that seeks to decenter and delegitimate the discourse of struggle. It is the new market culture that is defining how the universities ought to operate. Research is judged by its ability to produce new products. Teaching is assessed in terms of the marketable skills it develops. Bertelsen goes further to say that "[c]ost-efficiency requires that personnel be down-sized; 'peripheral' activities are eliminated; high-tech distance learning replaces inefficient classroom contact, and funding is regarded as an investment decision based on short-term production goals" (1998, p. 141).

Bertelsen argues that a new managerialism has taken hold in university administration and that administrators have expropriated the authority of academics. Core activities in the university have been put through the prism of business practices. In particular, research and teaching have had to be repackaged as "products," which add value and are measured with quality control measures borrowed from the market: " 'performance' rules, and productivity, cost-effectiveness and efficiency (jointly known as 'excellence') become the criteria of success" (Bertelsen, 1998, p. 149). She is particularly concerned with what she sees as the "entailment" of interdisciplinarity. For her interdisciplinarity, despite its "progressive" appeal and the undoubted challenge it constitutes to the conservatism of disciplines, cannot be seen independently of the changing nature of work in the new political economy from which the language currently used in the academy, such as performance indicators, comes. A convergence between interdisciplinarity and work protocols—post-Fordist in their character—has developed, which has the long-term potential for converting the academic experience into a commoditized product able to be accessed on-line and available in repackageable form. The impact, Bertelsen (1998, p. 153) argues, is the disciplining, de-skilling, and displacement of academic labor achieved through the post-Fordist repackaging of academic work in small highly flexible transportable modules.

Important as are both Kraak's and Bertelsen's characterizations of the new globalized informational economy and the context in which the university might be operating, the theoretical space in which they work, we argue (despite Bertelsen's qualification of her argument—she makes the point that discourse is always contested), is conditioned by its own teleology. In it resides a strongly centered hegemony alongside of a whole number of emasculated and decentered discourses. While the thrust of the new university, particularly, as we suggest below, in the presentation of the new curriculum in the form of programs, might be said to represent globalization at work, what Bertelsen's argument does not recognize is the continued presence of a variety of local dissident discourses, which limit the capacity of those in charge of the university to operate in an unimpeded way. Kraak's and Bertelsen's representations of the social order allows little of what Castells (1997, p. 109) calls "refusal" and even less of the recognition that marginalized discourses themselves intrude and enter into the very heart of the center itself.

To push the discussion ahead, the argument that will be made here, following Cloete et al. (1998), who in turn lean on Castells (1997), is that the stronger the insertion of a community into the global order, the more intense are the levels of differentiation and resistance within that community. Castells (1997, p. 308) points out that "the more they (states) triumph in the planetary scene, in close partnership with the agents of globalization, the less they represent their national constituencies." The basis of this argument is that the nation-state, far from withering away, is a crucial player in the new international order. While the free flow of capital has eroded the sovereignty of the state, elements within the state still have the power to block, obstruct, and regulate information, capital, and the flow of labor and commodities. It is in playing this role of impeding and/or facilitating the movement of intellectual and capital resources that state structures operate at both the international and the local level. Within this duality, the state, and by implication structures operating within it such as the university, are subjects of insistent and often dichotomizing stresses.

While it is important to recognize the paradigmatic frame of globalism within which we are working, simultaneously, we need to understand the multitude of tendencies and trends operating within this frame. It is this objective condition, we argue, which militates against any form of predetermined outcome in the state and its institutions. The case study presented below exemplifies the point.

CURRICULUM DEVELOPMENT AT THE UNIVERSITY OF CAPE TOWN AND THE CASE OF AFRICAN STUDIES

Program development at UCT began in 1996 when the university senate adopted an Academic Planning Framework (APF) that laid out the broad shape of the new curriculum. One of the consequences of this development was a process of faculty restructuring in terms of which the institution's ten faculties were reduced to six. Work on the APF had begun two years earlier. At the end of 1994 UCT's Academic Planning Committee initiated a lengthy process of consultations and workshops involving a broad range of academic and nonacademic staff: "strengths and weaknesses in most areas of the University were assessed; external opportunities and threats were evaluated; the culture and values of the University were explored" (Gillard, 1998, p. 9). A multitude of draft reports and draft proposals were subsequently discussed in faculties and the university senate. Developments were reported to the University Transformation Forum. Finally, in August 1996, the senate was ready to support a framework for academic planning which included "guidelines for program design, criteria for program strength, and an indication as to how priorities should be set" (Gillard, 1998, p. 9).

The context in which these changes were introduced is important to understand. The institution, like its counterparts elsewhere in the country, was having to respond to national pressures, particularly from government, and internal pressure, mainly from students, for the institution to transform itself.[3] Nationally, the university was faced with a declining subsidy from the state and had to confront the question of cost-efficient academic structures and programs. Internally, UCT had set up a Transformation Forum whose main task was to assist with the process of making the institution responsive to questions of its apartheid past and to correct its racial and gender imbalances. In terms of this context, toward cost-efficiency, faculties had already begun to assume financial responsibility for their own affairs. Faculties and departments were also put under pressure to respond to the need to change the profile of both the student body and the faculty.

The iterative process of designing and selecting programs within faculties took place in 1997 and 1998. Gillard has conceded that the "implementation of programmatic planning [was] much more complicated than expected" (1998, p. 9). In order to achieve program coherence, departments had to abandon the old ways of planning curricula, in which, for the most part, staff were responsible for coordinating the teaching of individual courses. The new approach called for the establishment of program committees to design whole courses of study in which the individual components related to each other and were consistent with the program's intention, defined at the beginning of the process in order to guide overall structure. Financial and staffing resources had to be taken into account at the same time and faculties were placed in the awkward position of planning for the coming year with hardly any sense of likely program demand. Deliberations were further complicated by faculty/departmental politics and the growing realization among staff that program planning was slowly revealing areas (i.e., staff) that were likely to be trimmed in order to remain within budget.

By the deadline for "program menus" in early 1998, the university's Academic Planning Office had received more than seventy program proposals, which amounted to almost seven hundred pages of reading. As expected, the fruits of the faculties' labors looked very different from conventional disciplinary majors, which students had hitherto put together in consultation with faculty program advisors. Individual student choice in program design had all but disappeared (requests to be exempted from what was on offer would henceforth have to be approved by the senior deputy vice-chancellor with responsibility for planning on the recommendation of the relevant faculty dean). These structured programs (some with three or four streams—variations within a program) came with names like "Development and Social Transformation," "Cultural and Literary Studies," "Historical Studies," "Molecular and Cell Biology," "Mathematical and Statistical Sciences," and so on. These names were perceived to provide clearer career directions for students.

These proposals were then subjected to intense scrutiny by an Academic Programs Working Group, which was given the responsibility for deciding (in negotiation with faculties) which programs it would recommend to the university Senate to be implemented.[4] The guidelines for determining the strength of a proposal were drawn from the APF's criteria, which stated that "programs are strong, when:

- they offer coherent teaching and learning, with well-structured core-course requirements in terms both of service components and the major(s), but with enough 'formative' pre-requisites and electives to give variety and breadth;
- they are designed so as to accommodate students from diverse educational backgrounds;
- they have a well-established reputation amongst potential recruits and subsequent employers;
- there is a recognized societal role for graduates, who meet national person-power needs;
- they produce graduates who are flexible in being able to adapt to new needs and opportunities and who are eligible for postgraduate study anywhere in the world;
- they attract excellent, highly motivated students of both sexes, from across the country and from all population groups;
- they reflect high success rates and low attrition rates, with a mixture of high [achievers] as well as solid performers;
- there is [a clear route] to postgraduate studies;
- they are taught by a critical mass of excellent staff with a keen interest in developing and maintaining the program, who are active in cutting-edge research in several sub-disciplinary areas;
- there is good support teaching by a substantial cadre of postgraduate students; and
- they are well-provided with library, laboratory (including equipment) and fieldwork facilities" (Academic Planning Framework, Interim Report for Discussion, 1996, pp. 6–7).

Other criteria were extrapolated from the university's mission statement, which emphasized, inter alia, notions of excellence and equity, lifelong education, research-based teaching and learning, the necessity for working within the framework of South Africa's location as an African nation, and the need for transcending the legacy of apartheid. Alongside of these, important too, was the vice-chancellor's frequently stated ambition, in a sense UCT's new motto, of making "UCT a world-class African university."

By the middle of the 1998 academic year (in order to allow sufficient time to prepare for program implementation in 1999), the process of selecting programs was complete. Programs had been classified, some given "blue-ribbon" status, some returned for revisions, and several not selected for implementation. A key feature of the process was the intense discomfort and anxiety that the process induced. Academics found themselves unable to navigate the semiotic arena of programs and frequently having to defer to the administration for guidance and clarification (see Currie, 1998; and Welch, 1998 for a discussion about similar developments elsewhere in the world).

It is important to note that the majority of the members of the Academic Programs Working Group were academics and six were full professors. All, except one, were heads of department and active teachers. However, this fact was lost on academics, who were mainly interacting with "the Administration" in the form of the academic planning officer and the senior deputy vice-chancellor (Planning) (himself a world-renowned medical biochemist) throughout the entire process. This interaction was appropriate since the senior deputy vice-chancellor had been the main sponsor of the APF on its way to and through the Senate, and, as the head of the academic planning department, the academic planning officer was responsible for managing the process of APF implementation. These two members of the administration often held lengthy meetings with academics in all the faculties during the complicated period of curriculum design. In addition, faculties were presented with detailed feedback on program design from the Academic Programs Working Group.

Despite this ongoing dialogue, there were hostile critics within the academic community who found much in the process that offended them, not least of all the encroachment on their academic freedom that the new multidisciplinary programs represented. They saw the new programs as the marketization of knowledge packaged in the discourse of skills acquisition at the expense of academic rigor (see Orr, 1997; and Kishun, 1998). For them, UCT was succumbing to the new globalized discourse of the market. Suspicion was fueled, moreover, by the administration's frequent invocation of the examples of the "great" American universities (the University of Chicago was often referred to), which were supposed to be leading the way in these developments.

This particular phase of South Africa's higher education history requires serious attention, which this study is unable to provide. What the remainder of our discussion seeks to show is how much the debate is about curriculum choice as it is also, and much more fundamentally so, about the way globalization both closes down and opens up issues. The discussion that follows is by no means meant to enter and develop the debate about the place and definition of African studies. It is instead meant to use the dispute to demonstrate a wider point.

THE AFRICAN STUDIES CURRICULUM DEBATE

As the contributions of Mamdani (1998a; 1998b), Hall (1998a; 1998b), Muller (1998), Ensor (1998), Jansen (1998), and Graaff (1998) in a special issue of the journal *Social Dynamics* show, the program debate took a particular turn around the question of the development of a foundation semester in the Faculty of Social Science and Humanities, which was meant to have an African Studies focus. The foundation semester was intended to serve as a pilot course that would be refined and eventually constitute the introductory phase to humanities programs once they were fully implemented in the faculty from the beginning of 1999. The African studies focus met the APF criterion for offerings to be "Africa-situated." (This process of refinement is still continuing, although it is mainly structural, as timetable constraints have inhibited the development of a common introduction for all students to programs in the humanities.)

The design of the course was initially entrusted to a professor who had been recently appointed to a new chair in African Studies. He was asked to work with a committee, convened by the deputy dean of the faculty, which comprised social scientists from the Departments of Social Anthropology, Sociology, and Academic Development. An outline he developed was supported by this group, but not the extended version, which included a reading list. It was in the course of the discussions around this extended outline that the participation of the professor was suspended by the deputy dean and the committee developed an alternative design for the course. The professor and the committee had disagreed fundamentally about the design of the course. One the one hand, the professor emphasized a particular organization of content and the use of materials he proposed. His approach precluded integration of the perspectives of the other disciplines represented on the committee. More importantly, the committee was careful to ensure that the structure of the course allowed the explicit mediation of "academic writing, argumentation and cognitive skills" in order to meet the needs of those first-year students whose educational background had ill-prepared them for the particular demands of university study (Graaff, 1998, p. 78). The professor was dismissive of this approach as patronizing students. His argument was that the course should expose students to African debates framed by African scholars. References he used included the work of Cheikh Anta Diop. The committee, on the other hand, thought that the appropriate approach to take was that of emphasizing skills development.

The controversy that followed this latter development is now a subject of national and international discussion. The professor protested at his suspension from the committee and withheld his services from all university duties except teaching. The issue reached the vice-chancellor's office, and various academic and administrative diplomats were asked to intercede. Apologies from members of the administration in the faculty followed and a public meeting took place in which the matter was fiercely debated.

It is not our intention to rehearse the arguments made in the course of what has now come to be known as the "great debate." What is important to draw attention to, however, in the context of the move toward programs at UCT, are issues of academic freedom and excellence, the role of the administration in academic affairs, and the relationship of pedagogy to content. At first glance these issues seem not to be about globalization. We argue that they are profoundly so. Even as the university seeks to respond to economic and academic forces that have their origin in the globalized arena, so too it finds itself constrained by the specificity of its local context, where local issues themselves become the object of the institution's attention.

CONCLUSION

While a micro-reading of the "great debate" shows the persistence of contestation in the quotidian of academic practice, read more expansively the dispute can be interpreted as a destabilization of the process of assimilation of the globalization discourse. Totalizing as the programmatic thrust might appear to be, what the dispute revealed was the continued existence and power of alternative projects deep within the institution. While the debate was being conducted within the framework of program renewal, the participants showed how hegemonic discursive thrusts (top-down policies in management language) take place in fields that are inhabited by already existing disputes and new disputes. The point is that while new terms of engagement (new regimens of power are installed to oversee the process of programization or new panoptica are devised) are being established, existing and/or new social projects continue to operate within the social space framed by the dominant discourse, which not only delays the progress of the intervention, but unsettles it. As the programs are installed in terms of the criteria of coherence, what constitutes coherence is placed under intense debate. Whose notions of coherence determine what goes into a program? Who decides that programs have met the criteria, administrators or disciplinary experts? How do questions get resolved around debates about pedagogy versus content? These are local questions that have the power to inhibit the momentum of the new hegemonic discourse.

Underlying the discussion is the motif of accountability. The new programs are surrounded by the familiar discursive markers of the globalized discourse. Prominent among these, is the signifier "accountability." The notion of accountability has become the foremost tool in the cut and thrust of the new academy and is invoked primarily in relation to funding. The pervasive and increasingly sophisticated debate around quality assurance and performance indicators is perhaps the most telling manifestation of this trend (see Bunting, 1997). What is done in universities and in the higher education sector as a whole cannot be divorced from other, wider social imperatives. The university is not an independent and free-floating structure; it is tied up with the destiny of the wider society. The logic upon which this argument rests is fundamentally that the people and their various proxies, the state, and the university authorities, need to know how their funds are being disbursed and wish to have those funds deployed meaningfully and equitably: "He who pays the piper calls the tune."

While there cannot be much argument against the idea that public institutions such as universities in South Africa have to be accountable, particularly financially, notions such as accountability are profoundly complex. Built into accountability as a signifier are ambiguities. Aside from meeting the needs of the market, programs at UCT have been presented in the rhetorical address of the university seeking to be a "world-class African university." This throws up distinctive possibilities and provides the space for the interrogation and indeed development of contradictory lines of thought and action right within the heart of the project of globalization. If programs do indeed represent the globalization of the South African university, they do so constrained by localized discourse. The address of the new order is held within the bounds of, on the one hand, the necessity for linking with the global market and, on the other, the need to deal with the local imperatives of redress, access, inclusion, and indigenization. The terms of the phrase a "world-class African university" simultaneously place the university in its international context and outside of it. The phrase promotes the possibility for the continued hegemony of the globalized world, but at the same time sets in place the possibility for the entry of rival local discourses. *African* as a signifier is not without its portent and power and brings into operation powerful rival accountability paradigms. Where is "Africa" and what is Africa in the programs becomes the question.

The curriculum debate at UCT is a fundamental expression of the ambiguity of accountability and brings to the very fore the complex question of the identity of the university. If it is to be international, and that seems an easily resolved part of the conundrum, the question is how, simultaneously, it is to become a vehicle for local issues and for promoting local identities. It is here that globalization forces encounter their strongest, and sometimes most unlikely, opposition. While the thrust of the globalized discourse is to operate in a homogenized and universalized world, local conditions have their own dynamics, and these dynamics do not operate independently of those that play themselves out internationally. What the juxtaposition of the local and the international produces is a national setting, which at one level has features that allow one to recognize it as a member of the global world, but at other levels, has features that demonstrate that it is profoundly distinct. At some moments the international discourse takes precedence, and at others the local debates take central stage. Often, the context is characterized by a complex dialogue between the globalized and the local, which creates new alliances and new divides.

What this argument sets up is the recognition that neither the global nor the local discourses are unfettered discourses. As Cloete et al. (1998, p. 35) say, "every individual in the world partakes of both the local and the global, albeit highly unevenly." In the case of the programmatic debate in South Africa, what we see is a discursive landscape dominated by the new demands of the epoch. Everywhere, however, are the insistent claims of the local; as the global seeks to assert itself, so the local seeks to pull it back.

NOTES

1. The South African higher education system is made up of the following structures: comprehensive universities, which emphasize, to different degrees, research and teaching; technikons, which seek to foster the development of technology; and a range of professional colleges aimed at education, nursing, agriculture, vocations, and so on. The sector has traditionally been hierarchically structured with universities at the top and vocational colleges at the bottom. The new South African Qualifications Authority, premised on the notion of lifelong learning, is seeking to build into the system increased possibilities for movement between the sectors and cross-articulation between different qualification levels.

2. Massification in Kraak's terms needs to be understood as a response to the demands for an expanded as opposed to a differentiated economic sector where differentiation is associated with the globalized post-Fordist labor process.

3. As Gillard (1999), a senior administrator, commented, students had accompanied a senior university deputy vice-chancellor on an international visit and returned with strong views of how UCT could develop relevant curricula that would articulate more directly with the world of work.

4. One of the subcommittees of the Strategic Planning Committee, within an integrated planning system, the Academic Programs Working Group is charged with all matters relating to academic program planning, in consultation with faculty planning committees. However, like many other committees at UCT that are overwhelmingly comprised of academics, the Working Group does not have decision making powers but has to have its recommendations ratified by higher committees including, ultimately, the university's senate and council (Board of Trustees).

REFERENCES

Academic Planning Framework, Interim Report for Discussion. 1996. Policy document, University of Cape Town.

Bertelsen, Eve. 1998. The Real Transformation: The Marketisation of Higher Education. *Social Dynamics*, vol. 24, no. 2, pp. 130–58.

Bunting, Ian. 1997. Performance Indicators for South Africa's Education Systems. *Social Dynamics*, vol. 23, no. 1. pp. 139–53.

Castells, Manuel. 1997. *The Power of Identity: The Information Age: Economy, Society and Culture*, vol. 2. Oxford: Blackwell.

Cloete, Nico. 1997. *Quality: Conceptions, Contestations and Comments*. Paper delivered at the African Regional Consultation Preparatory to the World Conference on Higher Education, Dakar, Senegal. <http://star.hsrc.ac.za/chet/debates/quality.html>.

———, Michael Cross, Johan Muller, and Sury Pillay. 1998. Culture, Identity and the Role of Higher Education in Building Democracy in South Africa. In Michael Cross, Nico Cloete, Edgar F. Beckham, Ann Harper, Jaya Indiresan, and Caryn Musil (eds.), *Diversity and Unity: The Role of Higher Education in Building Democracy*. Cape Town: Maskew Miller Longman, pp. 20–48.

Cooper, David. 1997. Introduction: Comments on the "Market" and/or "Development" University with Respect to UCT. Discussions on Changing Research Cultures. *Social Dynamics*, vol. 23, no. 1, pp. 23–41.

Currie, Jan. 1998. Globalization Practices and the Professoriate in Anglo-Pacific and North American Universities. *Comparative Education Review*, vol. 2, no 1, pp. 15–29.

Ensor, Paula. 1998. Access, Coherence and Relevance: Debating Curriculum in Higher Education. *Social Dynamics*, vol. 24, no. 2, pp. 93–105.

Giddens, Anthony. 1990. *The Consequences of Modernity*. Cambridge, UK: Polity Press.

Gillard, Erica. 1998. Programmes-Based Approach to Planning at the University of Cape Town. In open learning through distance education, 3rd Quarter, University of Cape Town.

———. 1999 (February 3). Interview conducted in Cape Town, South Africa.

Graaff, Johan. 1998. Pandering to Pedagogy or Consumed by Content: Brief Thoughts on Mahmood Mamdani's "Teaching Africa at Post-Apartheid University of Cape Town." *Social Dynamics*, vol. 24, no. 2, pp. 76–85.

Hall, Martin. 1998a. Teaching Africa at the Post-Apartheid University of Cape Town: A Response, *Social Dynamics*, vol. 24, no. 2, pp. 33–39.

———. 1998b. Bantu Education? A Reply to Mahmood Mamdani. *Social Dynamics*, vol. 24, no. 2, pp. 86–92.

Jameson, Fredric. 1991. *Post-modernism, or, the Cultural Logic of Late Capitalism*. London: Verso; and Durham, NC: Duke University Press.

Jansen, Jonathan. 1998. But Our Natives Are Different! Race, Knowledge and Power in the Academy. *Social Dynamics*, vol. 24, no. 2, pp. 106–16.

Kishun, Roshen. 1998. Internationalization in South Africa. Memo.

Kraak, André. 1997. Globalisation, Changes in Knowledge Production, and the Transformation of Higher Education. In Nico Cloete, Johan Muller, Malegapuru W. Makgoba, and Donald Ekong (eds.), *Knowledge, Identity and Curriculum Transformation in South Africa*. Cape Town: Maskew Miller Longman, pp. 51–76.

McGrew, Anthony. 1992. A Global Society? in Stuart Hall, David Held, and Anthony McGrew (eds.), *Modernity and its Futures*. Cambridge, UK: Polity Press in association with Blackwell Publishers and the Open University, pp. 61–116.

Mamdani, Mahmood. 1998a. Teaching Africa at the Post-Apartheid University of Cape Town: A Critical View of the "Introduction to Africa" Core Course in the Social Science and Humanities Faculty's Foundation Semester, 1998. *Social Dynamics*, vol. 24, no. 2, pp. 1–32.

————. 1998b. Is African Studies to Be Turned into a New Home for Bantu Education at UCT? *Social Dynamics*, vol. 24, no. 2, pp. 63–75.

————. 1998c (May 13). When Does a Settler Become a Native? Reflections of the Colonial Roots of Citizenship in Equatorial and South Africa. Inaugural Lecture, University of Cape Town.

Muller, Johan. 1998. Editorial Introduction. *Social Dynamics*, vol. 24, no. 2, pp. i–vi.

NCHE. 1996. *Report: A Framework for Transformation*. Pretoria: Government Printer.

Orr, Liesl. 1997. Globalization and Universities: Towards the "Market University?" *Social Dynamics*, vol. 23, no. 1, pp. 42–67.

Programme Planning and Implementation within UCT's Academic Planning Framework 1998. Internal UCT memorandum from the Head of the Academic Planning Department to Faculties.

Scott, Peter. 1997. Changes in Knowledge Production and Dissemination in the Context of Globalisation. Nico Cloete, Johan Muller, Malegapuru W. Makgoba, and Donald Ekong (eds.), *Knowledge, Identity and Curriculum Transformation in South Africa*. Cape Town: Maskew Miller Longman, pp. 17–42.

Subotzky, George. 1997. Pursuing Both Global Competitiveness and National Redistributive Development: Implications and Opportunities for South Africa's Historically Black Universities. *Social Dynamics*, vol. 23, no 1, pp. 102–39.

Welch, Anthony. 1998. The End of Certainty: The Academic Profession and the Challenge of Change. *Comparative Education Review*, vol. 2, no. 1, pp. 1–14.

16

The Impacts of Globalization on Education in Malaysia

Molly N. N. Lee

A quick survey of recent educational reforms in Malaysia includes the corporatization of public universities, establishment of branch campuses by foreign universities, mushrooming of transnational education programs in private colleges, setting up of "smart schools," emphasis on moral education, teaching of Islamic science in schools, and introduction of "double promotion" in primary schools. An obvious question would be, What has brought about these educational changes? Educational changes do not occur in a void, nor do educational policies materialize out of thin air. There is always a particular ideological and political climate and a social and economic context, which together influence the shape and timing of educational policies as well as their outcomes (Taylor et al., 1997).

Much that has been written about educational reforms in Malaysia tends to focus on socioeconomic and political forces internal to the country (Jasbir and Mukherjee, 1993; Lee, 1997a; Santhiram, 1997; Aziah, 1987). However, educational changes are only partially conditioned by internal forces. As some commentators point out, we should "move away from social change conceived as the internal development of societies to focusing on changes as the outcomes of struggles between the members of a figuration of interdependent and competing nation-states" (Featherstone and Lash, 1995, p. 2). We should also consider the influences of global trends on educational changes that have occurred in a particular country. As Archer notes (1991), global processes are now partly constitutive of local realities, so that local contexts cannot be completely understood in strictly local terms. But this does not mean these global trends offer a sufficient explanation for local policies either. Global trends provide a source of policy borrowing and a backdrop of policy choices. However, they are adapted to and blended with local conditions and options in a fluid and contingent policy process (Christie, 1996).

GLOBAL INFLUENCES

Many of the educational changes in Malaysia have been very much influenced by globalization, which "refers to all those processes by which the peoples of the world are incorporated into a single world society, global society" (Albrow, 1990, p. 9). Globalization can be viewed as a multidimensional process, which unfolds in realms such as the global economy, global politics, global communications, and worldwide cultural standardization and hybridization (Pieterse, 1995). The revolution in global communications, together with multinational investment, has given huge impetus to cultural globalization. The globalization of culture has been alluded to by many writers (Waters, 1995; Robertson, 1992; Featherstone, 1990), including a United Nations Educational, Scientific, and Cultural Organization (UNESCO) report that notes, "More generally, the same forces—trade, transport and communications—which are driving the globalization of science and technology are also driving the globalization of culture and are now reinforced by the relaxation of global political tensions" (UNESCO, 1991, pp. 69–70).

What have made the globalization process feasible were, of course, the communications and information revolutions, combined with an increased mobility of people, money, services, goods, and images (Appaduria, 1990). Likewise, Malaysia has been incorporated into the world capitalist economy, affected by technological changes, and assimilated into the global culture within which education operates.

According to Davies and Guppy (1997), there are two sets of arguments that use globalization as a conceptual framework for comprehending pan-national changes in education; one is "economic globalization," and the other is "global rationalization." The economic globalization perspective focuses on the ascendancy of the global marketplace in shaping educational reform. The opening up of world markets and the relatively free movement of capital and technology offer great potential for economic growth. However, the effects of globalization on a country's development potential depend critically on its educational or human resource capacity (Stewart, 1996). New market demands for better quality products and high technology jobs require a very skilled labor force, and rapidly changing tastes result in flexible and specialized production and greater worker responsibility.

Therefore, schools must adjust to this economic restructuring by making changes in the goals and contents of the learning process. Ilon (1994) notes that such changes would increase the need for a global curriculum, that is, "a curriculum emphasizing information gathering, manipulation, management, and creation" (p. 99). Furthermore, this economic transformation would also require curricula that concentrate on "consumer relations, problem solving, entrepreneurialism, and cross-cultural multi-skilling" (Davies and Guppy, 1997, p. 439). Basically, the need for change in education is largely cast in economic terms and particularly in relation to the preparation of a workforce and competition with other countries.

On the other hand, global rationalization stresses on the idea of a system of world culture. According to Meyer (1980), the world system is not simply a collection of nation-states engaged in economic exchange, but also an overarching social system of institutional rules and structural properties. These rules define the parameters within which nations operate and strongly influence the behavior of nations. At the same time, the behavior of nations helps to shape the institutional structure and pushes its evolution in new directions. Indeed, a central feature of the institutional perspective is its emphasis on evolving world cultural rules as a crucial aspect of the development of modern nation-states. As certain values and beliefs become institutionalized in the world polity, more and more nation-states are pressured to accommodate, at least symbolically, these cultural imperatives, since compliance with them is an important source of legitimacy and resources. According to this line of argument, the institutionalization of schools into rationalized bureaucratic forms is very much part of the world culture. Empirical studies have shown that there is a continual worldwide convergence of educational systems and curricula. Not only are subjects such as mathematics, science, and social studies standard, but the number of classroom hours devoted to each is almost identical across nation-states (Benavot et al., 1991; Kamens et al., 1996). Similarly, educational reforms like multicultural education, skill-centered curriculum, and standardized testing that have crossed national boundaries are very much part of the globalization process (Davies and Guppy, 1997).

Both economic globalization and global rationalization seem to point to processes of institutional convergence, but does it mean that all educational systems are going to be very similar because of increasing global influences? No doubt, in recent years, national educational systems may have become more porous, and educational reforms across nations may bear remarkable similarity because there has been much policy "borrowing," "transfer," or "copying," which "leads to universalising tendencies in educational reform" (Halpin, 1994, p. 204). As Ball (1998) observes, "National policy making is inevitably a process of bricolage: a matter of borrowing and copying bits and pieces of ideas from elsewhere, drawing upon and amending locally tried and tested approaches, cannibalizing theories, research, trends and fashions and not infrequently flailing around for anything at all that looks as though it might work" (p. 126).

However, this does not mean that there is a full-scale globalization of education and that the world has become more uniform and homogenized through a technological, commercial, and cultural synchronization emanating from the West. Rather, what we can observe is a plurality of national responses to the global forces. According to Pieterse (1995), globalization is a process of hybridization that gives rise to unique responses from different nation-states to global trends originating from various metropolitan centers, which are not necessary located in the West.

Cultural theorists are divided as to whether globalization means cultural standardization or increasing diversity. The most plausible deduction seems to be that it means both at the same time. This double movement produces cultural homogenization and, at the same time, a wide range of cultural hybrids and mixes (Green, 1997). Similarly, educational reforms are shaped by a complex interaction of local and global forces. It would be a mistake to view global influences simply as impositions on local contexts, since this would overlook the agency of local actors as well as different forms that adaptation to local context brings (Christie, 1996). Usually, policy ideas are received and interpreted differently within different national and cultural contexts. Therefore, in our attempts to understand education changes and policies, we need to examine how policy ideas are being "recontextualized" in specific national settings thus giving rise to local variations of generic policies (Ball, 1998).

IMPACTS ON NATIONAL CONTEXT

Malaysia has been a rapidly developing economy and was fast becoming industrialized until it was hit by the "East Asian economic crisis" that began in mid-1997. Under the National Front government, Malaysia has embarked on a state-directed development program that has transformed a previously commodity-export-based economy into an industrialized economy. In the past, Malaysia had depended on its natural resources like tin, oil, timber and agricultural products like rubber, oil palm, and cocoa, but now has joined the other newly industrializing economies in East Asia by expanding its manufacturing and service sectors. Malaysia has aggressively pursued an export-oriented growth strategy by encouraging foreign investments in its economy.

The accelerating pace of globalization of economy has been at the base of Malaysia's economic growth over the past two decades. The Malaysian economy interfaced with the global economy in what has been described as the "international division of labor." Multinational corporations from advanced countries went in search of politically stable offshore production sites and cheap labor in Third World countries, and in return they offered mass employment to the host countries. As a result of concerted effort to attract the multinational corporations by offering the comparative advantages of lower wages, the prohibition of unionization among a new industrial labor force, sound physical and social infrastructure, fiscal tax, and other incentives, the Malaysian economy became integrated with the globalization of industrial production (Khoo, forthcoming). A major measure taken by Malaysia to promote manufactured exports was the establishment of Free Trade Zones (FTZs) from 1971 onward. Nearly three-quarters of the FTZ firms are foreign-owned,[1] accounting for more than 90 percent of the total direct employment within the FTZs (Ariff, 1991). Much of the foreign direct investment (FDI) is in the electrical and electronic products, rubber products, and textile and wood products industries. Demands for these products come from export markets such as the United States, Singapore, Japan, and the People's Republic of China.

In the early 1980s, Malaysia ventured into a heavy industrialization drive based on the production of steel, automobiles, motorcycle engines, and cement. This heavy industrialization program was a combined effort of state investment (represented by HICOM, the Heavy Industries Corporation of Malaysia), "East Asian technology" (sourced from Japanese and South Korean firms through joint ventures), and indigenous management (Machado, 1994). This major shift in the industrialization program is a response to meet the challenges of a competitive global trading environment. To enhance the country's competitiveness at the present stage of industrialization, steps must be taken to increase the supply of skilled workers as well as upgrade technological capacity. The new emphasis is to develop high value-added, capital-intensive, and export industries, and the objective is to shift toward skill-intensive and high-technology industries producing more varied, better-designed, and competitive products that meet the demand of global markets. The Seventh Malaysia Plan (1996–2000) states, "In meeting the challenges arising from increased globalization and continued tightness in the labor market, priority will continue to be accorded to improving the competitiveness of industries through increases in productivity, research and development as well as the provision of adequate supporting infrastructure" (Malaysia, 1996, p. 263).

The move toward sophisticated technology industries has been most significant in the field of information technology (IT), which has been recognized as a strategic enabling tool to support the growth of the Malaysian economy as information has become the cutting edge of global competition. Malaysia has taken the initial step to promote the country as the IT hub of the region by establishing the fifteen by forty kilometer Multimedia Super Corridor (MSC) south of Kuala Lumpur (Malaysia, 1996). The MSC will have an information superhighway equipped with state-of-the-art telecommunications infrastructure comprising fiber optics, satellite, and wireless technology. World-class multimedia companies will be encouraged to locate in the MSC to undertake remote manufacturing and introduce high value-added IT goods and services, enabling Malaysia to become an IT hub. This implies that there will be a growing demand for a computer-literate workforce as well as professionals in specialized fields conversant with new technologies and their applications. Computer education and training programs will have to be intensified and expanded to cover all schools and higher education and training institutions. To compete in the global market, Malaysia needs to produce cadres of highly trained scientific and management personnel, as well as a highly productive and flexible workforce.

Global forces do not operate only in the economic sphere, nor do they originate only from the West. As discussed in the previous section, cultural globalization is occurring at the same time as economic globalization, and religion is very much a critical ingredient of cultural globalization (Robertson, 1991). In recent decades, one has witnessed the spread of Islamic resurgence in many Muslim countries,[2] including Malaysia. The intellectual characteristics of this global trend are the fervent belief that society should be organized on the bases of Islamic religion, advocacy of greater political freedom, and a general aversion to Western civilization (Chandra, 1987). The spread of Islamic revivalism has been attributed to various factors by different scholars.[3] According to Turner (1991), the fundamentalist revival in Islam is an example of the relativizing effect of globalization. He maintains that Western modernization in either its capitalistic or Marxist forms failed to deliver either material benefits or a coherent system of meanings to the Islamic world. Indeed, rapid industrialization and urbanization appeared to offer only stark inequality between the populace and the politically dominant elite. Islamic revivalism in various Muslim countries marks a rejection of Western modernization and secularism. In the context of Malaysia, the intra-ethnic group conflict among the Malays has resulted in the use of Islam as a political ideology both to maintain the status quo and to demand fundamental change in the political system.[4] Islam has become both an agent and a symbol of the many rapid social changes now occurring in Malaysia.

The manifestations of the Islamic influences take place at two levels: the individual and the organization. At the individual level, there is the rapid diffusion of what is regarded as Islamic attire[5] and a decline in social communication between the sexes among a significant portion of the Muslim population, the widespread use of Islamic forms of greeting,[6] an overt concern about Muslim dietary rules,[7] and strict adherence to religious duties[8] (Chandra, 1987, pp. 2–5). The Malaysian government launched its Islamization program in 1982 by promoting Islamic values such diligence, hard work, discipline, sincerity, honesty, respect, and loyalty in public administration (Mauzy and Milne, 1983) and by setting up Islamic institutions such as an Islamic university and an Islamic bank in 1983, an Islamic Foundation devoted to social welfare, and an Islamic insurance plan. The increased government intervention in Islamic affairs is an indication of the government's desire to increase its legitimacy among Muslims, as well as the impact of the spread of Islamic revivalism throughout the world. This Islamic movement in turn has its influence on what is being taught in schools, resulting in an emphasis on the teaching of moral values throughout the whole curriculum.

IMPACTS ON EDUCATION

What we have discussed so far are the changes that globalization has brought to the economic and social contexts of Malaysia. Now we shall examine, in greater detail, how these changes have influenced the education system in terms of access and equity, curriculum reforms, and higher education.

Access and Equity

The widening access of education to all people is very much part of a global trend that was emphasized at the World Conference on Education for All in Jomtien, Thailand in 1990 (UNESCO, 1989). Following this trend, starting from 1991, Malaysia has offered eleven years[9] of free basic education to every child in the country. Under this new policy, the educational system has changed an elitist secondary education into universal secondary education where all students can proceed to the upper secondary level even though they have performed poorly in the Penilaian Menengah Rendah (PMR) examination.[10] Corresponding to the widening access to education, the Ministry of Education has also taken steps to restructure the educational institutions so as to meet the diverse needs of the students.

Pre-school education and special education have been given more attention under the provision of the 1995 Education Act. With the globalization of the economy, more and more women are joining the workforce, thus resulting in the fast expansion of childcare centers and kindergartens. In 1998, there were 10,381 registered kindergartens with an enrollment of 446,302 children (*The Star*, 1999). To meet the needs of special children, the Ministry of Education planned to build thirty-one special schools throughout the country for hearing and visually impaired children and those with learning difficulties (Lee, 1998a). Another initiative has been the introduction of the "double promotion" for gifted children from Primary 3 to Primary 5, so that they spend only five years in primary schools instead of six. However, unlike other countries, there are no special programs for gifted children, other than shortening the primary school program for them by one year.

At the upper secondary level, the move toward universal secondary education resulted in a number of students who are academically weak being promoted to Form 4. To respond to the needs of these weak students, the Ministry of Education plans to revamp the Sijil Pelajaran Malaysia (SPM) examination[11] system by offering more subject choices and changing it from a rigid system that requires students to take between eight to ten subjects in the science or arts stream into an "open-certificate" system (*The Star*, 1998). Under the open-certificate system, students need to take six core subjects,[12] and they can choose two or more optional subjects based on their capabilities. By lengthening the provision of basic education from nine to eleven years, it is hoped that Malaysia will have a literate workforce to compete in the global economy and that it will subscribe to the universal ideology that equality of educational opportunity is one of the basic human rights.

The issue of social justice through education has been very much part of education discourse everywhere in the world. In fact, with the introduction of mass schooling, it was hoped that everyone would be given an opportunity for social improvement. However, this easy assumption was far from validated in reality, and thus it was challenged by educators, social activists, and some government officials worldwide. Governments today are increasingly forced to acknowledge that they have an important role to play in devising policies and programs that go beyond access, addressing some of the basic causes and special needs of the educationally disadvantaged.

In countries with culturally diverse populations, like Malaysia,[13] multicultural education is a very important aspect of policy making. There are different approaches to the task of constructing multicultural education (Lynch, 1986). The possible policies that can be pursued by governments range from assimilation of minority groups into the values and social norms of the majority group, to the integration of different groups until the divisive aspects of each group have been whittled away and a new culture has been created, to cultural pluralism that recognizes the cultural and social diversity of the different ethnic groups but seeks to create a political and economic unity from them (Watson, 1980).

Malaysia has opted for the integration approach. Education is seen as a means of redressing the ethnic imbalances and of creating a sense of national unity among the diverse ethnic groups. Ever since independence in 1957, educational policies have been concerned with how to bring about racial harmony and national identity in a national system of education and how to raise the economic status of Bumiputeras.

Under the provision of the 1961 Education Act, Bahasa Malaysia, which is the national language, became the main medium of instruction in all national schools. However, the minority groups had managed to negotiate with the Malay ruling class to allow for the provision of Chinese and Tamil primary schools with public funding. Furthermore, minority students can study their own mother tongue (Pupils' Own Language) as an optional subject at the secondary level. To foster national unity, all national schools are required to follow a common curriculum and a common set of public examinations. In actual fact, the educational system in Malaysia is highly centralized, with most of the major decisions and policy making taking place at the Ministry of Education in the capital city.

Another set of equity issues deals with access to higher education, for the Malaysian government views it as a means of restructuring the society to eliminate the identification of ethnic community with economic functions (Lee, 1997b). The restructuring of the Malaysian society has been one of the primary objectives of the New Economic Policy implemented in 1970, which involved providing more educational opportunities to the economically disadvantaged Bumiputeras so that there would be greater Bumiputera representation in the various professions and occupations in the modern sector. To achieve this objective, the government implemented a racial quota system for the admission of students into public tertiary education institutions. Besides this, the government also implemented various affirmative action policies to reduce the interethnic differences in educational attainment by giving government scholarships to Bumiputra students, establishing special secondary schools and programs to prepare them for the professional and technical fields. These policy initiatives were based on Rawls's theory of social justice, which has been enormously influential in the 1960s and 1970s in countries like the United States, India, and Sri Lanka. Rawls (1972) suggests that there should be equal distribution of primary social goods, unless unequal distribution is to the advantage of the least favored. He also maintains that the state has a special responsibility to create policy initiatives directed toward removing barriers, which prevent equity, access, and participation, arising from unequal power relations.

These various sets of educational policies pertaining to access and equity reflect the influence of worldwide concerns on educational opportunities, social justice, multicultural education, and national integration. As Malaysia interfaces with the global economy, it is paramount that the dominant ethnic group participates in the modern economy, which explains the government's effort to implement various affirmative action policies in favor of the Bumiputeras. The issues of access and the redistribution of educational opportunities are only part of the public discourse on education, for another important aspect is what is being taught in schools under the rubric of school curriculum.

Curriculum Reforms

Besides the democratization of education, another set of policy initiatives is directed toward the improvement of the quality of education, pupils' educational achievement, and school effectiveness. Starting from 1982, the school curriculum was totally revamped from primary level right up to upper secondary level in all Malaysian national schools. Following the global trends on "back to the basics," "child-centered curriculum," and the philosophy of an "all-rounded development of the individual," the New Primary School Curriculum[14] was implemented, giving emphasis to the acquisition of basic skills and knowledge through direct experiences, encouraging active involvement of pupils in various learning activities, using a variety of instruction materials, and practicing a variety of pupil groupings. This new curriculum also recognized the need to cater to different levels of ability among pupils by means of remedial and enrichment programs and the practice of continual assessment of the child's progress.

In 1988, the Integrated Secondary School Curriculum[15] was introduced as a continuation of the curriculum reform efforts. The emphasis of this new curriculum is on "integration," which stresses the teaching of language and noble values across the curriculum. Examples of such noble values are compassion, self-reliance, humility, honesty, diligence, cooperation, love, and justice. The importance of values in education is reinforced by the introduction of new subjects like moral education (for non-Muslim students) and Islamic studies (for Muslim students). The penetration of Islamic influence in schools can be further seen in the teaching of Islamic science, which stresses the teaching of moral values through science by highlighting the limitations as well as the strengths of science and relating science to the local environment and societal needs (Lee, 1992; Loo, 1996; Tan, 1997). As in many other countries, including the United States, there is a continuing debate as to whether high school science should teach "creation science," "evolution science," or both (Montagu, 1984). Malaysia has chosen the option of not teaching Darwin's evolutionary theory in schools because it is considered contradictory to the Islamic belief in Allah as the creator of the universe. In addition, a number of religious schools that place much emphasis on Islamic teaching—many of these are single-sex schools—have been established in line with the Islamic resurgence in the country. The Islamic influence in Malaysian schools can be seen as a defensive response to the onslaught of Western influences in all spheres of social life, which have been brought about by the process of globalization.

Another controversial issue is the role of the English language in the school curriculum. One of the major reforms in the 1970s was the conversion of all English-medium schools in Malaysia into Malay-medium. Since then, English has been taught in schools as a second language. As expected, there has been a general decline in the standard of English in the country, which is now causing great concern among the political leaders and employers in the commercial sectors. With the globalization of the economy, the importance of English as an international language for trade and the transfer of scientific knowledge and technical know-how cannot be further ignored. This realization has led the Ministry of Education to implement policy initiatives to arrest the decline of English in schools. In 1995, requirements for the English paper for the SPM examination increased the level of difficulty by incorporating some elements from the 1119 English paper[16] (*The Star*, 1997). Moreover, in December 1998, the minister of education announced that all pre-university students will have to sit for a special test called the Malaysian University English Test (MUET) from 1999 onward (*The Star*, 1998). As it is, the renewed emphasis on the importance of English is reflected in the 1996 Private Higher Educational Institutions Act, which allows courses to be taught in English with the approval of the minister of education. This policy shift away from the insistence on using Bahasa Malaysia as the main medium of instruction in earlier educational policies accounts for the need to produce a "globally oriented" workforce for the Malaysian economy. In making this shift, the Malaysian government has acknowledged a global imperative, which makes a national priority secondary.

In line with the Multimedia Super Corridor project and recent developments in educational technology, the Ministry of Education launched the Smart School project in February 1997 to prepare students for the information age. Under this project, ninety "smart schools" are to be set up by January 1999, and all schools will be converted into smart schools by the year 2010 (*The Star*, 1997). The concept of the smart school is one where learning is enhanced by the use of extensive multimedia technology. Besides the establishment of smart schools, efforts have been directed to promote computer studies, the use of information technology in distance education, virtual libraries, and the virtual university. All these recent educational developments can be attributed to technological change in the global context. Furthermore, the use of information technology in education can cause the gap between the "have" and "have-nots" to become even wider in terms of access to information.

However, there are two other global concerns, which do not seem to have had any effect on the Malaysian education system. One is the concern for the degradation of the environment and the other is the AIDS epidemic. None of the curriculum reforms that have occurred in Malaysian schools has given much attention to either environmental education or sex education. Although lip service has been given to some environmental issues, environmental education as a separate subject has not been introduced in the schools for fear of overloading the curriculum. Instead, teachers are told to incorporate environmental issues in the teaching of biology and geography. As for sex education, it is such a controversial issue among different groups of people, especially between the *ulama* (Islamic religious leaders) and the secular, that no definite policy has been formulated despite continuing public discourse on the matter.

Higher Education

In studying the globalizing practices in Anglo-Pacific and North American universities, Currie (1998) identifies a few interesting trends, which include a shift from elite to mass higher education, the privatization of higher education, the practice of corporate managerialism, and the spread of transnational education. Not surprisingly, the impacts of all these trends are found in Malaysia. Higher education in Malaysia may have started with a single university, the University of Malaya in 1962, but as of 1999, there are in existence ten public universities, nine private universities, six polytechnics, thirty-three teacher-training colleges, and 415 private colleges. The rapid expansion of higher education has been fueled by strong social demand for higher education, seen as the main avenue for social mobility and social justice, and facilitated by the universalization of secondary education (Lee, 1998b). The number of students enrolled in public tertiary institutions more than doubled from 86,330 in 1985 to 189,020 in 1995, whereas those in the private institutions had increased even faster, from about 15,000 in 1985 to 127,594 in 1995 (see table 16.1).

In fact, the increase has been even more pronounced in the past three years as shown by the annual student intake to all the public universities, which has leaped from 21,000 in 1995 to 77,600 in 1998 (Malaysia, 1998). About 30 percent of the development budget of the Ministry of Education is spent on higher education. Despite this large allocation, the Ministry of Education is constantly faced with tight budgetary constraints in meeting the ever-increasing demand for tertiary education. To overcome this problem, the government has been forced to seek alternative means of financing higher education. It is in this context that corporatization of public universities and the privatization of higher education have emerged as possible solutions. As in other countries, the major factor affecting universities has been the "economic ideology prevalent in globalization that calls for the primacy of the market, privatization, and a reduced role for the public sphere" (Currie, 1998, p. 17).

In 1995, the Universities and University Colleges Act 1971 (UCCA) was amended to lay the groundwork for all public universities to be corporatized. Under the new UCCA amendments, a board of directors would replace the university council, and the size of the university senate would be reduced from approximately three hundred members to about forty (Malaysia, 1995). By 1998, five of the public universities had been corporatized.[17] By corporatization, the public universities are freed from the shackles of government bureaucratic provision and would be run like business corporations. Corporatized universities are empowered to borrow money, enter into business ventures, raise endowments, set up companies, and acquire and hold investment shares. The government would continue to own most of the universities' existing assets and to provide development funds for new programs and expensive capital projects. But the corporatized universities have to shoulder the heavy burden of raising a major portion of their operating costs. Furthermore, these universities are expected to adopt a whole range of symbolic trappings of "corporate culture" like mission statement, strategic plans, total quality management (TQM), right-sizing, multi-skilling, and staff development. These management changes are designed to allow the universities greater financial and administrative autonomy. It is also expected that the adoption of business-like approaches will result in financial cost savings; increased administrative efficiencies; and, at the same time, arrest the "brain drain" among academic staff through the offering of competitive market remuneration. This policy shift reflects the global trend that higher education institutions are increasingly required to secure additional funds from external sources like students and industries, and to reduce dependence on the government.

Another alternative means of financing higher education is through privatization. Privatization means a reduction in the level of state provision, and a corresponding encouragement of the expansion of private provision. Since the 1980s, Malaysia has been following the global trend of privatization by privatizing the provision of many public utilities and infrastructure services like telecommunications, postal services, electricity, and the railways. The underlying ideology of privatization is based on the belief that the public sector is wasteful, inefficient, and unproductive, while the private sector is deemed as more efficient, effective, and responsive to rapid changes that are needed in the modern world (Walford, 1990). Privatization of education may imply (a) transfer of ownership of public schools; (b) shifting sectoral balance without redesignating existing institutions, that is, converting public institutions into private institutions; and/or (c) increased government funding and support for private schools (Bray, 1996). In the case of Malaysia, privatization of education has to date taken the form of shifting sectoral balance whereby there is a relaxation of restrictions affecting the establishment of private educational institutions. In 1995, about 35 percent of the students enrolled in higher education were enrolled in private institutions (refer to table 16.1).

A unique feature of this rapid expansion of private higher education is the emergence of offshore twinning programs that are offered by foreign universities in local private colleges. Twinning arrangements have a variety of forms, and most of them involve students taking the first one or two years of a degree program within a private college in Malaysia and then completing the remainder of the program in a twinning university overseas, thereby obtaining a degree from the foreign university (Lee, 1998b). These twinning arrangements came about because the Malaysian government did not allow the private colleges to confer degrees until recently. However, with the implementation of the 1996 Private Higher Educational Institutions Act, private universities have been established, and foreign universities are allowed to set up branch campuses in Malaysia. Since the beginning of the Asian economic crisis in 1997, several private colleges have begun to offer the "3 + 0" programs,[18] where students can obtain a foreign degree without having to go overseas.

This emergence of foreign-linked programs reflects a growing trend of transnational education, which means that there is a growing volume of higher education being delivered across national boundaries. In most cases, the curricula used in the transnational education programs are usually imported directly from the foreign institutions, although some institutions do try to adapt some of the curricula to the local context. Education is increasingly becoming commodified. In Australia, transnational education now exceeds wheat as an export earner. In the global context, boundaries around how, where, and under whose authorities education is carried out and certified are becoming less clear as universities, technical, and further education colleges internationalize their campuses, curricula, and teaching staffs. As some commentators astutely asked, "How can governments define their educational purposes and keep track of what is happening in their

Table 16.1   Estimates of Total Numbers of Students at the Tertiary Level, 1985–1995

Type of Institution	Student Enrollment		
	1985	*1990*	*1995*
Public	80,330 (52.5%)	122,340 (53.0%)	189,020 (51.5%)
Overseas	63,000 (38.3%)	73,000 (31.6%)	50,600 (13.8%)
Private	15,000 (9.1%)	35,600 (15.4%)	127,594 (34.7%)
Total	164,330 (100%)	230,940 (100%)	367,214 (100%)

Source: Molly N. N. Lee, Corporatisation, Privatisation, and Internationalisation of Higher Education in Malaysia. Paper presented at the conference on The Role of Private Higher Education in the Twenty-first Century, Boston College, May 27–30, 1998.

systems, given the tangle of institutional links now being created across regions and countries, and given the problems of regulating the borderless frontiers of cyberspace?" (Taylor et al., 1997, p. 74). With the expansion of transnational education, the Malaysian government is faced with the same dilemma. Therefore, in 1997, the Malaysian government set up the National Accreditation Board so that it could regulate the kinds of educational programs that are being offered in the private sector by giving legitimacy to programs it has accredited (*The Star*, 1997).

CONCLUSION

In this chapter, I have argued that an examination of the global forces impinging on education systems is just as essential as an examination of the global economy would be to an understanding of the dynamics of economic development in any one country. In analyzing the impacts of globalization on education, one notices two concurrent but opposing streams: one is homogenization and the other is particularization. While we can identify certain global trends in educational reforms across nations, we should not assume that there is total convergence of educational policies in all educational systems. In fact, the impact of globalization on the policies as well as content and process of education should take into account the sociopolitical and economic context of each nation. What usually emerges is a hybrid of local variations of educational policy ideas that may have originated from various metropolitan centers.

The Malaysian case study shows that many of the educational changes that have occurred are very much influenced by global trends as well as the internal dynamics of social, economic, and political forces. The democratization of education in Malaysia has taken the form of universal secondary education in terms of lengthening the years of basic education from nine to eleven years and by providing differential programs to meet the diverse needs of the students. As for equality of educational opportunities, the Malaysian government has made provision for education in the mother tongues of minority groups, at least at the primary level, and implemented various affirmative action policies to increase Bumiputeras' participation in higher education and employment in the commercial and industrial sectors. Language policies have always been a controversial issue in a multicultural society, but with the globalization of the economy, the importance of English has been re-emphasized in the Malaysian educational system. The Islamic influence from Middle Eastern countries is quite prevalent in Malaysia, especially in recent curriculum reforms with the continual stress on values education. On the other hand, the importance of information technology is recognized in the establishment of "smart schools." At the higher education level, one can observe the rapid expansion of private higher education, the corporatization of public universities, and the spread of transnational education.

Many of the educational changes that have occurred in Malaysia are the result of interaction between global challenge and national response. Whether an ideological belief gets political commitment in a particular setting depends on the interplay of conflict and compromise among diverse interests. Moreover, the translation of policy ideas into actual practice also depends on a whole host of factors like feasibility, resource constraints, bureaucratic routines, time, and the personalities of key actors in the implementation process. How ideas get translated into policies and practices depends greatly on the local settings, and, very often, what may at first appear to be similar policies may end up being quite different practices.

NOTES

1. Most of these foreign-owned firms are from Singapore, Japan, the United Kingdom, and the United States (Ariff, 1991).

2. Examples of such countries are Saudi Arabia, Egypt, Morocco, Pakistan, Afghanistan, Libya, Iran, Iraq, Syria, and Indonesia.

3. See Ayoob (1981), Chandra (1987), Nagata (1984), and Lyon (1979).

4. The two main political parties involved in this religious conflict are the United Malays National Organisation (UMNO) and Parti Islam Se-Malaysia (PAS).

5. Muslim females are supposed to cover their heads when appearing in public by wearing the *tudung*, and Muslim males are supposed to grow beards as their way of emulating the Prophet and his companions.

6. Islamic greetings mean the use of Islamic terminology, usually Arabic, in daily speech.

7. Muslim dietary rules include not only the avoidance of pork but also the avoidance of meat from animals that are not slaughtered in the manner prescribed by the religion.

8. Religious duties involve saying daily prayers, fasting in the month of Ramadhan, paying Zakat (Islamic tax), and performing the *haj* (pilgrimage to Mecca).

9. This eleven years of basic education consists of six years of primary education and five years of secondary education.

10. PMR is the Penilaian Menengah Rendah examination, which is taken at the end of Form 3 (Grade 9).

11. SPM is the Sijil Pelajaran Malaysia examination, which is equivalent to the O-level or the high school diploma, taken at the end of Form 5.

12. The six core subjects are Bahasa Malaysia, English, mathematics, science, history, and Islamic studies or moral education.

13. Malaysia has a population of 20.7 million, out of which 57.8 percent are Bumiputras, 25.6 percent Chinese, 7.2 percent Indians, and 3 percent others. Bumiputra means "native of the soil," and this term is used to include the Malays and other indigenous people in Sabah and Sarawak.

14. This is commonly referred to as KBSR, Kurikulum Baru Sekolah Rendah.

15. This is often referred to as KBSM, Kurikulum Berpaduan Sekolah Menengah.

16. The 1119 English paper is based on an O-level syllabus set by the Cambridge Examination Syndicate in England.

17. Universiti Malaya was corporatized on 1 January 1998, and this was followed by Universiti Kebangsaan Malaysia, Universiti Sains Malaysia, Universiti Putra Malaysia, and Universiti Teknologi Malaysia on 15 March 1998.

18. The "3 + 0" program is the latest variation of twinning programs between a private college and a foreign university where students can take a full degree program from the foreign university (usually three years) in Malaysia without having to fulfill any residential requirements in the foreign campus.

REFERENCES

Albrow, Martin. 1990. Introduction, in Martin Albrow and Elizabeth King (eds.), *Globalization, Knowledge and Society*. London: Sage, pp. 3–13.

Appaduria, Arjun. 1990. Disjuncture and Difference in Global Cultural Economy. In Mike Featherstone (ed.), *Global Culture: Nationalism, Globalization and Modernity*. London: Sage, pp. 295–310.

Archer, Margaret. 1991. Sociology for One World: Unity and Diversity. *International Sociology*, vol. 6, no. 2, pp. 131–47.

Ariff, Mohamed. 1991. *The Malaysian Economy: Pacific Connections*. Singapore: Oxford University Press.

Ayoob, Mohammed. 1981. *The Politics of Islamic Reassertion*. London: Croom Helm.

Aziah Abdul Rahman. 1987. Curriculum Innovation in Malaysia: The Case of the KBSR. Ph.D. thesis, University of London Institute of Education.

Ball, Stephen. 1998. Big Policies/Small World: An Introduction to International Perspectives in Education Policy. *Comparative Education*, vol. 34, no. 2, pp. 119–30.

Benavot, Aaron, Yun-Kyung Cha, David Kamens, John W. Meyer, and Suk-Ying Wong. 1991. Knowledge for the Masses: World Models and National Curricula, 1920–1986. *American Sociological Review*, vol. 56, no. 1, pp. 85–100.

Bray, Mark. 1996. *Privatization of Secondary Education: Issues and Policy Implication*. Paris: UNESCO.

Chandra, Muzaffar. 1987. *Islamic Resurgence in Malaysia*. Kuala Lumpur: Fajar Bakti.

Christie, Pam. 1996. Globalisation and the Curriculum: Proposals for the Integration of Education and Training in South Africa. *International Journal of Educational Development*, vol. 16, no. 4, pp. 407–16.

Currie, Jan. 1998. Globalization Practices and the Professoriate in Anglo-Pacific and North American Universities. *Comparative Education Review*, vol. 42, no. 1, pp. 15–29.

Davies, Scott, and Neil Guppy. 1997. Globalization and Educational Reforms in Anglo-American Democracies. *Comparative Education Review*, vol. 41, no. 4, pp. 435–59.

Featherstone, Mike (ed.). 1990. *Global Culture: Nationalism, Globalization and Modernity*. London: Sage.

Featherstone, Mike, and Scott Lash. 1995. Globalization, Modernity and the Spatialization of Social Theory: An Introduction. In Mike Featherstone, Scott Lash, and Roland Robertson (eds.), *Global Modernities*. London: Sage, pp. 1–24.

Green, Andy. 1997. *Education, Globalization and the Nation State*. New York: St. Martin's.

Halpin, David. 1994. Practices and Prospects in Educational Policy Research. In David

Halpin and Barry Troyna (eds.), *Researching Educational Policy: Ethical and Methodological Issues*. London: Falmer Press, pp. 198–206.

Ilon, Lynn. 1994. Structural Adjustment and Education: Adapting to a Growing Global Market. *International Journal of Educational Development*, vol. 14, no. 2, pp. 95–108.

Jasbir, Singh, and Hena Mukherjee. 1993. Education and National Integration in Malaysia: Stocktaking Thirty Years after Independence. *International Journal of Educational Development*, vol. 13, no. 2, pp. 89–102.

Kamens, David, John W. Meyer, Aaron Benavot. 1996. Worldwide Patterns in Academic Secondary Education Curricula. *Comparative Education Review*, vol. 40, no. 2, pp. 116–38.

Khoo, Boo Teik. Forthcoming. Economic Nationalism and its Discontent: Malaysian Political Economy after July 1997. In Richard Robinson, Kanishka Jayasuriya, Mark Beeson, and Hyuk Rae Kim (eds.), *From Miracle to Meltdown: The End of Asian Capitalism?* London: Routledge.

Lee, Molly N. N. 1992. School Science Curriculum Reforms in Malaysia: World Influences and National Context. *International Journal of Science Education*, vol. 14, no. 3, pp. 249–63.

———. 1997a. Education and the State: Malaysia after NEP. *Asia Pacific Journal of Education*, vol. 17, no. 1, pp. 27–40.

———. 1997b. Malaysia. In Gerard A. Postiglione and Grace C. L. Mak (eds.), *Asian Higher Education: An International Handbook and Reference Guide*. Westport, CT: Greenwood, pp.173–97.

———. 1998a. Malaysia: Review of Educational Events in 1997. *Asia Pacific Journal of Education*, vol. 18, no. 2, pp. 87–93.

———. 1998b (May 27–30). Corporatisation, Privatisation, and Internationalisation of Higher Education in Malaysia. Paper presented at the conference on The Role of Private Higher Education in the Twenty-first Century, Boston College.

Loo, Seng Piew. 1996. The Four Horsemen of Islamic Science: A Critical Analysis. *International Journal of Science Education*, vol. 18, no. 3, pp. 285–94.

Lynch, James. 1986. *Multicultural Education: Principles and Practices*. London: Routledge and Keagan Paul.

Lyon, Margo L. 1979. The Dakwah Movement in Malaysia. *Review of Indonesian and Malaysian Affairs*, vol. 13, no. 2, pp. 34–45.

Machado, Kit. 1994. Proton and Malaysia's Motor Vehicle Industry: National Industrial Policies and Japanese Regional Production Strategies. In Kwame S. Jomo (ed.), *Japan and Malaysian Development: In the Shadow of the Rising Sun*. London: Routledge, pp. 291–325.

Malaysia. 1995. Universities and University Colleges (Amendment) Act 1995. D.R. 42/95.

———. 1996. *Seventh Malaysia Plan 1996–2000*. Kuala Lumpur: Percetakan Nasional Malaysia Bhd.

———. 1998. Internet: <http://www.moe.gov.my/upstat.html>.

Mauzy, Diane K., and Robert S. Milne. 1983. The Mahathir Administration in Malaysia: Discipline through Islam. *Pacific Affairs*, vol. 56, no. 4, pp. 617–48.

Meyer, John W. 1980. The World Polity and the Authority of the Nation-State. In Albert Bergesen (ed.), *Studies of the Modern World-System*. New York: Academic Press, pp. 109–37.

Montagu, Ashley. 1984. *Science and Creationism.* New York: Oxford University Press.

Nagata, Judith. 1984. *The Reflowering of Malaysian Islam: Modern Religious Radicals and Their Roots.* Vancouver: University of British Columbia Press.

Pieterse, Jan N. 1995. Globalization as Hybridization. In Mike Featherstone, Scott Lash, and Roland Robertson (eds.), *Global Modernities.* London: Sage, pp. 45–68.

Rawls, John. 1972. *A Theory of Justice.* Oxford: Clarendon.

Robertson, Roland. 1991. The Globalization Paradigm: Thinking Globally. In David G. Bromley (ed.), *Religion and the Social Order: New Directions in Theory and Research.* Greenwich, CT: JAI Press.

———. 1992. *Globalization: Social Theory and Global Culture.* London: Sage.

Santhiram, Raman. 1997. Curriculum Materials for National Integration in Malaysia: Match or Mismatch? *Asia Pacific Journal of Education,* vol. 17, no. 2, pp. 7–20.

The Star. 1997 (December 8). What Made the News in '97?

———. 1998 (December 22). Pre-varsity Students to Sit for Special English Test.

———. 1999 (January 3). Regulating Kindergartens.

Stewart, Frances. 1996. Globalisation and Education. *International Journal of Educational Development,* vol. 16, no. 4, pp. 327–33.

Tan, Sok Khim. 1997. Moral Values and Science Teaching: A Malaysian School Curriculum Initiative. *Science and Education,* vol. 6, pp. 555–72.

Taylor, Sandra, Fazal Rizvi, Bob Lingard, and Miriam Henry. 1997. *Educational Policy and the Politics of Change.* London: Routledge.

Turner, Bryan S. 1991. Politics and Culture in Islamic Globalism. In Roland Robertson and William R. Garrett (eds.), *Religion and Global Order.* New York: Paragon, pp. 161–82.

UNESCO. 1989. *Meeting Basic Learning Needs: A New Vision for the 1990s.* Background document for the World Conference on Education for All, Jomtien, Thailand, March 5–9, 1990. Paris: UNESCO.

———. 1991. *World Education Report.* Paris: UNESCO.

Walford, Geoffrey. 1990. *Privatization and Privilege in Education.* London: Routledge.

Waters, Malcolm. 1995. *Globalization.* London: Routledge.

Watson, Keith. 1980. Education and Cultural Pluralism in Southeast Asia: With Special Reference to Peninsular Malaysia. *Comparative Education,* vol. 16, no. 2, pp. 139–203.

17

"Hanging onto the Edge": An Australian Case Study of Women, Universities, and Globalization

Jill Blackmore

Globalization has been the justification for the radical transformation of education in the late 1990s in most Western capitalist states. We are told that we must be more flexible, work harder, and develop our technological skills in order to make education contribute more to national productivity and to achieve international competitiveness. Universities are particularly susceptible to globalization discourses. They have always had an eye to the international and global, as key national sites of knowledge production and dissemination within international scholarly communities as well as sites of innovation in new information technologies, specifically, Internet and e-mail. Jane Kelsey (1995, p. 58) also sees universities as the primary sites of critique of the ideologies of liberal market theory and of alternative ideas, and thus an obvious target for "radical market oriented restructuring."

Globalization is often described as the changes brought about by global markets, new information and communication technologies, flexible labor markets, and mobile populations. While disputably not a new phenomenon, globalization is as much an *awareness* of the possibilities of new markets, ideas, and technologies and its ideological underpinnings, the speed of change, and its power as a discourse are an expression of a different "reality" arising from this awareness—reality in the making (Currie and Vidovich, 1998, p. 3). Some see globalization as putting the state at risk, if not rendering it powerless. Others see globalization offering greater democratic possibilities: global citizenship and global agreements on human rights and communication facilitated by the subversive capacities of the Internet. But at best such options are available only to 20 percent of the world's population, given that the concentration of trade flows still exists between

Western nation-states and within regional borders (e.g., European Union) (Hirst and Thompson, 1996). Paradoxically, political responses to globalization tend to be unifying (e.g., North Atlantic Free Trade Agreement, International Monetary Fund (IMF)/World Bank, World Trade Organization), a tendency evident in the high level of policy convergence in responses to globalization among Western nation states due to policy borrowing, a practice encouraged by international bodies such as the Organization for Economic Cooperation and Development (OECD) (Taylor et al., 1997). Yet the responses of civil society to globalization have tended to lead to social fragmentation (Currie, 1996).

One policy convergence is how structural adjustment policies implemented in many Western nations have produced a fundamental shift from welfare to post-welfare states, effecting those states historically more "welfarist" than others (e.g., Australia and New Zealand more than the United States). There has been a move away from state universal provision in education, health, and welfare to one of state subsidization of the "targeted" needy and steering providers from a distance through policy and regulation justified by discourses of self-help, self-interest, and self-promotion. On the one hand, the state seeks to privatize educational costs and reduce state educational expenditure, while on the other it seeks to control educational outputs to improve economic productivity (Taylor et al., 1997).

This chapter's case study of Australian higher education highlights the impact of global structural adjustment policies, the conservative policy response prescribed by key international financial bodies such as the OECD, World Bank, and IMF as the "drastic remedy" for "globalization woes"; on the more "marginal" Western states (e.g., Australia, New Zealand, and Canada); and on the more "marginal" in society, particularly women. It takes the feminist position that despite the gender-free language associated with globalization and education reform, the policies associated with globalization have fundamentally transformed gender relations by changing the very nature of the state and its relation to the individual, household, and community. "Gender relations can be defined in terms of the interplay between historical practices that are distinguished in terms of the masculine and feminine (theories and ideologies, including religious ideas), institutional practices (state and market) and material conditions (the nature and distribution of material capabilities along gender lines)" (Bakker, 1994, p. 3).

THE INTERNATIONAL DISCIPLINARY REGIME OF STRUCTURAL ADJUSTMENT

The power of globalization discourses during the 1980s about level trading fields, freely flowing markets, and financial deregulation is evident in the extent to which neoliberal market theories became dominant in World Bank and IMF policies. Whereas the welfare state previously disciplined the market within its national boundaries, in a globalized context the state is now disciplined by international markets. While the welfare state was seen to be against the market, the interests of the post-welfare state and the market are increasingly seen to coincide, even to the detriment of its citizenry (Yeatman, 1994).

Structural adjustment policies promoting small government, deregulation, and markets advocated by conservative economic think tanks have been adopted not only by conservative governments in the United States and United Kingdom, but also by Labour governments in Australia, New Zealand, and Canada (Kelsey, 1995). The latter states are marginal in the sense that they are located "on the edge" of the economic core of new regional trading blocs that arose in response to globalization (e.g., North American Free Trade Agreement, European Union, and Association of Southeast Asian Nations [ASEAN]) and therefore increasingly vulnerable to international exigencies and U.S. domination (Buchbinder and Rajagopal, 1996). Australian and New Zealand states are both within and outside dominant Western cultural, political, and economic enclaves, both with their own colonial and imperialist histories in relation to their own indigenous populations and postcolonial relations with neighborhood states, and are also subject to European and American economic and cultural colonization. Carnoy (1995) suggests that structural adjustment policies are selectively utilized. Smaller, more vulnerable Western states such as Australia, New Zealand, and South Africa, as well as Third World or developing nations, excluded from the political and economic collective responses of major nation states to globalization (e.g., European Union, ASEAN), have initiated more radical or "purer" modes of structural adjustment while larger and richer Western nation states undertook milder "self adjustment."

Feminists point to how structural adjustment policies, in general, in advocating less state intervention in the economy, financial and labor market deregulation, balanced national budgets, the replacement of domestic consumption with export production industries, and the privatization of public ownership and costs, impact on women more than men (Bakker, 1994). It is women who assume the responsibility for care, both in the workplace and at home, of the young, aged, and sick when the state withdraws its services. Neoconservative and liberal market ideologies are also gender inflected, invoking particularly conservative social views on women or ignoring gender altogether (Vidovich, 1997).

Education reform generally, and in higher education in particular, has meant a shift from semi-bureaucratic to corporate organizations. In Australia, the Labour government after 1987 sought to link higher education more closely to the economy. The corporatization strategies "retooling" education included privatization, marketization, and the commodification of educational work, as well as the introduction of new forms of "hybrid" managerialism with strong accountability regimes. Collectively, these strategies tightly couple education systems to the needs of the state and industry while deregulating, de-professionalizing, and casualizing what is increasingly feminized educational work (Blackmore, 1997). These reforms:

changed the way we practice research, as well as the way we define and value it. It changed the place of teaching, the modes of delivery and the relations between the education sectors, the pattern of rewards and incentives as well as the main lines of accountability. It opened up higher education to the wider world in a new way (Marginson, 1996, p. 8).

EQUITY: THE MISSING PARTNER IN THE COUPLING OF EDUCATION TO THE STATE

The reliance of the second wave of the women's movement in Australia and New Zealand on the state for equity reform has made gender equity strategies more vulnerable in the restructuring process as the state is transformed and indeed, some would argue, put at risk by globalization (Blackmore, 1999). Both Australia and New Zealand have histories of strong feminist "policy activism." As in Canada and Scandinavia, social democratic governments in Australia and New Zealand have been the central vehicle for changing the social relations between men and women. During the 1980s, feminist bureaucrats (femocrats) actively sought to work within the state for gender equity. Consequently, the dismantling of the social welfare state has had serious repercussions for equity. Indeed, the corporate triumvirate of big business, big unions, and big government under Labour in Australia and New Zealand, which rewrote education policy, largely excluded educators and women's interest groups. Equity has been marginal, if not absent, in the range of reports restructuring higher education in Australia (Blackmore, 1992). Even when equity policies were developed, see for example *A Fair Chance for All* (1990),[1] such policies rarely informed practice or became integral to individual institution's strategic plans, decision making, or institutional performance indicators (Burton, 1997). Increasingly, equity came to be perceived as inefficient and a cost against public sector reform. So in 1999, while women constituted over 55 percent of students in Australian universities, they continued to be underrepresented in the "hard" sciences and in senior and tenured academic positions (less than 10 percent of positions above senior lecturer were held by women).

Instead, the new managerialism in universities promoted a range of different structures, practices, and valuings. The specialist equity units, personnel, and policies developed during the 1980s under equal opportunity and affirmative action legislation were corporatized within human resource management during the 1990s. Devolution of responsibility down to the smallest unit meant responsibility for equity shifted onto individual managers, largely untrained in, and uncommitted to, equity work. The mainstreaming and downstreaming of equity either diluted the specialist expertise of equity personnel and policy units or meant the adoption of only those equity objectives that had immediate benefits for corporate ends. In Australia, the neoconservatism of the Howard Federal Coalition government after 1996 further weakened equity provision, curtailing the capacity and space for policy activism by femocrats as the national equity infrastructure built up during the 1980s has been downsized, downgraded, if not demolished. A variety of monitoring mechanisms have been dropped, relying upon self-reporting by large employers such as universities of equity outcomes. Recognition of group difference (between women, indigenous, ethnic, etc.) has been collapsed into an individualizing discourse about diversity, which treats all differences as equal and diversity as "a problem" to be managed. Notions of "group" disadvantage as a basis for citizenship claims upon the state have been supplanted by individual client demands upon a market state.

PRIVATIZATION

Central to structural adjustment is the reduction in public expenditure, largely achieved through public sector reform and downsizing. In Australia, the percentage of GDP spent on education has declined since 1995 from 4.2 percent to 3.8 percent (Marginson, 1996). As economic rationalism took over in federal and state bureaucracies in Australia by the late 1980s, efficiency rather than effectiveness or equity dominated decision making. Human capital theory took on a "purer" form in education policies operationalized by notions of individual choice. Human capital theory was premised upon notions of "economic man," and public choice theory assumed that "we all make rational choices to maximize our gains." This shift denied the social and cultural value of education, the basis for the welfare state's investment in free tertiary education after 1974 until 1988.

Labour's reinterpretation of human capital theory during the 1980s argued that both individuals and the state benefit from higher education; therefore individuals must contribute, as the nation-state can no longer afford free tertiary education in a competitive global world. Government disinvestment in education commenced with the introduction of the Higher Education Contribution Scheme (HECS) in 1992, a deferred tax, as a "fairer" alternative to up-front fees. Thus Labor temporarily resolved its traditional commitment to equity and access of the working class and women while addressing international pressure to reduce expenditure. Since then, the rate of increase of fees has been higher in Australian than elsewhere (Currie, 1996). The losers with HECS were middle-aged women and working-class males; the winners are middle-class school leavers (i.e., completers).

After 1996, under the conservative Howard government, privatization has intensified with moves to institute full fees in postgraduate courses. Women, still concentrated in the humanities, social sciences, and education, are most obviously effected, given their likely occupational destinations in the shrinking public sector. Furthermore, public sector employers (education, health, and welfare) tend not to fund professional development or training in the form of postgraduate education (Master of Education or Social Welfare) as do private business employers (MBAs or accounting degrees). In turn, this has repercussions on humanities, social science, and education faculties in terms of student demand, faculties where female academics are concentrated. With user pays, the student mix is also shifting emphasis from domestic to international students, as universities are pressured to become increasingly self funding (40 percent) by 2002.

"HYBRID" MANAGERIALISM IN THE "NEW" UNIVERSITY

An allied strategy to structural adjustment has been to adopt private sector management practices in university governance (de Boer and Goedegebuure, 1995). In Australia, the new managerialism led to a shift from more collegiate and quasi-democratic (although still patriarchal and bureaucratic) systems of university governance to "quasi-market managerial practices" (Lingard, 1999). The creation of the unified national system and new managerialism increased executive prerogative and shifted the locus of control away from academics and faculties to the CEO and upper level administrators (Currie, 1996). While universities were seen to have increased institutional autonomy, in return, they were more accountable for outcomes and efficiency. Devolution facilitated the shift from state regulation (and full provision) to state supervision of an increasingly privatized and deregulated system (Peters, 1998). Regulated deregulation allows for organizational heterogeneity, as personnel and resource decisions are made locally in response to specific niche markets, supposedly leaving curriculum and staffing up to individual institutions. At the same time the state steers (safely) from a distance, reducing education expenditure and effectively faxing the financial crisis of the state down the line.

These tensions hit hardest at the lowest end (sessional/contract/lecturer), with moves to contract and sessional staffing policies and intensification of academic labor, and at the middle management level where women are increasingly located. Heads of schools or departments do the emotional management work of a system in crisis, dealing with the competing demands of accountability upward for efficiency and downward by resource starved and overworked academics (Blackmore and Sachs, forthcoming). Deem and Ozga (1997) point to the evidence of women managers with regard to pressure and social isolation. The tensions also exacerbates the tendency in newer institutions, where women are largely located, with strong teaching and weak research cultures, to be more bureaucratic and practice surveillance. Older and generally more financially secure research-based institutions continue to enjoy the level of professional autonomy and trust typical of traditional universities (Deem and Ozga, 1997, p. 30; de Boer and Goedegebuure, 1995).

The new managerialism in universities is not a democratic and participatory model premised upon equal partnership between academics and management.

Studies of U.S. and Australian universities cite that the majority of academics see university decision making as being undemocratic, more bureaucratic, centralized, and autocratic (Currie, 1996). Even when power was devolved, it tends to be centered with deans and not staff, and deans have become line managers, not academic leaders. With the assertion of executive prerogative and commercial privilege, management has usurped the policy and decision-making prerogative, creating a growing divide between academics and managers within universities, marginalizing from key strategic decisions. University councils are no longer expected to be "representative" of educational communities, and university management establishes itself as different from academics in performance management, promotion, and salary structures. Women have not moved upward into executive positions as rapidly as could have been anticipated, although now six out of thirty-eight vice-chancellors are women (CEOs) (Burton, 1997).

The New Education Accountability

As in New Zealand, the imposition of private industry management practices through public sector reform has been performance based with the new contractualism. There is now explicit use of contracts in all relations in university life— performance agreements between universities and Higher Education authorities, between individual faculties and their university, between individual academics and management. Strategic planning links all levels: from national policies through to the CEOs down to faculties, then to schools/departments and individual performance plans of academics. These performance-based management systems require increased reporting and accounting mechanisms so the state and university management can steer from a distance through strategic plans and outcomes (Marginson, 1996). The increased emphasis on quantitative rather than qualitative performance indicators after 1995 was despite earlier reports that revealed that such "indicators were inadequate as sole sources of information leading to acceptable evaluation of quality" (Currie and Vidovich, 1998, p. 4). (Ac)-cruel accounting premised upon inputs and outputs means individual sub-units are expected to compete for resources in contracting for services under the principles of competitive tendering—a trend moving into teaching as well as research by 1999. These accountability regimes are now "global," with greater international linkages on quality assurance mechanisms, for example, the OECD, global assistance organizations (UNESCO), and the World Bank, encouraging global benchmarks of quality on which local universities can be judged internationally (Vidovich, 1997).

This outcomes orientation and emphasis on performativity has skewed the focus away from the core work of teaching and research and more onto recording, accounting, and measurement (Blackmore and Sachs, forthcoming; Lyotard, 1984). Stewart (1997) argues that universities are taking on private sector market activities, but without the same systems of financial management. The establish-

ment of new universities in other countries, offshore investment, and encouragement of individual faculties and centers to assume more aggressive enterprises
leaves universities open to financial failure. Likewise, downsizing is rarely monitored for its fairness, as there is no management information system premised
upon cost-benefit analyses or equity considerations. It is rarely asked whether the
trend to reduce tutorials and increase lecture size are actual cost savings, given
that lecturers still have to address student demands, administer the units, and
assess all students. Savings are gained through increased staff productivity resulting from increasing workloads.

The above factors have a number of implications for both equity and quality,
as women academics, concentrated in the lower echelons, usually teach more than
male academics and tend to be concentrated in the faculties that have lower research funding inputs or fewer marketable opportunities. The humanities, social
sciences, and education tend to have smaller grants (and therefore research input
funding) than the sciences, medicine, or engineering. In turn, this has the wider
effect of exacerbating institutional differences, as the newer universities tend not
to have medical or engineering faculties. Thus the funding and accounting mechanisms tend to privilege older institutions and "hard" disciplines where women
are not well represented.

Quality

The solution to reduced government funding has been to privatize costs but
also to differentiate funding between institutions on the basis of quality of teaching and research. Quality is critical to international performance. The quality assurance movement in Australia espoused three primary approaches: quality as excellence standards (the more traditional model), quality as improvement, and
quality as accountability. Yet after 1995, the system has been driven more by
quality as accountability (Vidovich, 1997). An array of mechanisms has been
brought into play to "test quality" in the student-centered university: student
charters and increased student evaluation. While welcomed by most, the teaching
quality focus is more rhetorical than real as quality is undermined by lack of resources, high staff workloads, or lack of institutional support for the staff who
undertake most of the teaching. Furthermore, while quality assurance increased
the focus on teaching, it also increased institutional and individual competition.
Academics are also accountable to a wide range of audiences—students, man-
ager/supervisors, institutional strategic plans, research bodies, ethics committees,
industry sponsors, research partners, etc. They increasingly practice forms of self-
regulation in terms of what research they do, how they do it, what is valued as
useful research, etc., thus producing narrow images of what constitutes a good
academic to the exclusion of difference (Peters, 1998).

Again, women academics at the lower level of the academic hierarchy do much
of the teaching and bear the brunt of student, managerial, and institutional sur-

veillance, through performance appraisal, customer satisfaction surveys, and student charters. Quality assurance has had contradictory implications for many women academics, as it captures their desire for quality learning and "perfectionism" and also exacerbates their guilt when they cannot achieve it. Women academics talks about "doing good and feeling bad" (Acker and Feuerverger, 1997; Blackmore and Sachs, forthcoming). Carmen Luke (1997) refers to how in her "newer" university the adherence to quality assurance made transparent the processes and put quality on the agenda. But this is undermined by big classes, little pastoral care, and fewer small tutorials. Increasingly, the teaching model of the postmodern university is one of the autonomous learner off campus using new learning technologies—the antithesis to the supportive and collaborative learning environments advocated by feminist pedagogies.

There are some entrepreneurial opportunities for individual women under this new regime as change agents or leaders, although often as the "colluded self" (Casey, 1996). The new work order produces the driven worker who is compliant, dependent on the company, manipulatable and ambitious. Many female academics express a strong sense of ambivalence about whether they are empowered or exploited by the new university, although they all agree they are overworked and undervalued (Deem and Ozga, 1997; Blackmore and Sachs, forthcoming). Clare Burton (1997) points to how performance-based management has built-in discriminatory practices "against those with family responsibilities, especially women who in our society are primary care givers, who cannot put unlimited time into the job, and this will tend to count against them . . . in judging performance" (p. 12).

Finally, corporatization, accountability, and quality surveillance constrain professional judgment and academic autonomy, discouraging those modes of independent critique that universities traditionally valued and have to some extent protected feminist critique in the 1980s.

CORPORATIZATION AND EDUCATION MARKETS

Universities are seen to be both the source of new knowledge wealth creation as an export industry and critical to skill formation for post-Fordist workplaces. Academic work has also been radically redefined as the globalized university is opened up to international markets. The market now penetrates every aspect of organizational life—creating new work identities, emphasizing individualistic and competitive over collegial relationships, redefining students as clients in contractual rather than a pedagogical relationships, and re-positioning efficiency over equity in Australian and New Zealand universities. Yet many nation-states in continental Europe have not taken up public choice theory and gone down the track of marketization and privatization with such vigor as in marginal nation-states (Currie and Vidovich, 1998, p. 5).

The market-led recovery has led to a shift in values and in ethos. Bakker (1994, p. 3) refers to "markets as institutions imbued with structural power relations and those have an asymmetrical gender dimension to them." Markets are "social settings that foster specific types of personal development and penalize others" (Bakker, 1994, p. 4). Gender is central to how the "managed education market" works differentially in terms of what is valued, images of academic or entrepreneurial leadership, and who has the opportunity to become the internationally mobile, strategic academic. Although seen to recognize merit, the market tends to protect those players already advantaged—older universities over newer universities (See also Deem and Ozga, 1997, for the UK). Internationally, the advantage rests with the United States and key European Union players (e.g., Germany) with their historically strong footing in academic and student markets softening the impact of globalization. Locally, the older, more established universities with strong research records in the "hard" sciences and elite student recruitment emerge as the winners over the newer universities.

Universities, in seeking to gain comparative advantage in the global market, as well as new sources of income, are ironically less able to provide comprehensive curricula to address diversity of student needs. Their focus is on niche markets, existing or potential research strengths, and short-term income gained from applied research in industry. The social sciences, humanities, arts, education, and nursing, where women are concentrated as academics and students, have less capacity to generate research funds from private industry or sponsors for programs or professors as their clients work in a downsized public sector.

Yeatman (1994) refers to another dilemma universities have, as strongholds of patriarchal and class elitism, of being market responsive to client diversity (cultural, gender, racial). Several "newer" universities have positioned themselves in niche markets by placing equity as central to their profile. Women academics and managers have often been positioned as change agents within these institutions, as both insiders and outsiders to the dominant masculinist cultures, with the expectation that they portray the institutions as being more culturally sensitive (Yeatman, 1994; Morley and Walsh, 1995). But equity is also high risk, as conservative governments reduce federal funding of student places, thus encouraging the push for increased fees and creating a tension between financial survival and access issues. In Australia, as in the United Kingdom, there is another tension between the desire to improve the quality and status of university teaching relative to research; enhance research funding in the humanities and the arts; and recognize lifelong learning, access, and community (where women are largely located in universities) and the necessity of increasing the use of part-time and short-term staff (more likely to be women) to provide the institutional flexibility required to maintain comparative international advantage.

"STRATEGIC" OR JUST PLAIN "FLEXIBLE" ACADEMICS?

Educational restructuring in Australian universities has had particularly harsh implications for women, given their historical location within universities as lower-level academics or general staff and students concentrated in the humanities (Castleman et al., 1995) While women constitute 30 percent of academic positions, they had only 26 percent of tenured positions, with 55 percent below lecturer status, part of a wider international pattern (3 percent of the United Kingdom's university professors are female).

In Australia, academic labor markets have been restructured by federal policies favoring "flexibility." After 1987, a new industrial relations regime of decentralized enterprise bargaining replaced the centralized wage bargaining system, which had protected women as premised on notions of the social and citizenship rights obligations. Enterprise bargaining is premised upon the power of individuals, individual workplaces, and individual unions to negotiate, and women tend not to have such power (Zetlin and Whitehouse, 1996). Evidence suggests that restructuring processes have tended to increase employer prerogative in determining hours and work conditions, "trading off" of earlier feminist gains such as family leave, and producing "women unfriendly" workplaces due to long hours.

There is also in Australia a widening gender gap in pay, as top level university managers, mostly men, receive considerably higher salaries (Burton, 1997), exacerbating a growing gender divide between academics and management, between high-flying researchers and teachers. Full-time equivalent staff have dropped 1.4 percent from 1997 to 1998, while student numbers increased 2 percent solely through international enrollments (Department of Employment, Education, Training and Youth Affairs [DEETYA], 1998). While women are now appointed in near equal numbers, promotion is not necessarily forthcoming (Burton, 1997). Any expansion in women's employment has occurred at the extreme ends: professorial and casual lecturer/sessional. This replicates in academic work the global polarization in labor markets between the functionally flexible (the tenured multifunctional core workforce) and the numerically flexible (the peripheral readily disposable workforce on contract or sessional work). Women also tend to make up the majority of the invisible class of "research staff" (research assistants, administrative and clerical, etc.) who are without career paths, do not have access to teaching, and are reliant upon "soft" research funds arising out of their academic employers' capacity to win grants (Organ and Svensen, 1995).

As student numbers increase relative to academic numbers, the trend in the United Kingdom, United States, Australia, and New Zealand has been for casualization of academic work. Institutional flexibility is achieved by increasing the number of contract (suggested 30 percent at all levels) and sessional staff (often never) (Castleman et al., 1995). There has been a drop of 2.4 percent in numbers of full-time staff and growth of 4.8 percent in part-time staff, with a radical drop of 30 percent of teaching-only staff, usually at lower levels and largely female (DEETYA, 1998). Again, this is a global trend. In the United Kingdom the rise of contract and casual labor has meant that on average a third of courses are taught by casual tutors and staff who are flexible and cheaper, also releasing universities from any responsibility for staff well-being, training, or career benefits (superannuation) (Allen-Collinson and Hockey, 1998, p. 497). General staff indicate a similar gendered division of labor; with most women located in the lower echelons, they are even more susceptible to globalization, as clerical and administrative skills are more generic and available "offshore," for example, financial reporting, salaries processing, and data processing.

The casualization and feminization of academic work has occurred at a moment when the nature of academic work is being radically altered: increased academic workloads, increased surveillance of academic work, a growing divide between teaching and research and teaching and research institutions, and reduced voice in institutional decision making (Castleman et al., 1995; Taylor et al., 1997). Deem and Ozga (1997, p. 34) comment, with regard to the United Kingdom but applicable elsewhere, "as salaries in the higher education sector fall relative to other professional occupations, there may be a greater feminization of certain sectors of the academic profession." Indeed, the vice-chancellors' industrial association argued that women *benefited* from the increased proportion of contract staff because it gave them access to fixed contracts at the upper levels of the academy, an argument refuted by the union.

Finally, academics are expected to promote themselves, their universities, and their courses locally and internationally in order to acquire fee-paying students. The expectation is that academics be culturally flexible and globally mobile workers, able to travel or to work "on-line" from home. Flexibility and mobility currently work against the career patterns of women academics, who enter the teaching force later and generally have family responsibilities. It reflects the dual processes that Janine Brodie (1996) calls the re-privatization of work with the privatization of educational costs of the institution (e.g., use of car between multicampuses, use of home office) and the invasion of private time by home/work underway in many Western liberal states as the state pulls out.

THE ANOREXIC CURRICULUM: COMMODIFICATION OF CURRICULUM, LEARNING TECHNOLOGIES, INSTRUCTIONAL DESIGN, AND TEACHERLESS COURSES

Then there is the trend to internationalization, facilitated by new information technologies and "just in time" courses. There is underway a commodification of academic curriculum as Australian universities increasingly provide "generic" and well-packaged international courses delivered on-line. Many universities have developed commercial arms that develop training units and courses for industry, the public sector, and unions and are workplace based. These units, while improving the articulation between training and university accreditation, are often delivered off campus and in the workplace, developed along principles of instructional design. Universities are increasingly expected to accredit courses produced by non-academics, with assessment often the only regulator or quality assurance. Many courses based on instructional design are highly behaviorist in their pedagogical assumptions, an approach exacerbated by the use of new learning technologies, which tend to put print materials on-line without regard for the different pedagogical spaces and different learning styles. These principles underlying flexible delivery not only mitigate against feminist academic traditions about the importance of particular modes of pedagogy that focus upon inclusiveness (Luke and Gore, 1992), but also tend to see the presence of the teacher itself as problematic—a hindrance to the flow of information to students via new learning technologies (McWilliam and Taylor, forthcoming). Not only is the status of the teacher put at risk, it is reduced to assessor or dispensable altogether with self-paced computer-assisted learning. This has significant implications, given that in the academy teaching is more often women's work. It reduces equity to getting access to high-tech on-line learning or what Janet Newson (1994) calls "technopedagogy" rather than the social relationships critical to pedagogy.

So while access for women students to universities has improved, there has been only marginal attention to curriculum inclusiveness in many disciplines. While feminism has made some inroads into the social sciences, many women see the new managerialism and market orientation devaluing particular knowledge areas, for example, women's studies or less popular subjects (e.g., anthropology) for their lack of use value. Client-focused curriculum provision, as well as student-centered consumption-driven evaluation systems, encourages giving students "what they want" and "immediate use value" rather than thinking about curriculum development based on professional and academic judgment. Gone are notions of getting students to understand key concepts of a discipline, helping them to grasp the full range of theory or empirical research, or encouraging them to engage in critical thinking. The utilitarian turn has led to the demise of some "pure" foundational disciplines (e.g., anthropology, history). Perceived student or industry demand (itself often constructed by policy) is the driving force. Slaughter (1993) points to the precedent in the 1980s in the United States of retrenchments in the humanities, social sciences, fine arts, and education as a "rational response to student choice." But management did not factor in future demand and growth (e.g., women's increased participation shifted demand). Indeed, the areas of high labor market growth in a postmodern society (e.g., human services, etc.) were primary targets in retrenchment because productivity was equated to the public and not the private sector in management and policymakers perceptions. Ideologically informed conservative discourses depict the public sector as inefficient, discourses that "gloss over the complex relationship between the state and civil society and [overlook] the state's part in maintaining growth in privileged fields" in the "managed market" (Slaughter, 1993, p. 271). The later increase in appointments after the early retrenchments have been part-time and sessional, largely given to women, and institutionally there has been a reallocation of resources to already privileged areas rather than reduction of expenditure, a pattern emerging in Australia.

Finally, curriculum is commodified and packaged into "consumable bites" for multiple audiences utilizing new learning technologies. This means "fat" pedagogies, which involve intensive student/ teacher interaction, are replaced by lean pedagogies in large lecture halls or on-line as more efficient ways to deal with increased student load. This produces an anorexic curriculum.[2] Feminists are ensnared in their own rhetoric. Practicing feminist pedagogies based upon group work, sharing, and listening is impossible in crowded lecture theaters. To do so only intensifies workload. If a feminist teacher does not do that caring and sharing work, she is seen to be untrue to her feminist principles (Luke, 1997). Women academics feel they are working excessively hard, doing more support work of colleagues and students. With higher teaching loads, women often do the emotional management work of institutions (Acker and Feuerverger, 1997; Blackmore and Sachs, forthcoming). Yet teaching gets substantively harder as the capacities to attract, retain, and pass students become key performance indicators, course requirements (e.g., advanced standing, length of courses, etc.) have been lowered, and international students have required greater language skill support (Deem and Ozga, 1997).

RESEARCH: THE NEW FAST COMMODITY

The pressure to publish in particular ways (international refereed journals) and in particular forums (international conferences) has also intensified in the performative university. The notion of what constitutes research has been reconstituted through new management practices and formulaic funding mechanisms. Research quantums have been developed, awarding points to individual academics (and their institutions) according to their productivity (measured by income earned by competitive bidding and publication output). The research quantum again has inherent biases, given that older universities have stronger research cultures and are well established in science, engineering, and medical areas, which bring in the highest research income (input), areas where women are underrepresented as researchers. Social science–oriented faculties and institutions tend to have productivity in terms of outcomes and publications, and these are increasingly devalued. The equation of "legitimate" research with funding and peer review among academic elites also devalues practitioner-based research that informs professional practice (the focus of humanities, education, and health). Ironically, while universities are being told they must be more client driven, research or publications written for nonacademic professional journals and practitioners do not "count." Industry, and not the community or "the public," is now the main client.

The above reasserts the old gender bifurcation between the soft humanities and hard sciences, one that has significant impact on who gets what in the academy. Emphasis on the immediate and applied has exacerbated the tendency of earlier research regimes to favor quantitative over qualitative research (science, math, engineering, medicine, IT, and management)—male-dominated disciplines and those that attract private sector funding, sponsorships, and partnerships. The female-dominated humanities, social sciences, education, and nursing disciplines with their interdisciplinary, community, and professional service orientation or practitioner research approaches have less scope for measurable, immediate commercial application. The monitoring procedures and definitions of what counts in research are narrowing, with edited books and editorial work, critical for the humanities and social sciences, no longer "counting" in many university research quantums. This changes the very notion of academics as intellectuals and academics as new knowledge workers—"the key question is not whether it is true, but whether it is salable. . . . Universities are all about creating skills and no longer ideals" (Lyotard, 1984, p. 48). Thus the focus upon strategic and applied research for the private sector rather than pure research or public policy research has regressive tendencies for women. Dependence on clients for funding under new commercial arrangements puts the capacity of academics to be independent and critical public intellectuals at risk. Feminists, as critical intellectuals, have been relatively protected in the past as the traditional knowledge production work of independent scholarship and research. Kenway and Langmead (1998) suggest that whereas feminists within the academy could use dominant knowledges to do counterhegemonic work for subordinate groups, the line of accountability for service practitioners in corporate universities is direct to the market.

CULTURAL SHIFTS—BUT WHICH WAY?

Thus the radical restructuring of Australian universities has exaggerated the historically constituted masculinist biases within its structures and processes that favor those in power. This has produced what could be called a structural as well as a cultural backlash against more inclusive, democratic, and female friendly practices that emerged, but were not institutionalized, during the 1980s. In terms of new work identities for postmodern academic workplaces it has meant the assertion of value systems of individual competitiveness and entrepreneurship more closely associated with "macho masculinity": "increasingly the evidence is mounting that competition, confrontation and 'macho' management styles are producing more workplace stress and less productivity" (Davidson, 1995, p. 19).

The shift to more overtly competitive cultures has significant effect on how women view their possibilities, as "culture is a key site in which issues of power and identity are enmeshed and in which male power is reproduced" (Itzin and Newman, cited in Deem and Ozga, 1997, p. 26). Even when women do get into leadership, the dominant institutional norms and practices place increased pressure on them because of their gender and minority status. Fay Gale, when vice-chancellor of the University of Western Australia and former chair of the Australian Vice-Chancellor's Committee, stated:

The culture of leadership today remains extremely male focused. The requirements of leadership do not fit with the expectations of female behavior. In universities, women have to positively establish their credibility as "non-standard" Vice Chancellors in a way that men do not. . . . Despite the fact that universities should be at the cutting edge of social change, the culture of university administration is very much a male culture. . . . Cultural expectations lead women to take a greater share of teaching and pastoral care in universities, rather than going on to research and administrative streams, which leads to promotion (Gale, 1996, p. 1).

GENDER EQUITY IN THE POSTMODERN GLOBALIZED UNIVERSITY: WHAT FUTURE?

Conservative social commentators now argue in Australia that equal opportunity policies have succeeded, given women's overrepresentation in tertiary education as students. This discourse has been brought into play at the time when changes in language practices in education have become market oriented: learners become consumers and courses are packaged into modules. These discourses signify a shift more generally in how individuals relate to others and society—away from notions of citizenship, obligation, and community to notions of being self-interested competitors. The trend to marketize teaching and research in close partnerships and sponsorship arrangements with industry has ethical and political implications.

For feminists, the issue is that globalization has threatened feminism's mode of engagement with the welfare state and its public agencies (e.g., universities). Discourses of globalization have been used to justify reshaping the nature of universities, which have been strategic sites for feminist political activism. The welfare state, while still patriarchal, had provided some advantages for women, and universities, while still highly conservative, provided an intellectual counterpoint for the wider women's movement. With both under threat, or at least dominated by market principles, gender equity work in universities is at risk.

Feminist academics have always experienced an uneasiness about their location among the privileged elite of the academy, working on a range of fronts simultaneously: multiple strategies for multiple situations. In Australia there has been a revival of community-based women's groups that now appeal to international bodies to bring government into line. Feminist academics are using their research to inform education, social, and economic policy. Feminists argue from a "liberal" market perspective that universities will be more productive and creative if they continue to value their traditional functions of pedagogy, research, and collegiality and that universities have to be more inclusive to address cultural difference in their student populations with internationalization. Feminists suggest that universities, now transnational companies,[3] must be good corporate citizens. Within institutions, quality assurance processes have been called upon strategically by women who demand transparency in institutional practices as equity is one measure of excellence and quality.

In conclusion, women academics, feminist or nonfeminist, strive to work and to enjoy their teaching and research in the restructured "postmodern" academy with highly unpredictable results. Life in the academy is fraught with ambiguities and tensions between long-held values of academic freedom, intellectual independence, and collegiality and entrepreneurial, competitive, and contractual values. But universities are also the base for new transnational professional elites and knowledge workers, and indeed transnational masculinities (Whitehead, 1999). In liberal Western states, on the one hand, there is the call for new ways of management and the person skills of women in the post-Fordist workplace, which provides some opportunities and spaces for individual women under the discourse of managing diversity. On the other, well-established modes of gender/power relations take on new forms through the processes of reform, specifically, emergence of new styles of flexible, mobile, and entrepreneurial academic images of masculinist leadership. The new work identities of academics are now being constituted through competitive and contractual relationships, with new modes of entrepreneurial or strategic masculinity, no less masculinist than earlier collegial and humanist relationships. What is different is that there is less space for the collective voice with the weakening of the basis of claims that can be made by women and other marginalized groups on a weak post-welfare state with few liberal humanist dispositions.

NOTES

1. The equity groups named here are Aboriginal and Torres Strait Islanders, women in nontraditional subjects, people with disabilities, rural and isolated people, people from socioeconomically disadvantaged and Non-English Speaking Backgrounds (NESB).

2. While tertiary funding has fallen radically (from AUST$11,600 per capita in 1983 to $10,800 in 1995) since 1983, class sizes increased radically with student growth of 44 percent since 1988, often unfunded as universities scramble to gain a niche in local and international markets (Bramble 1996, p. 8–9).

3. The marketing of educational services in Australia puts seventeen universities in the top 500 expert earning companies, led by Monash University ($45 million in 1995), RMIT ($36 million), and Curtin ($28 million).

REFERENCES

Acker, Sandra, and Grace Feuerverger. 1997. Enough Is Never Enough: Women's Work in Academe. In Catherine Marshall (ed.), *Feminist Critical Policy Analysis: A Perspective from Post-Secondary Education*. Vol. 2. London: Falmer Press, pp. 122–40.

Allen-Collinson, Jacquelyn, and John Hockey. 1998. Capturing Contracts: Informal Activity among Contract Researchers. *British Journal of Sociology of Education*, vol. 19, no. 4, pp. 497–515.

Bakker, Isabella. 1994. *The Strategic Silence: Gender and Economic Policy*. London: Zed Books and North-South Institute.

Blackmore, Jill. 1992 (Autumn). "More Power to the Powerful": Mergers, Corporate Management and their Implications for Women in the Reshaping of Higher Education, *Australian Feminist Studies*, vol. 15, pp. 65–98.

———. 1998. The Level Playing Field? Feminist Observations on the Global/Local Articulation of the Re-gendering and Re-structuring of Educational Work. *International Review of Education*. Special Issue edited by Anthony Welch. vol. 43, nos. 5-6, pp. 1–23.

———. 1999. Globalization/Localisation: Strategic Dilemmas for State Feminism and Gender Equity Policy. *Journal of Education Policy* Special Issue on Globalization and Education, vol. 14, no. 1, pp. 33–54.

———, and Judyth Sachs. Forthcoming. A Passionate Vocation: The Re-making of the Academic Self in an Era of Performativity. In Alison McKinnon and Anne Brooks (eds.), *Restructuring Women: Academic Women and the Politics of Restructuring*.

Bramble, Tony. 1996. Class and Power in the Ivory Tower. *Australian Universities Review*, vol. 39, no. 2, pp. 8–10.

Brodie, Janine. 1996. New State Forms, New Political Spaces. In Robert Boyer and Daniel Drache (eds.), *State against Markets: The Limits of Globalization*. New York: Routledge.

Buchbinder, Howard, and Pinayur Rajagopal. 1996 (April). Canadian Universities: The Impact of Free Trade and Globalization. *Higher Education*, vol. 31, pp. 283–99.

Burton, Clare. 1997. *Gender Equity in Australian University Staffing*. Canberra: DEETYA.

Carnoy, Martin. 1995. Structural Adjustment and the Changing Face of Education. *International Labor Review*, vol. 34, no. 6, pp. 653–73.

Casey, Catherine. 1996. *Work, Self and Society*. London: Routledge.

Castleman, Tanya, Margaret Allen, Wendy Bastalich, and Patrick Wright. 1995. *Limited Access: Women's Disadvantage in Higher Education Employment*. Sydney: National Tertiary Education Union.

Currie, Jan. 1996. Globalization Practices and Universities: Some Examples from American and Australian Universities. Paper presented at Ninth World Congress of Comparative Education Societies (WCCES), Sydney.

———, and Lesley Vidovich. 1998. Micro-Economic Reform through Managerialism in American and Australian Universities. In Jan Currie and Janice Newsom (eds.), *Universities and Globalization: Critical Perspectives*. Thousand Oaks, CA: Sage, pp. 153–72.

Davidson, Marilyn. 1995. Women in Management: Why the Glass Ceiling Is Thickening and Not Cracking. *Feminine Forces: Redefining the Workplace*. Women in Leadership Project, National Conference, 1994, Edith Cowan University Churchlands, Western Australia.

de Boer, Harry, and Leo Goedegebuure. 1995. Decision-Making in Higher Education: A Comparative Perspective. *Australian Universities Review*, vol. 1, pp. 41–47.

Deem, Rosemary, and Jenny Ozga. 1997. Women Managing for Diversity in a Postmodern World. In Catherine Marshall (ed.), *Feminist Critical Policy Analysis: A Perspective from Post-Secondary Education*. Vol. 2. London: Falmer Press, pp. 25–40.

DEETYA. 1998. *Selected Higher Education Staff Statistics*. Canberra: Australian Government Printing Service.

Gale, Fay. 1996 (March). Introduction. *Some Strategies to Redress Gender Imbalance in Numbers of Senior Academic Women*. Papers from the sixth session of the Association of the Commonwealth Universities Conference of Executive Heads, Malta.

Hirst, Paul, and Grahame Thompson. 1996. *Globalization in Question: The International Economy and Possibilities of Government*. Cambridge, UK: Polity.

Kelsey, Jane. 1995. *The New Zealand Experiment: A World Model of Structural Adjustment?* Wellington: Bridgit Williams.

Kenway, Jane, and Dianna Langmead. 1998. Fast Capitalism, Fast Feminism and Some Fast Food for Thought. *Winds of Change: Women and the Culture of Universities Proceedings*, vol. 2. Sydney: University of Technology.

Lingard, Bob. 1999. It Is and It Isn't: Vernacular Globalization, Educational Policy and Restructuring. In Nicolas Burbules and Carlos Torres (eds.), *Globalization and Education: Critical Perspectives*. New York: Routledge.

Luke, Carmen. 1997. Quality Assurance and Women in Higher Education. *Higher Education*, vol. 33, pp. 433–51.

———, and Jennifer Gore (eds.). 1992. *Feminism and Critical Pedagogy*. London: Routledge.

Lyotard, Jean François. 1984. *The Postmodern Condition: A Report on Knowledge*. Manchester: Manchester University.

Marginson, Simon. 1996 (March 14–20). 1983–96 Labor in Review: Higher Education Revolutionaries. *Campus Review*, pp. 8–9.

McWilliam, Erica, and Peter G. Taylor. Forthcoming. Teacher Im/material: Challenging the New Pedagogies of Instructional Design *Educational Researcher*, vol. 27, no. 8, pp. 29–34.

Morley, Louise, and Val Walsh (eds.). 1995. *Feminist Academics: Creative Agents for Change*. London: Taylor and Francis.

Newson, Janet. 1994. "Technopedagogy": A Critical Evaluation of the Effects of Academic Staff of Computerised Instructional Technologies in Higher Education. *Higher Education Policy*, vol. 7, no. 2, pp. 37–40.

National Board of Employment, Education and Training (NBEET). 1996 (April). *Equality, Diversity and Excellence: Advancing the National Higher Education Equity Framework*. Canberra.

Organ, M., and S. Svensen. 1995. Research Assistants in a Clever Country. *Australian Universities Review*.

Peters, Michael. 1998. Cybernetics, Cyberspace and the Politics of University Reform. In Michael Peters and Paul Roberts (eds.), *Virtual Technologies and Tertiary Education*. Wellington, New Zealand: Dunmore.

Slaughter, Sheila. 1993. Retrenchment in the 1980s: Politics, Prestige and Gender. *Journal of Higher Education*, vol. 64, no. 3, pp. 250–81.

———, and Larry L. Leslie. 1997. *Academic Capitalism: Politics, Policies and the Entrepreneurial University*. Baltimore: John Hopkins University Press.

Stewart, Jan. 1997. Rethinking University Management. *Australian Universities Review*, vol. 40, no. 2, pp. 36–41.

Taylor, Sandra, Miriam Henry, Bob Lingard, and Fazal Rizvi. 1997. *Policy and the Politics of Education*. St. Leonards, New South Wales: Allen and Unwin.

Vidovich, Lesley. 1997 (December 3–4). A "Quality" Policy Trajectory: From Global Ho-
megenisations to Localised Differentiation. Paper presented at AARE, Brisbane.

Whitehead, Stephen. 1999. From Paternalism to Entrepreneurialism: the Experience of
Men Managers in UK Postcompulsory Education, *Discourse*, vol. 20, p. 2.

Yeatman, Anna 1994. *Postmodern Revisionings of the Political*. London: Routledge.

Zetlin, Di, and Gillian Whitehouse. 1996 (Sept. 30–Oct. 2). Citizenship and Industrial
Regulation: A Feminist Perspective. Paper presented to the Culture and Citizenship
Conference, Griffith University, Brisbane, Australia.

Index

access to higher education, 160, 226, 231
accountability, 224, 328, 339–341, 344
accreditation, 224, 328, 339–341, 344
adult education, 16, 105–112, 197–215, 256, 302
affirmative action, 322, 328
Africa, 10, 22n4, 37, 50, 51
AID USAID. *See* international organizations
Americanization, 7
Asia, 5, 22n4, 22n6, 43
Asian Pacific trade organization, 5, 20

brain drain, 13, 18

capital, 12, 18, 20, 43, 45, 305; distribution, 6; mobility of, 6, 10, 21; private, 12, 21
capitalism, 3, 5, 9, 20–21, 31, 33
Caribbean, 13
citizenship, 21, 161, 186, 207, 209–213, 348
civil society, 16
class, 7, 14, 53
commodities, 4, 5
communication, 30, 31, 36; impact of faster communication, 3, 4, 11, 28, 46. *See also* telecommunications
community colleges, 149–171
comparative education, 66
competition and competitiveness, 5, 12, 13, 18, 46, 127. *See also* education, knowledge

computer-assisted communications. *See* telecommunications
computers, 7, 43, 46, 87. *See also* microelectronics
consumers, 11, 17
corporatization. *See* entrepreneurship
critical thought, 13, 14, 15
culture: diversity, 28, 29, 34–35; effects of globalization on, 4, 6–11, 30, 166, 316; homogenization of, 7, 28, 29, 34; influence of local cultures on globalization, 29; local cultures, 7, 28; traditional, 7–8; values, 7, 11
currency, 5, 18
curriculum, 12, 19, 43, 47, 77–98, 137, 185, 233, 243, 249, 300, 316, 345

decentralization, 13, 17, 38, 44, 47–51, 58, 202, 255–274, 285
deconstruction, 79, 80
demilitarization, 27, 31. *See also* peace
democracy, 4, 16, 22, 30, 31, 32–36, 39, 54, 154, 338
dependency, 4, 35
deregulation, 17
developed countries. *See* industrialized countries
developing countries, 4, 17, 18, 22n2, 50–51
development, 102
Development Alternatives with Women for a New Era (DAWN), 20

353

distance education, 152, 228, 233
diversity. *See* culture
donor agencies. *See* international organizations

East Asian trade bloc, 5, 20
economic polarization, 7
economy: economic policies, 4; effects of globalization on, 3, 1, 4, 29, 78, 123, 187, 192, 335; global economy, defined, 43; informal, 4, 22n1; primacy of in world relations, 29
education: administration, 43; basic, 13, 50; as a commodity, 12–13, 18, 19; decline in importance of non-market-related subjects, 13, 14; for efficient production, 13, 56–57; and employment, 9, 12, 206; finance of, 43, 44, 46–51; funding of, 16; homogenization of, 17, 151, 232, 280; impact of globalization on, 12–13, 19, 21, 342, 346; internationalization of, 19; and market efficiency, 12, 56; as a means of achieving national competitiveness, 12, 13, 18; national education systems, 17, 19, 44; and parents and community, 39, 47–48, 49, 53; policy, 19, 58; primary, 13, 53, 242, 243, 257, 286, 315, 349; secondary, 13, 47, 49, 53, 242, 244–246; special 321; and women, 9, 10, 16, 44, 53–54. *See also* international organizations, non-governmental organizations, schools, schooling, tuition, university
efficiency. *See* education, market
electronic media. *See* telecommunications
electronics industry (assembly), 10
elites. *See* class
employment, 9, 10, 20, 52. *See also* labor
empowerment, 153
English language, 3, 7
entrepreneurship, 128, 140, 308, 326, 349
environment, 5, 30–31, 78, 80, 210, 263
equality and equity, 123, 211, 225, 302, 340. *See also* ethnicity, gender
ethnicity, 7, 13, 153

families, 54, 86, 102, 175, 182, 190, 192, 197, 344; division of labor within, 10; impact of globalization on, 4, 9, 10.
feminists and feminism, 10, 11, 16, 74, 114–116, 174, 181, 223, 226, 334, 336, 341, 346
financial markets, 4, 5, 20; control of, 27; internationalization of, 4, 29

garment industry, 10
gender, 8–11, 15–16, 53–54; gender-equal vs. gender-neutral conditions, 8, 13; issues, 173, 178, 258, 342; studies, 14, 15–16. *See also* labor, women
global culture, 4, 29, 34. *See also* culture
global education, 83
globalization: and changing power structures, 17; counterefforts, 20–21, 28; defined, 3–4, 27–31; and dissent, 17; effects on outsiders, 30; governance of, 27, 30; of the market, 5–6, 127, 182; and profit motive, 16. *See also* education, gender, international order, schools, transnational corporations, university
global solidarity, 7
governance. *See* nation-state
government, 6, 104, 234

health, 78, 140, 197, 263, 337
higher education, 44, 47, 49, 123–147, 219–236, 299–314, 333–352. *See also* university
homogenization, 21, 154. *See also* education, global culture
households. *See* families
human capital, 204
human rights, 4, 15, 16, 30, 32, 35, 39. *See also* social justice

identity, 7–8, 10, 21, 30, 161, 176, 208, 240, 251, 341
ideology, 17, 37, 44, 49–50, 53, 58
IMF. *See* international organizations
immigration. *See* migration
indigenous populations, 7, 16, 207. *See also* ethnicity

individuality and neoliberal theory, 29, 30.
See also neoliberal agenda/theory
industrialization, 4, 102
industrialized countries, 18, 19, 20
industry, 4, 142
informal sector of the economy. *See*
economy
information distribution, 11, 28, 45–46.
See also communication, telecommunications
information industry, 9, 10, 51
information technology, 43, 45, 54, 56, 78, 86, 248, 319, 324, 328, 347
international development agencies. *See* international organizations
international institutions, 4, 5, 6, 33
internationalism, 27–42; and globalization, 31, 34, 35, 36, 37; defined, 31
internationalization, 4, 238
international law, 31
international order, 30, 31, 32, 33
international organizations, 16, 32, 33, 36–39; International Monetary Fund (IMF), 6, 100, 112, 124, 283; NATO (North Atlantic Treaty Organization), 6; United Nations Childrens Fund (UNICEF), 36–37; United Nations Development Programme (UNDP), 113; United Nations Educational, Scientific, and Cultural Organization (UNESCO), 16–37, 80, 113, 229, 275, 290; United Nations Environment Program (UNEP), 81; World Bank, 6, 12, 37–39, 46, 47, 49, 50, 56, 57, 107, 112, 256–257, 283, 286–287; World Trade Organization (WTO), 6
Internet, 162, 164

knowledge, 11–12; and competitiveness, 5, 12, 13, 15; and globalization, 11–12, 43, 45, 84–91, 242; technological, 11, 12, 13, 18
knowledge workers, 128

labor: corporate attitudes toward, 8; costs, 5, 6, 9; division of labor, 4, 9, 10, 28, 30, 343; domestic and menial work, 9;
10, 11, 13; effects of globalization on, 3, 7, 8, 9, 10, 13, 46, 51–52; home-based, 10; immigrant, 6, 9, 10, 13, 22n5, 51; informal, 4, 197, 212; international mobility of, 6, 20, 28; labor market, 3, 5, 6, 10, 27, 29, 44, 52, 161, 177; masculinization and feminization of, 9, 22n3; part-time and temporary, 8; skills, 5, 6, 9, 51–54, 55; uneducated labor, 8, 13, 18, 54, 55; youth, 20, 55. *See also* education, women
language, 245, 247, 250, 283, 322
learning, 11. *See also* education
literacy, 20
local effects of globalization, 21, 28, 34, 81

macro-institutions. *See* international institutions
management, 5, 43, 124, 127, 268, 335, 338, 345
marginalized populations. *See* ethnicity, gender, poverty, race, women
market (global), 5–6, 10, 12, 36; control of, 27–28; efficiency, 5, 11, 27, 57; and knowledge, 341, 348; and the state, 16–17. *See also* financial markets, globalization, labor
marketing, 12
Marxism, 29
masculinity, 179, 342, 347
media, 7, 8, 20, 87, 94, 175, 240
microelectronics, 14, 19, 43
migration, 4, 11, 13, 22n1, 22n5, 51. *See also* labor
military power, 103
moral education, 249, 315, 323
multilateral funding agencies. *See* international organizations
multinational corporations. *See* transnational corporations

NAFTA. *See* North American Free Trade Association
nation-state, 10, 19; and competitiveness, 18, 45; development policies, 17; external influences on, 3; economic differentiation of, 28; and ecomomic regulation,

45; and education, 18, 49, 51; and governance, 17, 27, 30, 34; impact of globalization on, 3, 4, 6, 30, 44–46; as mediator, 4; national economies, 44–46; relationship with the international market, 16–18, 27–28; role in a globalized world, 5 ,6, 17, 18, 21, 27, 28, 32, 34, 36, 46; and social policies, 17, 27, 30, 34; sovereignty of, 29–30, 31, 33, 34. *See also* politics

NATO. *See* international organizations

natural resources, 12, 20, 21

neoliberal agenda/theory, 3, 9, 10, 16–17, 133, 284, 335

non-governmental organizations (NGOs), 16, 201, 208; and international development agencies, 37

women-led, 11, 16

North American Free Trade Association (NAFTA), 5, 20, 22

Organization for Economic Cooperation and Development (OECD), 20, 22n6, 53, 56, 83, 124, 133, 149, 275, 283, 334

partnerships, 137, 138, 140, 338

patriarchy, 10, 16, 67

peace, 30, 31–36

pedagogy and globalization, 13

perestroika, 66

political aspects of globalization, 3, 4, 5, 18, 27

politics, 35, 36; and globalization, 3, 4, 5, 18, 27, 29–30; political allegiance, 7. *See also* university

poverty, 12, 16, 20, 21, 22, 58

power, 20. *See also* globalization, women

privatization, 13, 15, 19, 47, 68 70, 127, 219, 262, 264, 325, 337; of services, 4, 17, 47. *See also* education, schools, university

production and productivity, 3, 5, 7, 9, 10, 20, 22n6, 49; cost of, 5; change in processes of, 8; internationalization of, 4; relocation of, 22n2

prostitution, 10, 11, 22n4

public policy, 5, 16–19, 46,

public schooling, 72, 75

public services, 7, 28, 29, 30, 37, 46, 47

race, 9, 10, 34

raw materials. *See* natural resources

reflexivity, 84, 174

reform movements, 70

regional trade blocs. *See* trade blocs

religion, 30

research, 14, 18, 107, 128, 141, 193, 226, 282, 349, 343. *See also* university

SAPs. *See* Structural Adjustment Programs

Scandinavia, 12

schooling, 12–16, 19, 44; impact of globalization on formal schooling, 5, 11, 12–14; responsibility of state toward, 13, 18

schools: administration, 13, 48; corporate influence on, 6; and market efficiency, 12; privatization, 13, 48–49

science, 5, 11, 44, 56

services. *See* public services

skills. *See* labor

slavery, 101

social class. *See* class

social inequality, 17, 20. *See also* ethnicity, gender

socialism, 5, 66, 74

social justice, 11, 14, 21, 321. *See also* human rights

social sciences, 11

state, 63, 129. *See also* nation-state

students, 94, 179, 184, 190, 233, 343

Structural Adjustment Programs (SAPs), 6, 17, 50, 51, 106, 108–111

subcontracting, 4

supranational institutions. *See* international institutions, international organizations

taxation, 17, 27

teachers, 44, 48, 50, 178, 184, 256, 276, 288–289, 291; loss of classroom autonomy, 13, 50

technology, 3, 4, 6, 10, 12, 18, 20, 22n6, 43, 45, 128, 162, 220, 227, 283; techno-

logical production capabilities, 5, 12, 20; training in, 13, 14, 15, 53
telecommunications, 4, 8, 43, 54, 162
textile and garment industry, 10
Third World. *See* developing countries
trade: free, 4, 17, 27, 31; international, 4, 6, 43; and peace, 31–32, 35
trade blocs, 5, 17, 20. *See also* North American Free Trade Association
transnational capital, 99
transnational corporations (TNCs), 5, 6, 9, 10, 13, 14, 18, 21, 44–45, 18, 128, 198, 209, 318, 348
tuition, 13, 49, 160, 268, 337

unemployment, 179, 187
UNESCO. *See* international organizations
UNICEF. *See* international organizations
unions, 11, 55
United Nations. *See* international organizations
university, 14–15, 16, 49, 53. *See also* higher education

USAID. *See* international organizations

values. *See* culture
vocational training, 12, 13, 165, 173, 195
vouchers, 57

wages, 54–56
wealth 20, 35
welfare state, 6, 16, 17, 55, 67, 337
women: employment and family responsibilities, 9; empowerment of, 16; in the labor force, 8, 9, 10, 11, 53–54; part-time and temporary employment, 8, 9; "the personal is political," 8; politicization of, 8; and social discrimination, 10; as a source of cheap labor, 9, 44, 54. *See also* employment, education, gender, labor
women's movement, 16
women's organizations, 11. *See also* nongovernmental organizations
workers. *See* labor
World Bank. *See* international organizations

About the Editors and Contributors

Jill Blackmore is associate professor in the School of Social and Cultural Studies, Faculty of Education, Deakin University, who teaches undergraduate and postgraduate teacher education and specializes in educational administration and policy. She is co-director of the Deakin Centre for Education and Change and editor of the *Australian Educational Researcher*. She has researched and published in the area of feminist perspectives on organizational change, leadership, globalization, educational restructuring, teachers' work, school governance, gender equity reform, the parent movement, and citizenship education.

Rosa Nidia Buenfil Burgos (Ph.D. in government/discourse analysis, Essex, UK, 1990) is professor at the Departamento de Investigaciones Educativas, Centro de Investigación y Estudios Avanzados, and also part-time lecturer in the Faculty of Philosophy, Universidad Nacional Autónoma de México. She is author of three books about the educational discourse of the Mexican revolution and of chapters, articles, and papers about philosophical debates on education and recent educational policies in Mexico in the context of globalization and postmodernity.

Martin Carnoy is professor of education and economics at Stanford University and heads its International and Comparative Education Program. He is the author of a number of books on education, economic development, and labor markets, including *The New Global Economy in the Information Age* (1993), *Faded Dreams: The Economics and Politics of Race in America* (1994), and most recently *Sustaining Flexibility: Work, Family, and Community in the Information Age* (1999).

Carol Corneilse recently completed a MPhil in Education at the University of Cape Town under the guidance of Associate Professor Crain Soudien. Her research focused on international trends in quality assurance in higher education. She is currently a researcher in the university's Centre for Higher Education Development developing a framework for quality assurance at UCT. Prior to this appointment she spent nine years as an assistant academic planning officer.

Jan Currie, Ph.D. (Chicago), is associate professor at Murdoch University in Perth, Western Australia. She co-edited (with Janice Newson) *Universities and Globalization: Critical Perspectives* (1998) and has published articles in *Gender and Education, Comparative Education Review, Discourse, Women's Studies International Forum,* and *Australian Universities' Review,* among others. She has received major national grants and has researched in the areas of academic work, Aboriginal education, gender and organizational culture, and women and work. She is an active feminist and unionist.

Noel Gough is associate professor in the Faculty of Education, Deakin University, and a director of the Deakin Centre for Education and Change. His current research focuses on narrative theory and popular media culture in education, with particular reference to qualitative research methods, curriculum change, environmental education, and science education. He is the Australian editor of the *Journal of Curriculum Studies,* reviews editor of *The Australian Educational Researcher,* and coeditor of the *Australian Journal of Environmental Education.* His publications on globalization and curriculum have appeared in *Educational Policy,* the *Journal of Educational Policy,* and the *Southern African Journal of Environmental Education.*

Anne Hickling-Hudson is senior lecturer in education at the Queensland University of Technology in Brisbane, Australia. Born and raised in Jamaica, she earned degrees in history, education, and media studies in the Caribbean, Hong Kong, and Australia. She taught in the United Kingdom, worked for over a decade as a teacher educator in the Caribbean, and has continued in teacher education in Australia since 1987. Her academic focus is on crosscultural and international studies in education, and she is committed to developing teacher education curricula that reflect a postcolonial perspective, to encourage teachers to challenge the negative legacies of colonialism that still characterize Western education systems. Two research themes engage her attention: cultural issues in the teacher education curriculum in Australia and the development of the higher education system in postcolonial societies such as the Caribbean.

Phillip W. Jones is head of the School of Social, Policy, and Curriculum Studies at the University of Sydney, Australia. He is the author of several well-known books in international education, including *World Bank Financing of Education: Lending, Learning and Development* and *International Policies for Third World Development: UNESCO, Literacy and Development.* He is currently completing a major project on the impact of globalization on the educational work of major multilateral organizations.

Peter Kelly is lecturer in behavioral studies in the Faculty of Social and Behavioural Sciences at the University of Queensland. His research interests lie in the analysis of youth-related policy and discourses and the forms of youthful identities produced and regulated in spaces structured by these policies and discourses. He is particularly interested in the changing nature of government and of the nation-state in the context of globalization and the consequences for the regulation of youth transitions under these conditions.

Jane Kenway is a member and professor of of the Language and Literacy Research Centre, University of South Australia. Her research expertise is in education policy sociology with reference to schools and education systems in the context of wider social and cultural change, with specific interest in issues of justice. She is co-author of *Answering Back: Girls, Boys and Feminism in Schools* (1997) and is now working on *Selling Education: Consumer Cultures, Consuming Kids*. She has also published distance teaching monographs: *New Kids, New Times* (1997), *Marketing Education: Some Critical Issues* (1995), and *Economising Education: The Post-Fordist Directions* (1994).

Molly N. N. Lee is associate professor in education at Universiti Sains Malaysia, teaching sociology of education and science teaching methods. She is the author of articles on higher and teacher education, private education, science education, and educational policies. Recent publications include "Reforms in Higher Education in Malaysia: Emergent Issues," "Corporatisation, Privatisation and Internationalisation of Higher Education in Malaysia," "Education and the State: Malaysia after NEP," "Public Policies toward Private Education in Malaysia," and "The Politics of Educational Change in Malaysia: National Context and Global Influences."

Karen Monkman is assistant professor in the International and Intercultural Development Education Program at Florida State University. Her areas of interest include gender and education, sociocultural and transnational contexts of learning, community service learning, social change, and nonformal education. She has published articles in the *International Journal of Educational Development* and *Education as Change* (South Africa) and in *Women in the Third World: An Encyclopedia of Contemporary Issues* (1998), for which she was also assistant editor.

Catherine A. Odora Hoppers is distinguished professional and chief research specialist at the Human Sciences Research Council (HSRC), Pretoria, South Africa, and coordinator of their Project on the Integration of Knowledge Systems. Previously she was the deputy director of the Centre for Education and Policy Development in Johannesburg and a visiting scholar at the Southern African Regional Institute for Policy Studies in Harare, Zimbabwe. She is an expert for UNESCO and has been adviser to the UNESCO Institute of Education and other international agencies in areas of gender, education and social policy, and international development. Her recent publications include *Structural Violence as a*

Constraint to African Policy Formation: Repositioning Education in International Relations (1998) and *Public Policy Dialog: Its Role in the Policy Process.* (1997).

Lynne Parmenter is associate professor in the Faculty of Economics, Fukushima University, Japan. She completed a doctoral thesis on internationalization in Japanese education in 1997 and is currently interested in children's construction of identities in the world.

Rosalind Latiner Raby is lecturer at California State University, Northridge, in the Educational Leadership and Policy Studies Department of the College of Education. She also serves as the director of California Colleges for International Education, a consortium whose membership includes sixty-four California community colleges. She is also the community college coordinator of the UCLA International Teacher-Training Institutes. Among her publications on the topic of international education and community colleges, she is co-editor with Norma Tarrow of *Dimensions of the Community College: International and Inter/Multicultural Perspectives* (1996).

William M. Rideout, Jr., is professor at the University of Southern California and program leader of the International and Intercultural Education Specialization. His academic degrees were completed at Stanford University with a Master's degree also earned at the School of Advanced International Studies, Johns Hopkins University. He has been especially interested in studying the role of education in promoting directed change and is presently focusing on educational reform, including educational decentralization, in Africa and Southeast Asia.

Val D. Rust is professor of education at UCLA where he serves as director of the UCLA Education Abroad Program. He currently serves as the associate editor of the *Comparative Education Review.* His recent books include *The Unification of German Education* (1995), *Education and the Values Crisis in Central and Eastern Europe* (1995), and *Toward Schooling for the Twenty-first Century* (1996).

Crain Soudien teaches at the School of Education at the University of Cape Town, South Africa. He holds a Ph.D. in Sociology of Education from the State University of New York at Buffalo. While his major work is in the area of educational policy, race, class, and gender and the school, he is also a well-published public historian. He has edited a number of books and monographs and has written over forty articles and book chapters.

Nelly P. Stromquist (Ph.D., Stanford University) is professor of international development education at the University of Southern California. She has considerable experience in formal and nonformal education, particularly in Latin America and West Africa. Her research interests focus on issues of gender equity, educational policies and practices, and adult literacy, which she examines from a critical theory perspective. She has published widely; her most recent works include authoring *Literacy for Citizenship: Gender and Grassroots in Brazil* (1997), editing *Women in the Third World: An Encyclopedia of Contemporary Issues* (1998), and co-editing (with Michael Basile) *Politics of Educational Innovations in Developing Countries* (1999). She is past president of the Comparative and International Education Society.

George Subotzky is acting director of the Education Policy Unit at the University of the Western Cape in Cape Town, South Africa, which conducts higher education policy research. He has conducted numerous studies on higher education transformation in South Africa, focusing on the historically black universities. He has also contributed to a number of national higher education policy studies. His current research interests include higher education–community partnerships and community service learning, knowledge production, higher education and development, higher education institutional and organizational change management, policy research methodology, foreign donor aid to education and training, and equity in higher education. He has published in these areas in various journals and books and is co-author of *The Skewed Revolution: A Handbook of South African Higher Education*.

Shirley Walters is professor of adult and continuing education at the University of the Western Cape, South Africa, and founding director of the Centre for Adult and Continuing Education. She is also implementing head of a new Division for Lifelong Learning on the campus. Her most recent edited collections are *Globalization, Adult Education and Training: Impacts and Issues* (1997) and, with Linzi Manicom, *Gender in Popular Education: Methods for Empowerment* (1996). She has been involved in anti-apartheid civil society organizations and particularly the women's movement over many years.